'This new contribution to the debate on legal education in general and experiential legal education in particular is all the more valuable because it spans both the common law and civil law world; the latter being too often neglected in previous literature.'

—*Anthony Bradney, Professor of Law, Keele University, UK.*

Re-thinking Legal Education Under the Civil and Common Law

Whilst educational theory has developed significantly in recent years, much of the law curriculum remains content-driven and traditionally delivered, predominantly through lecture format. Students are, in the main, treated as empty vessels to be filled by the eminent academics of the day. *Re-thinking Legal Education Under the Civil and Common Law* draws on the experience of teachers, practitioners and students across the world who are committed to developing a more engaging and, consequently, a likely more effective learning process.

Little attention has, historically, been paid to the importance of the application of theory, the role of reflective learning, the understanding and acquisition of lawyering skills and the development of professional responsibility and wider ethical values. With contributions from across the global north and south, this book examines the history of educating our lawyers, the influences and constraints that may shape the curriculum, the means of delivering it and the models that could be used to tackle current shortcomings. The whole is intended to represent what might be desirable and possible if we are to produce lawyers who are fit for purpose in the 21st century, be that in either in civil or common law jurisdictions.

This book will be of direct assistance to those who wish to understand the theory and practice of legal pedagogy in an experiential context. It should be essential reading for academics, researchers and teachers in the fields of law and education, particularly those concerned with curriculum design and developing interactive teaching methods. It is likely to be of interest to law students too – particularly those who value a more direct engagement in their learning.

Richard Grimes is a senior consultant with Les Deux Ltd, a training and development service specialising in access to justice and legal education. He was, until recently, Director of Clinical Programmes at the York Law School, University of York, UK.

Legal Pedagogy

Series Editor
Kris Gledhill, Auckland University of Technology, New Zealand

This series consists of high-quality monographs, each of which explores best practice in an aspect of the law school curriculum. Books will cover teaching methods and curriculum design in the main areas of law, how to integrate themes, areas of jurisprudential thought, and wider questions about legal education more generally. With contributions from around the world, this series explores innovative thinking and practice within the context of a generally conservative branch of academia, with the aim of promoting discussion as to how best to teach the various aspects of the law degree and ensure the ongoing validity of the law degree and vocational and continuing legal education as a whole. Typical topics addressed include the value of variety in teaching methods and curriculum design, how best to incorporate educational research, the role for more practical courses, and the need to ensure that law schools provide degrees of relevance to the needs of students and of society.

The books in this series will be of great interest to academics, researchers and students (undergraduates and postgraduates) in the fields of law and education, as well as teachers of law who may be interested in revising curricula and need guidance in doing so. In addition, the legal profession, and in particular those who regulate entry into the profession, will find much to interest them within the series.

https://www.routledge.com/law/series/LEGPED

Books in this series:

Re-thinking Legal Education Under the Civil and Common Law
A Road Map for Constructive Change
Edited by Richard Grimes

The Teaching of Criminal Law
The Pedagogical Imperatives
Edited by Kris Gledhill and Ben Livings

Re-thinking Legal Education Under the Civil and Common Law

A Road Map for Constructive Change

Edited by Richard Grimes

Routledge
Taylor & Francis Group
LONDON AND NEW YORK

First published 2018
by Routledge

2 Park Square, Milton Park, Abingdon, Oxfordshire OX14 4RN

52 Vanderbilt Avenue, New York, NY 10017

Routledge is an imprint of the Taylor & Francis Group, an informa business

First issued in paperback 2018

British Library Cataloguing-in-Publication Data
A catalogue record for this book is available from the British Library

Library of Congress Cataloging-in-Publication Data
A catalog record for this book has been requested

ISBN: 978-0-415-79200-4 (hbk)
ISBN: 978-0-367-18193-2 (pbk)

Typeset in Bembo
by Apex CoVantage, LLC

To Rebecca: best friend, wife and ‘fellow’ clinician

Contents

Foreword

Re-thinking Legal Education under the Civil and Common Law seeks to establish through analysis, argument and example that learning and teaching, curriculum and course design and the structure and regulation of education are not determined by the organization and design of law, the attributes of the legal system, modes of legal reasoning or the nature of legal process. Arguments about the unsuitability of experiential legal education to scientific, theoretical, sophisticated understandings of law are confronted, dealt with and politely rejected. Nor, it is shown, is experiential learning uniquely qualified to facilitate the learning required for professional functions. Learning is learning – and the best learning always results from the best instruction, teaching and assessment. How we organize learning and teaching depends not on the structure of knowledge but on the goals of the curriculum.

Lest one think the authors have stirred a tempest in a teapot, be assured they have not!

Everywhere, experiential, active, student-oriented learning has faced obstruction and rebuff. There are many plausible reasons why the movement towards experiential learning in law has been bedeviled by detractors. Primary among these reasons are the many types and aspects of entrenched culture one finds in higher education, within legal regimes and among the leaders and practitioners of both legal education and legal practice. "We have always done it this way." "It can't be done that way." "They need to master substance, then process and much later, the how-to." "Universities are about advancing the study of theory and do not serve the interests of professional practice." "Law is not about clients and their needs; it's about ideas, their formation and elucidation."

Until recently both those engaged in tertiary education and those in the leadership of the law, courts, bureaucracies and the profession have had little if any background in learning theory, principles and practices. They learned and excelled through traditional university practices and honestly believe that what worked for them will work for others, if they are suited to the study. And while common law lawyers have long been comfortable with experience as a core to the development of law, this is less true for the development of lawyers. Civil lawyers have been much more comfortable with the cathedral of law and its jurisprudential and scientific magnificence: experience is for later, or at least for a different place from the academy.

In some common-law jurisdictions, the advent of clinical legal education (CLE) leapt over more conventional experiential learning models, including problem-based learning, role-play and simulation. It arose not only from an urge to improve student learning but also, and for the most part, to right the wrongs regularly occurring within a flawed, hierarchical and intrinsically discriminatory legal system. Law was to be used to achieve the goals in a cause. The educational rationale often followed the practice, to justify it on learning grounds. In a common-law tradition, trial and error, reflection and the search for theories, principles and practices by induction, both within and without CLE, have strengthened and justified the learning model. But experiential learning is not without its detractors to this day.

The civil law's commitment to intellectualism has long prevailed as the dominant reason for the dismissal of experiential learning from the instructor's armamentarium, as if to say that experience provides no pathway to learning, discovering or deducing general legal propositions. The law's majesty was traditionally experienced in the magisterial tradition, by the teaching provided by manifestly superior experts, whose words and phrases reflected learning of the systematically structured, if not provable, sets of theories, propositions and dictates. Nonetheless, clinical and other forms of experiential learning flourish in many civil law locations. In China, East Asia, South America and many parts of the civil law's ancestral home, Europe, legal educators daily demonstrate the utility of experiential learning to acquiring civil law concepts and principles – and much more.

Re-thinking Legal Education under the Civil and Common Law demonstrates and advances how experiential education deepens, broadens, reinforces and secures learning, not only of law, legal theory, legal skills and the values underlying each, but also of the discovery of self, other and society – and each person's individual comprehension.

Neil Gold
Professor Emeritus
Faculty of Law
University of Windsor
Canada

Opening thoughts

Legal education has, for many years, seemingly struggled with its identity and purpose. Is it a liberal study intended to produce analytical, critical and reflective graduates, or is it one stage in the process of producing practising lawyers? To what extent do these academic and vocational foci lead to tensions in terms of the form, content and delivery of legal education?

This book is an attempt to examine some fundamental issues that may impact how we educate our lawyers and looks at ideas and initiatives across the globe, giving examples of how legal education may be improved and made more relevant to all stakeholders, be they students, universities, the legal profession, other employers, government and the public as ultimate consumer or subject of the legal education product.

Recent developments in curriculum design and development have resulted in more emphasis on the value of learning through application and reflection – experiential or 'hands-on' study. The presence of learning by doing and reflecting on that experience has been widespread (if not fully integrated) in some countries for many years – for example, and notably in the USA and in parts of South America. Experiential or 'clinical' education is now a common feature in the majority of law schools in the UK and Australia and in many countries of the former Eastern Bloc. In continental Western Europe, experiential learning has emerged in the last five years but is now to be found in at least half of the countries currently forming the European Union. Clinics and other forms of experiential learning too can be located in law schools in the Middle East, in Central and South East Asia and on the Indian sub-continent.

Following recent conferences, workshops and in wider debates, questions are now being asked as to what such learning methods have to offer from both the academic and vocational perspective and whether there are significant differences in terms of structuring legal study depending on the nature of the legal system concerned.

In 2013 I attended a workshop in Luxembourg. The topic for discussion there was how legal education in countries represented by delegates might be reformed and improved. Colleagues from a range of mainly Western, continental, European jurisdictions were present, along with invited speakers from the

USA and the UK. Coming then from an institution (University of York) where experiential learning and clinical legal education was (and is) very much at the heart of the undergraduate and postgraduate curriculum I thought, naively perhaps, that delegates would be receptive to such concepts and interested in how these might be adapted for implementation under the civil law system.

Whilst I was politely listened to as I described the options and extolled the virtues of 'learning by doing', the majority of the audience appeared at best perplexed at and at worst sceptical, even highly critical, of the role of 'clinics' in legal education. From comments made at the workshop, it was clear that many attendees considered such common law models inappropriate in a civil law context.

Interesting discussions were had in the symposium sessions and afterward in various networking opportunities. In these exchanges, one frequent comment was that legal education under the civil law system was more about theory than practice and jurisprudential concepts rather than judicial decisions. Education under the civil law was said to be more akin to teaching a form of legal 'science'. Whilst, even then, I appreciated that there were significant differences in both philosophy and approach under the civil and common law, I was not convinced that the differences were as profound as were being suggested, at least in terms of pedagogy and effective learning and teaching. Of course, the common law relies heavily on the role of judicial precedent whereas the civil law traditionally does not (although interesting, the role of judicial decisions in shaping future interpretations is certainly not unknown under the civil law and has been said to be expanding, particularly so in the context of the European Union). Judges in the civil law system might be seen more as factual inquisitors and legal administrators applying codified principles than as interpreters of the law. When I pressed colleagues on how the suggested differences impacted on the legal education process, their overwhelming responses were that challenging underpinnings of principle could not be learnt by students without them having the benefit of direct instruction from experienced professors who were acknowledged experts in their particular fields. Only then could they be in a position to apply theory to practice. As attractive and persuasive a notion as this might be, especially from the professor's lofty position, the seemingly unquestioned presumption clearly was that basic concepts could only be understood if the students received imparted wisdom from above.

I asked for some specific examples of legal principles that had to be provided for students by academic staff. The first was the intention to create legal relations. Another was overlapping interests in land. A third was the idea of a trust, where one person holds property for the benefit of another. A further concept raised was proportionality under EU law.

Any law student, from a civil or common law position, has to come to terms with such basic principles. Contractual intent, land tenure, trusts and beneficial interests and possibly, proportionality are all issues that students are required to study in law schools in the common law world too.

If the curriculum that is to be taught and learnt is perhaps not so far apart as might otherwise be thought, where might other differences lay, and how could these impact of legal education – both in terms of form and content?

The structure of the legal and related professions may be one area of significant divergence. Although rules vary from one jurisdiction to another under the common law, the route to qualification for a lawyer typically involves a university education, followed by a period of overt vocational training and/or a some work-based learning or apprenticeship. The recruitment of judges, other senior administration of justice officials and state-based lawyers (for example public prosecutors) are often from the ranks of the initially qualified lawyer. By contrast, in most civil law countries following a university law degree the aspirant lawyer is expected to complete further training in a setting specific to career destination – be that as a judge, notary or prosecutor. Given that there are at least structural differences here, how does that impact on legal education? As is explored and explained later in this book, I suggest relatively little.

If we are to consider changes to what and how we teach and learn the law, might the regulation of the legal profession in civil compared with common law countries have a bearing on what can be done? Similarly, the law school itself may have to follow wider university regulations and policies, and there may be an overarching obligation to meet statutory requirements in the form of rules that dictate what and how a subject can be taught and assessed. Any attempt to introduce a clinical component where members of the public are advised and possibly represented by law school staff and students may well require compliance with professional codes of conduct and possible legislative rules and/or institutional policy. The position here is likely to vary considerably from country to country.

That said, if the thrust of this book is that students engage with their studies and learn more effectively if they are actively involved in the educational process, as compared with those who sit passively and listen to the wise words of their 'olders and betters', reform to what and how we teach can be examined in the context of applicable regulation. Compliance may have to be assured, but having to be compliant should not be a reason for educational inertia and stagnation.

Following this introduction the book is divided into 3 parts – paraphrased here as Context, Content and Countries. In each section, authors with extensive experience of legal education as teachers, administrators, regulators and/or recent students explain the given subject matter on the basis of either a set themes or from the perspective of a particular jurisdiction. At the beginning of each section, there is a brief introduction explaining what each contribution covers.

The themes of parts, B and C have a common focus – how teaching and learning can or could be improved from the viewpoint of both the educator and the law student. The contributors to this book look at not only the study of the substantive law and legal doctrine but also the relevance of skills (legal and transferable) and the ethical context in which law operates – on philosophical/jurisprudential and practical or applied levels. The expectations of the legal profession and other prospective employers are also taken into account, as is regulation, be that imposed by the profession, government, federal or transnational bodies or the educational institution.

Specific examples are given of how legal education operates in particular jurisdictions and what steps have been or might be taken to improve provision in that context. Wherever possible, concrete examples, including sample scripts, are given of what re-thinking legal education can actually look like in practice and how challenges in achieving such change might be handled.

Contributions include the North and South American experience, encompassing the USA, Canada and Chile, the situation in Western Europe, legal education in the countries of the former Soviet Bloc, reports from West and South Africa, legal education in India and the current position in Australia.

In both instances – Content and Countries – the authors develop their arguments to show what the historical legacy of legal education has been from their perspective and how matters might be improved in the future for the benefit of all. Many contributors have vast experience in legal education and have been highly influential in effecting change. Some have a background in both the civil and common law worlds. Others have more limited experience and in many instances only of one particular system and jurisdiction. To make greater sense of the whole and to give the book the necessary 'fit', I have provided brief commentary at the start of each section attempting to make the link between the contributions and the salient points raised by the relevant contributors as obvious as possible. I hope I have done justice to the richness and value of the individual submissions.

This juxtaposition of contributions from the civil and common world in many of the chapters is designed to illustrate both differences and similarities and to promote a discussion on constructive ways forward. The result is intended to inform a wider debate on what we (whoever that might be) want from our lawyers in future and importantly, how we can we get that.

Richard Grimes

Contributors

Cristina Amato, LLM, PhD in comparative law, Esquire Milan Bar Association, is associate professor of comparative law at the Brescia Law Faculty, Italy. Her areas of expertise are private comparative law, continuing education training for the legal profession and clinical legal education. She has been a visiting professor in several European and South American law schools and has published widely on civil law, particularly around consumer protection, civil liability, contract and damages.

Juan Pablo Beca is a qualified lawyer in Chile. He holds a master's in law from the Università deglistudi di Genova (Italy) and at Universidad Católica de Temuco (Chile), where he is associate professor.

Katarzyna Gromek Broc teaches at the University ofYork, Law School at undergraduate and postgraduate levels. She was appointed in 2008 to develop postgraduate programmes in law. She obtained her PhD from EUI/Florence and has other postgraduate qualifications from Paris II (Panthéon/Sorbonne). She has taught widely in Europe, Asia, Australia and South America and has held visiting professorships at the Institute of European Studies of Macau; Golden Gate University, San Francisco and Stetson College of Law, Florida. Her research has attracted numerous grant awards, including from the Arts and Humanities Research Board (2003) and the British Academy (2004). She won the Strategic Fund Competition in 2006 for her research on discrimination and has been sponsored by the Sir Reckitt Foundation on several occasions. Her research interests include European law, comparative law, labour law, cross-border insolvency law, bioethics and human rights. She has published widely in these areas.

Laura Bugatti holds a PhD in comparative law. She is currently a research fellow at Brescia Law School, Italy. She is a supervisor in the Brescia Legal Clinic specialising in civil liability. Her main fields of research interest are: professional liability (with a particular focus on legal profession), the regulation of lawyers and legal education. She has published several articles on professional and civil liability and not-for-profit legislation. She has been involved in national/international research projects, mainly in collaboration with the Center of European and Comparative Studies in Brescia.

Meredith Daniel studied for her undergraduate law degree at the University of York, becoming the first person to be awarded first-class honours (with distinction) in law. Her engagement with clinic as an undergraduate sparked an interest which led to her undertaking her LLM in the theory and practice of clinical legal education, providing experience of interacting with clinic as both a student and a supervisor. Now undertaking the Bar Professional Training Course, Meredith has continued her interest in clinical legal education by taking a position as a student director in the Housing Clinic at the law school, BPP.

Pilar Fernández-Artiach, PhD, is an associate professor of labour law and Social Security at the University of Valencia, where she is Director of the Migrants' Law Clinic. She is a member of the Global Alliance for Justice Education (GAJE) and the European Network of Clinical Legal Education (ENCLE). She has published extensively in her fields of interest.

José García-Añón is professor in the School of Law and researcher in the Human Rights Institute at the University of Valencia. His main research interests and publications are around human rights, especially minorities' rights, migrant rights, women's rights; discrimination and the law; racial and ethnic discrimination (specifically racial profiling); multiculturalism and human rights (specifically female genital mutilation); innovation and methods on teaching and learning law (specifically using ICT tools for teaching, and clinical legal education). He is member of the board of directors of the Global Alliance for Justice Education (GAJE) and a member of the Steering Committee of the European Network for Clinical Legal Education (ENCLE)

Philip M. Genty is the Everett B. Birch Innovative Teaching Clinical Professor in Professional Responsibility at Columbia Law School. He teaches professional responsibility, civil procedure and the Incarceration and the Family Clinic. His research interests are in legal ethics, prisoners' rights, family law and clinical education. He has taught and consulted on legal ethics and clinical legal education in Central and Eastern Europe the Middle East. He received a Columbia University Presidential Award for Outstanding Teaching in 2014, and Columbia Law School's Willis L.M. Reese Prize for Excellence in Teaching in 2008.

Jenny Gibbons is a lecturer at the University of York. She is responsible for the delivery of public law and employment law modules and is actively involved in the ongoing design of the law curriculum. She qualified as a solicitor in 2003 and continues to supervise live cases in the York Law Clinic.

Jeff Giddings is a professor of law at Monash University, Melbourne, Australia. He has written extensively on experiential learning, and his book *Promoting Justice Through Clinical Legal Education* was published in 2013. Jeff developed the clinical programme at Griffith University, Brisbane, where he worked for 22 years. He also teaches and researches in the fields of access to justice and alternative dispute resolution.

Richard Grimes qualified as a solicitor in 1977 and worked initially in a law centre and later as a full-equity partner in a law firm, handling a wide range of, principally, publicly funded cases. He has retained an interest in law teaching and research as well as legal practice in the belief that the one informs the other. In 1990 he joined Sheffield Hallam University, where he established an in-house solicitors' practice in which undergraduate law students handled real cases under professional supervision. He was seconded to the University of the South Pacific from 1995–1997, where he became the Director of the Institute for Justice and Applied Legal Studies. In 1998 he was appointed Head of Law and Professor of Legal Education at the University of Derby and in 2000 joined The College of Law as Professor and Director of Pro Bono Services and Clinical Education. From 2006 to 2010 Richard acted as an independent consultant on a variety of legal education projects, including in Afghanistan, Georgia, Iran and Nigeria, working with national governments, donor agencies, law schools, the legal profession and NGOs. He was Director of Clinical Programmes at the York Law School, University of York, from 2010 to 2016 and helped to pioneer a fully integrated clinical approach to study using problem-based learning. He has now returned to a consultancy role. He has published widely on clinical legal education issues and in the legal skills field and remains committed to learning by doing and to improving access to justice more generally.

Richard Hedlund has recently been awarded his PhD from York Law School (YLS) at the University of York, where he also worked as a part-time PBL tutor and a mentor in the Law Clinic. He had previously graduated from YLS with an LLB and LLM, both studied using PBL methods. Richard has now secured his first academic position as a lecturer with the Law School at the University of Lincoln.

Katarzyna J. Kowalska, PhD, is an assistant professor in the Legal Clinic at the University of Warsaw. She is also a legal practitioner, trainer and author of various publications devoted mainly to clinical legal education, access to justice and the pro bono movement in Poland and Eastern Europe. She is also a member of the board of the European Network for Clinical Legal Education (ENCLE).

Liubou Krasnitskaya graduated from the Belarusian State University with a law degree and has been appointed supervisor and manager of the legal clinic there. Having gained the experience in clinical legal education in the USA, Poland, Russia and Belarus, she was invited to Vietnam to support the establishment and development of the legal clinics in 2012–2013. Currently she is studying for a PhD University of Bialystok in Poland under the title: "Higher legal education through the prism of the human right to education".

Stephen Levett is a solicitor and former deputy dean at the University of Sunderland, and previously set up and ran Student Legal Advice Centres at the University of Law in York and in London. He has spoken at a number of clinical legal education conferences and is a former steering committee member of the Global Alliance for Justice Education. He is now the Director for the newly established law clinic at the Dickson Poon School of Law, Kings College London.

Chris Maguire is Professor of Professional Education and Dean of Academic Affairs and proctor at BPP University, London. He has worked for a number of regulatory and professional bodies, including the Bar Standards Board and the Solicitors' Regulation Authority. He is a Quality Assurance Agency assessor and was formerly the chair of the Association of Law Teachers. He has acted as a consultant to the World Bank and the British Council in several countries worldwide. His research interests lie in professional identity, quality and the affective domain.

David McQuoid-Mason is a professor at the Centre for Socio-Studies, University of KwaZulu-Natal, South Africa; an honorary visiting law professor at Strathclyde University, Scotland; an adjunct professor of Law at Griffith University in Australia and President of the Commonwealth Legal Education Association. He has published more than 150 articles in law and medical journals, written two books, co-authored 20 books and manuals, contributed more than 70 chapters to books and delivered over 300 papers at national and international conferences. He has visited over 120 countries and drafted legal aid legislation, helped establish law clinics and Street law programmes and conducted numerous clinical legal education training sessions in 60 of these.

Ruth M. Mestre i Mestre is a professor of jurisprudence and legal theory at the University of Valencia and member of the Human Rights Institute. She holds a master's in legal theory (Brussels, 1995) and master's in sociology of law (Oñati, 1997). Ruth has been Marie Curie Fellow at CRER-Warwick University (2003–2004). Her research interests are in feminist legal theory, equality and non-discrimination, citizenship, multiculturalism, women's rights and clinical legal education. Ruth is currently the director of the Clínica Jurídica per la justicia social at Valencia.

Donald Nicolson (BA, LLB, PHD) is a law professor at the University of Strathclyde, Scotland. He is founding director of the school's law clinic and was also founding director of the University of Bristol Law Clinic. Donald has written extensively on legal ethics and ethical education, as well as on evidence, criminal law, clinical education, evidence theory, affirmative action and adjudication. He is on the editorial board of *Legal Ethics* and the *International Journal of the Legal Profession*, a trustee of Law Works Scotland established to promote voluntary legal work and of the Clinical Legal Education Organisation and a member of Law Society of Scotland's Access to Justice Committee.

Ernest Ojukwu is a senior advocate of Nigeria and partner at OFY-Lawyer Abuja. He is president of the Network of University Legal Aid Institutions

(NULAI) Nigeria; Professor of Law Baze University Abuja Nigeria; and was deputy director-general and head of quality assurance at the Nigerian Law School (2013–2014), deputy director-general and head of Augustine Nnamani Campus Enugu, Nigerian Law School from 2001 to 2013 and dean, Faculty of Law Abia State University (1995–2000). He established the Nigerian Bar Association's Institute of Continuing Legal Education and designed the rules and guidelines that drive the mandatory continuing legal education programme for the legal profession and was its director 2007–2010 and 2012–2014. Ernest has a deep interest and experience in legal education. He was alternate chairman of the Nigerian Bar Association's Summit on Legal Education 2006 and secretary of the federal government of Nigeria Committee on the Reform of Legal Education in Nigeria, 2006–2007. He is at present the Secretary of Nigerian Council of Legal Education Committee on the Review of the LLB Programme of Nigerian Universities. He has published widely on legal education including: *Legal Education in Nigeria: A Chronicle of Reforms and Transformation under Tahir Mamman*. He is editor-in-chief of *African Journal of Clinical Legal Education and Access to Justice*.

Sue Prince is an associate professor at Exeter University. She has extensive research interests in alternative dispute resolution, clinical legal education and pro bono, particularly in a Canadian context. Sue led the establishment of a student advice clinic, the Community Legal Helpdesk, at her university, which won the LawWorks Attorney-General's Pro Bono award in 2013. She is currently reviewing online dispute resolution processes in British Colombia and has developed a Canadian Negotiation Competition, in conjunction with a global law firm, aimed at contextualising skills, practice and education.

David Roccaro is a graduate in law from the University of Palermo with a dissertation on the clinical legal education under civil and common law. He is co-author of the first handbook in Italian on legal clinics, *Clinica legale. Un manuale operativo* (2015). He gained experience abroad under the Erasmus scheme at the Georg-August-Universität in Göttingen and has undertaken an internship in a law office in Wien and worked in a legal clinic, the Escritório de prática jurídica, at the Universidade de Fortaleza (Unifor) in Brazil. He spent time researching clinical legal education at the York Law School Clinic and is now undertaking his studies in theory and practice of law.

Shuvro Prosun Sarker is a Researcher at the Center for Regulatory Studies, Governance and Public Policy at the West Bengal National University of Juridical Sciences (NUJS), India. He holds an LL.B from Calcutta University, LL.M and a PhD from NUJS. He is an Assistant Editor of *Asian Journal of Legal Education*.

Anne-Lise Sibony is Professor of European law at the University of Louvain. She read law and economics in Paris, graduated from the École Normale

Supérieure (Paris) and holds an MsC in regulation from the London School of Economics. Anne-Lise wrote her PhD on the judicial use of economic reasoning in competition law. Her main research interest lies more broadly in how scientific knowledge (mainly economics and psychology) is used in the legal sphere. Her current focus is on behaviourally informed law making at EU level. She is a visiting professor at University Paris II and at the European Law and Governance School.

Michal Urban, JUDd, PhD, is a senior lecturer in the Faculty of Law, at Charles University in Prague, Czech Republic. He also runs the Street Law programme there (see www.streetlaw.eu) and participates in other clinical education programmes (simulations and externships).

Tanya Walker completed her postgraduate degree in the theory and practice of clinical legal education at York Law School, University of York, having studied for her LLB there under the PBL method. This followed a lengthy career as a civil servant and trade union officer. She is currently working as a freelance researcher with an interest in clinical pedagogy and ethics prior to finalising her PhD research proposal (please see the postscript to "Final words" at the end of this book).

Part A

Context and concepts

Introduction

The first section of this book is about scene-setting in which the contributors ask and try to answer specific and significant questions. What makes the civil and common law traditions so distinctive? To what extent does this impact on legal education provisions in the respective jurisdictions? Is there sufficient common ground for certain models of educational best practice to be shared and adapted or are the fundamentals so entrenched or different as to mean that current forms of pedagogy are immovable?

Philip Genty opens the discussion by looking at the civil and common law traditions and welcoming the diversity encompassed by both. Although he sees ample shared ground and interest, he feels that one can inform the other and although both types of legal jurisdiction can, and should, focus on improving legal education, much can be gained from dialogue and an exchange of ideas.

Cristina Amato takes a somewhat different stance and suggests that the civil law has, in fact, always linked law and practice even if it does not recognise or accept that. Taking a journey through the history of legal education, she highlights the characteristics of the civil law, shows how it affects perceptions of law and in consequence legal education and concludes by predicting the further development of experiential learning methods throughout the civil law world.

In the final chapter of this section, Richard Grimes and Anne-Lise Sibony take the clear position that there is nothing in principle in either the civil or common law systems that prevent us from first, being constructively critical of how and what we teach and learn with a view to improving legal education provision and secondly, using modern, innovative and educationally robust ways of delivering that service. They identify the stakeholders in the process – the student, the client, the law school, the university as a whole, the legal (and other) profession(s) and the wider public and set a challenge to law schools to 'up their game'.

Chapter 1

Celebrating the difference

A U.S. educator's perspective on legal education under the civil and common law

Philip M. Genty

1.1 Introduction

I have been a legal educator for almost 30 years, and during that time, my primary focus has been on clinical education and professional responsibility or legal ethics. I also coordinated my school's legal writing and moot court programs for many years. Like many of my U.S. colleagues, I have also spent time doing international work to take this experiential message "on the road." I have made many trips to Europe and Israel to engage with educators and students in classes, discussions, conferences, and workshops on these topics.[1]

I say all of this to establish at the outset that I am well aware of, and have benefitted tremendously from, the networks of legal educators and academics around the world who are focused on preparing students for the legal profession. Members of this community – both those who teach clinical and other experiential offerings and those who teach more traditional doctrinal courses – meet regularly in international fora, collaborate on teaching and writing projects, and form close personal relationships.

Given this widespread and growing trend, it is tempting to suggest that international differences – and particularly differences between the civil and common law systems – no longer matter very much. But I want to challenge this view and offer a different perspective based upon my own experiences and observations as an American "outsider." In this chapter I want to suggest that the traditional civil/common law distinctions still matter, although perhaps for reasons that are more practical than philosophical. And while a sense of shared purpose is both desirable and necessary for effective international collaboration, I believe that those of us who are involved in developing legal pedagogies that will educate students for the 21st century legal profession do ourselves and the students a disservice if we ignore these differences.

In this chapter I will start by briefly exploring the historical differences between the civil and common law systems. I will then discuss ways in which these differences have narrowed over time. Next I will argue why, despite this convergence, the differences still matter. Finally, I will offer some concluding thoughts.

1.2 Our "uncommon" origins

Many of the differences between the civil and common law traditions and systems are well known and obvious.[2] The civil law is rooted in codes going back to Roman times, while the common law grew out of English court decisions, beginning after the Norman Conquest of 1066.[3] The core of the civil law is therefore doctrinal, with an emphasis on "pure" determination of legal principles. The common law is more fact based; legal principles evolve as law is applied to new factual contexts.

I have previously summarized five main characteristics that distinguish civil law from common law systems:

1 the importance of substance, rather than process;
2 the importance of mastering, rather than creatively interpreting, legal doctrine;
3 the limited importance of the attorney-client relationship;
4 the central role of an informed authority figure; and
5 the lack of a concept of cause lawyering.[4]

These differences have implications both for how law is taught and how it is practiced. Legal education in a civil law system is structured around the teaching of legal doctrine. While legal doctrine can certainly be taught in a variety of ways, the lecture is a logical and efficient way of doing this, and it is therefore no accident that traditional civil law education is lecture-based.[5] In contrast, legal education in the common law system whilst relying on lectures is often is much more interactive. In the traditional "Socratic" method of teaching, the professor presents the students with a series of hypothetical scenarios, asking the students to articulate and continually re-examine legal principles and conclusions as the professor modifies the facts in the scenarios.[6]

With respect to the way law is practiced in the two systems, a similar dichotomy exists. In civil law systems, because the principles of doctrinal law are "fixed" and do not depend on specific factual applications, the job of the judge and the lawyers is to determine the law. The judge controls the case, as the arbiter of legal doctrine. Because it is not necessary to spend significant time on fact-finding (other than in the initial investigation[7]), there is often no need to conduct in-person examinations of parties and witnesses; written submissions about the law will suffice. In the common law system, this is all reversed. Because legal principles are applied to the specific facts in the case, fact-finding is crucial. Lawyers earn their living arguing about what precedent is factually relevant and presenting facts through the testimony of their clients, although in the U.S. this testimony is likely to occur in pre-trial depositions given that most lawsuits do not end up going to trial. Thus, civil law lawyers look to codes for clear answers, while common law lawyers look for factual distinctions that will change the way the law will be applied.

1.3 The narrowing of the gap

The previous section provides a brief summary of the historical differences between the civil and common law traditions and the way these differences affect legal education and the practice of law. Over time these differences have narrowed. As a result of increased international interactions – commercially, culturally, academically – we no longer have "pure" civil or common law systems. For example, in civil law continental Europe, inter-European human rights tribunals have taken on a decidedly common law quality, as decisions of these courts are less grounded in code-based doctrine than in judge-made law. At the same time, law in the United States, as well as other common law countries, has increasingly become codified, making it look much more like the law of civil law countries. In addition, in the U.S. federal court judges increasingly take on a "managerial role"[8] that looks a lot like the role of judges in the inquisitorial civil law system. Finally, law is practiced on a global level, with international law firms based in multiple countries.

The changes in legal education are even more pronounced. In Europe the Bologna Declaration, adopted by the European Ministers of Education in 1999 (commonly referred to as the "Bologna Process"), has been transformative. There is a new emphasis on giving students the practical skills they will need to become successful practitioners. Lusine Hovhannisian has described the effects of the Bologna Declaration:

> [The Declaration] places great importance on the need for institutes of higher education in Europe to become more competitive internationally, so as to better rival American universities. It further recognizes the link between education and employment, casting the suggested reforms as a way to increase the labor market for graduates in a "globalized market for a high-grade work force."[9]

The Bologna Process has created a greater need to link education to the legal profession, and this has led to an expansion of experiential and clinical legal education throughout Europe. This trend was formalized in 2012, with the founding of the European Network for Clinical Legal Education ("ENCLE"), which now boasts more than 140 members from 30 countries.[10] A related development is the creation of the International Journal of Clinical Legal Education ("IJCLE"), a peer-edited law review published by Northumbria University in the United Kingdom. In addition to publishing two issues a year, the IJCLE conducts annual conferences, which have been hosted in a variety of European countries, as well as Australia and South Africa.[11]

The expansion of experiential and clinical education has not been limited to Europe. The Global Alliance for Justice Education ("GAJE") has grown steadily since its founding in 1996.[12] GAJE conducts biannual conferences throughout the world. Conferences have been held in India (twice), South Africa, Poland,

Argentina, Philippines, Spain, and Turkey.[13] The GAJE Mission Statement notes that GAJE's focus extends beyond clinical legal education:

> Clinical education of law students is a key component of justice education, but this organization also works to advance other forms of **socially relevant legal education**, which includes education of practicing lawyers, judges, non-governmental organizations and the lay public.[14]

An additional development in international legal education has been an expanded focus on the teaching of legal ethics. Since 2004, an International Legal Ethics Conference has been held every two years. The success of these conferences led to the formation of the International Association of Legal Ethics in 2010.[15]

Another interesting international initiative is the weeklong Professional Responsibility and Ethics in the Global Legal Market course that has been taught at Moscow State University in Russia for the past five years. The course is a collaboration among the international law firms White & Case and DLA Piper, Microsoft and Verizon, and the NGO PILnet. The course brings in students from universities throughout Russia for four days and covers issues such as the regulation of the legal profession, conflicts of interest, confidentiality and disclosure, anticorruption, corporate social responsibility, and pro bono.[16] Beyond its role in this weeklong program, White & Case, through its Moscow-based associates, offers legal skills courses to students at Moscow State University and other law schools in Russia.[17]

These are some of the most tangible examples of a worldwide trend in legal education away from an exclusive reliance on traditional doctrinal, lecture-based teaching, to more interactive educational models focusing on practical skills and professional roles. Educational approaches associated with the U.S. specifically or common law countries more generally have clearly taken hold in a significant number of countries and schools throughout the world.

1.4 The differences and why they still matter

Fellowship and a wonderful sense of community characterize international gatherings such as those described above – conferences organized by ENCLE, the IJCLE, GAJE, and the International Association of Legal Ethics. These gatherings bring together educators who share many goals for legal pedagogy, the practice of law, and the standards of the legal profession. Participants speak a common language, both figuratively and usually, literally (English). The conferences involve a fairly standard mix of plenary sessions and more interactive small group sessions in which the presenters often model experiential teaching methods. For many participants, these conferences provide opportunities for reunions with old friends and colleagues around issues of mutual importance. There is a sense among both the old and new faces that the international community of legal educators is one big (civil and common law) happy family. And this is not an illusion – there truly is a profound, sincere, and deeply rewarding feeling of shared values and aspirations.

While all of this is quite real, it obscures several important differences. The first of these is the issue of culture. The participants from civil law countries were raised and educated in systems and traditions significantly different from their U.S. and Commonwealth colleagues. Those of us in the legal professions are all products of our legal traditions. We are "hardwired" to think in ways that are particular to our respective civil or common law upbringing. To take a simple example, a civilian faced with a legal question will instinctively think in terms of an answer grounded in doctrine. She or he will automatically look for the relevant code. In contrast, a common law legal professional will think factually; she or he will certainly start with the law, whether in statutes or in cases, but will almost immediately begin to ask, "How is my case factually similar to or different from other cases that have been decided on this issue?" In short, we *think* differently about law.

Second, legal education continues to be structured differently in the two systems. Civil law education continues to be governed by a strict top-down doctrinal model – the ministry of education frequently dictates the curriculum, which is traditional and doctrinal. While practice and profession-oriented education (clinics, classes in legal ethics, etc.) are increasingly taught, they are "add-ons" to the curriculum, rather than core components. Students may not even receive credit for these courses, and faculty will be expected to teach the courses on an overload basis, receiving no teaching credit for these additional experiential offerings. In addition, because legal education continues to center around the teaching of doctrine, large lecture classes continue to be the dominant educational model.

In contrast, the common law model is much more decentralized. For example, in the U.S., while the American Bar Association (ABA) and the state courts prescribe guidelines in accreditation and bar admission standards, these are framed much more generally than the curricular requirements of the civil law countries.[18] Individual law schools therefore have a good deal of freedom to structure their curricula. To the extent that content is prescribed by the ABA and the courts, the trend is toward requiring more experiential offerings,[19] so the law schools are offering students a greater range of clinics and other innovative and interactive, practice-oriented educational opportunities.

Third, there continue to be important differences in the way the legal professions are structured in the two cultures. In contrast to common law systems, which typically treat law as a single profession, albeit with varied career options, civil law systems tend to divide law into several separate professions (e.g., advocates, judges, prosecutors and notaries, each of which has its own educational track that students choose early in their legal studies).[20]

Fourth, in many respects law is practiced differently in the two systems. In "The Common Law/Civil Law Divide: Residual Truth of a Misleading Distinction,"[21] Professor Mirjan Damaška, while concluding that the historical differences between the two systems are overstated and have also diminished over time, observes that a number of important differences remain.[22] Professor Damaška offers the following reflections about the division of responsibility between attorneys and judges in the two systems, as well as the way pre-trial discovery is conducted:

> In early stages of lawsuits, a prominent relic is the different approaches toward gathering the material for decision. In common law countries, the task is entrusted to partisan counsel: the judge merely supervises their activity and intervenes only when a dispute between them arises. On the Continent, the task is still performed by the judge, or some delegated official. This distinction between "privatized" and "officialized" action is reflected in different regimes for the mandatory disclosure of information. Common law "discovery" implies an exchange of information between the parties and is independent from the submission of evidence: litigants freely decide what information received from the opponent shall be used in proof-taking. . . . On the Continent, disclosure of information assumes an official flavor, since it requires inclusion of the relevant items in the official file of the case: the item becomes evidence in the case and of potential use in other proceedings. But the existence of the official file is, in itself, a telling sign of the persisting hierarchical and bureaucratic arrangements. From the inception of the lawsuit until its end, the file serves as the backbone, or the nerve center, of proceedings that are expected to take place before several levels of authority. In common law jurisdictions, we still find no real counterpart of such official documentation: here, parties preserve their separate files.[23]

Professor Damaška concludes that the role of the judge may be the most important practical difference between the two systems:

> Common law judges do not view accurate fact-finding as central to their task, and experience little difficulty in deciding lawsuits on the basis of the evidence presented to them by the parties. . . . [J]udges do not engage in fact-finding activities, but merely supervise the development of evidence by the litigants. Continental judges, on the other hand, are heirs to the longstanding tradition that accurate fact-finding is at the heart of their vocation. . . . Feeling responsible for finding out the truth, judges are reluctant to be limited by evidence as put to them by self-interested parties. . . . Thus, if one's interest in the differences between common and civil law extends beyond their normative frameworks to cover the systems' actual

> functioning, these discrepant understandings of the judicial office assume great importance.[24]

Thus, despite a good deal of cross-fertilization and convergence that has brought the two systems closer together, significant differences remain. The question is whether these differences still matter in our increasingly integrated international legal community. I want to argue that they do and that by suggesting otherwise, we lose a critical opportunity for mutual learning.

In the clinical course I teach in my law school, I, like most of my colleagues, cover, among other things, interviewing and counseling. The text I use and the classes I teach on this subject stress the importance of attempting to find ways to connect with clients. However, I caution the students about the danger of making "false" connections. We discuss the ways in which superficial similarities can obscure fundamental differences between lawyer and client and prevent them from communicating effectively and working successfully together. The lawyer may not fully understand, and may therefore undervalue, the client's goals and priorities. The client may become frustrated at what he or she perceives as the lawyer's lack of caring and commitment.

While this is obviously not a perfect analogy, similar concerns arise in cross-cultural collaboration among legal professionals. The comfort and familiarity among legal educators and academics – and the fact that international conferences are typically conducted in English – mask the very real differences described above in the ways law is taught and practiced. The risk is that the international conferences will be dominated by the native English speakers – particularly those from the U.S., but also those from Commonwealth countries. These will be the "loudest" voices, and the workshop topics and teaching approaches that are modeled will reflect the values and assumptions of the common law societies, rather than being a true cross-fertilization and mutual exchange of ideas. And much of the potential benefit of these gatherings will be lost as a result.

I want us not only to recognize, but also to *revel in*, our differences. In institutions of higher learning, including law schools, in the United States, there is an increasing emphasis on the importance of recognizing, appreciating, and teaching about diversity (e.g., race, gender, ethnicity, culture, economic background). This trend reflects a recognition of the importance of understanding the ways people's backgrounds define their perceptions and experiences. These principles apply fully to backgrounds of legal culture, and hence legal education, as well.

1.5 Conclusion

Those of us in civil and common law societies are coming from different places in every sense – we have long and deep legal histories, and our respective traditions have left their mark on the way we think about our professional roles and carry out our day-to-day work. Again, the important differences are practical as much as theoretical.

Creating a cross-cultural conversation in which these differences can be examined, discussed, and understood requires careful and conscious planning.[25] One concrete approach would be to structure portions of international workshops in a way that is specifically designed to accomplish this goal. When choosing topics for our international gatherings, a starting point might be to frame the opening discussions around the question – how do you do this in your society/courtrooms/law faculties, and why? While there is an understandable desire to move beyond the purely descriptive to conversations that are more prescriptive, it may be that we actually need to spend more time using description as a vehicle for achieving understanding.

Another possibility would be to move away from an exclusive reliance on English at such conferences. More of the discussions could be conducted in the language of the participants, with translation provided for others. While this would probably slow things down and require more time for each conference session, the potential benefits would outweigh these concerns. The conferences I have attended that include such translation have generally provided for more participants to speak comfortably and express their ideas fully, and thus to ensure that more voices are heard, and that they are heard accurately and completely.

Whatever the means chosen, we need to find ways to appreciate our diverse legal backgrounds and traditions. The differences between the civil and common law systems are rich and varied, and there is much to be learned from each other as we continue to build a global community of educators who will prepare our students for their futures as legal professionals.

Notes

1 To date I have done work in Albania, Armenia, Bosnia-Herzogovina, Bulgaria, Croatia, the Czech Republic, England, Georgia, Hungary, Israel, Macedonia, the Netherlands, Poland, Romania, Russia, Serbia, and Spain.

2 Drawing on the work of others, I have previously explored these differences and what I see as their implications for clinical legal education. See: P.M. Genty, *Overcoming cultural blindness in international clinical collaboration: the divide between civil and common law cultures and its implications for clinical education* (hereafter "*Overcoming cultural blindness*"), Clinical Law Review, 15, 2008, 131.

3 Ibid., 137, citing G.F. Bell, The U.S. legal tradition among the legal traditions of the world, in J.C. Ginsburg (ed.), *Legal methods cases and materials* (revised 2nd edn), New York, Foundation, 2014, 63.

4 See: Genty, *Overcoming cultural blindness* (n 1), 149.

5 This is not to suggest that lecturing is the only way to teach legal doctrine but only that it is the most obvious method for doing so. See: M. McAuley, *On a theme by Ren'e David: comparative law as technique indispensable*, Journal of Legal Education, 52, 2002, 42, 47 ("There is nothing so peculiar about the civil law that reserves learning of its principles and rules solely to the lecture style of instruction. The civil law need not be taught in the Continental mode, in huge amphitheaters, or magisterially.")

6 Again, the "Socratic" method is not the only way of teaching in a common law system. Lecturing, among other methods, may also be used.
7 For a discussion of the relevance of fact-finding see the Amato's comments in the following chapter of this book.
8 See, e.g.: E.D. Elliott, *Managerial judging and the evolution of procedure*, University of Chicago Law Review, 53, 1986, 306.
9 L. Hovhannisian, *Clinical legal education and the Bologna Process*, PILI Papers, Number 2, December 2006, 5. (citations omitted), available at: www.pilnet.org/public-interest-law-resources/25-clinical-legal-education-and-the-bologna-process.html, accessed 14 October 2016. See, also: L.S. Terry, *The Bologna Process and its impact in Europe: it's so much more than degree changes*, Vanderbilt Journal of Transnational Law, 41, 2008, 107.
10 See: website of European Network for Clinical Legal Education, www.encle.org/membership-directories/mdir, accessed 6 April 2017. See also: website of PILnet, "Project Updates" webpage, *PILnet welcomes the European Network for clinical legal education*, 3 October 2012, available at: www.pilnet.org/project-updates/166-pilnet-welcomes-the-european-network-for-clinical-education.html, accessed 6 April 2017.
11 See: website of International Journal of Clinical Legal Education, "Journal History" webpage, www.northumbriajournals.co.uk/index.php/ijcle/about/history, accessed 6 April 2017.
12 See: website of Global Alliance for Justice Education, "About GAJE" webpage, www.gaje.org/about-gaje/, accessed 6 April 2017.
13 See: website of Global Alliance for Justice Education, "Past Conferences" webpage, www.gaje.org/conferences/past-conferences/ and "8th Worldwide Conference" webpage, www.gaje.org/8th-worldwide-conference, both accessed 6 April 2017.
14 See: website of Global Alliance for Justice Education, "Mission Statement" webpage, www.gaje.org/about-gaje/mission-statement/, accessed 6 April 2017 (emphasis in original)
15 See: website of International Association of Legal Ethics, "History of IAOLE" webpage, www.iaole.org/history-of-iaole/, accessed 6 April 2017.
16 See: website of White & Case, "Social Responsibility" webpage, www.whitecase.com/social-responsibility/legal-education-programs, accessed 6 April 2017. See also: P.M. Genty, *Dichotomy no longer? The role of the private business sector in educating the future Russian legal professions*, Fordham Urban Law Journal, 40, 2013, 213, 288–290 (describing the 2011 conference, in which the author participated).
17 See: ibid. See also: White and Case, *Those who do, also teach*, Social Responsibility Review, 2014, available at: www.whitecase.com/publications/story/those-who-do-also-teach, accessed 14 October 2016.
18 Apart from prescribing the minimum number of credits a law student must take to obtain a law degree, the ABA standards require only that a student have completed a professional responsibility course, a writing requirement, and as noted below, six hours of experiential education. See: American Bar Association, *2016–2017, Standards and rules of procedure for approval of law schools*, Standard 303(a) and Standard 311, available at: www.americanbar.org/content/dam/aba/publications/misc/legal_education/Standards/2016_2017_standards_chapter3.authcheckdam.pdf, accessed 15 October 2016 (requiring the completion of 83 credit hours for graduation and stating that "at least 64 of these credit hours shall be in courses that require attendance in regularly scheduled classroom sessions or direct faculty instruction.").
19 See: ibid. Standard 303(a)(3) (requiring one or more experiential course(s) totaling at least six credit hours. "Experiential course" is defined as a simulation course, law clinic, or field placement.)
20 See, e.g.: R.J. Wilson, *General report: the role of practice in legal education*, 18th International Congress on Comparative Law, Washington, D.C., July 2010, 10–14; M.G. Bolocan (ed.),

Professional legal ethics: a comparative perspective, ABA Central European and Eurasian Law Initiative, Legislative and Research Program, 2002, 4; L.S. Terry, *An introduction to the European Community's legal ethics code, part I: an analysis of the CCBE code of conduct*, Georgetown Journal of Legal Ethics, 7, 1993, 1, 10–11.

21 M. Damaška, *The common law/civil law divide: residual truth of a misleading distinction*, Supreme Court Review (2nd edn), 49, 2010, 3.

22 Professor Damaška also notes that there are differences between the U.S. and other common law systems that are, in some respects, as significant as the differences between civil and common law systems. See: ibid., 12–13.

23 Ibid., 15–16.

24 Ibid., 17.

25 For a discussion of a method for doing this in the context of legal ethics, see: P.M. Genty, *The challenges of developing cross-cultural legal ethics education, professional development, and guidance for the legal professions*, Journal of the Professional Lawyer, 2011, 37.

Chapter 2

Experiential learning from the continental viewpoint

If the cap fits . . .

Cristina Amato

2.1 Academic teaching in continental Europe: a short historical overview

It is well known that in Italy at first – and later on all over western continental Europe[1] – the growth of professional lawyers was strictly linked to the birth and rise of universities. From the very beginning of the 12th century, the presence in Bologna of nearly one thousand students coming from all over Italy and Western Europe[2] to become acquainted with the Roman ancient texts enhanced legal culture, as well as the book industry.[3] At this time, the *Corpus Iuris* was *the* law: a treasure chest where the jurist could find anything he or she needed to understand and solve a real case.

Since the 12th century, universities and their legal teaching spread across continental Europe, accompanied by the development of didactic study methods drawing heavily on universities' bylaws, informed by Aristotle's legacy ('*scuola dei Commentatori*'). The importance of an ordered method in teaching had already been determined by the masters of the *trivia* (*grammatici, dialettici, retori*), aided by philosophers[4] and later on by the jurists. Cino da Pistoia, in particular, gives us evidence of the importance attributed to the didactic methods, publishing a treatise dealing with the need for and importance of order.[5] Early jurists affirmed the legitimacy of legal text by conferring to the law the status of a science, or *ars*.[6] According to the classical method adopted by the *Commentatori,* as described by Cino da Pistoia,[7] the lecture was strictly structured into: *lectio literae* (reading of the legal text); *divisio legis* (logical distinctions of the different components of the law); *expositio* (critical exposition of the legal text); *positio casum* (presentation of a particular case with pedagogical aims); *collectio notabilium* (presentation of the main issues raised by the law); *contraria* (possible objections); and *quaestiones* (controversial issues). *Contraria* would consist of a discussion of different possible constructive solutions offered by previous or contemporary scholars, in order to solve an apparent legal inconsistency. Usually the *Magister* (the professor) would supersede such opinions according to his own construction, often adopting the technique of distinguishing. *Quaestiones*, on the other hand, were raised by the legal texts' ambiguities: the

Magister himself would highlight such ambiguities offering his own solution to cases not envisaged by the legal text. *Contraria* and *quaestiones* would thus give the Magister the possibility of discussing pro and cons and eventually providing the best solution (or the solution that might be considered as more probable among others, in compliance with a 'probabilistic logic'), according to the typical dialectic method (*ars opponendi et respondendi*).[8] They both had a central role of exposing the legal text in its entire *ratio*, as an expression of a rational, perfect, total order. In a historical perspective, though, they had the merit of expressing the opposite forces of conservative *versus* progressive opinions; the former represented by the *ius commune* sponsored by the imperial authority; the latter imposed by the local legislator in the *ius proprium*, result of modern market economy of the Italian Cities as autonomous States. The *quaestiones*, in particular, would often be disputed not only in the classroom during the lecture (*lectura de mane*); but in separate seminars (usually held once a week, in the afternoon) attended by young apprentice scholars as well. In the latter case (public *disputatio*) the magister would pose the questions to the participants a few days before the discussion; *doctores* and students participating to the discussion would then dispute the questions following a structured hierarchy (imposed by the university bylaws), and the *magister* would eventually disclose the solution at the end of the debate.[9]

It is important to stress the methodology applied in arguing legal cases, which can be described as a two-tier process: inductive at first and then deductive. The inductive reasoning would consist of a first step, where the jurist would distinguish facts (*quaestio facti*) from the legal issue (*quaestio iuris*).[10] In particular, the *quaestio facti* consisted in searching for truth – that is to objectively ascertain factual issues established by evidence describing in sufficient detail to establish factual credibility. It is clear from the very beginning that the *questio facti* was itself rooted into two *legal* concepts: which rules of evidence applied and which may be used to eliminate or select the facts at stake, implying the necessary knowledge of legal texts (*Corpus iuris* above all), where similar facts had already been addressed and problems resolved (*casus legis*). Once the *questio facti* was clarified, the second step would consist of a deductive process: the ancient legal texts were examined carefully, in order to find a *nomen iuris* to the facts at stake, and consequently pick up the adequate rules to be applied. Most often the adequate rules were not automatically discovered, but they went through a construction process where questions, pros and cons and general discussion took place. At the end of this process, it was presumed that any doubt would be settled and the legal issue (*questio iuris*) would eventually reach a rational and certain outcome. For the purposes of this paper, there are three important characteristics of such a teaching method. Understanding this helps to explain why traditional teaching across continental Europe is how it is.

First, the ancient Roman texts were accurately learned by the students,[11] even by heart, as they were considered the very essence of legal reasoning. Second, the essence of a *questio facti* depended on the construction of the *casus legis*, that is of a similar case faced and solved by the Roman texts. Third, *questio facti* and *iuris* were two parts of the same issue.

The didactic method can therefore be considered as an advanced approach to study given the historical context: while the lectures introduced the student to the required knowledge and construction of the legal texts, the questions that called for debate that – using Aristotelian logic – led to the resolution of practical cases. Knowledge, dialectic skills and professional abilities were eventually transmitted to students, who would participate actively to the lessons. Because students and teachers gathered in Italy first, and later on all over Europe (using Latin as the common language), the *mos italicus* spread everywhere in the Continent: universities – as 'republics of legal culture' – offered a pedagogical model of legal education that lasted for centuries, especially outside Italy, as a scientific, international and uniform didactic methodology.[12]

This two-tier process changed after the 13th century, in that the importance of the research of true facts almost disappeared in favor of the discussion of the legal issue, that is in favor of certain and unquestionable facts treated in the Roman texts, thus concentrating the legal arguments around the relevant rules to be applied to a *specific* case.[13]

Such evolution may be explained by the desire and need for certainty and absolute order so important in the turbulent days of the Medieval era. This has undoubtedly conditioned continental legal reasoning during the following centuries with its legacy still felt today.

While the early jurists' goal was to find the *ratio legis,* this changed during a period referred to elsewhere as emergence of humanistic jurisprudence.[14] For the first time the Roman *Corpus Iuris* was now being questioned, even criticized.[15] There was a transition with the formation of governmental authorities and consequently, the need for a new *jus commune* based on statutes passed by the king or emperor. The new conception of legal order later led to the German legal dogma method of the 19th century ('*Pandettistica*').

Leibniz represents one of the best examples of such a new perspective.[16] His treaty on the new method of teaching and learning jurisprudence[17] is entirely founded on the elaboration of logic (later on defined as 'symbolic'), able to construe a rational legal order based on axiomatic arguments and postulates, where the solution to real cases would be the only one possible, as based on 'scientific truths'. Nevertheless, notwithstanding his obsession for a rational legal order, Leibniz did not mix this goal with the teaching (and learning) methodology. What is extraordinary, especially given the subject of this book, is that Leibniz was writing in the 17th century. This highly respected and influential philosopher had a clear idea of pursuing education through active engagement and even play: teaching through games is suggested as the best way to achieve a good learning.[18] In Part II of his treatise (dedicated to education methodology in legal teaching), the author imagines the ideal path of legal education, which should consist of didactic and polemic courses. Didactic courses would provide students with a basic knowledge of legal texts and materials, founded on clear definitions of word or sentences, and on strict demonstrations of concepts; polemic courses would use simulated cases,[19] thus enabling students to apply principles and raise new legal issues. Leibniz affirms that legal education cannot consist in didactic and polemic courses only. Otherwise students would be *practitioners*, instead of *jurists*: a real jurist is expected, instead, to handle historical and exegetical competences.[20] How true that rings in certain academic quarters today!

In sum, the new natural method envisaged by Leibniz describes a complex path, whereas the deductive methodologies – directed to teach knowledge – were strictly applied with Aristotelian logic to maintain a rational legal order and eventually provide students with *practical* skills.

Despite these advances in thinking, by the end of the 17th century a distinction between academic and practical teaching – theory and praxis – was claimed: theory should be taught at university, while praxis should be acquired in the courts and tribunals and through the community of lawyers. In truth, before this age, the training of lawyers and practitioners was not clearly assigned to such communities or guilds: while the education of a jurist had been entrusted to the universities, the vocational course – though existing – had never acquired official autonomy.

A separate training course, in fact, did exist, even in Italy, from Medieval times. By the beginning of the 12th century a first guild of practitioners was registered (*Collegio dei Giudici*).[21] Since then, the legal profession has always been subject to the successful completion of legal studies at university.[22] Provided that the candidate has this credential and then passed an admission test to the bar (along with proving certain other requirements, such as residency in the borough where the bar was located), admission as a lawyer was granted. It was only after the Napoleonic reforms that the bar's full autonomy in legal training was recognized. In order to sit the bar examination, besides a university degree, the new regulations[23] required completion of a *vocational course*, that is, a two-year training period during which the candidate would acquire the necessary practical skills under the supervision of a qualified lawyer.[24]

Though the distinction between theory and praxis was still apparent, up to this period, in the Western civil law tradition legal education never lost its intrinsic characteristic of social science. Law was (and is) not (only) made out of concepts and universal principles but has been applied with social needs in mind – even in Medieval times.[25] My argument, therefore, is that a clear distinction between the educational role of universities and vocational guilds was not necessary because legal science taught at university from a didactic methodology had much respect for the practical goals of the law, a common denominator for the professional training of the students.

The shift toward natural law and positivism (in the 17th and 18th centuries) further underpinned the didactic method. Abstract legal thinking became a pedagogical tool enhancing the preservation of middle-class privileges.[26] According to this jurisprudence, private law should be interpreted and taught as pure science, based on reason and on social contract, separated from its historical base and factual demands – because the law was seen to provide rational answers to any social problem, valid for ever and for any society.[27] This approach has conditioned legal teaching in Italy and other countries of the civil law ever since.

In terms of authority, law became synonymous of the king's will, later on embodied into national (civil) codes. Codes were in fact promoted and promulgated as the supreme expression of the acknowledgment of state authority – a complete collection of rules and principles. Codes fulfilled the request of logic and became models of formalism resulting in a passive response from jurists who shied away from their potential role of serving the real needs of a growing society.[28] By the second half of the 19th century, a gap between legal 'scientists' and socio-economic reality was patent, deeply influencing legal education.[29]

By the end of the 19th century, the first signs of a crisis emerged: some Italian scholars started to show concern for social issues, questioning individualism and starting to assume a collective social responsibility. Interest began to emerge in the hitherto largely unknown and 'exotic' common law.[30] This movement would gain momentum during the 1930s alongside the American realistic movement. Following the upheavals of the Second World War, the majority of civil law scholars (as opposed to practitioners), however, still indulged in a formalist, positivistic and conceptual approach to study and importantly teaching, where norms were observed, interpreted and taught as *dogma*,[31] without any reference to particular facts, and with a strong compliance to statutory provisions. This followed the German school of 'Pandette' (or 'new critical school') and was at a time when the second civil code in Italy was passed. According to this perspective, the task of jurists and legal science was limited to construe the law through abstracts concepts and strict legal categories: any attempt to evaluate the law, by attributing goals of social justice, or searching for a more rational or convenient setting of the rules, should belong to the domain of the philosophy or sociology of law.[32] Clearly a tension was arising between the critical thinkers and the traditionalists.

Meanwhile, the law practitioners' guilds were prevalent across Europe as the places where practitioners could learn lawyering skills and apply their theoretical knowledge.

Soon after the Second World War, things began to change in the world of law and legal education: principles and rules began to be reflect the real world through the consideration of actual cases.[33] The Italian Constitution has played a pivotal role; a clear example is given by the meaning and contents of the principle of equality, otherwise presumed by the Italian Civil Code (in line with the libertarian ideas of the French revolution). The Constitution now made specific provision (art. 3, § 2 It. Const.) for equality – a fundamental principle to which private law should be submitted.[34]

During the 1970s, several legal movements appeared in Italian academic teaching.[35] For example, and in contrast with the dogmatic approach, the application of the law to current social needs was now considered in the context of the constitutional provision of equality.[36] The jurist's task was now said not to be limited to the mere construction of the written law, considered in an applied social setting. In addition, there was a call for law to be studied comparatively – taking into account theory and practice from both the civil and common law traditions.[37]

Such a legal revolution was supported by a new legislative era characterized by the appearance of statutes (most of them implementing European legislation) that took away rules and prestige from the civil code. The result was a breaking down of previously established order and a final admission of the complexity.[38]

It is also important to note the active role attributed to the state in Italy and other civil law countries in the latter third of the 20th century, particularly with shifts in the ideological base with frequent changes in the political flavor of government and as a consequence of membership of the (now) European Union.[39] Rigid rules imposed, top down, by the state have been partly superseded by a regulation of the market formed by laws and policies that arise from the very essence of economic needs and (for better or worse) rooted in freedom of the market.[40]

The current position in many countries under the civil law tradition, and reflected in approaches to legal education, can now be described as the turning from the dogmatic to the problematic – the latter allowing for consideration of practical issues and socio-economic demands.[41]

2.2 Universities and the legal profession – two institutions in decline?

What I tried to demonstrate in the first section of this chapter is that the characteristic of the civil law tradition, especially in Italy, rooted in a particular view of and adherence to legal science, does not mean that approaches to teaching and learning necessarily reject an applied pedagogy and a wider social mission – even if the format for delivery was (and is) still dominated by the lecture.

To find inspiration for effective learning, we might go back the ancient lessons of the Romans, when it was clear that questions of law and questions of facts were but different aspects of a same problem.

Since the 1930s, some more enlightened scholars realized there was a connection between the old dogmatic approach to teaching and the efficacy of learning:

> We currently teach in our universities as Irnerio used to teach in Bologna. The teacher climbs on the desk, and he gives a speech for one hour; he goes on with his speech, without wondering whether the students do understand what he is saying. [. . .] A method that does not have any reason in an era where the press gives students the opportunity of reading and learning by themselves. [. . .] If we do want to go on teaching,

> we should then assign a goal to our teaching, different from mere reading. Teaching is an intellectual exercise; it should be the very example of the intellectual elaboration of an advanced mind transmitted to younger students' minds eager to learn; it is by means of such a transcendent, intellectual infection that the Master shall influence his students. [. . .] I should teach my students how to learn, how to reason, how to criticize, how to research: in other words, to do whatever an active and positive mind is expected to do.[42]

It is now time to rethink the continental methodology of transmitting legal knowledge and of educating jurists more widely. We may discover that by a simple but reasoned pedagogy, the crisis that I believe exists both in the law school and the law profession can be tackled to the benefit of all.

There is, today, a greater demand on law to promote modern commerce whilst protecting human values,[43] not only in a socio-economic context, but also in the sphere of individual existence. Marriage, heterosexuality and homosexuality, raising and looking after children, technology, privacy and human rights are all part of the ever-complex world law is now and increasingly called upon to play its part in.[44] We are currently experiencing a neo-liberalist ideology, mitigated (in the case of Italy at least) by a (Catholic) attention to values, fundamental constitutional rights and trans and international treaties and charters. Jurists and practicing lawyers are, in consequence, required to understand contemporary society in its complexity, in its plurality of values and inconsistencies rather than playing a mere mechanical or declaratory role. It follows that legal education must, if it is to best serve all stakeholder interests, reflect this changing context.[45]

The challenge that our law schools face goes further to the entire university system:[46] "what is deeply incorrect in the current university setting is the method of teaching; if we do not accept to reform it, any other reform shall be worthless."[47] This is the case despite numerous changes that have taken place.[48] Whilst the university remains a place of liberty, discussion, dialogue, discovery and in-depth analysis, its methods have not moved with the times.[49] In Italy, as in many civil law jurisdictions, the university is predominantly a public service, and it is surely our duty to provide students (and the public who will be directly affected as taxpayers and indirectly as possible consumers of legal or educational services) with the highest quality of provision, within the present and foreseeable future social and economic context. The effective transmission of knowledge necessarily means a change in the strategy in terms of both 'what' and 'how' we teach (and learn). The 'what' in most civil law countries may be government-regulated (with some degree of flexibility passed down to the law school). The 'how' is more in the university domain and for members of the law faculty. The importance and limitations of traditional didactic methods have recently been addressed with several alternative approaches proposed.[50] These cover not only non-lecture-based approaches but rightly embrace e-technology, multi-disciplinary studies, problem solving and cooperative or team learning.[51] This is often posed as an addition to rather than instead of the traditional lecture.

Alongside this we are currently experiencing major changes to the various branches of the legal profession with accompanying complaints about quality of provision.[52] In a globalized society, particularly in a European context, lawyers are transforming their *modus operandi* and in consequence, status. This impacts on regulation (as is seen in Part 1 of Chapter 6 of this book). The challenge here is how to maintain the quality of service, preserving and promoting ethical values (particularly professional responsibility) whilst embracing and enhancing new functions.

The social composition of lawyers is changing (in relation to gender, ethnicity and economic background).[53] The organization is very different – with larger firms predominating and specialism increasing.[54] The guild-like institution is now turning into a larger and fragmented[55] professional sector, where a variety of practitioners offer their legal services within multiple forms of professional structures.[56] Increasingly, lawyers are becoming employee practitioners – a change from the self-employment/small firm approach of earlier years.

In terms of regulation and reputation, bar associations generally provide ethics codes and have the machinery to investigate, and where necessary discipline, transgressors. Additionally, the bar sets entry barriers to the profession, in order to control the human capital and quality of their members.

This background of largely self-regulatory mechanisms – which national bar associations have so far relied upon – is contrary to the EU policy of free movement and competition,[57] thus forcing many member states within the EU to modify their original models,[58] for national bar associations to adopt new regulatory frameworks and for lawyers to re-think the future of the legal profession.[59]

Against this backdrop, clinics in law schools are an ever-increasing phenomenon. As has been noted elsewhere: 'Unbundling and fragmentation are also equally relevant and raise questions about how we train the lawyers of the future': legal clinical teaching is in fact growing everywhere in Europe.[60]

What can be, then, the role of experiential learning in general and clinical legal education in particular in tackling the challenges mentioned above – inertia in law schools' delivery modes and pursuance of a contemporarily relevant and high quality of legal professional? To this I will now turn.

2.3 Experiential learning in civil law schools: an Italian case study

A seminal article appeared in a prestigious law review in 1935.[61] Even at that time, the author was able to claim that it was a mistake for law schools not to have clinical teachings: like students of medicine, law students as well should attend such courses. Critics protest that a clinical methodology is nothing more than a duplication of the vocational course students may (depending on jurisdiction) have to take post-graduation. Let us counter that objection.

First, law students are not necessarily going to become practicing lawyers. They may go on to be judges, notaries, consultants, administrators, politicians or legislators. They may work in commerce and industry or in human resources. Some may choose to teach or work in the not-for-profit sector. To all of them, a clinic provides the challenges, the opportunities and the responsibilities of applying theory, skills and values in the context of a real or realistic (in the case of simulation) case.[62]

Instead of simply immersing themselves in codes or books, students can take an educational lead, first experiencing the law and then, with the help of professors and their peers, analyzing and debating the legal content be it a contract, a code, a judgment or a draft document. The significance of the content can fall to discussion, including the need for law reform, the comparative position in other jurisdictions and the wider role of law in society. Such an opportunity can inform any student not just those bent on a career in a law office.

Second, a vocational course under a lawyer's supervision is substantially different from a clinical teaching in a university setting,[63] in that the latter is a *reasoned* application of the law,[64] it does not consist in illustrating the rule deriving from case law or statute law: it rather consists in *how* to find the rules and *how* to apply them.[65] Moreover, clinical teaching is also concerned with developing lawyering skills: building a relationship with the client, fact-finding, dispute resolution methods, legal drafting, teamwork and the like.[66] The requirement in a legal clinic to reflect on experience differs from both the traditional lecture setting and a vocational training program in that the process of reflection is an overt expectation with encounters between students and professors/supervisors designed in a way that visits and revisits relevant experience, building in the students' minds the need to ask and answer questions such as what happened and why, what might have happened and whether there is anything different that could be done to improve on either the student performance for the future or the law in general. The careful selection of cases and clients can be controlled in the clinic to ensure a variety of casework that serves both the interest of the client and the teaching and learning needs of the student.

Third, clinical teaching consists of a methodology that applies the inductive method, from the particular case to the general doctrine.[67] Such a methodology allows students (particularly those in civil law countries) to extend their experience from the traditional deductive approach enshrined in the commitment to 'legal science'. Deductive and inductive methods, therefore, come together to mutual benefit.

Fourth, clinical teaching is also (though not exclusively)[68] a tool to pursue social justice and promote advanced legal ethics,[69] as real cases most often involve those with unmet legal needs who are unlikely, for financial, logistical or cultural reasons, to get help elsewhere. Many are highly vulnerable.[70] Universities can be ideal places to address these needs whilst at the same time enhancing educational provision. The relative lack of economic pressures and the human and other resource-rich environment makes for a highly responsive context for public service. This also can serve the mission of the university in terms of building meaningful relationships with the public, NGOs and government, as well as with the legal profession in its various guises.

Setting up legal clinics in law schools comes with challenges, but these are surmountable, as evidenced by the growing number of such initiatives in Italy and further afield in the civil and common law worlds.[71] I have the privilege of working in the University of Brescia, where the first Italian clinical courses were implemented.[72] The Brescia clinic is a multidisciplinary model. Courses are run over the two semesters, focusing on a wide range of what might be broadly termed human rights cases. Real issues are tackled by students under close supervision of professionally qualified staff (academic and practitioner), in cooperation with local NGOs. Small groups of students (three to seven) work on each case handling matters selected by the clinic board (which consists of the entire clinic). The casework comes first (our professional obligation to the client) and then the theoretical and deductive reflection follows. Specific seminars may be held to address particular issues, and all clinic students are invited to attend these. The students report that they are extremely satisfied with their experience, and clients say they are very grateful for the prompt, professional and sympathetic service they receive.

Notwithstanding some practical difficulties,[73] and the absence of a coherent strategy in clinical legal education across my law school and I suspect, in others across the continent, it is now a case of developing a measured and strategic way to ensure that future provision of legal services and applied legal education can be improved and sustained.[74]

Notes

1 Irnerio is said to have taught from 1112 to 1125, and after him his students Bulgaro, Martino, Iacopo and Ugo, known as the four doctors; Naples followed in 1224, and later on Padova (1222) and Rome (1244). Outside Italy, the legal teaching at Universities spread out in the south of France first (Montpellier), and later on in Paris, Reims, Oxford and Prague, followed by developments in Ireland, Spain, Germany: A. Padoa Schioppa, *Storia del diritto in Europa: Dal medioevo all'età contemporanea*, Bologna, Il Mulino, 2009, 82–85.

2 Students coming from Italy were identified as *citramontani*, while the others coming from any other territory beyond the Alps were called *ultramontani*.

3 The *Corpus Iuris* was divided into five parts, each copied out by several writers (*stationarii*) into standardized *folios* (the *pecies*). Once each part had been reproduced into thousands of identical *folios*, the five parts were unified (into thousands of complete copies, or *quinterni*) and distributed to the students: A. Padoa Schioppa, op cit., 125–127.

4 R.M. Spiazzi (ed.), *S. Thomae Aquinatis in Decem Libros Ethicorum Aristotelis ad Nicomacum*, Torino, Marietti, 1964, 3, at 1.1.: 'sicut dicit Philsophus in principio Metaphysicae sapientis est ordinare. Cuius ratio est, quia sapientia est potentissima perfectio rationis'.

5 *Lectura super Codice*, 1314: A. Padoa Schioppa, *Storia del diritto in Europa: Dal medioevo all'età contemporanea*, Bologna, Il Mulino, 2009, 153; A. Padovani, *'Tenebo hunc ordinem':*

Metodo e struttura della lezione nei giuristi medievali (secoli XII-XIV), The Legal History Review, 2011, 353 ff.

6 See: P. Grossi, *L'ordine giuridico medieval*, Bari, Laterza, 2006, in particular at 80–85, 144–151.

7 A. Padovani, '*Tenebo hunc ordinem*': *Metodo e struttura della lezione nei giuristi medievali (secoli XII-XIV)*, The Legal History Review, 2011, 354; F. Calasso, *Medioevo del diritto, I: Le fonti*, Milano, Giuffré, 1954, 594.

8 M. Bellomo, Legere, repetere, disputare: Introduzione ad una ricerca sulle 'quaestiones' civilistiche, in M. Bellomo (ed.), *'Medioevo edito e inedito', I: Scholae, universitates, studia*, Roma, Il Cigno, 1988, 53 ff., 68–70. The relevance of the *quaestiones* is also stressed by: A. Padoa Schioppa, op cit., 153.

9 A detailed description of the different literary forms of the *Quaestiones disputata* (treaties, selected extracts) can be found in: M. Bellomo, Legere, repetere, disputare: Introduzione ad una ricerca sulle 'quaestiones' civilistiche, in M. Bellomo (ed.), *Medioevo edito e inedito, I: Scholae, universitates, studia*, Roma, Il Cigno, 1988, 75–97.

10 M. Bellomo, 'Factum' e 'ius': Itinerari di ricerca tra le certezze e i dubbi del pensiero giuridico medievale, in M. Bellomo (ed.), *'Medioevo edito e inedito', II: 'Scienza del diritto e società medievale*, Roma, Il Cigno, 1997, 67–79.

11 From the beginning of the 13th century, lectures on the five parts of the *Corpus Iuris* lasted for at least two years and were repeated twice. Therefore, the education of a jurist might last for 7 to 8 years: A. Padoa Schioppa, op cit., 128.

12 Ibid., 130.

13 The scenario became much more complicated from the end of the 13th century by the rise of a market economy due to the phenomenon of urbanization and the emergence of local laws (*ius proprium*) that superseded Roman texts. The rise of a market economy created new legal cases that could not be found in the ancient texts and therefore could not be easily solved according to the existing rules. The rise of *ius proprium* forced jurists to harmonize local statutes and orders with the authority of ancient sources in order to find new solutions adequate to new problems. See: M. Bellomo, 'Factum' e 'ius': Itinerari di ricerca tra le certezze e i dubbi del pensiero giuridico medievale, in M. Bellomo (ed.), *Medioevo edito e inedito, II, 'Scienza del diritto e società medievale*, Roma, Il Cigno, 1997, 80–89.

14 V. Piano Mortari, *Diritto, logica, metodo nel secolo XVI*, Napoli, Jovene, 1978, 281–282, 342.

15 The most important scholars whose humanistic approach would have influenced the modern legal methods were Budé (who was not a jurist, but a *gramaticus*), Zasius and Alciato: I. Birocchi, *Alla ricerca dell'ordine: Fonti e cultura giuridica nell'età moderna*, Torino, Giappichelli, 2002, 12 ff. Budé, in particular, believed in the importance of pedagogy applied in legal education, where clarity and simplicity would represent the rational pedagogical order necessary to 'reach' the student. See: V. Piano Mortari, *Diritto, logica, metodo nel secolo XVI*, Napoli, Jovene, 1978, 335–345.

16 C.M. De Iuliis, *Leibniz e la scienza giuridica tra topica e dogmatica*, Europa e diritto privato, 711 (3), 2010, 711–748.

17 G.W. Von Leibniz, *Il nuovo metodo di apprendere ed insegnare la giurisprudenza: in base ai principi dell'arte didattica premessi nella parte generale, e alla luce dell'esperienza*, Milano, Giuffré, 2012 (original edn: Frankfurt, 1667).

18 Ibid., 19.

19 Ibid., 98–101.

20 This definition of the jurist's competences can be found in: M. Bellomo, Una nuova figura intellettuale: il giurista, in M. Bellomo (ed.), *Medioevo edito ed inedito, II, Scienza del diritto e società medievale*, Roma, Il Cigno, 1997, 12–18.

21 A. Padoa Schioppa, op cit., 137.

22 In 1158 the bylaws of the University of Bologna stated that the law profession was reserved only for practitioners who had successfully studied law at university for five

years; subsequently, though, university's bylaws would impose different durations of legal teaching, up to a maximum of seven years.

23 *Nuovo metodo giudiziario*, April 14, 1804: S. Parini Vincenti, Ad Auxilium Vocatus: Studi sul praticantato da Napoleone alla Legge professionale del 1874: l'esperienza normativa, in A. Padoa Schioppa (ed.), *Avvocati e avvocatura nell'Italia dell'Ottocento*, Bologna, Il Mulino, 2009, 59 ff.

24 The length of the vocational period has changed over the centuries: since the 19th century, several reforms concerning the training period have been passed. At present, the vocational course stands at 18 months.

25 F. Macario and M. Lobuono (eds.), *Il diritto civile nel pensiero dei giuristi*, Padova, Cedam, 2010, 102–104.

26 This is a basic historical assumption: P. Grossi, *La cultura del civilista italiano: Un profilo storico*, Milano, Giuffré, 2002, 1–2.

27 A. Padoa Schioppa, op cit., 328–331.

28 P. Grossi, *La cultura del civilista italiano: Un profilo storico*, Milano, Giuffré, 2002, 12–14.

29 See the father of the Pandette school in Germany: B. Windscheid, *Diritto delle pandette, II*, Torino, Utet, 1904; P. Oertmann (ed.), *Gesammelte Reden und Abbandlungen*, Leipzig, Duncker und Humblot, 1904.

30 See G. Venezian, *Opere giuridiche*, 2 vols., Roma, Athenaeum, 1930.

31 A smart and appreciated representative of the civilian dogmatic approach can be found in: F. Santoro Passarelli, *Dottrine generali del diritto civile*, Napoli, Jovene, 1944.

32 F. Santoro Passarelli, Quid jus?, in S. Passarelli (ed.), *Ordinamento e diritto civile: Ultimi saggi*, Napoli, Esi, 1988, 25.

33 For an approach that describes the current European private law position see: P. Grossi, Il diritto civile italiano alle soglie del terzo millennio, in F. Macario and M. Lobuono (eds.), *Il diritto civile nel pensiero dei giuristi*, Padova, Cedam, 2010, 417–418.

34 P. Grossi, Il diritto civile italiano alle soglie del terzo millennio, in F. Macario and M. Lobuono (eds.), *Il diritto civile nel pensiero dei giuristi*, Padova, Cedam, 2010, 405 ff., 412.

35 On the alternative use of the law, see: P. Barcellona (ed.), Introduzione, in *L'uso alternativo del diritto*, Roma – Bari, Laterza, 1973, i–viii.

36 'Alternative use of the law' is clearly defined by P. Grossi, op cit., 160: "According to the vision of those who have created this expression, 'alternative use of the law' means the use of legal tools in order to satisfy different interests than those belonging to the dominant social class which has created the traditional legal tools".

37 See in particular: G. Gorla, *Il contratto*, II vols., Milano, Giuffré, 1954; R. Sacco, Il contratto, in diretto da F. Vassalli, *Trattato di diritto civile*, Torino, Utet, 1975.

38 G. Vettori (ed.), *Persona e mercato – Lezioni*, Padova, Cedam, 1996, 1.

39 G. Zagrebelsky, *Il diritto mite*, Torino, Einaudi, 1992.

40 G. Alpa, *Trattato di diritto civile: Storia, fonti interpretazione*, vol. I, Milano, Giuffré, 2000, 464 ff.

41 F. Macario and M. Lobuono (eds.), *Il diritto civile nel pensiero dei giuristi*, Padova, Cedam, 2010, 373; L. Mengoni, Problema e sistema nella controversia sul metodo giuridico, in L. Mengoni, F. Modugno and F. Rimoli (eds.), *Diritto e valori*, Bologna, Il Mulino, 1985, 55.

42 V. Scialoja, Sugli studi giuridici e sulla preparazione alle professioni giudiziarie (discorso in senato nella tornata del 20 maggio 1923), in V. Scialoja (ed.), *Scritti e discorsi politici, II, Sul bilancio della giustizia – Ordinamento giudiziario – Istruzione superiore: La scuola e la guerra*, Roma, Anonima Romana Editoriale, 1936, 199–200. See also: P. Calamandrei, *Troppi avvocati*, Firenze, ESI, 1921, 114; and W. Bigiavi, *La riforma degli studi giuridici in Francia*, Rivista di diritto civile, 1956, 131. More recently, a scholar very sensitive to the needs of legal pedagogy has proposed the metaphor of the jar: teaching law at university means pressing as much information as possible in the student's course, stamping the jar with a final thesis and labelling it with the university degree: V. Zeno Zencovich, *Ci vuole poco per fare un'Università migliore*, Il Sirente, e-book, 2011, 36.

43 A. Padoa Schioppa, op cit., Bologna, Il Mulino, 2009, 641.
44 N. Lipari, *Luigi Mengoni, ovvero la dogmatica dei valori*, Rivista trimestrale di diritto e procedura civile, 1063 (4), 2002, 1063–1113.
45 P. Perlingieri, Il diritto civile e la complessità del sistema, in P. Perlingieri (ed.), *L'ordinamento vigente e i suoi valori*, Napoli, Esi, 2006, 231; and A. Padoa Schioppa, op cit., 657–658.
46 V. Zeno Zencovich, *Ci vuole poco per fare un'Università migliore*, Il Sirente, e-book, 2011.
47 V. Scialoja, op cit., 199.
48 From 1999 and 2010 there have been three main statutory reforms, along with a raft of governmental decrees and regulations: L. n. 509/1999; L. n. 2003/53; L. n. 240/2010.
49 V. Zeno Zencovich, *Ci vuole poco per fare un'Università migliore*, Il Sirente, e-book, 2011, 6–7.
50 V. Zeno Zencovich (ed.), *Come insegnare il diritto: metodi, modelli, valutazione*, Torino, Giappichelli, 2004: in the Introduction, Zencovich stresses the importance of how to teach law, especially given that higher education is predominantly a public service in Italy.
51 G. Pascuzzi, *Avvocati formano avvocati*, Bologna, Il Mulino, 2015; G. Pascuzzi, *Giuristi si diventa*, Bologna, Il Mulino, 2008; G. Pascuzzi, *Scienze cognitive e formazione universitaria del giurista*, Sistemi intelligenti, 137 (1), 2007, 137–139.
52 G. Alpa, *L'avvocato*, Bologna, Il Mulino, 2011.
53 According to the data published by the Italian Bar National Bar Association, 47.02 percent of the Italian lawyers are women at present. See: www.consiglionazionaleforense.it/documents/20182/50638/Statistiche+Albo+Telematico+Nazionale+Avvocati/65b9991e-6ead-42cb-974d-7752fb00f42e, accessed 24 October 2016.
54 H. Sommerlad, S. Harris-Short, S. Vaughan and R. Young (eds.), *The future of legal education and the legal profession*, Hart, Oxford and Portland, 2015, 1–5.
55 L. n. 226, August 2, 2006, art. 2, par. 1, let. c) has abolished the original statutory prohibition of interdisciplinary partnerships, provided that the legal service is supplied by a lawyer, who can be liable of any damage as member of the local bar: See C. Amato, I 'nuovi rischi' da obbligazioni di risultato e da svolgimento di professioni liberali: riflessi sui profili contrattuali dell'assicurazione di responsabilità professionale, in F.D. Busnelli and G. Comandé (eds.), *L'assicurazione tra codice civile e nuove esigenze: per un approccio precauzionale al governo dei rischi*, Milano, Giuffré, 2009, 17 ff.
56 As regards the legal professional structures in Italy, according to the L. n. 96, 2 February 2001 (arts. 16–26) legal practices can now be exercised in the form of partnership (unlimited corporations are still prohibited), provided that the sole object of the partnership is the collective exercise of legal service, and that all the members are qualified as lawyers. See also: T. Heremans, *Professional services in the EU Internal Market*, Oxford and Portland, Hart Publishing, 2012, 38.
57 See: European Commission: *Communication 'Professional Services – scope for more reform' of 5 September 2005* – COM (2005) 405 final; *Communication from the Commission, Report on Competition in Professional Services*, COM (2004) 83 final, Brussels, February 9th, 2004. See also: OECD, *Competitive Restrictions in Legal Professions*, DAF/COMP(2007)39, January 28th 2008; and L.S. Terry, *The European Commission project regarding competition in professional service*, Northwest Journal of International Law & Business, 1 (29), 2009.
58 In the UK, the Legal Service Act (2007) brought to an end the total self-regulatory powers of the legal profession. See: H. Sommerland, el al, op cit., 7. In Italy, the Italian legislature now imposed new rules concerning the operation of lawyers (the 'Bersani law') and L. n. 247/2012.
59 The situation in the United Kingdom is well captured in: J. Webb, *The LETRs (still) in the post: the legal education and training review and the reform of legal services education and training – a personal (re)view*, in H. Sommerlad, et al (eds.), op cit., 5. The report, *Setting standards: the future of legal service education and training regulation in England and Wales*, is available at: www.letr.org.uk, accessed 26 October 2016.

60 H. Sommerlad, et al, op cit., 13.
61 See: F. Carnelutti, *Clinica del diritto*, Rivista di diritto processuale, 169 (I), 1935, 169–175.
62 The distinction and correlation between knowledge, skills and competency or ability has been defined in the Annex I to the Recommendation 23 April 2008/C 111 of the European Parliament and Council on the establishment of the European Qualifications Framework for lifelong learning. Lett. '(g) "'knowledge' means the outcome of the assimilation of information through learning. Knowledge is the body of facts, principles, theories and practices that is related to a field of work or study. In the context of the European Qualifications Framework, knowledge is described as theoretical and/or factual". Lett. (h): "'skills' means the ability to apply knowledge and use know-how to complete tasks and solve problems. In the context of the European Qualifications Framework, skills are described as cognitive (involving the use of logical, intuitive and creative thinking) or practical (involving manual dexterity and the use of methods, materials, tools and instruments)". Lett. (i), defines *competence* as " the proven ability to use knowledge, skills and personal, social and/or methodological abilities, in work or study situations and in professional and personal development."
63 F. Carnelutti, op cit., 170–171.
64 Ibid., 172.
65 Ibid., 173.
66 E. Poillot, *Comparing legal clinics: is there a way to a European Clinical Culture? the Luxemburg experience,* Proceedings of the Naples Conference 15–16th October 2015.
67 F. Carnelutti, op cit., 174.
68 E. Poillot, op cit. Poillot argues in favor of a European clinical model essentially based on teaching skills, rather than the pursuit of social justice.
69 See the contribution in this book by L. Bugatti, *Ethics, professionalism and the law* (Chapter 5, part 3).
70 F. Carnelutti, op cit., 174.
71 C. Bartoli, *Legal clinics in Europe: for a commitment of higher education in social justice*, Diritto & questioni pubbliche, special issue, May 2016, available at: www.dirittoequestionipubbliche.org/page/2016_nSE_Legal-clinics-in-Europe/index.htm, accessed 24 October 2016.
72 The Brescia model, is described in: C. Amato, Developing strategies for academic and financial sustainability: the Brescia Legal Clinic's experience, in E. Poillot (ed.), *L'einseignement clinique du droit*, Larcier, Luxembourg, 2014, 141–154.
73 G. Smorto, *Clinica legale: Un manuale operative*, Palermo, Next, 2015: the book provides a useful toolkit for setting up and running a clinic from a teaching and learning perspective.
74 F. Carnelutti, op cit., 175.

Chapter 3

Experiential learning

Just for 'common lawyers' – really?

Richard Grimes and Anne-Lise Sibony

3.1 A starting point

In the Introduction to this book, a symposium is mentioned. One of us (Grimes) shared his experience of clinical teaching in various settings (literally from **A**fghanistan to **Z**imbabwe) and explained more broadly the benefits he saw in experiential learning. As explained earlier, many civil law participants at this event expressed considerable concern and in some stages showed overt resistance to the idea of developing experiential learning methods in the civil law world. Meanwhile, the other author of this chapter (Sibony), who was educated and teaches in a civil law environment, albeit with limited 'clinical experience', felt a strong urge to disagree with these apparent opponents. Her intuition was that the civil/common law distinction was not in fact the relevant dividing line between experiential learning enthusiasts and experiential learning sceptics. Clinical legal education may have seemed foreign territory to these continental colleagues, but this was perhaps bedded less in the differences between the two systems and more in a lack of familiarity and specific cultural contexts and perceptions found there.

A core of delegates showed sufficient interest to explore this hypothesis, and Grimes hosted a further meeting in York in June 2014. The purpose of the *Cooks, kitchens and the law*[1] workshop was to analyse the potential of learning by doing across the two legal worlds. Delegates from a wide range of Western and Eastern European countries along with representatives from South America, Australasia and Asia came together to exchange views. The deliberations at that gathering further convinced us of the potential for major reforms and consequential improvements in legal education in our respective countries using clinical and other experiential learning and teaching methods.

This chapter seeks to flesh out this intuition, which other contributions in this volume then put to the test.

We first attempt to expose the thesis of the accusation ("clinical legal education is good for common lawyers – only") and then seek to rebut it. In the process, we attempt to critique the notion that learning must start with idées reçues (received wisdom), which appears to be the case at present in both (predominantly) civil and (to a lesser extent) common law education systems.

Here we look at a set of themes that lie at the heart of the form and content of legal education in any jurisdiction. To what extent does legal knowledge and do skills and values matter? What is the role of a law school, and to what extent should other stakeholders with a vested interest in what law schools produce be recognised and their agenda served?

In addressing these important concerns, we ask whether and how the legal environment of a civil or common law system affects the design of a legal curriculum. Do the acknowledged differences between the civil and common law worlds impact on how legal education is structured and delivered? Is there a role for experiential learning, and if so why and how?

Our short answer to these questions is that, contrary to a widely shared notion among civil law professors, teaching methods based on experiential learning are not good just for 'common lawyers'. Rather, we argue that experiential learning brings benefits that enhance the learning and teaching experience in any subject and under any system, including legal ones.

This assertion is founded both on personal experience and educational theory. Personal experience will be alluded to at various points in this and following chapters. Educational theory pertaining to experiential learning is briefly reviewed in section 3.2 below. Section 3.3 is devoted to reflecting on contact points between experiential learning and legal education under the civil and common law traditions. Importantly, we find connecting factors in both. Section 3.4 offers our views on why there is room for convergence between civil and common law educational methods around experiential learning, namely because the value of experiential learning is not linked to content. Section 3.5 briefly concludes.

3.2 A theoretical framework

The recognition of the value of learning through observation and practical application is nothing new. Confucius is credited with saying: 'By three methods we may learn wisdom: First, by reflection, which is noblest; Second, by imitation, which is easiest; and third by experience, which is the bitterest.'[2] Whilst we might agree neither with the proposition and order nor with the idea that experience is necessarily a painful encounter, it is interesting to see the concepts of reflection, imitation (role-play and simulation) and experience mentioned at such an early point in history and linked together in this way.

The following quotation is also attributed to Confucius: 'I am told, I forget; I see, I remember; I do, I understand'.[3] Learning by doing is seen (rightly, we say) as a fundamental stepping stone to learning, especially when integrated with other forms of educational delivery – yes, even we see a place for more traditional forms of learning!

Whilst dwelling on some of the world's influential thinkers, it is worth mentioning what Einstein apparently said: 'Information is not knowledge. The only source of knowledge is experience'.[4] Whether these words were uttered by the great man we cannot be certain, but as a pithy saying, it fits well with what early writers have recorded and what subsequent scholars have written. We will be more specific on sources shortly, but the above quotations, whatever their true origin, accord with the gist of our arguments and a host of personal and reported anecdotal evidence. They also set the scene for a more thorough analysis of pedagogic theory.

Much of what has been written and debated in this realm relates to education generally, rather than to legal education specifically. As we show below, it is only in relatively recently times that those responsible for the design and delivery of legal education have focused on how teaching and learning might be improved based on a relevant theoretical framework.

At the turn of the 20th century John Dewey, an American philosopher and educational reformer, extolled the virtues of using practical experience as an integral part of learning and teaching.[5] Seeing the education process as very much a shared experience between teacher and learner, Dewey broke new and, at the time, radical ground in his attempts to improve students' education and the educational system. The use of an application context also accords with longer-established practices, of practical training periods for lawyers under the common law system as, also, in many civil law countries.

Much more recently, Donald Schön's seminal work on experience and reflection (remember Confucius) describes what effective learning can look like using the analogy of the swamp. Schön suggests that, in order the make sense of the world or specific aspects of it, one needs to descend into the swamp and take what might now be referred to as a 'reality check'. That experience alone, however, is insufficient to extract and digest the relevant learning. One then needs to retreat to higher ground in order to have both the distance and time to deconstruct and make sense of what was encountered down below. The obvious setting here, in the context of this book, would be the classroom – where the student and teacher can engage in an in-depth discussion of what happened and why, what could have happened and how this might inform future action and analysis.[6] In other words and in educational terms, one needs to retreat to higher ground to analyse and make sense of the 'mess' that is life.

Around the same time (early 1980s), David Kolb developed similar ideas. Although Kolb has subsequently been criticised for presenting an over-simplistic and one-dimensional model for learning,[7] we suggest the learning cycle originally presented in Kolb's work is a very helpful representation of the nature and process of learning (Figure 3.1).

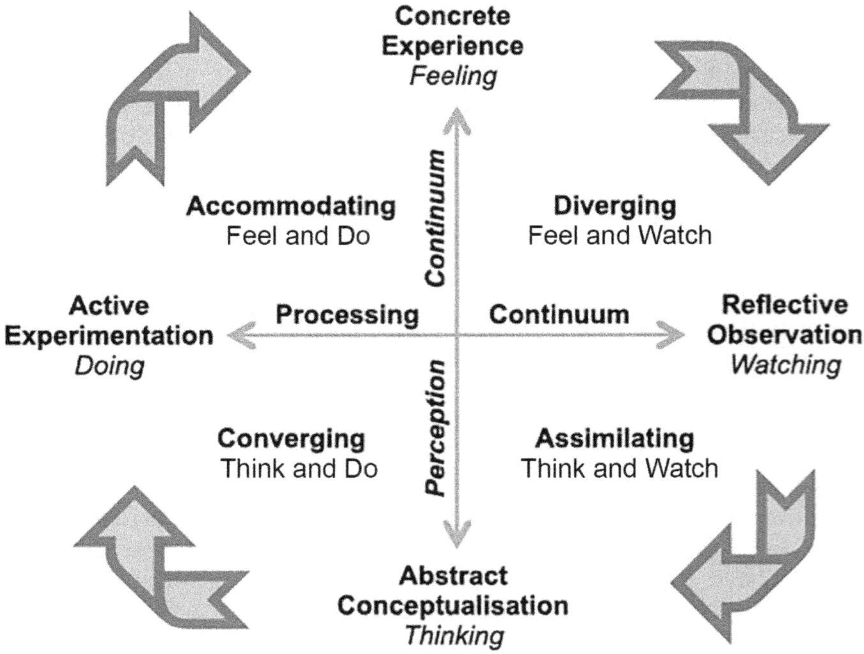

Figure 3.1 Kolb's learning cycle

This cycle encompasses, at various points, the acquisition of experience, reflections on that experience, abstraction to identify the issues/theory at stake and then application (or further application depending on how often the cycle is repeated) of theory to practice.[8] As the process is circular (albeit not necessarily sequential as described above), one stage may well inform another and the learning process may see several, if not more, revolutions of the circle as understanding advances. Anyone who has considered the value of continuing professional development (CPD) will be familiar with this concept.

Further important work can be found in the publications of Graham Gibbs. Gibbs coins the terms 'surface' and 'deep learning'. The former fits with the early stages of development shown in Bloom's taxonomy as remembering and understanding.[9] Deeper (and by implication, more effective) learning[10] is more likely to occur if the learner is exposed to a process of structured reflection where initial knowledge acquisition is scrutinised through discourse between learners and teachers – a facilitated reflective process.[11] Gibbs not only gives us the pegs on which to hang the proverbial hats in terms of concepts but then provides us with a set of tools for ensuring that the pegs stay on the wall – even down to the nuts and bolts (or possibly screws) for ensuring effective facilitative pedagogic practice.

The continued mention of reflection perhaps suggests an intuitive exercise – think about it and you will think 'deeper' as a result. We suggest this is not the case and reflection needs, as all aspects of learning and teaching do, content, form and the relevant expertise, in order to maximise the learning opportunity.[12] It is also not a one-way street – reflection 'in' and 'on action'[13] can inform all participants in the learning process. We are all never too old or wise to learn. To assist with this, Jennifer Moon's more recent work on strategies for reflection is worth mentioning here.[14] Moon discusses both the why and how of reflection, providing not only a theoretical framework for understanding the principles for effective learning and teaching but a set of resources for putting reflection into practice.

As can be seen, experience as a starting point for knowledge acquisition (and, as we later argue, skill and value development) is clearly underpinned by educationalists. A structured and facilitated reflective component is said to enhance the process and maximise the learning potential.

What about theories of experiential learning specifically in legal education?

As suggested above, learning about the law and the legal system is surely no different in principle from learning anything else. It is perhaps not surprising that academics in the generic education field have historically given more thought and published space to the process of learning and how we might learn more effectively. That is, after all, their business. Over the past decade, however, legal educators have been catching up with extensive writings on learning in general and experiential learning in particular. Much of this has been spearheaded by Julian Webb, many of whose publications have focused on learning by doing and the need for theory as a basis for development and change.[15] Several journals of international standing now focus on how we learn the law rather than what we learn in terms of substantive rules and doctrine.[16]

Recent publications have looked at the development of clinical legal education,[17] the use of simulation as a basis for education and reflective practice[18] and the use of e-technology in the context of experiential learning.[19] Most of the source materials cited so far have emerged from common law jurisdictions. The civil law world may have been slower to pick up this particular baton, but it is catching up and developing its own discourse, as evidenced by Jamin's book referred to above (who also notes the general paucity of legal education scholarship in France) as well as in several other recent and peer-reviewed publications.[20]

The scene is therefore set. We maintain that what makes up 'good' education – that serves the interests of all concerned by promoting and supporting a deeper, contextual and socially relevant learning – is not determined by country, region, history or culture. Of course, all of these variables may colour what legal education looks like, but in the light of educational theory, there are no longer any excuses for ineffective educational systems and processes. We maintain that we (as educators) owe it to society (including our students, present and future clients, the legal profession, other employers and the wider public) to educate to the highest standards and using established best practice.

This does not mean homogenising the product or process. As law is largely a reflection of societal values, this will necessarily impact on the content and form of legal education. Nonetheless, any of the stakeholders with an interest in how lawyers are educated and trained should have regard to how the curriculum is designed and delivered to ensure it is as effective as possible.

The specific features of civil law system do not detract from this very general position. In this chapter, we criticise the claim that the intrinsic nature of civil law systems justifies the traditional model of legal education with its emphasis on doctrinal content, a lecture-led student interface, extensive rote learning focused on written examinations, a narrow syllabus that ignores or devalues a range of legal and transferable skills and an overt ethical/professional practice consideration.

In the next section, we review a number of potentially sensitive issues. We start with the position taken by Kronstein, who in the 1950s identified and then dismissed the argument that if the case method were introduced into continental Europe's legal education curriculum, it would inevitably transform the 'scholarly' law faculty into a school for practitioners.[21] For us, introducing interactive experiential learning and teaching methods is no less likely to corrupt the doctrinal purity of the civil law faculty than any other form of pedagogy. To the extent universities in civil law countries deem it appropriate to emphasise doctrinal content, that content – like any other – can be more effectively taught experientially than in a traditional top-down manner. Indeed, if students are not familiar with how the principles of the law apply to practical problems, is that not indicative of a lack of understanding of the relevant doctrine or theory?

3.3 How does experiential learning fit with the civil and common law traditions?

It is common perception in many common law jurisdictions and most civil law ones that legal education is *not* about experiencing learning. To understand why the concept seems so foreign, we need a historical perspective.

Experiential learning and the common law tradition

In the UK and many other common law countries, legal education, such as it was, was largely based on work-related experience. The Inns of Court (the organisations through which one side of the legal profession – barristers – operate) provided an effective apprenticeship coupled with instruction from more experienced practitioners. Other legal professionals (solicitors) also worked through a period of supervised practice – then termed articles of clerkship.[22] It is only in relatively recent times (around 100 years ago) that the route to qualification for a lawyer required completing a course at university. For better or worse the divide between the 'academic' and the 'vocational' is now a key feature of UK legal education although this is currently under review. Both within the UK and throughout the former British colonies, legal education systems display variations on that theme.[23]

Whilst some universities in the UK, particularly the longer-established institutions, maintain that law is a subject of liberal study, the reality is that the majority of students enrolling in a university law degree programme have the intention of qualifying as legal practitioners – at least at the start of their studies.[24] In other common law countries, notably the USA, the academic and vocational stages of legal education are not separated in the same way – law is not taught as an 'academic' subject but rather as a discipline for those wanting to become lawyers. Law school in the US is graduate-only entry and aimed at producing practitioners.

Regardless of these differences in some common law countries, the role of the legal profession and its regulators is key to the form and content of legal education. Let us take two examples. In the USA, the American Bar Association (ABA) accredits law schools. Graduation from a non-accredited law school may prevent a student from qualifying to sit for a state bar examination. The ABA dictates much of what is taught and to an extent how legal education is carried out. For instance, there is currently a requirement that a law school has a defined programme of pro bono/work-based experience – an in-house clinic (the norm) or some alternative, for example placements with organisations external to the law school.[25]

In the UK, at present (this is currently under review) students must acquire a 'qualifying law degree' (QLD) before entering the overtly vocational stage of the Legal Practice Course (for would-be solicitors) and the Bar Professional Training Course (for barristers). The joint statement by the relevant regulatory bodies governs what is required for a programme to qualify a QLD. This is largely content and resource/facility-driven and does not address the way in which legal education is actually delivered. Subject to the above, law schools are largely free to present programmes as they think fit – provided they comply with requirements in terms of assessment and consider guidance of the UK Quality Assurance Agency and the Benchmark Standard for Law.[26]

This can be contrasted with situation in continental Europe.

Experiential learning and the civil law tradition

Although the situation varies from country to country, it is largely the case that law schools are solely responsible for curriculum design, without interference from the bar. A university degree is a prerequisite for applying to the bar, but practitioners typically do not consider that a law graduate is equipped for practice after five years of law school. Bar associations usually organise a period of work-based study and in many jurisdictions, additional training, notably on matters not covered at all in the university curriculum, such as professional ethics.

The divide between the academic study of law and the professional training is the product of historical evolution.[27] In France, the 19th century is a crucial period to understand to make sense of the current situation. Legal education was completely revamped after the revolution. In the early years of the 19th century, under Napoleon, the mission of law school was very clearly to teach the (then novel) civil code and train practitioners.[28] This imperial model is criticised for instrumentalising law schools, denying academic freedom and downgrading the teaching of law to professional training, as opposed to the study of a 'science'.[29] By the turn of the century (after the defeat of France against Germany in the 1870 war), France emulated the German model, where the study of law is seen as 'truly scientific'. Arguments of (internal) consistency are highly valued in scholarly discussions (more than consequentialist arguments). As far as teaching is concerned, the emphasis is on giving students an orderly overview of the whole legal system and its various branches. Law professors write treaties and construct their lectures as sections of a cathedral.[30]

To prepare students for the practice of law, the focus is on developing the ability to link particular situations to general principles.[31] This occurred (in France only in the second half of the 20th century) by means of introducing class teaching in addition to lectures. Two types of exercises are practiced under the supervision of teaching assistants: dissertations and case comments (but still no practical problems). Students do develop argumentative skills about the law and useful writing skills but are not exposed to professional-like situations. With the exception of some specific programmes, for which there is a selection process (otherwise prohibited by law to French universities), emulation of professional situations is left for after law school, for the training organised by professional bodies (or in the case of judges, by the state but in a specific professional school). While many agree this is not a satisfactory state of affairs, innovation in legal education is slow and takes place in part outside of universities.[32]

This being said, we do not want to paint too negative a picture of experiential learning on the continent. To be sure, it constitutes the fringe rather than the core of legal education, but there are two reasons to think the situation could evolve and is indeed evolving towards a greater role for experiential learning. First, experiential learning actually fits well with an existing tradition in continental legal education (although this may not be immediately apparent). Second, the current EU-wide shift towards a skill-based approach helps to bring this good fit to the fore.

Experiential learning and desired outcomes

To illustrate the first point, let's take the German example. Arguably, Germany is, within continental Europe, a country where traditions are particularly strong in legal education, so much so that Germany refused to implement the 'Bologna process' (so named after the city where the blueprint of an EU-wide harmonisation was agreed among education ministers, but on a voluntary basis, outside of the EU framework). The main features of the Bologna agreement are that university studies have the same two-tier structure: a bachelor's degree (three years) followed by a master's degree (two years), with each course carrying a certain number of credits (ECTS). Both elements aim to facilitate free movement of students and mutual recognition. While this has been largely implemented across Europe,[33] including in Law, Germany resits the change: it would jeopardise the all-important *Staatsexamen*, a set of two state exams, which students take at the end of their studies and need to pass if they want to join any legal profession. While the exams were initially devised to select public legal officers (judges, prosecutors and civil servants), they constitute a must-pass not only for public legal offices but also to join the bar. Needless to say, the requirement for these exams exerts a considerable influence on what is taught in law schools and how it is taught.[34]

In the words of Lehmann, the ideal candidate for the *Staatsexam* is a modern Renaissance man (or – more often – woman), with a broad knowledge spanning across all areas of law. However, the exams are not designed to test abstract knowledge of legal principles or command of doctrinal scholarship. Rather, the exams test the ability of the candidate to genuinely understand the law and apply it.[35] The tests, therefore, are quite practical. In the first state exam, students are asked to solve problems applying rules they do not know (often invented statutes). The aim is to test their ability to reason their way in novel situations. To prepare for this, university education emphasises reasoning techniques. More precisely, four methods of interpretation are traditionally – since Savigny –[36] considered to constitute the basic toolkit of any self-respecting German lawyer: literal, systemic, historic and teleological interpretation. In the second state exam, candidates are confronted with a hypothetical case (a traditional exercise theorised by Jhering, another revered German law professor of the 19th century). Candidates are asked to draft a court order or an act of accusation (but rarely submissions on behalf of a party).

This brief overview of the German situation suggests that, even in continental countries where the legal education system is very attached to the national tradition, there may be elements within that tradition on which to build when it comes to introducing experiential learning in the legal curriculum. In the German case, while it is unlikely that the idiosyncratic state exams will go,[37] the requirement that these exams test a genuine understanding of the law and the ability to apply could in our view only be well served by injecting a dose of experiential learning in the curriculum. Indeed, this is what is beginning to happen in several continental European countries.

Ongoing innovations in continental Europe

There is a myriad of local initiatives which seek to introduce some experiential learning in the law curriculum. At the time of writing, a French-speaking network of law clinics comprises 22 members of which 16 are located in France and one in Luxembourg.[38] In Belgium too, some law schools offer law clinics.[39] In addition to clinics, other ways of channelling teaching innovation should be mentioned. Some examples from Belgium may be used to illustrate this point. Although they owe in some respect to common features of Belgian universities, these examples tell a story which could resonate in other continental jurisdiction because they are directly linked to the shift towards a skill-based approach, which is a pan-European evolution.[40]

A skill-based approach is characterised by the fact that aims of the curriculum are explicitly formulated in terms of skills (what a law graduate should be able to do) rather than in terms of content. Implementing a skill-based approach usually requires revamping curricula initially structured to accumulate knowledge. The guiding principle of such reform, once the skill set has been agreed upon, is to ensure the curriculum as a whole provides enough learning opportunities for students to acquire target skills. Skills are normally not subject-specific. Writing skills, for example, may be acquired by writing a paper on contract law just as well as on constitutional or environmental law. Under this approach, teaching still covers specific contents, but a list of contents taught is no longer considered sufficient to define the curriculum. The skill-based approach facilitates mutual recognition of diplomas and qualifications. When the focus is on content, it is enough that subjects taught differ, as they usually do in Europe, for a graduate from Germany to be refused full recognition of her degree in Belgium. If the focus shifts to skills, it becomes easier to recognise that two diplomas that attest to the same skill set are equivalent even if the contents of the curricula differ. For this reason, the skill-based approach is promoted by the European Union.

In Belgian universities, law schools have all started a transition to a skill-based approach (usually prompted by national quality evaluation bodies). In this process, they may count on support offered by learning labs. Learning labs (whose appellation varies across universities and over time) are resource centres which are part of each university and whose mission it is to offer pedagogic training to young recruits as well as continuing professional development modules to anyone holding a teaching position. They are not attached to any faculty or school and provide cross-subject methodological support for teaching innovation. The training sessions offered in this framework create opportunities for law professors (those who choose to attend) to realise that many of the issues they face are not specific to the teaching of law. These issues include, of course, depth of learning and ability to use the new methodologies and technology. In this regard, one particularly important contribution of these trainings is that they equip participants with a conceptual framework. It makes a world of difference to learn – even only the basics – of a language that enables one to speak about the core issues of course design, which would otherwise remain unformulated in the shadow of solitary course preparation.

For instance, discovering Bloom's taxonomy (the different stages of learning referred to above) allows one to make sense of the otherwise abstract requirements of the skill-based approach which the dean is pressing with more, or less, enthusiasm upon faculty. It might be useful here to recall, at least in outline, what this attempts to show. In this seminal work, Bloom and his colleagues attempt to classify stages in learning in the cognitive, affective and sensory domains by setting out a hierarchical structure, with 'knowing' at the foot and evaluation at the apex and with increasing levels of sophistication and complexity, in terms of learning, being demonstrated as one moves along the learning axis. The process of development involved includes, in ascending order, the recall of knowledge, application, analysis, synthesisation, evaluation and innovation or creation.[41]

The distinctions between the learning stages may allow one to realise, for example, that all that is implicitly required from students for a course as it stands is merely to remember and understand, but not to apply (rules to real cases) or analyse (rules, discourses about the rules), far less to evaluate (an opponent's statement about the correct interpretation of rules) or to create (write own opinion on rules/draft alternative rules). This may prompt revision of the course's aims and even more importantly, makes those aims explicit in a concrete manner. Indeed, the formulation of expectations, which is the cornerstone of good practice in general and in a skill-based approach in particular, is a necessary first step in realising what experiential learning can bring. It is from there that clinics and all other techniques that require students to actively do something with the knowledge rather than passively receive it turn from pedagogic gimmicks to meaningful tools to achieve a goal defined by the teacher him or herself (taking into consideration the target skill set defined for the programme).

Directly or indirectly (through word-of-mouth between teachers), such training, which includes hands-on sessions on various active teaching tools, contributes to instilling student activity in an otherwise traditional setting typical of law schools in civil law countries.

3.4 Convergence?

In spite of cultural differences between the UK and continental Europe (as well as other manifestations of the common and civil law worlds), the requirements imposed on the law curriculum and the relationship between universities and the relevant professional bodies is not, we suggest, so very different. We accept that in some specific instances there may be regulations that impact on this relationship and the nature of legal education in consequence. Where this is the case it is noted in the text. We maintain, as do many of the book's other contributors, that there are no principled reasons linked to the role of universities in legal education that would explain why what works for university education under the common law should not apply equally to the education of 'civil lawyers'. Practical differences (numbers of students, resources, bar association rules, higher education regulation) may create *obstacles* to the expansion of experiential learning in civil law contexts – indeed they do – but that needs to be distinguished from any sustainable *objection*.

Order vs. cases: can one experience a system?

We feel obliged, because of the strength and frequency that the matter is raised, to deal with one particular objection to experiential learning in the civil law context. We both heard an extraordinary expression of this objection at the previously mentioned conference in Luxembourg. A civil law colleague who was afraid neither to offend nor to amuse common lawyers in the room objected with great force and conviction: "But you see, in civil law, we have *principles*, we have *concepts*!" The self-evident consequence of this assertion seemed to be that, therefore, experiential learning could not possibly be suited to legal education under the civil law. Likewise, there was the inference that such fundamental issues were not applicable or not as prevalent under the common law to which experiential learning may, in consequence, be more suited. Our colleague's remark was very much in keeping with what might be termed the 'traditional view' that the core mission of a law professor in civil law countries is to teach *structures* (i.e., how the law on a subject matter is divided and sub-divided). The emphasis on the systematic aspects of the law (the civil code as a cathedral) is a longstanding feature of legal culture in civil law systems and a value that shapes professional attitudes to this day.

A crucial step in making the case for experiential learning in civil legal education is, therefore, to adduce evidence that concepts, distinctions and systems can be taught experientially. We claim this is the case and the reader will find examples of this in subsequent chapters of this book.

As a preliminary point, it may be worth stating the obvious, namely that common law too, of course, has structures and concepts. As mentioned at the beginning of this book, concepts such as co-existing tenures in land ownership or the intention to create legal relations in forming binding contracts are just two examples. The common law may well display peculiarities, but like any law, it operates on the basis of concepts. Certainly, the common core of legal education in any jurisdiction is to acquaint students with such legal principles and underlying notions and introduce them to how these concepts are applied to facts.

More fundamentally, our French colleague was assuming that the one and only way to teach concepts and structures is a lecture where knowledge is effectively handed down from expert to novice. In our view, this is a serious error in both principle and practice. Structures and distinctions can very well constitute the learning outcomes of teaching modules in which students are active participants rather than passive recipients of words of wisdom – in much the same way, a guided tour of Notre-Dame Cathedral in Paris is not the only (or best) way to learn about French gothic buildings. To extend the analogy, one can invite visitors to compare different shapes of lancet windows, the motives of cross-shaped vaulting or the sophistication of stain glass. In other words, one can create opportunities for students to experience differences. What is true of architecture works for legal concepts too. Designing a law course for adults, be it about a highly structured civil law content, need not be very different from designing a children's programme in a museum albeit that objectives, language and testing comprehension may differ depending on the age, level and ability of the learner.

The real difference between civil and common law context is not the degree to which the law is structured or conceptualised. It is to do with the dominant view about how one becomes a lawyer – academic, practising or otherwise. The historical differences between the two legal traditions, the approach to the practice of law and the implications for legal education under common and civil law systems is well described elsewhere.[42] In a previous publication one of this book's contributors, Philip Genty, takes up this discussion further when he compares what he sees as the 'bottom-up', inductive approach taken in the former (with judges acting as arbiters and social engineers) with the 'top down', deductive method found in the latter[43] (where the judges act as technicians and operators of what Genty refers to (in discussing Merryman's analysis of civil law as social science) as a 'machine built by others'.[44]

Cultural traits respectively associated with common/civil law worlds – rather than intrinsic features of the legal systems – may help to explain why common law environments are more receptive to experiential learning. But one should not overstate the link between common law and experiential learning on the one hand and civil law and lecturing on the other. This is both because, positively, experiential learning can equally well be associated with civil law and negatively, because the association with common law is not always present. As we have shown above, the value of experiential learning is to do with the learning process itself, not with the content taught. Therefore, active learning is also better learning when, as in civil law countries, the focus is on teaching the architecture of the legal system. Conversely, the association between experiential learning and common law ought not be overstated. In case it be thought that the common law world uniformly uses an interactive pedagogy as a matter of course, let us dispel that notion. The Socratic method, so often raised and praised as being central to learning the law,[45] especially in the USA, may be more spoken of than acted upon. In other countries of both the common and civil law persuasion (including the UK and France), a discourse on the law using pure Socratic techniques is, in our experience, largely missing or replaced by lecture-driven and content-led delivery.

Both in civil law and common law countries, therefore, there is room to expand experiential learning.

3.5 Conclusion

European countries, including civil law jurisdictions, are experiencing pressure for a change from purely knowledge-based content to more of a skill-based approach in education generally. This is reflected by developments at specific educational institutions, political and strategic initiatives (for example, as initiated by the Bologna process) and globalisation of commerce and (in consequence) the law and the legal profession. The move for change is also fuelled by employability and the realities of an ever-increasingly competitive job market.

Jurisdictionally, specific factors such as the introduction of student fees in the UK may also have had an impact – the student being seen and reacting more as a consumer than traditional learner. In addition, one might think that advances in educational theory have had an effect with the knowledge, skills and values dimensions of learning being seen more holistically and the application of these educational objectives now recognised for their worth.

As will be seen elsewhere in this book, countries further afield, from the Far East and Indian sub-continent to Australasia and across to South America similarly are responding to demands for change from a range of stakeholders.

These development are specifically hitting legal education. The inclusion of a target skill set as part of the law curriculum constitutes an excellent opportunity for law schools in both systems to conduct a thorough review of existing provision – in terms of both content and delivery. In particular, the implementation of an integrated and more skill-based approach invites law schools to reflect on whether current provision is suited to achieve the goals and aspirations formulated by the academy, the legal profession, government and the wider public. Producing lawyers fit for purpose in the 21st century has been discussed extensively elsewhere.[46]

We argue that the transition to a curriculum where the subjects studied and the methods used to study them require a degree of application of legal principle, lawyering skills and ethical awareness, will only be effective if at least some measure of experiential learning is introduced into the law school. We accept that there are major differences in the legal process under the civil and common law. We have suggested in this chapter that those differences neither explain nor justify why there needs to be such a rigid adherence to traditional means of curriculum delivery. The nature of the lawyer/client relationship and role of lawyer or judge in the fact-finding process, for example, do not, in principle, mitigate against suggested improvements to legal education through the inclusion of structured experiential opportunities.[47]

Let us now widen the discussion and turn to some concrete examples of re-thinking legal education

Notes

1 So named not because it had anything to do with the rules regulating cooking or chefs but because of the pioneering work of Christophe Jamin, set out in his book: C. Jamin,

La cuisine du droit, Paris, Lextenso, 2012. This title was inspired by the criticism of other academics in France that a more hands-on focus to legal education would simply produce technicians and those versed in practical skills – like cooks in a kitchen! The 'legal' kitchen seemed to use a very good analogy for a forum in which the application of theory to practice could occur and one that gave the York workshop its own working title.

2 See: Confucious, The sayings of Confucious, Barnes and Noble, 1994 and available at www.gurteen.com/gurteen/gurteen.nsf/id/X0055C026/, accessed 4 January 2016.

3 Ibid, but see: http://english.stackexchange.com/questions/226886/origin-of-i-hear-and-i-forget-i-see-and-i-remember-i-do-and-i-understand, accessed 4 January 2016.

4 This quotation has no definitive citation. See: https://answers.yahoo.com/question/index?qid=20141227074325AA1nTxw, accessed 4 January 2016.

5 See: J. Dewey, *How we think: a restatement of the relation of reflective thinking to the educative process*, Lexington, D.C. Heath and Company, 1933.

6 See: D. Schön, *Educating the reflective practitioner*, San Francisco, Jossey-Bass, 1987.

7 For example see: R. Miettinen, *The concept of experiential learning and John Dewey's theory of reflective thought and action*, International Journal of Lifelong Education, 19 (1), 2000, 54, 61–62.

8 D.A. Kolb, *Experiential learning: experience as the source of learning and development*, New Jersey, Pearson Education, 2015. This relatively recent (and second) edition of his 1984 classic text importantly contains a revision of his theories and in particular addresses the critiques of his earlier work.

9 We are referring to the amended Bloom taxonomy (L.W. Anderson, D.R. Krathwohl, P.W. Airasian, K.A. Cruikshank, R.E. Mayer, P.R. Pintrich, J. Raths and M.C. Wittrock, *A taxonomy for learning, teaching, and assessing: a revision of Bloom's Taxonomy of Educational Objectives*, New York, Pearson, Allyn & Bacon, 2001. In Bloom's original formulation, the first two stages of learning were termed 'knowledge' and 'comprehension' See: B.S. Bloom (ed.), *Taxonomy of educational objectives, handbook i: the cognitive domain*, New York, David McKay, 1956.

10 In the terminology of the above taxonomy: applying, analysing, evaluating and creating.

11 G. Gibbs, *Teaching students to learn*, Milton Keynes and Philadelphia, Open University Press, 1981.

12 R. Grimes, *Reflection in teaching, learning and practice*, in C. Ashford and J. Guth (eds.), *Legal academics' handbook*, Basingstoke, Palgrave, 2016, 106.

13 See, D.A. Schōn, *The reflective practitioner: how professionals think in action*, Farnham, Ashgate, 1983.

14 See: J.A. Moon, *A handbook of reflective and experiential learning: theory and practice*, Abingdon, Routledge Farmer, 2004.

15 See for example: J. Webb, *Ethics for lawyers or ethics for citizens? New directions for legal education*, Journal of Law and Society, 25 (1), 1998, 134.

16 For examples of relevant peer-reviewed journals see: The Journal of Legal Education (USA), The Law Teacher (UK), The Asian Journal of Legal Education (India), and the Clinical Law Review (USA).

17 K. Kerrigan and V. Murray (eds.), *A student guide to clinical legal education and pro bono*, Basingstoke, Palgrave Macmillan, 2011.

18 See: C. Strevens, R. Grimes and E. Phillips (eds.), *Legal education: simulation in theory and practice*, Farnham, Ashgate, 2014.

19 In particular see: P. Maharg, *Transforming legal education*, Farnham, Ashgate, 2007.

20 See Jamin, op cit., 29; Elise Poillot (ed.), *L'enseignement clinique du droit: experiences croisées et perspective pratique*, Brussels, Larcier, 2014; and Xavier Aurey and Marie-Joelle Redor-Fichot, *Les clinques juridiques*, Caen, Presse universitaires de Caen, 2015. P. Ancel and L. Heuschling (eds.), *La transnationalisation de l'enseignement du droit*, Brussels, Larcier, 2016.

21 See: H. Kronstein, *Reflections on the case method – in teaching civil law*, Journal of Legal Education, 3, 1950, 271.

22 For a helpful overview of the history of legal education in the UK and further afield, including continental Europe see: Mary Ann Glendon, William P. Alford and Lionel Astor Sheridan, *Legal education*, available at: www.britannica.com/topic/legal-education, accessed 6 October 2016.

23 LETR, *Setting standards: the future of legal services education and training regulation in England and Wales*, IPS, BSB and SRA, 2013 and available at: www.letr.org.uk/wp-content/uploads/LETR-Report.pdf, accessed 6 May 2016. The impact of this report can be seen on the relatively recent promulgation of the Quality Assurance Agency for Higher Education in the form of the new QAA, *Benchmark Standard for Law*, 2015, available at: www.qaa.ac.uk/en/Publications/Documents/SBS-Law-15.pdf, accessed 6 May 2016. The outcome of the all-important consultation process, conducted over the past 2 years, of the Solicitors' Regulation Authority (SRA) is currently awaited. This will most likely result in a re-shaping of legal education at least to the point of recognising the importance of applied learning and an assessment process that is linked to outcomes and competencies established over a defined period of time and most probably centrally controlled. The last of the SRA's consultative papers, dealing in particular with assessment, is: SRA, *Training for tomorrow: assessing competence,* 2015 and available at: www.sra.org.uk/sra/consultations/t4t-assessing-competence.page#, accessed 6 May 2016. Note: since the above was written the SRA has committed itself to the principle of a centralised bar examination although the details of exactly what this will consist of and who will conduct it are yet to be published (April 2017).

24 Well under half of all undergraduate law students in the UK currently end up as qualified practitioners – a reflection, we suggest, more of the state of the employment market than perhaps career aspiration. See: Law careers - becoming a solicitor, Law Society, 2016, available at www.lawsociety.org.uk/law-careers/becoming-a-solicitor/entry-trends/, accessed 6 October 2016.

25 American Bar Association, *Standards and Rules of Procedure for Approval of Law Schools,* Rules 303–304, ABA, 2015.

26 QAA, *Benchmark Standard for Law*, 2015, available at: www.qaa.ac.uk/en/Publications/Documents/SBS-Law-15.pdf, accessed 6 May 2016.

27 On which, see Jamin, op cit., chapter 1 (focusing on France with and drawing comparisons with both common law jurisdictions and with Germany).

28 Jamin, op cit., 38.

29 Ibid., 60.

30 Ibid.

31 Ibid., 57.

32 In France, Science Po is a case in point. The creation of Sciences Po law school is narrated by Jamin (op cit.). For (one of many) critical comments, see L. Vogel, *L'Université, une chance pour la France*, Paris, PUF, 2010.

33 See: The Bologna Process and the European Higher Education Area available at: http://ec.europa.eu/education/policy/higher-education/bologna-process_en, accessed 6 October 2016.

34 The following account draws on Matthias Lehmann, Examen d'État (Staatsexamen) en Allemagne – Un obstacle insurmontable à la transnationalisation du droit?, in P. Ancel and L. Heuschling (eds.), *La transnationalisation de l'enseignement du droit*, Brussels, Larcier, 2016.

35 In the original: '*das Recht mit Verständnis erfassen und anwenden können*', v. § 2 II Juristenausbildungsgesetz Rheinland-Pfatz (legal education statute of the state of Rhineland Palatinate), cited by Lehmann, op cit.

36 F.K. Von Savigny, *System des heutigen römischen Rechts*, vol. 1, Veit und comp, 1840, 213sq, cited by Lehman, op cit.

37 In this regard, Lehmann notes, somewhat cheekily perhaps, that the express wish of Chancellor Merkel to see the German education system brought in line with the Bologna process, vested interest at State (Länder) level makes it an unlikely development. See Lehmann, op cit., 162.

38 For the website of the network of these legal clinics see: www.cliniques-juridiques.org, accessed 6 October 2016.

39 To our knowledge, the Human Rights Clinic in Gent was the first in the country. For an overview of the activities of this clinic see: www.hrc.ugent.be/human-rights-law-clinic, accessed 1 October 2016. ULB offers an Equality Law Clinic, available at: www.iee-ulb.eu/fr/equality-law-clinic. The law school in Leuven has a 'clinic' programme but the word is used to refer to seminars with practitioners rather than hands-on work done by the students themselves.

40 Recommendation of the European Parliament and of the Council of 23 April 2008 on the establishment of the European Qualifications Framework for lifelong learning (OJ C 111, 6.5.2008, 1–7). For more details, see A.-L. Sibony, 'La transnationalistation de l'enseignement juridique: et si c'était (aussi) une question de pédagogie?' in P. Ancel and L. Heuschling, op cit.

41 A very helpful description and slight modification of Bloom's taxonomy can be found in R. Modaniel, *Bloom's revised taxonomy - a framework for assessing student learning* available at: https://cft.vanderbilt.edu/guides-sub-pages/blooms-taxonomy/, accessed 10 January 2017; and see fn 9.

42 See: G. Bell, The US legal tradition among the legal traditions of the world, in J. Ginsburg (ed.), *Legal methods: cases and materials*, St. Paul, Foundation Press, 2004, 66.

43 See: P.M. Genty, *Overcoming cultural blindness in international clinical collaboration: the divide between civil and common law cultures and its implication for clinical education*, Clinical Law Review, 15, 2008, 131.

44 Op cit, 137 and 139.

45 As dramatically portrayed by a professor and his students in John Jay Osborn Jr., *The paper chase*, Houghton Mifflin, Boston, 1971.

46 See: R. Grimes and C. Smith, *Reviewing legal education – what do we want from our lawyers and how do we get it?* (with C. Smith), Delhi Law Review, XXVII – XXIX, 2007, 1.

47 See: J.H. Merryman, *The Civil Law tradition: an introduction to the legal systems of Europe and Latin America*, Redwood City, Stanford University Press, 2007 generally and in relation to the examination of witnesses (something normally done by civil law judges in private and in a non-adversarial way) at 55.

Part B

Content and careers

Introduction

The second section of this book is an attempt to drill down into the key issues facing law schools if they are serious about reviewing legal education provision and improving both its coverage and the means by which the content is taught and learnt.

Chapter 4 has been written by a set of 4 contributors (Richard Hedlund, Tanya Walker, Meredith Daniel and David Roccaro), all of whom have 3 things in common. First, they studied, relatively recently, at one particular law school that centres its entire programme on experiential methods (albeit it that David was on a short-term placement as part of his master's degree at home in Italy – with a thesis on experiential learning). Secondly, they have all played a part in supporting other students, as tutors or mentors. Thirdly, they reach similar conclusions – that properly structured and resourced experiential learning in general and clinical legal education in particular present a win/win situation for all concerned and one in which students can study law in context whilst developing their legal knowledge, their skills set and an appreciation of the professional and wider ethical considerations relevant to law in the real world. That said – there is room for improvement.

The relevance of professional responsibility and ethics is the subject of Chapter 5. Here three contributors look at the 'why' and the 'how' (as well as the 'who' and the 'when') of ethics. Donald Nicolson makes an impassioned and powerful plea for the inclusion of ethics in the law curriculum – from the very start of a student's programme of study – giving clear reasons why. Jose Garcia Anon makes much the same arguments but from the continental European law perspective and uses examples from his own jurisdiction – Spain – to make the case. This is followed by Laura Bugatti, who again links the history of law and legal education to the current resistance to changing the curriculum but concludes, as do the two other chapter contributors, that it is essential that ethics becomes a major component of the legal education portfolio.

Much is said throughout the book on the role of the legal profession (and other employers) in influencing the legal education system. In Chapter 6

Chris Maguire looks at the extent to which legal education is and should be influenced by regulators and other stakeholders. He draws on his considerable experience as a quality assurance driver to conclude that clear tensions and contradictions exist and that dialogue is needed between law schools, the profession(s) and the professional bodies to ensure that the outcomes for socially, economically and professionally relevant education are achieved. In a post-script to the chapter Stephen Levett then looks at apprenticeships on degree programmes and reaches interesting conclusions on how these might fit with the educational and regulatory objectives and constraints. Unsurprisingly perhaps experiential learning comes to the fore once again.

The final chapter in this section tackles the vitally important but difficult issue of assessment. What are we assessing in law schools? Is it more than just an exit mark or grade? How can assessment be incorporated into the learning process, and what models exist to assist with this process? Jenny Gibbons sets out a vision for effective assessment – one that meets the educational needs of students whilst fulfilling the responsibilities of the law school.

Chapter 4

Re-thinking the learning and teaching

Part 1 – A case study from York

Richard Hedlund

4.1.1 Background

As evidenced in this book and elsewhere, there is a growing debate worldwide about the design and delivery of legal education and a discernible and increasing demand for clinical and/or experiential approaches to study.

In England, as elsewhere, the pathway into legal practice is changing, with increasing numbers of law graduates now going straight into the legal professions as paralegals as opposed to completing established vocational training programmes – the usual route to qualification and practice. At the same time, pedagogical research suggests that distinct and profound advantages are associated with experiential learning. This is now impacting on the nature of and recruitment to undergraduate law degrees and a call more generally, as echoed elsewhere in this volume, for more thought to be given by law schools to both the form as well as the content of the curriculum.

The challenge for the modern law school is squaring the traditional ways of teaching law, primarily in the format of lectures and set-question seminars, with the need for theoretical studies linked to experiential and skills-based learning. In light of this, this chapter will discuss the role of experiential learning in undergraduate law teaching in English law schools, with a particular focus on how these questions have been addressed at one particular and innovative university through the LLB programme at York Law School (YLS). I use two examples of how 'conventional' subjects can be taught using experiential methods.

As part of this discussion, this contribution will also look at a small-scale survey in which student feedback was canvassed in response to questions on the perceived benefits (and challenges) of experiential learning. In conclusion, I suggest there is a need to draw on different modes of learning to enhance the student experience and to ensure that the experiential and more traditional forms of delivery are complementary.

4.1.2 The LLB programme at YLS

York Law School opened in 2008 and that year accepted its first undergraduate law cohort. I will always be proud to say that I was one of those students, who, ignoring the warnings from family and teachers, voluntarily joined a new law school with an overtly radical agenda in terms of how law is studied. Being a new law school, YLS had a perfect opportunity to create an innovative programme reflecting best practice in education and meeting the needs of students in the 21st century. As will be seen, this approach very much broke with tradition and embraced new pedagogical thinking. The key way in which YLS did so was by adopting a fully integrated 'problem-based learning' (PBL) approach to studying each of the core modules of the curriculum. The PBL model adopted at YLS has been fully discussed elsewhere, and will only be outlined briefly here.[1] PBL as a learning tool more generally has also been extensively debated.[2]

4.1.3 Problem-based learning

The essence of PBL is a student-oriented and engaging way of learning through pre-set problem scenarios. The problems take centre-stage in the process rather than, as in many seminar designs, simply being add-ons after a series of substantive questions.

Students work in small groups, pointedly referred to as student law firms (SLFs), usually around 12 to 14 members. Each week, depending on the schedule, the group is presented with a number of realistic legal scenarios (ranging from one problem a week to three), which are designed, where possible, to fit within the framework of the substantive modules that form the curriculum. This further differentiates the PBL problems from problem questions in traditional module seminars, which normally only address current issues in one module. Frequently, again depending on the structure of the syllabus, any given problem will involve more than one legal issue and will relate back to what the curriculum designers intended the student to study at a particular juncture. For example, a problem may have issues of civil liability (say a road traffic accident with a compensation claim for injuries suffered) but may also have criminal implications (the other driver was perhaps drunk at the wheel) and may have public law concerns (involving perhaps the role of the police or the courts). As well as fitting with the curriculum, the idea is to present problems in a realistic way in which the law is not divided neatly into compartments or sub-divisions called negligence, crime or judicial review.

Each week, SLF members choose one of the firm to chair the discussions. This role focuses on leading the group through the stages of the PBL process. One student also acts as scribe or note taker for recording the group's deliberations on a 'smart' (e)-board (or on paper if the IT fails). Scribing ensures that the thought process is captured so that students can revisit it during their later research or revision. It also frees up the other members from having to take notes. The roles of chair and scribe alternate each week, so every student get the opportunity to do both. The students are guided by a tutor – a member of academic staff and occasionally a practitioner, whose main goal is to facilitate discussion but allow the group to take responsibility for their learning. Tutor intervention is kept to a minimum.

The students follow a set procedure in which they must progress through defined stages. All students are inducted into this system, so everyone is familiar with what is expected. Whist the students remain in control of the process, the structure for each PBL session (rather than the content and outcomes) is pre-set for them. First the students, in their group, read the problem out loud and then start to analyse the scenario. They must identify the prospective parties involved and what their interests might be. Those interests are not necessary overtly legal ones. This allows the students to place the law into its wider social context. Issues of policy and practise may arise as well as the substantive law. The students must also identify the key facts in the scenario. Understanding the importance of facts and evidence is crucial to comprehending how law functions. This leads on to a general discussion which culminates with the students identifying a set of research questions (termed learning outcomes) – what it is the students need to find out to 'answer' the problem. At the end of the initial session the tutor will ensure that the students' research questions correspond to the outcomes agreed by the module leaders who designed the scenario. The key is to ensure that all PBL groups and their members undertake all of the same research, even if the way they have worded their questions differ. After all the PBL approach is targeted at all students not just the particular SLF.

After this initial session, which lasts up to 2 hours, the students will go away for self-directed study, conducting their research in response to the questions they have identified. They are encouraged to work collaboratively but must produce a set of their own conclusions on which they will report back to the whole group.

They are assisted by a handbook (referred to as the block guide) which covers the syllabus content and contains suggested readings. There are also weekly plenary sessions (mistakenly but understandably referred to by the students as lectures!) where academic staff use the Socratic technique to look at key issues arising in that 'block'. These sessions are designed to place the week's topics in context, provide background information, or focus on particular case analysis, or other theoretical approach. The plenary sessions are meant to assist the students in getting the necessary overview or insight but do not directly answer the research questions. The students conduct their research independently, albeit they can collaborate. This is another key difference to the traditional lecture-seminar design, where the lecture comes before the seminar. In the PBL process, the students begin by analysing the problem and plenary sessions (of which there may be several looking at different aspects of a problem or problems) comes after.

After 3 or 4 days of independent research, and assisted by the plenary session, each PBL group reconvenes, and the students discuss their research findings. The feedback session will be led by the chairperson who led the initial session. Again, the role of the tutor is meant to be minimal but of course will vary according to the extent to which the students have identified the relevant research and how far their analysis addresses the given problem. Students then get 2 to 3 days to finalise their findings and then report back to complete the cycle before being given the next problem. The cycle is then repeated for the rest of the term, year and complete period of study.

Ultimately the tutor has to ensure that all of his or her the students have come to terms with the required and expected content. Each tutor is guided by a set of notes, which are centrally prepared by the module leader.

The role of the tutor and the extent of his or her intervention is important: in a study on tutorials, it was found that some students favoured listening to the tutor rather than fellow students, based on 'judging the authority of the *speaker*'.[3] In the context of PBL this can undermine group discussions if the expectation is that only the tutor has 'authority' and can or will provide the 'correct' answers. Many tutorials in the traditional format have a tendency of turning into mini-lectures due to a lack of student engagement, which can be blamed on many factors, including the stated perception about authority, as well as the logistical problem of class sizes and understandable reluctance and natural timidity in the face of one's 'betters' and peers.

A problem in all group work is the potential for lack of participation, which can happen for several reasons and not just the perceived authority of the tutor. One theory used to explain this phenomenon is known as 'social comparison', and in particular 'upward' social comparison. This theory states that in any social context, people compare themselves to everyone else in the group. In upward social comparison, the students compare themselves to 'perceived superior others'. In this situation, one student may feel inferior to another, for instance a dominating student (who may or may not have the right answers), and because of that the student will withdraw from the process and will not participate.[4] This concern is of course present in the PBL process, but is addressed, so far as it possibly can, in a number of ways. Importantly, the role of chairing the session and scribing are rotated, and every student must take his or her turn. The PBL group is also actively encouraged to consider options for ensuring that everyone participates, including by adopting innovative feedback processes. From the very start, the students understand that they are the focus of the process and that the tutor is meant to be as non-interventionist as possible. This places a particular challenge on the tutor to not jump in and try to lead or direct the debates but to carefully judge where any intervention is necessary. PBL thus challenges the problems with non-participation and perceived authority of the tutor by emphasising student participation and tutor non-participation from day one, and also encourages student participation by keeping group sizes deliberately small.

At any one time the students may have up to 3 PBL problems on-going, some of which will require them to revisit issues raised in previous sessions. The process is therefore one which asks for a regular review of knowledge and understanding through further application of theory to practice.

4.1.4 Experiential learning beyond PBL

Beyond the use of PBL in the core modules, a number of optional modules at YLS have also made use of varying types of experiential learning. Some adopted and at times adapted PBL outright, though as options the PBL problems will normally focus on only that one subject area. Some optional modules have opted for a more traditional lecture-seminar approach, which ironically, for all its pedagogical flaws, some students appreciate as a breath of fresh air. Some further options have adopted different types of experiential learning. This chapter will look at two of those.

Company law

At YLS, Company Law is a third-year optional module. There are no prerequisites for studying this subject. It used to be taught over two terms (20 weeks) but was later shortened to one term (10 weeks) in line with university modularisation policy. Research into learning would suggest that this change is a mistake as students learn better where their learning is spaced out over a longer period of time, including where they are given the opportunity to revisit subjects.[5] A study carried out by Budé et al. into a statistics course showed that students understood and retained less information when the course was shortened from six months to only eight weeks.[6]

In its original two-term incarnation the module was taught by weekly lectures and fortnightly experiential learning sessions. This was then condensed into weekly lectures and weekly experiential learning sessions over one term, which cut about half the lectures. The lectures that were cut were primarily the more heavily doctrinal ones. It was felt that the experiential work brought out the theoretical issues in a way that passive participation in a lecture could not.

The course as a whole was based around a simulation. Unsurprisingly, it revolved around a fictional client who wanted to set up a new company, and then followed the adventures of that company and its officers and shareholders. The students began by considering the various business structures available, before choosing a format for their client – a private limited company. As a guided simulation, the students of course did not have a real choice in terms of which business structure to choose. For the purposes of the module, the facts of the hypothetical business naturally lent itself towards a private limited company. Nonetheless the students had to consider relative business structure pros and cons.

The students then went about filling in the incorporation documents for the business. Critics will question the utility of having students spend time on mundanities such as filling in fictional addresses into the incorporation form.[7] There are many reasons for using the real incorporation form. It brings to life the requirements of the relevant legislation, in this case the Companies Act 2006.

It naturally puts into context a whole host of technical terms which would otherwise take a long time to explain – as the saying goes, a picture is worth 1,000 words.

The students then had to deal with various challenges to the business. This included amending the company's constitution (the articles of association) and holding a shareholders' meeting to remove a director from office. The students, using the facts of the simulation, had to identify the correct procedures for each and then carry them out in practice. This enhanced their learning in that they did not only have to read the statute but had to understand it sufficiently to actually be able to carry out what it prescribes. Again, this brings to life technical terms. For instance, why try to explain what a shareholders' resolution is when one can (a) show an example to the students (which is an interesting if relatively passive form of teaching) and (b) ask the students to write their own (which then becomes a very active form of teaching)?

Running a simulation of this kind also takes the teaching to places that I, as the tutor, had not expected. A shareholders' resolution (I will have to explain it now) is simply a written order issued by the shareholders (usually after a simple majority vote) instructing the directors in general or particular aspects of company management. Resolutions should be short and to the point. One year, a student tried to write his resolution with at least two or three chunky paragraphs, where most other students managed with only one or two sentences. The student objected by saying that a one-sentence resolution did not look "legal" enough. This led to an interesting discussion about legal drafting, and the pros and cons between short, simple writing and absurdly long legalese prose. We also discussed professionalism and whether a client would pay for half a page of text when a single sentence would suffice. These kinds of discussion see the law holistically and are unlikely to emerge from a seminar discussion which is simply about reading and debating the statutory provisions.

In my last year of teaching company law at YLS the module was changed. The simulation was cut down, and doctrinal seminars were mixed in. There should be no immediate objection to that. A mix of doctrinal learning and experiential learning has worked in other courses and has been beneficial to the students.[8] It recognises that the law is both practical and theoretical; it is worth emphasising that the law is not exclusively one or the other. As seen at various points of this book, it is frequently both appropriate and advantageous to teach theory and practice side by side. The doctrinal seminars allowed the students to consider bigger questions about the role and purpose of company law that do not organically flow from a simulation. This includes important questions around corporate governance and the relationship between businesses and employment, environmental or human rights law.

In the end, I felt the module found a constructive balance between theory and practice. It allowed the students to get their 'hands dirty' with some of the fundamentals of company law, such as incorporation, directors' meetings and shareholders' resolutions. It also allowed the students to think critically about some of the bigger issues facing businesses, both today and in the past. That is law.

Modern uses of trusts

The second module was called Modern Uses of Trusts (MUT). It has later been renamed but without any fundamental change in content. Again, it is a third-year optional module. Equity & Trusts is a mandatory module in English LLB programmes, and indeed in many parts of the common law world. Unfortunately, because of the sheer size of the topic, the mandatory module is usually only able to cover the basics of trust law. It can easily fail to go into some of the modern usages of trusts, especially financial/tax management structures in "off-shore" jurisdictions.[9] Despite the importance of the written trust deed (the written document that outlines the trust arrangement), many, if not most, LLB students will leave the Equity & Trusts module without having seen such a document. At YLS, Equity & Trusts is taught in the second year, and being mandatory all third-year students choosing MUT will have had a grounding in the basics of trust law.

The purpose of the MUT module was to remedy these shortcomings. The module uses a different type of experiential learning from running a full-scale simulation. The students were assigned to small groups with only two or three students in each. A week prior to each session, the students would be introduced to a new trust deed, together with a series of questions about it. One group would be asked to take the lead on each trust deed, by having the primary role of presenting the answers to the questions in the following week's seminar (of course, all students were expected to contribute to the general discussion that followed). By taking turns, each group would take the lead on at least one trust deed.

The trust deeds covered a wide range of modern uses of trusts, from family and corporate tax arrangements to investment and off-shore trusts. The trust deeds used were generally templates provided by various actual law firms. They were, as such, the real deal, rather than templates mocked up by the professor. From feedback given the students appeared to appreciate this level of realism in the teaching documents.

The questions that were asked all related to the trust deed itself. What was the rationale for each trust? The students were asked to go through the trust deed, sometimes clause by clause, to consider and explain the purpose of each clause, and how the meaning of each could be manipulated by alternative drafting. As relevant, the students could discuss decided cases to show how the courts might interpret a clause if it was litigated on. The questions also addressed more general issues, such as when a particular type of trust would be used, and the arguments around its use. There is of course great scope to have discussions around the legality and morality of tax planning and moving (hiding?) assets overseas in so-called tax havens.

In using the trust deeds the module bridges the gap from addressing the basic rules of trust law to looking practically and theoretically at how trusts are actually used. The first is very abstract (and because of trust law's heavy use of technical rules, many students find trust law challenging – even dull) and the second is applied and gives the students a real insight into how this area of law works.

4.1.5 Moving towards learning experientially

English law schools (and I suspect law faculties elsewhere) increasingly run the danger of having to be all things to all students.

They need to recognise the career aspirations of students. Some (perhaps the majority at the start) want to enter the legal profession. Others (the majority by the time graduation comes around) do not (or recognise they are unlikely to be able to).

Whatever the attractions of experiential learning in English law schools, this development has not been universally welcomed. An anthology promoting the use of simulations was recently reviewed by Nicholas McBride, who raised a number of criticisms and objections to experiential learning.[10] It is a solid example of the rear-guard action fought by those academics who think the LLB programme should be exclusively 'academic'. However, his arguments are important.

The first issue to raise is the link between experiential learning and the common law. Without making any observations on the civil law system in this context (although many other contributors in this volume do and reach similar conclusions to me), the common law system lends itself very well to experiential learning. The common law is still to a large extent based on the development of case law, where judicial pronouncements can have binding effect. The common law system thus gradually creates law and theories of law out of analysing and in particular synthesising judicial decisions, as opposed to primarily basing the law on a central legal code.[11] It is therefore wholly appropriate for common law students to base their learning around legal cases, such as through a PBL approach.

Most, if not all, common law students initially struggle to appropriately deal with the judgments, and the traditional lecture/seminar format is not necessarily the best way to assist them. Seminars generally ask questions about the cases rather than setting out a clear framework for how to analyse them. Seminars also seldom introduce students to real material – for example contracts or other relevant legal forms and documents – meaning that students have no point of reference when seeing such documents mentioned in judgments.

PBL, as noted, on the other hand, asks students to identify key parties, their interests, and key facts, which is a similar task to analysing aspects of a judgment. Having this structure helps the students understand how to deal with judgments, and how to understand the interests of the parties in the judgment, the relevant key facts, and, then, the legal principles that comes out of those facts.

There are additional links depending on the relevant area of law. In civil disputes, such as contracts, property, company law, or trust law, the case will centre on the particular agreement between the parties, be that a contract, trust deed or corporate documents. It is thus appropriate that students have the opportunity to practice dealing with such documents, such as negotiating and writing them. It will give students a better understanding of how real documents are used in judgments. All around, a range of experiential learning will help students understand and use the common law system.

The second issue to raise is the range of transferrable skills that students can gain from undertaking a range of experiential learning. Some proponents of experiential learning support it not only because it prepares students for legal practice, which has been discussed above, but also because of the transferability of the skills.[12] It has been suggested that "communication, teamwork and leadership skills" have too often been lacking from graduates, not just in law, entering the work force.[13] This is immediately addressed through PBL, as discussed above, but also comes out of other forms of experiential learning, which generally involve students working together in groups.

McBride strongly challenges aspects of experiential learning, saying that law degrees instead are about, and should be about, teaching students to think, reason and argue persuasively, and implicitly queries whether simulations are appropriate for that.[14] Both sides to the argument are, to an extent, correct. But there is no reason why experiential learning (which, as seen, is not limited to simulations) cannot both teach students critical reasoning as well as a range of transferrable skills.

Seeing and using the practical realities of law, be that filling in incorporation forms or analysing trust deeds, is just as much 'the law', if not more so, than the theories that underpin the law. When studying law it surely makes sense to look at both the practice and the theory.

The third issue is the identified pedagogic benefits of experiential learning. Though not in law, there has been substantial educational research into different teaching methodologies. In summary, they suggest there are significant benefits to teaching through experiential, practical learning methods over lectures and seminars.[15] One issue is knowledge retention, which is arguably vitally important, and not just for completing and passing assessments! A study by Duderstadt et al. suggests that students retain only 5 percent of information given in a lecture as opposed to a full 75 percent of information gained through practical experience.[16] That is a remarkable difference in information retention. Despite this, McBride only reflects on ways of improving lectures – undoubtedly with good intentions but this is unlikely to solve the deeper pedagogical problem with lecturing. Indeed, it has been argued that lecturing is the least effective method of teaching, and in its predominately passive format has been 'blamed for [the] lack of student engagement' in higher education.[17]

It has even been suggested that lecturing might be worse than not having any lectures at all, since students attending a lecture might feel less inclined to pursue additional independent reading.[18] Indeed, anecdotal evidence suggests that some students come to seminars with only the lecture slides and notes taken during the lecture. It is vital that lectures 'stimulate self-study' as opposed to being just about the 'transmission of knowledge'.[19] Passive recipients of knowledge are unlikely to be successful at reasoning or arguing persuasively. This suggests that the focus of the course should be on other learning activities and that lectures, if retained, should take a backseat role. The PBL format at YLS seems to satisfy that requirement, in that the plenary session is designed to assist students in their wider research, rather than being the primary learning encounter.

Traditionally designed seminars, which usually come with a set list of questions and perhaps a problem-question, are also subject to criticism. They are meant to be the forum in which students use the learning from the lecture (or at least the 5 percent they do remember) to critically formulate arguments. A study into traditional tutorials found a worrying concern that tutorials do not automatically lead to greater student participation and engagement, since many students perceive them as 'little more than an interactive lecture', and do not develop critical thinking and analytical skills.[20] Anecdotal evidence suggests some merit in this. As noted above, some students question the authority of fellow students.[21] This is no doubt in part due to the fact that seminars are not designed to be student-focused or student-led; they are designed for a tutor to walk the students through set questions. It suggests a deep rethink is needed on the mode of teaching and a recognition that tutorials are not automatically student-centred and do not necessarily lead to interactive sessions.

The critiques of lectures and seminars and corresponding benefits of experiential learning have nothing to do with law specifically. It demonstrates that the use of experiential learning in law has objective pedagogic benefits and is not automatically about preparation for legal practice. There is also the thorny issue of cost. Certainly live-client clinics can be resource-intensive (depending on the client service offered and student numbers involved) but I suggest that simulation can be made very cost-effective using, for example, the approach outlined in the two examples given above (Company Law and Trusts). Also, there is the value-added factor to consider.

And one further point – although I (and others) make a strong case for experiential learning, it is not a case of all or nothing. A healthy and varied mix of delivery diet may act to stimulate students and capture the best in those different means for learning and teaching. The golden words of wisdom in a carefully structured lecture by an expert in the field may speak volumes to students who before or after (or both) have had the opportunity of putting theory into practice and applying relevant principles.

4.1.6 Testing the water

Whilst educational research clearly shows that experiential learning has its benefits that in itself might not be enough to warrant an overhaul of legal education. In designing a module, or indeed a whole LLB programme, it is always important to get student feedback into the content, structure and delivery. You want to know that the subject matter you are trying to impart is actually being received, understood and utilised. I therefore contacted a number of former students who have studied the Company Law and Modern Uses of Trusts modules referred to above to see what they had to say about the experiential elements involved on their LLB programme. Although the numbers involved were relatively small (the module numbers were low in any event and not everyone responded to my survey), the results were interesting especially given the nature and extent of student commentary on the questions posed.

Let us consider some of the responses:

Student A was enthusiastic about experiential learning but emphasised its 'proper' role, arguing that experiential learning is something which comes after learning law in the 'traditional sense', by which was meant undertaking doctrinal lectures/seminars in which initially legal rules are taught. This student thus suggests that experiential learning is something which best comes after doctrinal learning, and that it should not be in 'isolation' or as a substitute for the latter. This student writes that 'context is essential' and warns against the risk that experiential learning enthusiasts might skip the doctrinal/theoretical background to the law (which explains what the law is and why it is there). This warning is very apt. Merely using the law without understanding its proper role, purpose and rationale is likely to confuse and mislead, thus undermining the learning experience. In essence, one cannot build a house without a proper foundation. With these caveats in mind, the student is nonetheless supportive of experiential learning. The student uses a baking metaphor to explain its proper role vis-à-vis purely doctrinal teaching, saying "it's the difference between preparing the ingredients for a cake and leaving them on the worktop and mixing the ingredients and baking them to make something new". This is an important sentiment to which I relate, namely that experiential learning allows the students to fully understand the meaning of a rule by seeing its practical application; the rule is a living thing rather than merely a (potentially inaccessible) abstraction.

Student B was also enthusiastic about experiential learning. This student described himself as a hands-on learner, and it is of course very important to reflect on the many different learning styles that students might adopt or more naturally conform to.[22] Student B suggested that the simulation activities allowed him to understand how the law works rather than, as in doctrinal seminars, having to try to visualise it. This student saw the value of seeing what lawyers might do in practice, rather than, again, having to personally imagine how doctrinal law applied to given facts.

Student C was also impressed by the experiential component. The reasons given included gaining greater confidence in applying the law when starting his first legal job as well as the potential application of the interdisciplinary skills learnt. This student noted that the skills learnt in reading and analysing trust deeds gave him a sense of the whole when later working with commercial contracts. Importantly, student C states that undertaking skills tasks, such as filling in the incorporation documents for a company, helped with the long-term retention of the law – the requirements of the Companies Act 2006 and wider issues of whether or not to incorporate. Whilst the subject matter of lectures and seminars can melt into the memory over time, this student explained that the retention of information was made easier by having specific tasks to link the knowledge to. Further, she went on to say that participating in the simulation helped to 'break up the monotony of a heavy subject'. This is an important point to make – disinterested students are unlikely to fully engage and the extent of their disengagement understandably links to understanding and knowledge retention. She also said that it is a tutor's responsibility to make the sessions interesting, engaging and memorable. A fair point! Experiential learning is one, but certainly not the only, way of doing that. Student C also came with some appropriate cautions, which are important to acknowledge. Some students may opt for experiential courses as a 'soft option' – an easy module with hopefully an easy mark. The student aptly warns that this view can undermine the 'effectiveness' of experiential learning, which only works when all students put the required time and effort into the work.

The student feedback received was unanimously positive about the value of experiential learning.

Whilst supportive the responses are perceptive and reflect on both the benefits and possible dangers that arise in this context.

4.1.7 Conclusion

As I have shown, the LLB programme at YLS includes a wide range of experiential learning methods, including the centrepiece PBL model as well as a live-client clinic. These approaches blend practice and theory, recognising that the law encompasses both. A good law programme, in the sense of meeting the needs of today's student, prospective employers and wider society is unlikely to be exclusively practical or entirely theoretical. I suggest that theory informs practice but application helps us to understand principles and doctrine.

What is without doubt is that reality (competition, recruitment, employability and cost) will increasingly compel law schools to consider how far their programmes meet modern needs. I hope I have shown through my own use of theory and practice that experiential learning has much to offer and carefully integrated can bring out the best for all and indeed the two work most effectively when joined together.

Notes

1 See, for instance, R. Grimes, *Delivering legal education through an integrated Problem-Based Learning model – the nuts and bolts*, International Journal of Clinical Legal Education, 21, 2014, 1–26.

2 N. Sockalingam, J. Rotgans and H.G. Schmidt, *Student and tutor perceptions on attributes of effective problems in Problem-Based Learning*, Higher Education, 62, 2011, 1–16.
3 K. Jesper Herrmann, *Learning from tutorials: a qualitative study of approaches to learning and perceptions of tutorial interaction*, Higher Education, 68, 2014, 591, 597–606.
4 M. Micari and P. Pazos, *Worrying about what others think: a social-comparison concern intervention in small learning groups*, Active Learning in Higher Education, 15, 2014, 249–262, 251.
5 W. Binford, *How to be the world's best law professor*, Journal of Legal Education, 64, 2015, 542–561, 548.
6 L. Budé, T. Imbos, M.W. van de Wiel and M.P. Berger, *The effect of distributed practice on students' conceptual understanding of statistics*, Higher Education, 62, 2011, 69–79, 75.
7 I thought the addresses were fictional, but the students found some of them on Google Maps.
8 J.L. Mnookin, *Reflections on law teaching*, UCLA Law Review Discourse, 62, 2014, 126–238, 135.
9 The 'off-shore' jurisdictions include Jersey in the Channel Islands, and various Caribbean jurisdictions, including the Cayman Islands and the British Virgin Islands.
10 N. McBride, *Publication review: legal education: simulation in theory and practice*, Cambridge Law Journal, 74, 2015, 637–639, 638.
11 J. Hutcheson, *This thing men call law*, University of Chicago Law Review, 2, 1934/5, 1–13, 3; R. Pound, *What is the common law*, University of Chicago Law Review, 4, 1936/7, 176–189, 186; R. Posner, *Legal reasoning from the top down and from the bottom up: the question of unenumerated constitutional rights*, University of Chicago Law Review, 59, 1992, 433–452; Ringsted v Lady Lanesborough (1783) 3 Dougl 197, 203; 99 ER 610, 613 (Lord Mansfield); Roxborough v Rothmans of Pall Mall Australia Ltd [2001] HCA 68, 208 CLR 516, [72] (Gummow J)
12 Consider C. Strevens and R. Welch, *Simulation and the learning of the law: constructing and using an online transactional assessment in employment law*; N. Ross, A. Apps and S. Campbell, Shaping the future lawyer: connecting students with clients in first-year law, in C. Strevens, R. Grimes and E. Phillips (eds.), *Legal education: simulation in theory and practice*, Farnham, Ashgate, 2014, 50, 67.
13 D. Hall and S. Buzwell, *The problem of free-riding in group projects: looking beyond social loafing as reason for non-contribution*, Active Learning in Higher Education, 14, 2012, 37–49, 38.
14 N. McBride, op cit., 638.
15 W. Binford, op cit., 553.
16 J. Duderstadt, D. Atkins and D. Van Houweling, *Higher education in the digital age: technology issues and strategies for American colleges and universities*, American Council on Education, Praeger Publications, 2002, 64–65.
17 K. Jesper Herrmann, *Learning from tutorials: a qualitative study of approaches to learning and perceptions of tutorial interaction*, Higher Education, 68, 2014, 591–606, 592; G Hillocks Jr., *What works in teaching composition: a meta-analysis of experimental treatment studies*, American Journal of Education, 93, 1984, 133–170, 159.
18 W. Binford, op cit., 549.
19 K. Lonka and E. Ketonen, *How to make a lecture course an engaging learning experience?*, Studies for the Learning Society, 2012, 63–74, 66.
20 K. Jesper Herrmann, op cit., 604.
21 Ibid., 597.
22 Consider, e.g., C. Maughan and J. Webb, *Lawyering skills and the legal process* (2nd edn), Cambridge, Cambridge University Press, 2005, 50.

Part 2 – Don't talk at me, talk to me

Tanya Walker

4.2.1 Introduction

The student perspective of experiential learning presented this author with an insight of how Schön's theory of reflective practice can be indirectly affected by demographics.[1] Today's student body has become an intergenerational, international, mixed-gender group[2] who bring with them a profusion of experiences, responsibilities and expectations. As a non-traditional former student whose first degree was predominantly built around problem-based learning (PBL) and simulation, I question how and why experiential learning works and whether its use could be affected by demographic factors.

Constructivism and experiential learning are at the core of experiential learning.[3] With a hint of inquisition born out of experience I question, whether the timing of PBL and simulation, or the duration of its use, can affect a student's skill acquisition and ability to achieve high-order thinking. The experience and theory of how these programmes work in reality does not always meet expectations, and the repetition of a process in the absence of real life unpredictability can result in apathy and surface learning. I sense that higher education in the future may need to adjust established best practice to meet the demands of a rapidly changing student body and society.

The motive for completing a law degree varies from professional aspiration to curiosity and personal gratification,[4] and though our initial reasons may differ, we are united by our desired outcome. Although conventional lectures play a part in many (if not most) study programmes a methodology that principally focuses upon the 'traditional' educational values of 'replicability, reliability, communication and control'[5] may prevent a student making a connection between the information and its real life application.[6] It is this link that forms the foundation of experiential learning. As evidenced elsewhere in this book, recent strides in legal education delivery mean that students are often exposed to a combination of teaching methods including, of course, traditional lectures and seminars but increasingly featuring experiential learning.[7]

This mix is, I suggest, crucial to our development and ability to interpret and apply factual or theoretical information in a manner that addresses the adversarial nature of a common law legal system. This shift in educational best practice and institutional dynamics is an evolving process in higher education as providers adjust to the increasing focus on work and lifelong learning.[8] Law students are not immune from these changes.

4.2.2 PBL and other forms of experiential learning

PBL owes its origin to medical schools.[9] Since its introduction in the 1970s, the model has been developed and refined to make it suitable for audiences across the educational and professional sectors as it encourages participants to seize, absorb and understand information before building and reconstructing it alongside the, knowledge and experiences they already have.[10] Several models of PBL now exist though the majority encompass small groups of students, a facilitator, the problem scenario and on occasion a scribe and a chair.[11] With the spotlight on the 'problem' it is here that our cognitive skills take priority over the discipline as students work together, aided by a facilitator-tutor, to identify the outcomes of the 'problem'.[12]

More broadly, simulation (which frequently forms the cornerstone in PBL) harnesses constructivist-learning theories to create an interactive exercise or role-play underpinned by situational realism and a contextualisation of the subject.[13] Although it is impossible to recreate the unpredictability of a real-life incident, the objective is to expose students to experiences that are normally the preserve of the legal profession. This engagement with the subject allows all students, irrespective of their learning style, the space needed to confront and reflect upon knowledge limitations, abilities or beliefs and skill levels.[14] By watching or taking part in a such exercises, we are provided with the freedom to explore and experiment with our own styles and solutions to the task, which could incorporate case-oriented activities, such as drafting a client letter or conducting an interview, to a debate or full mock trial.[15] Each of these tasks, however, will incorporate our personal experiences; a student with extensive experience of client interaction, for example, is unlikely to adopt the same interviewing technique or ask the same questions as a person with no experience, and this in turn will be mirrored in their reflection and shared with the study group.

When I think about life's vital lessons, I periodically hear the ominous words 'you won't do that again, will you'? PBL and simulation need the same honest, understandable and supportive feedback if the reflection upon our decisions, actions and mistakes is to be effective.[16] Exposing students to experiential learning can be beneficial, even enjoyable, when undertaken in a positive and well-facilitated group environment, but the group setting and exercise need to be flexible and adaptive if different experiences, learning styles and knowledge are to be accommodated.[17] This evolution of moral development and knowledge is essential to high-order thinking, yet the probability of students being able to make a successful link between their education, skills, work and lifelong learning could be severely impeded if groups are not arranged effectively or the facilitation of the 'problem' or simulation is not taken into account.[18]

4.2.3 University transition and experiential learning

A student's involvement with PBL, simulation and live-client clinical activities varies immensely and many, me included, will report positive and negative experiences due to complications with group cohesion and dynamics, levels of participation or poor group selection.[19] Granted, such difficulties are well documented, but experiential learning can be severely affected by other, less obvious factors raising questions about when a programme should be initiated.[20] Such modes of learning are characteristically very different from that of a secondary (high) school or professional setting, and while a pedagogy built upon a mixed scholastic model should theoretically accommodate student learning styles and achieve the required benchmarks, the reality can be very different.

Higher education can be a nerve-racking experience but accommodating multiple learning styles, using mixed pedagogic methods, may not be enough to address the 'no man's land' as we adapt to the changes and demands that are placed upon our social, academic and technological time.[21] Student support, particularly in the early days, plays a vital role in helping transition. Yet universities often gear their academic and peer support structures towards a student community living on or close to campus, resulting in the omission of non-traditional students' needs.[22] At school we are surrounded by peers who share many demographic characteristics.[23] The common bond that campus-centred services focuses on can work well for exercises like PBL where students participate in collaborative group work, as it is easier to facilitate meetings and study sessions. This can pose complications for students living farther afield.[24]

To meet this challenge head on, faculty needs to take account of students' environmental and emotional support needs.[25] Peer and academic support should not be underestimated as the number of law schools continues to grow[26] and student numbers rise again (even after the 2012 English fee increase).[27]

The increased use of PBL, simulation and clinics in law has yet to be reflected by relevant research as to its efficacy – unlike in the medical world. There is, however, compelling evidence of a demographical imbalance between those completing a medical qualification and other higher education studies, including law. Unlike other study fields, students completing a qualification in medicine, dentistry or veterinary science (referred to here as 'medical' students) primarily commence their studies between the ages of 21 and 24.[28] Contrast this with law students, who predominantly start their undergraduate studies after completing their secondary education – around the age of 18. It is reported that 94.3 percent of law students are under the age of 20 than over 30 years old.[29] Disconcertingly, the disparity between the numbers of students who fail to complete their first year of study is marked with only 1.5 percent of medical students leaving compared to 5.7 percent of UK-domiciled law students. Non-completion rates for students aged 21 or over is 15.6 percent of law students compared to 2.5 percent of medical students who fail to complete their studies. Noticeably many of these law students had previous examination grades that were similar to that of medical students.[30]

It would appear that the deferred starting age of medical students could benefit experiential learning as the initial upheaval and trauma associated with the transition from adolescence to emerging adulthood starts to dissipate.[31] Unlike their younger counterparts who form the student majority elsewhere in higher education the older student intake reduces the impact associated with this period of development including fluctuating emotional, residential, educational and employment situations.[32]

Even if experiential learning does have the ability to develop the skills needed for higher education it does not necessarily address all of the needs of non-traditional students, who could be disproportionately affected by the time and personal commitment PBL and clinics demand. Failing to use PBL and simulation judiciously could have a disproportionate impact on non-traditional students. There are a significant number of non-traditional students who have secondary responsibilities, such as childcare, family and employment, that can affect the creation of peer support networks and friendships with whom the PBL burden can be shared, which could in turn lead to feelings of isolation, fear and not belonging or fitting in.

Addressing academic and peer support needs has the potential to improve the learning experience, retention figures and exam results as students will have the potential to engage with the subject on a personal level.[33] Encouraging and supporting students should help to tackle the student complaints and concerns that the module or coursing is wanting, course structure poor and academic staff unsupportive.[34] Nevertheless, adjustments to experiential programmes may require a fresh approach to team building as research now indicates that techniques such as the Belbin test are unable to support the psychological and socio-technical concerns of students which can, in turn, affect a groups cohesion.[35]

Subsequently, the question is less whether PBL or other forms of hands-on learning should be introduced at a certain time, but more how student groups are formed[36] particularly taking into account non-traditional students.

4.2.4 Traversing the swamp

"What am I doing here?" frequently crossed my mind in those first few weeks at university. After leaving an enjoyable job, it soon became apparent that I was in the boggy marshlands of Schön's 'swamp', doubtful where the other side was, let alone if it was accessible.[37] Often used to emphasise the high ground of pure knowledge compared to the unpredictable lowlands of real life, the swamp is an environment faced by professionals, but the concept is comparable to the early months of student transition.[38]

In spite of the view that PBL fails to emulate the complexities or unpredictability found in the swamp,[39] the initial transitionary uncertainties when combined with plenary sessions and experiential learning methods[40] are analogous to those first days of professional employment when you desperately seek to utilise your knowledge and past experiences with the new environment, information and requirements.[41] If law schools were to take a step back and acknowledge that students may feel that they receive insufficient feedback and that they are insufficiently supported then a possible solution might actually be found within the PBL and simulation process.[42]

Introducing PBL and simulation exercises to small groups of students early in their learning may have the potential to bridge the uncomfortable transitionary gap between the world of work or a school environment to one where you are expected to be a team player, an autonomous researcher and a judicious author.[43] The early group sessions I experienced utilised simulation and team-building exercises to illustrate group dynamics and decision-making processes, thus combining basic legal application with group support. Seemingly innocuous activities helped form bonds, especially for students with limited experience of education or from diverse working environments.

There is an idealism (admirable as that may be) in PBL theory that overlooks both the psychological impact of personal experiences and the educational struggles a person may be experiencing.

Although, in my experience, PBL and simulation were initially enjoyable, motivational decline did emerge as time progressed and cliques developed particularly where there was a noticeable variance in the student demographic. The rigid adherence to the PBL process did cause apathy in some sessions, and students found ways to skirt over the surface of the problems by using the module 'block guide' to establish adequate responses to the questions but not the multifaceted answers or reflection required for deep learning.

4.2.5 Learning and improvement: a journey of discovery

The picture may appear negative. It is not intended to be, nor is it. Progressive knowledge and skill acquisition is achievable by making adjustments to established PBL pedagogy and introducing live-client clinical work.This would improve motivation and acknowledge the needs of an increasingly diverse cohort.[44] A small increase in the extent a student considers a module to be worthwhile could improve motivation or interest in the subject which in turn could increase enjoyment now or in the future through improved retention and exam outcomes.[45]

If PBL is to support student learning from the transitionary to the final year, its use needs to occur alongside multiple facilitation models, modes and pedagogic stances to maintain its efficacy and provide a developmental programme of study for students.[46] Using Heron's three modes of facilitation in conjunction with a PBL model that increasingly promotes competence, professional action and critical contestability would facilitate a pedagogic approach that provides students with support and feedback at the start before reducing input, thus enabling students to improve their self-direction, confidence and autonomy.[47] This staggered approach to PBL, along with alignment of live-client clinics, might alleviate some of the problems in the transitionary period and later in the learning cycle. This is likely to have particular resonance for students from non-traditional backgrounds.[48] The need, at least in the early stages, to reduce the cognitive load and increase explanatory feedback for students who have little or no prior knowledge of the material, process or subject, is clear.[49]

Problem-based learning could form a solid pedagogic cornerstone of legal education, but unlike medicine, where PBL is undertaken by a student body largely aiming for the same profession, law students have a multiplicity of employment futures, in spite of the fact that a substantial majority initially intend to pursue a career in the legal sector.[50] Nevertheless, an education that teaches skills alongside knowledge extends far beyond the confines of legal practice and equips students with the qualities demanded by employers[51] and the cognitive[52] and affective qualities[53] outlined in Bloom's taxonomy.

Progressive skill acquisition is nothing new as best practice advocates a curriculum of observation, simulation, externships and in-house clinics to increase students' independent thinking and levels of autonomy and independence.[54] Even though British students do not have the right to practice law upon the completion of their degree, moving through a progressive experiential learning sequence would allow the student to progress with a supportive mix of PBL and simulation, before moving onto live-client work.

Knight and Yorke in their work on employability have observed a need for a heuristic approach to undergraduate education, developing the USEM model to incorporate **U**nderstanding of the subject, general and subject specific **S**kills, an **E**ffiacy of beliefs and personal qualities, and finally **M**etacognition and reflective practice.[55] This is increasingly important as life beyond graduation will see students return to a profession or enter into the world of work for the first time and irrespective of the education you receive, books you read or advice you believe, nothing in life prepares you for the first time you encounter a client's distress or anger or a moral, ethical or professional dilemma.

Even though I do not believe that real client work must be done through an in-house practice (though this provides more control and consistency), there is a need to develop the ability to assimilate multiple tiers of knowledge, respond to deadlines, be an effective team player and manage human expectation and demands, and exposure to real cases aids this process. Evolution is inevitable; Reich asserted that learners must develop the four essential skills of abstraction, system thinking, experimentation and collaboration before understanding can be employed to optimum effect while Stephenson ascertained that capability is determined when a person can take appropriate action, explain why they are doing it, engage fully in teamwork and continue to lean from their experiences.[56]

Dealing with people requires us to challenge our own beliefs and morals, and while it is possible for doctrine, skills, principles of diversity and equality and professional values to be taught using didactic methods, PBL, simulation and live-client clinics can focus minds on the application of that theory and the practice of those principles.[57]

4.2.6 Conclusion

The insight provided while completing this piece of work has been cathartic. I am convinced having been through the experiential process that this form of study plays a major role in meaningful education. Its ability to bring unconscious and conscious actions and thoughts to the fore are fundamental to core skills development that is vital within an adversarial legal system. Knowledge is unattainable if I do not know where to find it, interpretation is problematic if I am unaware of the beginning and end, application is impossible if I don't experience it.

Whilst there is much to be positive about in legal education, especially with advances in pedagogy, adjustments still need to be made, for example, to the way PBL groups are organised and facilitated. Although I am an enthusiast for PBL, in a rigid format and across an entire undergraduate degree it may be inappropriate and can have a disproportionate demographic impact.

In contrast, other forms of 'clinic', from team-building exercises to mock trials and a host of activities in between, to live-client case work, have much to offer. It is not until a student is confronted with the real-life problem of professional ethics and rules, coupled with a person (real or simulated) who is reliant upon them for help, that they can start to make wade purposefully through Schön's swampy conditions where learning is a process of doing, building and reflecting. Whilst legal education is certainly not broken, it certainly needs some servicing and fine-tuning.

Notes

1 D.A. Schön, *The reflective practitioner: how professionals think in action*, Basic Books Inc., 1983, 49–69.

2 Higher Education Statistics Agency (HESA), *Higher education student enrolments and qualifications obtained at higher education providers in the United Kingdom 2014/15*, HESA, 2016, Chart 1 and Chart 2.

3 Richard Grimes, Faking it and making it? Using simulation with Problem-Based Learning, in C. Strevens, R. Grimes and E. Phillips (eds.), *Legal education: simulation in theory and practice*, Farnham, Ashgate Publishing, 2014, 171.

4 M. Hardee, *Career expectations of students on qualifying law degrees in England and Wales*, The Higher Education Academy, 2012, 11–13, 29–33, available at: www.heacademy.ac.uk/sites/default/files/resources/hardee-report-2012.pdf, accessed 8 March 2016.

5 D. Lebow, *Constructivist values for instructional systems design: five principles toward a new mindset*, 41 (3), 1993. ETR&D 4, 5 citing Robert Heinich, *The proper study of instructional technology*, 1984, 32 ECTJ 67.

6 P. Ramsden, *Learning to teach in higher education* (2nd edn), RoutledgeFalmer, 2003, 21–37, 40–59, 80–83, 125–129.
7 G. Light and R. Cox, *Learning and teaching in higher education; the reflective professional*, Paul Chapman Publishing, 2001, 47–62, 86–89.
8 Ron Dearing, *Higher education in the learning society, Report of the National Committee of Enquiry into Higher Education*, HMSO, 1997.
9 J.R. Savery and T.M. Duffy, *Problem based learning: an instructional model and its constructivist framework*, Educational Technology, 35 (5), 1995, 31.
10 Ibid.
11 B.J. Dutch, Models for problem-based instruction in undergraduate courses, in B.J. Dutch, S.E. Groh and D.E. Allen (eds.), *The power of problem-based learning*, Stylus Publishing, 2001, 39–45.
12 M. Savin-Baden and C. Howell Major, *Foundations of problem-based learning*, Open University Press, 2004, 3–7.
13 K. Barton, P. McKellar and P. Maharg, *Authentic fictions: simulation, professionalism and legal learning*, Clinical Law Review, 14 (1), 2007, 143, 144–148, 155–160.
14 S.M. Shellman and K. Turan, *Do simulations enhance student learning? An empirical evaluation of an IR simulation*, Journal of Political Science Education, 2 (1), 2006, 19, 21–23, 28–30.
15 R. Burridge and N. Duncan, Role-play and simulation in the clinic, in H. Brayne, N. Duncan and R. Grimes (eds.), *Clinical legal education: active learning in your law school*, Blackstone Press Ltd, 1998, 173–193.
16 R. Corrada, 'Ill Structured' simulations in two American law classes: Labour Law And Administrative Law, in *Strevens, Grimes & Phillips*, op cit., 243–262.
17 E. Jenson, *Teaching with the brain in mind* (2nd edn), Association for Supervision and Curriculum Development, 2005, 33–59.
18 M. Savin-Baden, *Facilitating problem-based learning: illuminating perspectives*, Society for Research into Higher Education and Oxford: OUP, 2003, 48–60.
19 C. Schuler and A. Finchman, 'To admit or not to admit? That is the question?', in Peter Schwartz, Stewart Mennin and G. Webb (eds.), *Problem-based learning: case studies, experience and practice*, Kogan Page Ltd, 2001, 126–134; and J.B. Shaw, *A fair go for all? The impact of intragroup diversity and diversity-management skills on student experiences and outcomes in team-based class projects*, Journal of Management Education, 28 (2), 2004, 139, 139–169.
20 D.H.J.M. Dolmans, W. De Grave, I.H.A.P. Wolfhagen and C.P.M. Van Der Vleuten, *Problem-based learning: future challenges for educational practice and research*, Medical Education, 39 (7), 2005, 732, 733–736.
21 E. Tindle and D. Lincoln, *Mature age students in transition: Factors contributing to their success in first year*, 4th Pacific Rim First Year in Higher Education Conference: Creating Futures for a New Milennium, Brisbane 5–7th July 2000, 1–6.
22 Tanya Kantanis, *Same or different: issues that affect mature age undergraduate students' transition to university*, 6th Pacific Rim – First Year in Higher Education Conference: Changing Agendas, 'Te Ao Hurihuri' 8–10 July 2002, 1–10.
23 Schön op cit., 16–30.
24 J. Macfarlane and J. Manwaring, *Using problem-based learning to teach first year contracts*, Journal of Professional Legal Education, 16 (2), 1998, 271, 281–284.
25 HESA Enrolments and Qualifications, op cit, Table 6a
26 Lord High Chancellor of Great Britain, *Report of the Committee on Legal Education* (Cmnd 4595 1970–71) s.97, s.118, s.119, s.122, s.159, Appendix C Part 1.
27 HESA Enrolments and Qualifications, op cit, Chart 1 and Chart 2.
28 Ibid., Table 6a.
29 Ibid.
30 Ibid.
31 L. Wallis, *Is 25 the new cut-off point for adulthood?*, BBC, 23 September 2013, available at: www.bbc.co.uk/news/magazine-24173194, accessed 10 April 2016.
32 C. Munsey, *Emerging adults: the in-between age*, Monitor Staff, 37 (6), 2006, 68.

33 M. Yorke and B. Longden, *The first-year experience in higher education in the UK: final report*, York, The Higher Education Academy, 2008, 7–9, 13–14, 16–52.
34 R. Brinkworth, B. McCann, C. Matthews and K. Nordström, *First year expectations and experiences: student and teacher perspectives*, Higher Education, 58 (2), 2009, 157, 157–173.
35 N. Anderson and S. Sleap, *An evaluation of gender differences on the Belbin Team Role Self-Perception Inventory*, Journal of Occupational and Organizational Psychology, 77 (3), 2004, 429–437.
36 Macfarlane and Manwaring, op cit., (n 46), 281–284.
37 C. Maughan and J. Webb, *Lawyering skills in context* (2nd edn), Cambridge: Cambridge University Press, 2005, 34–44.
38 H. Brayne, N. Duncan and R. Grimes, *Clinical legal education: active learning in your law school*, London, Blackstone Press, 1998, 35–44.
39 Ibid., 35–36.
40 Strevens, Grimes and Phillips, op cit., 87–106.
41 Schön, 49–69.
42 Macfarlane & Manwaring, op cit, 281–284, 292–294
43 Brinkworth, McCann, Matthews and Nordström, op cit., 159, 163–171.
44 G. O'Neill and T. McMahon, Student-centred learning: what does it mean for students and lecturers?, in *2005–1: Emerging issues in the practice of university learning and teaching*, The All Ireland Society for Higher Education (AISHE), 2005, available at: www.aishe.org/readings/2005-1/toc.html, accessed 20 April 2016.
45 S.M Glynn, L. Price Aultman and A.M Owens, *Motivation to learn in general education programs*, The Journal of General Education, 54 (2), 2005, 150, 152–163.
46 Savin-Baden, op cit., 28–32.
47 Ibid., 28–29.
48 R. Moreno, *Decreasing cognitive load for novice students: effects of explanatory versus corrective feedback in discovery-based multimedia*, Instructional Science, 32 (1), 2004, 99, 102.
49 Ibid., 102, 109–111.
50 Hardee, op cit., 11–13, 34–37.
51 M. Humburg and R. van der Velden, *Skills and the graduate recruitment process: evidence from two discrete choice experiments*, Economics of Education Review, 49, 2015, 24, 25–26, 30–38.
52 B.S. Bloom (ed.), *Taxonomy of educational objectives: the classification of educational goals, book 1 cognitive domain*, Longman, 1956, 25–43 and 62–207.
53 B.S. Bloom, D.R. Krathwohl and B.B. Masia, *Taxonomy of educational objectives: the classification of educational goals, book 2 affective domain*, Longman, 1964, 25–43, 62–207.
54 R. Stuckey, et al (eds.), *Best practices for legal education: a vision and a road map*, Clinical Legal Education Association, 2007, 121–174.
55 P.T. Knight and M. Yorke, *Employability through the curriculum*, Tertiary Education and Management, 8 (4), 2002, 261, 264–266, 271–273.
56 Ibid., 262, 264.
57 Brayne, Duncan and Grimes, op cit., 70–72, 83–106.

Part 3 – Clinic, employability and educational need

Meredith Daniel

4.3.1 Introduction

Clinical legal education (CLE) in the UK sprang out of the "fertile environment of post 1968 Europe,"[1] and was largely driven by the desire to combat unmet legal need in the 1970s. The tension between facilitating social justice and maximising educational benefit has been a constant presence in academic debate in CLE, yet there has been little discussion about whether recent changes within higher education should affect this debate. Furthermore, the social and economic landscape of the country has also significantly altered, impacting on what students expect and need from their law degrees. This contribution focuses on the needs of the modern-day law student and ways in which experiential learning in general, and clinics in particular, can be used to meet such an agenda by utilising the strengths of simulated and live-client models.

In England and Wales, apprenticeships for would-be lawyers, training contracts for solicitors and pupillage for barristers, are becoming increasingly competitive. The number of students, even just those with high marks on graduation, far exceeds the number of job opportunities, meaning that academic success is no longer enough. The academic stage of education, where students undertake a law degree or another degree followed by a conversion course, is separate from the vocational stage where course content is more practical and focused on skills development. Students are expected to apply for jobs during the academic stage, yet employers are increasingly looking for candidates who have life experience – preferably in lawyering and people skills together with a sense of commercial awareness – when they apply for positions. It is clearly never too soon to start.

I wish to look at the comparative strengths and weaknesses of simulated and live-client CLE in what they can offer today's student. Simulation has the potential to outperform live-client models in areas such as skills development and may have other benefits. For example, simulated exercises can be constructed which mirror those used at assessment centres or mini-pupillages, and integrated into the curriculum. When it comes to employers' perception of experience, however, live-client clinics are vital. Law firms value students with a knowledge of access to justice issues and experience of working with real clients.

I conclude with suggestions for relatively minor, but significant, changes to experiential programmes that could increase the impact that CLE has on student learning and employability.

Overall, it is shown that the discussion surrounding CLE might usefully move away from whether CLE should be focused on social justice or education. Instead practitioners must be asking what the needs of the student are outside the scope of these two competing issues and how CLE can be best used to address these.

4.3.2 Changing needs and educational impact

There have been many fundamental changes to higher education and the legal profession which have created a need for greater emphasis to be placed on student employability. There are three particular developments that warrant mention: the introduction and progressive increase in university tuition fees, the decline in apprenticeships following completion of the academic and vocational stages of a student's education and the early testing and recruitment practices undertaken by employers. By focusing on the pressures and challenges facing students, the subtle changes that can be made within clinical programmes to better meet student needs become clear.

In 2012 in England and Wales, university tuition fees rose by almost 275 per-cent to a maximum of £9000 per year. Prior to the changes, there were numerous discussions about the impact that such changes would have on students. Initial studies indicated that increasing fees would cause greater financial competition between universities,[2] but in fact the variation in cost between courses at different universities is minimal, with the vast majority charging the full £9,000.[3] Hardee's 2012 study into law students' expectations of their degree asked students how their expectations would change if tuition fees rose to £7,500. The results indicated that students would have overall significantly higher expectations. Interestingly, however, it was skills-based areas which students argued needed the greatest improvement.[4] Hardee also showed that in selecting a degree, students indicated that having a stable and secure future was a key factor in choosing to study law.[5] The recent introduction of Unistats' Key Information Sets (KIS), which allow students to more thoroughly assess the quality of education supplied by different providers, demonstrates the increasing interest of students in their future employment prospects.[6] Such developments are justified by the government body, the Quality Assurance Agency, by the "increasing tendency to see higher education as a product with a price tag."[7]

Anecdotal evidence also indicates an increasing focus on employability as part of an increased demand for value for money following the tuition fee increase. As such, universities and their departments have a lot to gain from meeting student demands due to the increased transparency regarding student satisfaction and employability. The increase in tuition fees, as well as encouraging an increased focus on employability within CLE, also raises moral questions. The debate about whether the focus of CLE should be the education of students or the promotion of social justice and client care has been ruminating since the origins of CLE. Since the introduction of, and then subsequent raising of tuition fees, however, university law clinics present the interesting quandary of students paying significant sums of money to represent clients. CLE must therefore proceed cautiously, with a focus on student benefit and employability, if it is not to be accused of exploiting students' need for experience to combat deficiencies with social justice.

It is not just tuition fees which have changed the needs of students. The legal employment market has altered significantly since the introduction of CLE in the 1970s. Unfortunately, it is almost impossible to objectively assess how much. The rapid changes in legal education, especially the introduction of the Bar Vocational Course (BVC) in 1989 and the Legal Practice Course (LPC) in 1993, make it difficult to make consistent comparisons between yearly employability statistics even where they do exist. This is further exacerbated as the statistics are presented in a form from which it is difficult to draw meaningful conclusions. Comparing the number of students who undertake the LPC with the number of training contracts available ignores students who may have given up on a career in law rather than self-fund the LPC. Comparing the number of law graduates with the number of training contracts ignores the fact that some law students do not attempt to enter law and that graduates from other disciplines do. None of the statistics recognise the impact of recent graduates who are still trying to enter the profession. Despite these limitations, the most up-to-date Law Society Annual Report for 2014 paints a bleak picture.

In 2014 there were 16,120 law graduates and 5,001 training contracts. This does not include students undertaking the GDL, second-year LLB students, graduates from previous years or people changing careers later in life.[8] More worrying than these statistics, however, is that there is a trend in the data indicating a consistent increase in law graduates and a decline in training contracts. At the Bar, the statistics demonstrate just how competitive law has become, with 86 percent of students who completed the BPTC (the successor programme to the BVC) in 2013 not having gained a pupillage within 18 months.[9] The situation is worse when considering the number of students who gain tenancy after their pupillage. In 2010–2011, 477 pupils undertook a second six,[10] the final stage of pupillage. However, in 2011 only 335 tenancies were registered.[11] This represents a further loss of 30 percent of students. In this increasingly competitive job market, small changes within CLE can make a significant difference to students' chances of standing out.

The final factor to consider is the stage at which many law firms are recruiting students. Vacation schemes, a period of paid work experience with a law firm, are seen as the most reliable way to secure a training contract. Students are usually required to apply in the first or second term of their second year. The scheme itself takes place during the summer of their second year. An assessed mini-pupillage is the equivalent for the Bar, with students usually applying at the end of their second year for experiences during their third. During these assessments students are often expected to demonstrate research, presentation, advocacy, written and other skills which inform the decision as to whether to employ them. It is therefore crucial that CLE is implemented as early as possible in students' legal education both so that they can highlight it as work experience to assist them in securing interviews, and so that they can develop the skills necessary to pass the assessments. It is worrying that skills and experience gained during students' third year of university are often too late to help them during the prime window to secure a training contract.

The three fundamental influences on student need outlined above show a distinct movement away from the needs and demands of students at the beginning of the CLE movement. CLE, available to all students regardless of connections or finances, offers an unrivalled opportunity to improve employability. In many cases this will not involve significant change but simply a refocusing of existing CLE to either place greater emphasis on, or simply make students more aware of, the skills they are developing.

4.3.3 The pros and cons of simulation and live-client models in improving employability

Simulation has become increasingly popular both in forming clinical modules but also in adding elements or assessments to existing modules within law degrees. Simulation carries a number of benefits over live-client models: it is more cost effective; it provides more control and consistency in course content; it can often be offered to greater numbers of students and, as a manipulable device it can be superior in teaching skills faster and more thoroughly. When it comes to using CLE to improve student employability, many of these advantages are crucial.

The control and consistency in course content is important to provide students with relevant and equivalent learning experiences.[12] On simulated courses, content can be adapted to provide students with more opportunities to develop the skills most sought after by employers. Given the prevalence of formal presentation skills in vacation schemes, and letter drafting in mini-pupillages, additional focus could be given to these skills. Furthermore, simulation offers students the opportunity to perform advocacy, an experience which would often be too difficult to control in live-client models, and one which is increasingly required at pupillage interviews. Simulation also provides the opportunity to receive informed feedback from the person simulating the client, more accurately mirroring employment assessments where your interviewer may play your client.[13]

Owing to lower supervision requirements (with no real client care considerations), simulation can also more frequently be offered to more students. Given the potential impact that CLE can have on employability, restricting student access or allowing some students to undertake CLE in their second year whilst others have to wait until their third year, could seriously disadvantage some students in the job market. Where student numbers are capped, in both simulated and live-client models, it is important to consider how we are selecting the students exposed to these experiences. Francis discusses the difficulties that students from lower socio-economic backgrounds, with fewer industry connections or lower self-belief in their career prospects, have securing work experience.[14] Although work experience is not the only barrier to entry in the profession, it is a significant advantage in showing commercial awareness and interest. Where clinical programmes do select students, clinicians should be cautious not to exclude those who are already disadvantaged.

Research into the efficacy of simulated CLE is still limited. In medical education, on the other hand, simulation has been far more widely implemented and assessed both independently of and in conjunction with live-client clinics. High-fidelity simulations in medicine have been shown to facilitate high levels of learning.[15] Two independent reviews conducted in 2011, of over 20 years of data, determined that simulation outperformed traditional clinical education when it was used for the development of clearly defined skills.[16] Studies have also shown that simulation can outperform traditional clinic in areas such as patient care.[17] Key skills are becoming more essential to students at earlier stages of their academic lives. Simulation provides a level of control, an ability for repetition and a flexibility in feedback which can lead to greater levels of proficiency and improved confidence. Both of these are vital if students are to thrive in an increasingly competitive job market.

One of the key criticisms of simulation is that it creates less-intrinsic motivation and emotional engagement from students. Where high-fidelity simulation is used, studies into both medical and legal simulation have shown some capacity to engage students emotionally.[18] Overall, however, live-client clinic is better at eliciting emotional responses.[19] It also has the capacity to confront students with the reality and commonality of the problems that the legal profession faces.[20] In simulation it is far easier to see barriers to justice as manufactured, or tools to promote thought, making it far easier to dismiss them. It seems, therefore, that in ethical and emotional learning, live-client models still outperform comparative simulations. The problem is that it is difficult to ensure the educational value of live-client experiences.[21] Whilst they may be better at showing injustice and ethical conundrums, it may be that students are not exposed to cases which highlight these issues. Far more concerning is that students' skills development is entirely dependent on their cases, leaving some students without key employability skills. It has also been shown that the fear and anxiety produced among some students in live-client interactions may actually inhibit their learning and skills development.[22]

Despite all of this, live-client clinic retains an importance for employers that is unmatched by simulation. The graduate recruitment websites of many top law firms and chambers espouse the value of pro bono work and advise students to undertake activities with organisations such as the Free Representation Unit, while simulation is barely mentioned. It seems therefore, that when it comes to employability students need simulation to engage and develop the skills that they will be both assessed on and asked to discuss, and live-client models to show an engagement with the profession and a proven track record of handling clients.

4.3.4 Small changes, big impact?

This final section outlines some practical ways in which clinics can adapt to better meet the needs of modern students. Whilst many clinics already implement some of these principles, the following suggestions are provided to encourage clinicians to consider some programme re-alignments which may make a big difference to students.

- Offering clinical programmes earlier:
  - Providing clinical opportunities in students' first two years of university will significantly assist them in the recruitment process. The problem of limited legal knowledge can be overcome by offering groups which span year groups or providing an observational role for first-year students.
  - Clinicians should also consider the disparity of opportunity when some students can engage in clinic during their second year of university whilst others have to wait until their third.
- Changing selection processes to consider the employability needs of students:
  - Students often find it difficult to secure their first piece of legal work experience because many work experience schemes presuppose prior experience. Clinic has the opportunity to counter this, but only if clinical selection procedures do not prioritise students who are better placed to complete application forms due to prior experience.
  - Randomly selecting students also poses difficulties. Given that clinical programmes have the opportunity to boost student employability, any random ballot risks advantaging and disadvantaging students, who are all paying for a service, on the basis of luck.
- Integrating more skills which are assessed by employers:
  - Many of the skills assessed by employers are not currently prioritised in clinical programmes. One key example of this is presentation skills which are frequently used to assess students in both legal and non-legal graduate recruitment programmes. These could be introduced through students presenting details of their cases to one another on a regular basis. This would both improve their skills and increase their exposure to legal principles and social justice issues.

- At the Bar, students are frequently tested on opinion-writing skills. In practice, these are very similar to the letters which students draft to clients. As such, students could be asked to redraft advice letters as opinions. Having already done the vast majority of the work, this would be a simple way for students to develop an additional skill.

- Offering students realistic expectations of what their law career will involve:
  - Live-client clinic can paint an unrealistic expectation of what legal practice is like as many cases are vetted based on interest and academic relevance. Students also receive a high level of satisfaction from casework because the importance of that case to them is high and they build a relationship with their client. This is not always reflected in practice, where you may never meet your client and the case you undertake is one of many.
  - One way to counter this is by offering clinical programmes alongside local work experience placements. This could be a day spent shadowing a practitioner or even a half-day court visit. Such opportunities also provide students with an opportunity to cement their learning.
  - Where this is not possible, talks given by local practitioners who are prepared to be candid with students would also be beneficial.

- Encouraging students to actively explore the skills that they exhibit through clinical programmes:
  - Where clinics focus predominantly on providing a service to the community as opposed to education, students often do not understand the full range of skills they demonstrate during the programmes.
  - This tacit learning can be hard for students to formalise by writing it on an application form or analysing it in an interview.
  - Clinical programmes should encourage students to discuss this skills development throughout the course and highlight the ways in which comparisons can be drawn between skills used in the clinic and key skills which employers value.

- Using oral exams (*viva voce*) as a method of examination:
  - Vivas allow students to learn to both articulate and justify their achievements. An experience which is directly comparable to a job interview.

- Allowing opportunities for international visits using connections built between clinicians:
  - Clinical legal education is fortunate to operate in a very open international community which provides the opportunity for clinicians to organise international vacation placements for students. This would be highly advantageous, as employers cite international work experience as a very important factor in modern employment.

4.3.5 Conclusion

The combination of increased tuition fees and unstable employment prospects make it ethically questionable to justify using law students to bridge the legal aid gap if there isn't a significant benefit to them. Whilst CLE already serves a key role in improving student employability, it is important for educators to reflect on the extent to which their programme design maximises value for the modern student. It is, perhaps, time to step back and question whether programme designs fully meet student needs. CLE has always been rooted in the concept of exposing students to the reality of the legal landscape. The proposals outlined above are simply widening that original purpose to accommodate the changing needs of the student body.

Notes

1 J. Giddings, R. Burridge, Sam Gavigan and C.F. Klein, The first wave of modern clinical legal education, in F.S. Bloch (ed.), *The global clinical movement*, Oxford, Oxford University Press, 2010, 6.

2 *University study examines impact of higher tuition fees*, Leicester: University of Leicester, 2010, available at: www.le.ac.uk/ebulletin-archive/ebulletin/news/press-releases/2010–2019/2010/09/nparticle.2010–09–20.html, accessed 2 April 2016.

3 *Foundation and undergraduate tuition fees 2016–17*, Complete University Guide, 2016, available at: www.thecompleteuniversityguide.co.uk/university-tuition-fees/reddin-survey-of-university-tuition-fees/foundation-undergraduate-tuition-fees-2016%E2%80%9317,-ukeu/, accessed 1 August 2016.

4 M. Hardee, *Interim report: comparing the first year of the Cohort study in 2012–2013 with the UKCLE study March 2012*, The Higher Education Academy, 2014, available at: www.heacademy.ac.uk/system/files/resources/hardee_interimreport_2014final.pdf, accessed 2 April 2016.

5 M. Hardee, *Career expectations of students on qualifying law degrees in England and Wales*, Hardee Consulting, Higher Education Academy, 2012, 83.

6 HEFCE, *Unistats and key information sets*, HEFCE, 2016, available at: www.hefce.ac.uk/lt/unikis/, accessed 2 April 2016.

7 QAA, *Skills for employability*, available at: http://qaa.ac.uk/assuring-standards-and-quality/skills-for-employability, accessed 2 April 2016.

8 The Law Society, *Trends in the solicitors' profession: Annual Statistics Report 2014*, London, Law Society Publishing, 2014.

9 Bar Standards Board, *BPTC key statistic 2011–2014: an analysis of students over three academic years*, BSB, 2015, available at: www.barstandardsboard.org.uk/media/1713286/bptc_key_statistics_report_-_301115.pdf, accessed 2 April 2016.

10 BSB, *An analysis of the backgrounds of pupils registered in 2010/11*, Bar Standards Board, 2012, available at: www.barstandardsboard.org.uk/media/1408372/pupillage_supplementary_survey_201011.pdf, accessed 2 April 2016.

11 Bar Standards Board, *Bar barometer: trends in the profile of the Bar*, BSB, 2014, available at: www.barstandardsboard.org.uk/media/1599997/bsb_barometer_report_112pp_june_13.pdf, accessed 2 April 2016.

12 R. Tyler and R. Catz, *The contradictions of clinical legal education*, Cleveland State Law Review, 1980, 693, 706.

13 K. Barton, C. Cunningham, G. Jones and P. Maharg, *Valuing what clients think*, Clinical Law Review, 2006, 1.

14 A. Francis, *Legal education, social mobility, and employability: possible selves, curriculum intervention and the role of legal work experience,* Journal of Law and Society, 43 (2), 2015, 173.
15 S. Issenberg, W. McGaghie, E. Petrusa, D. Gordon and R. Scalese, *Features and uses of high-fidelity medical simulations that lead to effective learning: a BEME systematic review*, Medical Teacher, 2005, 10, 24.
16 W. McGaghie, S. Issenberg, E. Cohen, J. Barsuk and D. Wayne, *Does simulation-based medical education with deliberative practice yield better results than traditional clinical education? a meta-analytic comparative review of the evidence,* Academic Medicine, 2011, 706.
17 B. Singer, T. Corbridge and C. Schroedl, *First-year residents outperform third-year residents after simulation-based education,* Critical Care Medicine, Simulation in Healthcare, 2013, 67.
18 K. Khan, T. Pattison and M. Sherwood, *Simulation in medical education*, Medical Teacher, 2011, 1, 2.
19 S. Witzner, *Teaching and doing: the role of law school clinics in enhancing access to justice*, Fordham Law Review, 2004, 997, 1008.
20 J. Webb, *Inventing the good: a prospectus for clinical education and the teaching of legal ethics in England and Wales,* The Law Teacher, 1996, 270, 278.
21 K. Kerrigan and P. Plowden, *Who benefits? – case management and clinical education,* The Law Teacher, 1996, 315.
22 R. Vince, *Behind and beyond Kolb's learning cycle,* Journal of Management Education, 1998, 304, 307.

Part 4 – Shared potential despite the difference?

David Roccaro

4.4.1 Introduction

The presence of the legal clinic as an integral part of the law school curriculum has been recently spreading in civil law countries who were traditionally reluctant to the introduction of such methods. Many universities in Western Europe now have clinical and other experiential programmes within and alongside the curriculum. What has caused this shift and where are we heading?

I first learned of the role of clinics during a programme about innovative didactic methods in legal education.[1] I wondered why in some institutions this was commonplace whilst in others it was not. In researching the theory and practice of 'clinics', I am increasingly convinced that the civil law is no greater attached to tradition than its common law counterpart. Rather, the reluctance to develop clinic under the civil is more one of context and perception. I will try to explain.

As early as the first few decades of the 20th Century some continentally-based academics such as Carnelutti in Italy and Frommhold in Germany, supported the introduction of a hands-on approach to learning the law as part of the law school curriculum (respectively in Cliniche di diritto and Juristische Kliniken).[2] A clinical movement was also discernible in the USA at this time too but where jurisdictions did rely on law schools to produce lawyers (as compared with the apprenticeship system found in many countries of the common law) it was still a rarity.

4.4.2 The connection between legal education and legal tradition

In 1905 Carnelutti wrote a paper on the relevance of introduction of legal clinics in Italian legal education. He wrote that:

> we [jurists] as much as them [medics] operate on human beings; what varies is the point of view since they consider man himself, as *individual* and therefore as a whole, and we in relationship with other men, as citizen and as party besides; but one is the substance in any case: divine human nature.[3]

He continued saying that both doctors and lawyers needed an education that involved looking through the lens of reality – in modern-day parlance experiential learning and the application of theory to practice.

Whilst, with hindsight, we may see the virtues of learning experientially, particularly in an applied professional context such as medicine or the law, I suggest (and it is said by others including the contributors to this book) that it is not possible to isolate models of legal education from their specific context or system and from the relevant cultural setting.[4]

Accordingly, on the one hand legal education reflects the way law is conceived, structured and practised. To be precise, teaching methods are the consequence of applicable cultures and traditions. On the other hand, however, the form and content of legal education necessarily contributes to those very perceptions, traditions and conventions. Using Merryman's words:

> through legal education the legal culture is transferred from generation to generation.[5]

It is clearly not possible to separate legal education from legal tradition or *vice versa*.[6] For this reason, a descriptive analysis of a legal education system and its methods goes hand in hand with that of the legal tradition to which it is part. Elsewhere in this book, the value of learning through application of theory to practice is stressed – we might term this generically as 'clinical legal education' (CLE). As I will attempt to show here, and as others show elsewhere in this volume, whilst legal clinics (working with real clients or based on simulation) are now increasingly being found in civil law-based law schools, their adoption has neither been wholesale nor without adaption. There is, of course, considerable risk in taking a seemingly successful clinic 'package' from one jurisdiction and introducing it into another. Whilst CLE may be fit for purpose in both civil and common law countries the form and *modus operandi* may be quite different. The common denominator is that the student must have the chance to experience the application of the law and to have the opportunity to deconstruct that experience with members of the academy (ideally with professors, other students and all those with a vested interest e.g., NGOs). The process of adaptation may be challenging, but I suggest any problems encountered in doing so are not insurmountable.[7]

4.4.3 Clinical legal education as a product of common law experience

And now to the movement for change in legal education. Clinical legal education was largely the product of developments in common law countries. It is now increasingly found in the civil law world.[8]

Why has Western Europe been so hesitant in the acceptance of such an approach to learning in the university curricula?[9]

We have already looked, elsewhere in this book, at the historical development of and the cultural differences between the civil and common law in general terms.

In relation to the origins of CLE, it is important to recognise traits in the US legal system that favoured the development of clinics in law schools.[10]

First, the US legal profession was and remains strong and largely unitary (although some regulatory and substantive law differences can be found between the individual states that make up the federal structure). Large law firms are just one of the consequences of this strength. Bench and bar come from the same educational background – law school – with judges chosen (or elected) from the ranks of the practising bar. Professional identity is strong, and members really identify with the overarching professional entity.

Second, although the legal profession is subject to federal and state law, the profession itself is largely self-regulating. The American Bar Association (ABA) prepares models for regulation (including prescribing the form and content of much of the law school curriculum that falls to be implemented by individuals, and law schools in each state).[11] The ABA, alongside the Association of American Law Schools, imposes minimum standards for law schools wishing to obtain accreditation – making their graduates eligible to sit the applicable state bar examination – a precursor to qualification as a practising lawyer. In this way, the profession indirectly (and more recently in some instances, directly, for example the insistence in the Standards on students getting some work-based [including clinical] experience) impacts on teaching content and delivery.[12] Using Merryman's words, "in the United States, legal education is primarily professional education".[13] Couple with this the coincidence and importance of the scholarly work of educationalists such as Dewey, Schön and Kolb[14] (extolling the virtues of learning through the application of theory to practice and the value of reflection) then there was clearly fertile ground for the development of experiential learning methods in legal education.

One other factor needs mentioning to explain the initial growth of clinics in the USA. In the 1960s the civil rights movement was in full swing. The fight for racial equality, radical politics, an increasing public awareness (including private and state funding opportunities) of the anti-poverty agenda and the development of cause lawyering all contributed to a movement to deliver legal services to those variously disadvantaged. Clinical legal education could be said to have been born to compensate for the absence of state-driven legal aid services. This is why today it is possible to identify two dimensions of clinical legal education, both essential to its nature: a teaching method and an instrument of social justice. It is, indeed, before the war on poverty and overt welfare policies that legal aid clinics began to provide free and focused legal services and in doing so providing the potential for the growth of law school pro bono activity.[15] The significance of charitable funding also must be mentioned, and this is discussed elsewhere.[16]

4.4.4 Transplanting experiential learning

In re-thinking legal education, in the civil law world at least, it is important to identify its shortcomings. Students are in the main passive participants in the learning process. They listen, often in large numbers in the lecture hall, to the words of wisdom of their professors. They have little opportunity to discuss or debate what they hear, nor is there much opportunity, except informally, to test their understanding through the application of principles and theory to practice and reality. The only time the students receive any indication of their educational progress is at exam time, and frequently no feedback is given on student performance other than implicit from the mark or grade awarded. Substantial numbers fail to pass. In addition, the subjects taught largely ignore the skills that students need to embrace – regardless of whether they intend to practice law at some later stage. The ability to research thoroughly, evaluate critically, write accurately and precisely and time-manage and collaborate effectively in a team are attributes that all students will need at some point in their lives regardless of career destination.

As seen above the main form of instruction in law schools under the civil law is the lecture. Whilst it is *the* means of delivery, attendance is not normally compulsory. A student could arrive at the exam hall having never attended a lecture. Whether he or she has been attentive or not, the exam requires little by the way of critical thinking of application of principle to practice and is more a repetition of what was said in the lecture and/or read in the recommended books (often written by the lecturer). What is left in students' minds after this performance? I suggest that it is reasonable to mistrust the assessment method and more broadly the educational approach.

Lastly, dialogues on legal education are not important in academic discussion, except in rare instances when educational reform is necessary.[17]

Even though these are the general characteristics of civil law legal education, exceptions exist. Sometimes professors on their personal initiative (rarely by institutional choice) organize activities other than lectures: for example, visits to court and contributions from experts or professionals such as practising lawyers, notaries or politicians. Moreover, some student associations organize mock trials. Clinical essence lingers deep down in these kind of programmes, even if these are fragmented and not integrated in curriculum.

The civil law legal education system falls short on these counts.

How might a re-think shape up to address this?

It would be easy and attractive to say that law clinics fit the bill here. Many contributors to this volume and elsewhere say that the law clinic provides the vehicle for study in which knowledge, skills and values can be studied holistically and where the student is required and supported to take responsibility for his or her learning.[18] Having worked in clinics personally at home and abroad, I would not disagree with that assessment in principle. What I would say is this: taking into account the value and potential of CLE, is it possible to take a proven but pre-packaged model and export it into new contexts without the risk of legal (and probably cultural) imperialism resulting?[19]

Taking a historical perspective, I suggest that it is not correct to say that clinical method is 'better' than lectures per se, but that any legal education system approaches to learning and study are the result of a certain legal culture. This however doesn't prevent the transplanting of good practices from one system to another.

In my view there is a common core within CLE that is transferable without undue risk. There are then factors that must be taken into account to ensure that the clinic is legally, culturally and socially appropriate.

The core centres on active student participation, structured feedback, the opportunity to revisit experiences – with the same or another client or in simulation – and close and adequate supervision to protect the client's interests. The clinical programme might be focused on learning and teaching or may be more driven by local unmet legal need.[20]

The adaptations depend on the particular context and will reflect applicable laws and professional regulation, social norms and expectations and a range of other considerations from the political to the religious. Whether the clinic forms an integrated, credit-bearing, part of the curriculum or not (and if so how it is assessed) will necessarily depend on the will of the law faculty and the requirements of the university more generally. The essence of clinic, however, is to give the student the opportunity of exposure to the real or realistic application of the law and to have the chance to deconstruct that experience.

There are many activities that the student can engage in under direct supervision or in self-directed activity. For example, this might include: legal research, fact-finding inquiry, assisting qualified lawyers, interviewing clients and witnesses, drafting letters and other documents and depending on applicable rules, engaging in negotiations and even advocacy before courts and tribunals.

The focus of the clinic itself can be many and varied – from advice and possibly representation on areas of local unmet need such as immigration, employment, housing or juvenile crime to public legal education programmes such as Street Law.[21] The siting of the clinic is equally flexible and may be within the law school's building, elsewhere on campus, in the town or in another lawyer's or NGO's office.

Experiential learning through clinic, be it for actual clients or in simulated role-play, has the adaptability to fit into particular settings and situations without the fear of inappropriate cultural domination.

4.4.5 Today and the future for legal education under the civil law

Whilst increasing numbers now accept the worth of CLE (as evidenced by the published works cited in this contribution and the growth of clinics across the region), there are obstacles to be overcome – in terms of perceptions, conventions and logistics.

The first is that governments in the civil law world commonly define which educational activities are required and which are left to the discretion of the individual university.[22] The law school curriculum is, for reasons given above, generally standardised on the basis that the study of law is the study of legal science – a fixed diet of topics and categorisations. This leaves little room for optional courses at least in the first few years of study.[23] Therefore, students may have to wait before being able to elect to take optional offerings (such as a clinic).

Second, little attention has, until recently, been given to the notion that the theory and practice of law are inextricably linked. However, this is now being challenged, with some writers suggesting that a new way to conceive law should start with the idea that practice is not the antithesis of theory but is its completion. This notion was in fact raised many years ago and is now enjoying something of a revival.[24] The separation of the academic and vocational stages of legal education is further pronounced in most civil jurisdictions as a result of the specialisations law graduates may opt to follow post university. To be a lawyer in private practice or to be a notary, a prosecutor or a judge requires further study. The university seldom provides that opportunity and instead graduates go to a professional school to undertake the necessary instruction and practice experience.[25] By contrast, US students do not undertake a practice stage after graduation. They can progress straight to the bar exam (although many go to intensive classes in preparation for that).[26]

But even after considering the history and engrained concepts and traditions of the civil system, what improvements might prove possible and how might clinic play a part in this?

The future can be summed up in four words: active participation of students. Educational theory and a wealth of scholarly writings in the specific context of legal education all suggest that students learn more and more deeply if required to apply their knowledge and understanding. The sense of this is clear – think of any discipline – do tasks, get feedback and do them again and performance normally improves.

Experiential learning is, I suggest, a highly appropriate educational method for a law student, because it allows him or her to contextualise theoretical studies in the frame of problematic legal experience. It is also an instrument through which the university can make its human and cultural capital available to wider society – going beyond its limited brief of teaching and research.

There are three aspects of civil law legal education that, I suggest, can be improved by adopting and adapting clinical methods.

First, there is the relationship between the 'academic' and the 'vocational'. Civil law systems reserve the former to the universities and the latter to the professional providers, post-graduation.[27]

However, the dichotomy between theory and practice unnecessarily fragments the reality of law at a point when the student is attempting to make sense of law as a whole. Clinical legal education is a hybrid, on the one hand enhancing knowledge of doctrine and substantive rules and on the other hand developing legal and transferable skills and a sense of professional responsibility. It also provides a forum for discussion between teacher and student and potentially across jurisdictions.[28] The mix of theory and practice also provides the opportunity for greater co-operation between academic and legal practitioner.

Second, clinical legal education allows students to observe law in context. They can look at the general and abstract rule in relation to the social, economic and cultural context where it operates. Students can also address extra-legal aspects of law, reflecting on philosophic or economic justifications, possible law reform issues, the role of law in society and ethical considerations of law and the legal system.

As noted above the civil law curriculum currently has little room for the introduction of additional subjects and options, particularly where this does not fall neatly in the established legal science classification.[29] However, clinical programmes might be included as subjects of 'procedural' study. Although this might risk the clinic being sacrificed in terms of its real pedagogic significance.[30]

Third, the nature of clinic results in a steady flow of feedback for students from those who supervise their casework and from peers. Mostly, assessment and (where it is given) feedback on the rest of the law course comes at the end of a period of study and the student has little or no opportunity to discover beforehand how he or she is progressing nor how improvement can be made. By contrast, assessment is inevitably part of the clinical learning process and is used as an opportunity for learning rather than a one-off measurement of achievement at a particular juncture – where the student has little chance to improve further at least in that context.

4.4.6 Conclusions: towards a continental model of clinical legal education

What is the role of the university in the 21st century? Is it to pass on knowledge in the hope, even expectation, that through a system of osmosis it is absorbed and retained by the student regardless of what he or she intends to do with it? Or is the role of the law school to prepare students for later life? Do universities also have a responsibility to use their extensive resources to better society and serve a wider social mission?

I suggest the universities owe a duty, morally and economically, to society to serve students and the public more effectively. Clinical legal education is a versatile tool which, if carefully structured and properly supervised, can meet a variety of needs – student, client, university, legal profession and public.

In the continental European context, legal education is an undergraduate programme of study. Students are inevitably mostly young and inexperienced and need many aspects of their education addressed.[31] A clinical programme can assist through a holistic approach to study that involves not just applied doctrine but skills and values too.

The case for experiential learning in general and clinic in particular is, I suggest, compelling. That said, such an approach may be seen as too radical a step for many. Hence my recommendation in re-thinking legal education is to embrace the clinic in a small and gradual way so that all – student, teacher and client – can become used to the nature, demands and impact of the clinic. A safe way of managing such an introduction is to start with simulation and possibly placements (externships) in legal practice and with NGOs. The full-blown in-house law school clinic offering legal advice and representation may then follow.

I believe that the clinical method can give lifeblood to legal science and to extend the medical analogy (and remember that the norm for most medics is to learn clinically) enable students to properly dissect and diagnose the law.

Notes

1 For more information see: http://clinicalegale.it, accessed 1 October 2016.

2 F. Carnelutti, *Clinica del diritto*, Rivista di diritto processuale I, 1935, 169; G. Frommhold, *Juristische Kliniken*, Deutsche Juristen-Zeitung 5, 1900, 448.

3 The term *jurist* here is defined as: "all those who dedicate themselves to professional activities concerning education, application, exposition and transmission of law", see: G. Pascuzzi, *Giuristi si diventa*, Bologna, Il Mulino, 2013, 29; F. Carnelutti, *Clinica del diritto*, I Rivista di diritto processuale, 1935, 169.

4 Merryman evaluates difficulties and relevance of comparison among legal education systems. Moreover, he sees the tight relationship between legal education and cultural context in this way: "a legal system is a component part (a subsystem) of a social system, and the system of legal education is a component part (a sub-subsystem) of the legal system. The system and its subsystems are organically related and give meaning to each other. A change in any part resounds throughout the whole." See: J.H. Merryman, *Legal education there and here: a comparison*, Stanford Law Review, 27, 1974–1975, 859.

5 Ibid.

6 Indeed a *legal tradition* is: "a set of modes to think, apply and teach law that is historically conditioned and deeply-rooted in legal mentality", A. Gambaro and R. Sacco, *Sistemi giuridici comparati,* Utet giuridica, 32–33. 2008.

7 D. Blazquez Martin, The relative significance of legal tradition and legal education reform, in D. Ikawa and L. Wortham (eds.), *The new law school*, Public Interest Law Institute, 2010, 23–32.

8 See for example the material and discussion through the European clinic network, available at: www.encle.org, accessed 8 October 2016.

9 Pre-existing form of apprenticeship, large number of students, the undergraduate nature of legal education, limitations on practice of law for non-qualified people, some legal aid (state) provision for the poor people all mitigated against the initial growth of law clinics in Western Europe. See: R. Wilson, *Western Europe last holdout in the world wide acceptance of clinical legal education*, German Law Journal, 10, 2009, 838–839.

10 Unfortunately, it is not possible to avoid again some generalisation due to the presence of slightly different legal education models within the USA.

11 U. Mattei, T. Ruskola and A. Gidi, *Schlesinger's comparative law: cases, text, materials*, Foundation Press, 2009, 637–643.

12 J.R. Ostertag, *Legal education in Germany and the United States: a structural comparison*, Vand Journal of Transnational Law, 26, 1993–1994, 305.

13 J.H. Merryman, *Legal education there and here: a comparison*, op cit., 866.

14 J. Dewey, *How we think*, New York, D.C. Heath, 1910; D. Schon, *The reflective practitioner: how professionals think in action*, New York, Basic Books, 1983; D. Kolb, *Experiential learning: experience as the source of learning and development*, New Jersey, Pearson, 2014 (2nd edn).
15 M.M. Barry, J.C. Dubin, and P.A. Joy, *Clinical education for this millennium: the third wave*, Clinical Law Review, 7, 2001, 1.
16 S.Wizner, *The law school clinic: legal education in the interests of justice*, Fordham Law Review, 70, 2001, 1929.
17 By contrast, common law legal education is a common genre in legal literature. J.H. Merryman, *Legal education there and here: a comparison*, Stanford Law Review,27, 1975, 874; A. Dondi, *Qualche considerazione in tema di educazione giuridica istituzionale*, Politica del diritto, 1–2, 2013, 107.
18 See: H. Brayne, N. Duncan and R. Grimes, *Clinical legal education: active learning in your law school*, London, Blackstone Press, 1998, 1 and more generally.
19 R. Wilson, *Training for justice: the global reach of clinical legal education*, Penn State International Law Review, 2004, 428–429; D. Bonilla, *Legal clinics in the global north and south: between equality and subordination-an essay*, Yale Human Rights & Development Law Journal, 16, 2013, 1–40.
20 F.S. Bloch, *Access to justice and the global clinical movement*, Washington University Journal of Law & Policy, 28, 2008, 126.
21 For more information on Street Law see the sebsite of Street Law Inc, Washington, DC and available at: www.streetlaw.org, accessed 9 October 2016.
22 N. Picardi, *La formazione del giurista di base*, Rivista di diritto processuale, 60 (2), 2005, 356–360.
23 R. Wilson, *Western Europe last holdout in the world wide acceptance of clinical legal education*, German Law Journal, 10, 2009, 838–839.
24 E. Gianturco, *Crestomazia di casi giuridici in uso accademico: Lettura di Ferdinando Treggiani*, Arnaldo Forni Editore, 1989, 9; V. Scialoja, *Diritto pratico e diritto teorico*, Rivista del diritto commerciale, 9, 1911, 941–948.
25 For example: *Pratica Forense* in Italy or *Referendariat* in Germany.
26 For an explanation of the various routes to qualification and how the clinic can complement this progression see: R. Grimes, Clinical legal education and problem based learning: an integrated approach to study fit for purpose?, *Transformations in legal teaching and learning publication: proceedings of the fifth national Spanish Conference on legal education*, Tirant lo Blanch, 2014, 34–66.
27 A.H. Campbell, *Comparison of educational methods and institutions*, Journal of Legal Education, 4, 1952, 31–32.
28 L. Hovhannisian, *Clinical legal education and the Bologna Process*, Public Interest Law Initiative Papers, 2, 2006, 6.
29 R. Grimes, *Clinical legal education and problem based learning: an integrated approach to study fit for purpose?*, op cit., 18.
30 A. Dondi, *Qualche considerazione in tema di educazione giuridica istituzionale*, Politica del diritto, 1–2, 2013, 105–125.
31 The undergraduate nature of continental legal courses is not an obstacle to the clinical method (as it is not in common law countries that offer law as first degree study) but live-client clinical work does require close supervision to compensate for any lack of knowledge and experience on the part of the student.

Chapter 5

Ethics and professional responsibility

Part 1 – Teaching and learning legal ethics: what, how and why?

Donald Nicolson

5.1.1 Why teach legal ethics?

It is increasingly being recognised in both common law and civil law systems that legal education should include an ethical element. Most obviously introducing students to the ethical dimension of lawyering is important in seeking to ensure that law graduates understand their considerable power as representatives of clients and the fact that they can adversely affect both the client and others. Such 'harm' of course may be professionally justified by the needs of the clients and the demands of the lawyers' role.[1] Legal ethics also matters because many, if not most, societies do not guarantee access to a lawyer, at least in civil cases, and it can be argued that an – if not *the* most – important ethical duty on lawyers is to help ensure that no one is denied justice because he or she lacks access to legal advice and representation.[2]

Less obviously, ethical lawyers are also more competent lawyers.[3] First, they are likely to be more effective in the long run than unethical lawyers, given that they are more likely to be trusted by other lawyers in the far more common task of negotiating as opposed to litigating cases. Second, lawyers who eschew moral detachment from their clients are arguably more likely to exercise more effective judgment on their behalf and are certainly more likely to take account of a client's moral and emotional as well as practical needs, and to treat them as autonomous human beings rather than bearers of legal problems. Exposing students to the dangers of lawyer paternalism will also discourage lawyers from impinging on their clients' autonomy while still seeking to act in their best interests. More generally, because clients might entrust important and often emotionally charged issues to the lawyer, the relationship is a highly personal one, which involves – or should involve – trust, commitment, care and consideration. Consequently, every single interaction with and action on behalf of a client (or in the case of corporate clients, their human representatives) involves an ethical dimension.[4]

Finally, legal ethics matters for law graduates themselves. Just as legal education could be said to fail if students are not prepared in terms of legal knowledge and skills, so should it be regarded as failing if they are not prepared for the ethical dilemmas, and the pressures and temptations to act unethically that they will face in practice. Forewarned, graduates can seek careers, if needs be, which are more compatible with their moral values or at least cope better with the dilemmas they do go on to face.

5.1.2 The goals of ethical education

For all these reasons, it can be argued that legal education should strive to develop ethical lawyers. However, it has to be recognised that this is no easy task. It is now received wisdom that in order for people to act ethically, they need to develop four different psychological components.[5] First, they need moral sensitivity in order to recognise moral problems in the first place. Second, they need the moral judgment to work out the correct response. Third, moral commitment is required to ensure that they regard morality as important enough to take precedence over competing considerations like self-interest. Finally, moral actors need moral courage to sustain this commitment in the face of competing pressures, for example, the demands of senior law firm colleagues.

If this received wisdom is correct, legal education has a mountain to climb if it is going to ensure that law graduates leave university capable of acting ethically (whatever that might involve). There is little it can do to change the pressures to act unethically once graduates enter practice. However, it currently rarely gets beyond base camp in providing them with the tools to act ethically. In common law countries, ethical education is usually limited to the formal rules adopted by the professional bodies, delivered in the form of lectures, albeit often reinforced by small group discussions in which students are required to spot ethical issues in hypothetical problems and apply the rules to them. Moreover, ethical teaching is usually confined to courses preparing graduates for practice, but even if incorporated into earlier stages of legal education, ethics is rarely accorded more than one class among many others and often an elective at that.

As many have argued, there are numerous problems with this approach to teaching ethics.[6] First, even if ethics teaching takes place alongside other law courses, it is likely to be too limited and especially if it follows a general legal education where ethics teaching is usually conspicuous. by its absence, too late to counter what is described variously as the hidden,[7] latent,[8] implicit[9] or informal[10] curriculum in legal education. These unarticulated value assumptions are communicated to students by example, by teaching methods, by curriculum choice as to what courses are or are not taught and what is or is not compulsory, at what level and for what credit points and by student culture and contacts with the legal profession. According to critics, by concentrating primarily on the teaching of legal rules and 'thinking like a lawyer', by separating issues of law from those of justice and ethics and largely disregarding the latter, by failing to challenge images of the lawyer as a legal technician whose function is confined to manipulating law and facts in the interests of paying clients, traditional legal education conveys the implicit message that issues of ethics and justice are of little relevance to the real business of law. Rather, rules are either there to be formalistically followed or manipulated in the interests of clients, and a legal career is a means to success and financial rewards. And according to research albeit largely in the US, this tends to undermine student idealism about using law to promote justice, engenders moral and political cynicism and encourages, albeit tacitly, a propensity towards ethically dubious behaviour.[11]

At best, teaching the ethical rules contained in profession's codes of conduct will only help develop the sensitivity and judgment to recognise possible breaches of the rules and how to apply them. But leaving aside the fact that merely providing students with knowledge of rules does little to encourage, let alone a develop, a critical approach to their content, the rules promulgated by many professions are too vague and general to provide the solutions to ethical problems and thus teaching them will not go far in equipping students to identify and solve ethical problems. And even when the rules are very detailed, they will always contain gaps, suffer from language's inherent ambiguity and vagueness, while also struggling to deal with the contextual nuances of actual moral dilemmas. Rules thus always need to be complemented by judgment. However, simply teaching rules does very little to develop such judgment. And even if it did, moral agents might know what morality requires but lack the motivation or courage to convert such knowledge into behaviour. Empirical research repeatedly confirms that knowing what is morally right by no means guarantees moral behaviour.[12] In fact, most moral behaviour is a more or less automatic rather than a conscious response to moral issues.[13] Consequently, instead of naively hoping that teaching students the rules will lead to obedience simply out of fear of threatened sanctions – a hope undermined by the difficulty of detecting breaches of professional rules[14] and the frequently lax approach to those who do so[15] – the aim of legal education should be to seek to ensure that law graduates display an soundly embedded 'reflex' response to moral problems once in practice.

According to Aristotle and other virtue ethicists, the solution lies in fostering students' moral character so that they gradually develop relatively stable character dispositions, or habits of perception, thinking, feeling and behaviour through actual engagement with moral issues in a way similar to how expertise is developed in other walks of life.[16] By emulating others, by trial and error, by instruction from authoritative others, by experiencing and reflecting on the appropriate pride or regret at the outcome of one's actions, moral habits or dispositions are said to gradually develop to the point that appropriate moral behaviour and feelings become embedded in the individual's character. In other words, character formation results not so much from direct teaching but from the experience of frequent immersion in moral dilemmas, the frequent exercise of one's moral muscles and learning from one's mistakes and successes in moral behaviour.

If appropriately developed, moral character can be said to equip individuals, not just with moral sensitivity and judgment, but also moral motivation and courage. Where all four moral components are developed to the extent that virtue becomes a way of life, moral behaviour is far more likely to ensue. Thus, moral 'saints', such as Gandhi, Nelson Mandela and Oskar Schindler, seem to act out of deep-seated and spontaneous feelings of compassion, empathy, etc. – by 'habits of the heart' – rather than conscious deliberation. This is confirmed by studies of moral exemplars who acted more or less automatically. According to contemporary psychologists, this automaticity derives from the fact that frequent activation renders moral considerations and categories easily accessible and readily utilized.[17] Based on empirical studies, it is argued that moral behaviour is more likely for those for whom moral considerations are central to their personal identity and sense of self.[18] For such individuals, immoral behaviour will diminish, and moral behaviour will enhance their sense of self and self-esteem. Indeed, where moral motivations are central to the individual's self-identity, moral action is argued to flow from a kind of 'spontaneous necessity' without the need for willpower or moral courage to overcome temptations or pressures to act unethically.

Admittedly, it is not possible to positively affect the moral character of all incoming law students. Radical changes to a person's essential character are likely to be rare, so there is probably little that universities can do in relation to those who enter university with, or quickly develop, a deep-seated cynical attitude to legal practice and hence are likely to be impervious to attempts to encourage students to see ethics as a central part of their professional identity – what can be called ethical professionalism. However, universities can reinforce the existing moral character of those more inclined to act ethically and adapt it to the ethical demands of legal practice and perhaps even influence those without predispositions towards either cynicism or ethical professionalism to choose the latter path. Whether they can achieve these goals depends, at least in part, on how much time is devoted to ethics in the curriculum, what is taught and how.

5.1.3 The *what* and *how* of legal education

Ideally, all law students should have some compulsory exposure to legal ethics. Even if there is no hope of affecting the moral character of some students, they can at least be made aware of what might constitute unethical conduct so that they can make informed choices about risking formal sanctions and peer condemnation. If the argument for compulsory ethical education is accepted, the first question that needs to be answered is whether ethics should be taught pervasively throughout the curriculum as and when ethical issues arise in other classes or in compulsory dedicated classes. Ideally, as many argue, both approaches should be adopted.[19] However, if a choice has to be made, the latter seems preferable. No doubt, teaching ethics pervasively redresses its current marginalisation and demonstrates to students that ethical considerations are integral to legal practice and vary according to contextual factors, such as the practice setting, the type of case and the client's status. However, there are well-recognised problems with pervasive teaching. By giving ethics 'a home everywhere, it effectively deprives its core concepts of a home anywhere'.[20] There is therefore a need for a dedicated class to provide an in-depth analysis of overarching theoretical and institutional issues, and an introduction to the sort of ethical issues which arise in different contexts, such as client confidentiality and conflicts of interest. Moreover, all academics are currently unlikely to give ethics the attention it deserves if required to deal with ethical issues relevant to their classes. Instead, they are likely to cut corners to ensure adequate coverage of their specialist topics and may even make clear their disdain for having to waste precious time, thus actually making the current situation even worse. Consequently, it seems best to leave ethics teaching to those who are committed to taking it seriously, and this is more likely occur within dedicated, hopefully compulsory, but if not optional, classes.

As regards such classes, our discussion thus far suggests that they should have four aims:

- *inspiring* an interest in ethics;
- *illuminating* the general and professional ethical tools available to resolve issues of professional ethics;
- *illustrating* these tools and issues through exposure to situations involving moral dilemmas; and
- *inculcating* the habit of identifying, evaluating and caring about ethical issues so that this becomes a more or less spontaneous response in practice.

In terms of illuminating professional ethics, while the formal rules obviously have to be taught at some stage, I suggest that this should occur *after* students have been exposed to legal ethics literature so that they develop the ability to critically evaluate these rules and their underlying morality, apply them in ways which are sensitive to the contexts of legal practice and fill in the gaps where they are silent, vague and conflicting. As many recognise, this also requires introducing students to various ethical theories which both underlie and may challenge dominant approaches in legal ethics and to the realities of modern legal practice so that students understand problems of access to justice and the ways in which various factors like increasing specialisation, fragmentation, bureaucratisation, commercialisation and globalisation of legal practice affect lawyers' ability to act ethically.[21]

While such knowledge can be conveyed in traditional lecture format, interactive teaching methods are more likely to inspire and help students develop their own moral stance and moral reasoning. Here, dialogue in small classes will produce a deeper understanding of issues through exposure to different views, whereas debates can be brought to life and students ethically inspired by exposure to legal biographies, fictional accounts of legal practice in literature, films and television or even short dramas filmed by academics, and the personal accounts of local lawyers, clients and those affected by lawyer behaviour.[22]

When it comes to developing moral sensitivity and judgment, role-play and simulation are more likely to engage their interest and emotions and hence potentially develop moral commitment than the discussion of hypothetical scenarios.[23] This is because, according to adult learning theory,[24] learning is more profound where student experiences are more personal, immediate and realistic, and relate to the fulfilment of their future social roles. This is particularly so if such experience is accompanied by critical evaluation of student performance by others in class and by themselves in reflective journals. Learning is also more profound when prior assumptions and settled values jar with experienced reality causing 'disorienting moments' involving moral crises and cognitive conflict.[25] By encouraging participants to see issues from the 'other side', role-playing may encourage the development, not only of moral judgment but also empathy and other emotional sentiments, which virtue ethicists and others see as so important to morality.[26] This is particularly likely in ongoing and realistic simulations. When the results seem to 'count' in contexts which accurately reflect practice, students are more likely to emotionally invest in and learn from their experiences.[27]

However, it is generally accepted that ethical learning is best achieved in student law clinics.[28] By engaging with actual (or simulated) clients, students are far more likely to develop the empathy and emotional maturity which is so important to ethical behaviour. Lessons learnt are likely to go deeper when students bear responsibility for decisions which have consequences in the 'real' world and where the presence of flesh and blood clients with actual problems make learning seem more useful than traditional legal education. Moreover, because of their perceived practical knowledge and skills, clinic supervisors may function as influential moral exemplars, modelling good client relations, concern for how their actions affect others and an altruistic commitment to the community. And crucially for character development, any feelings of satisfaction or regret at their actions in representing actual clients and resolving real dilemmas may affect character development. Finally, clinics reveal the extent of unmet legal need, and social and legal injustice, that legal practice can involve helping others, and that this can be rewarding as well as intellectually challenging. Thus, according to the anecdotal evidence of many clinicians[29] and a growing body of empirical work,[30] clinical work may inspire, or at least reinforce, students' aspirations to being an ethical and altruistic professional, especially if combined with a theoretical basis to help them make sense of their experiences.

Thus, without being alerted to the sort of ethical dilemmas which arise in practice, students might overlook those staring them in the face, whereas without exposure to a wide variety of ethical theories or positions on issues of legal ethics, they will not have the opportunity to explore alternative approaches to resolving dilemmas and to develop their own sense of professional values in order to supplement or even supplant existing professional roles and rules. Moreover, according to clinical educational theorists '[l]earning occurs not in the doing but in the reflection and conceptualisation that takes place during and after the event'.[31] Such reflection, aided by the critical evaluation of others, may help students develop the lifelong learning skills of the reflective practitioner. Thus according to Kölb's well-known learning circle, reflection may lead to the adoption of new, or the adaptation of existing, theories about how to handle issues which can then be put into practice when similar situations arise.[32] This new experience provides the material for further reflection, theory adaption and theory testing, and so on.

5.1.4 Conclusion

Admittedly, teaching ethics clinically can be highly resource-intensive. Even if one runs law clinics on as cost-effective basis as at my own institution,[33] only a relatively small number of students can receive the intensive moral apprenticeship that is required in order to ensure character development. Consequently, one cannot ignore other forms of ethical education. Indeed, legal education is currently so far from taking ethics seriously that any means of illuminating and illustrating professional legal ethics and inspiring student interest is worth pursuing even if it does not necessarily inculcate the sort of habits of moral conscience argued for in this chapter.

Notes

1 See: D. Nicolson and J. Webb, *Professional legal ethics*, Oxford, OUP, 1999, Chapters 6–9.

2 See: D. Nicolson, *Legal education, ethics and access to justice: forging warriors for justice in a neo-liberal world*, International Journal of Legal Profession, 22, 2015, 1.

3 D. Nicolson, *Problematizing competence in clinical legal education: what do we mean by competence and how do we assess non-skill competencies?* International Journal of Clinical Legal Education, 23, 2016, 66.

4 S.J. Burnham, *Teaching legal ethics in contracts*, Journal of Legal Education, 41, 1991, 105; and, J.E. Moliterno, *An analysis of ethics teaching in law schools: replacing lost benefits of the apprentice system in the academic atmosphere*, University of Cincinnati Law Review, 60, 1991, 83.

5 See in particular: and Kurtines and J. Gewirtz (eds.), *Morality: Moral behaviour and moral development*, Wiley, 1984; D. Narvaez and J. Rest, The four components of acting morally' in W.M. Kurtines and J.L, Gewirtz (eds), *Moral development: an introduction*, Allyn and Bacon, 1995, 385.

6 For example see: A. Boon and J. Levin, *The ethics and conduct of lawyers in England & Wales*, Hart Publishing, 2008; and R. Burridge and J. Webb, *The values of common law legal education: rethinking rules, responsibilities, relationships and roles in the law school*, Legal Ethics, 10, 2007, 72.

7 C. Cramton, *The ordinary religion of the law school classroom*, Journal of Legal Education, 29, 1978, 247.

8 R.M. Pipkin, *Law school instruction in professional responsibility: a curricular paradox*, American Bar Foundation Research Journal, 4, 1979, 247.

9 H. Lesnick, *Infinity in a grain of sand: the world of law and lawyering as portrayed in the clinical teaching implicit in the law school curriculum*, UCLA Law Review, 37, 1990, 1157.
10 K. Economides, *Learning the law of lawyering*, Legal Problems, 52, 1999, 392.
11 Usefully summarised in: J. Chapman, *Why teach legal ethics to undergraduates?*, Legal Ethics, 5, 2002, 68.
12 See: J. Rest, *Can ethics be taught in professional schools? The psychological research*, Ethics Easier Said Than Done, 1, 1988, 22.
13 See: D. Lapsley and C. Power (eds.), *Character psychology and character education*, University of Notre Dame Press, 2005.
14 R. O'Dair, *Legal ethics: text and materials*, London, Butterworths, 2001.
15 For example see: R.L. Abel, *English lawyers between market and state: the politics of professionalism*, Oxford University Press, 2003.
16 See: Aristotle, *The Nicomachean ethics,* Prometheus Books, 1987 and also: J. Kupperman, How not to educate character, in D. Lapsley and C. Power (eds.), op cit. 201; and H.L. Dreyfus and S.E. Dreyfus, What is moral maturity? A phenomenological account of the development of ethical expertise, in D. Rasmussen (ed.), *Universalism vs. communitarianism*, MIT Press, 1990, 237.
17 See: D. Narvaez and D.K. Lapsley, *Moral psychology at the crossroads*, in D. Lapsley and C. Power (eds.), op cit, 18.
18 For example see: A. Blasi, Moral understanding and the moral personality: the process of moral integration, in W.M. Kurtines and J.L. Gewirtz (eds.), *Moral development: an introduction*, Mass, Allyn & Bacon, 1995, 78.
19 For example see: Nicolson and Webb, op cit.; O'Dair, op cit.; and A. Paterson, Legal ethics: its nature and place in the curriculum, in R. Cranston (ed.), *Legal ethics and professional responsibility*, Clarendon Press, 1995, 175.For the relative merits and drawbacks of each approach see: e.g. Boon and Levin, 2008, op cit.; and J. Webb, Conduct, ethics and experience in vocational legal education: opportunities missed, in K. Economides (ed.), *Ethical challenges to legal education and conduct*, Hart Publishing, 1998, 271.
20 S.M. Bundy, *Ethics education in the first year: an experiment*, Law and Contemporary Problems, 58 (3), 2004, 19, 33.
21 For example see: A. Boon, *Ethics in legal education and training: four reports, three jurisdictions and a prospectus*, Legal Ethics, 5, 2002, 34; A. Goldsmith, *Heroes or technicians? The moral capacities of tomorrow's lawyers*, Journal of Professional Legal Education, 14, 1996, 1; and R. Granfield and T. Koenig, *'It's hard to be a human being and a lawyer': young attorneys and the confrontation with ethical ambiguity*, University of West Virginia Law Review, 105, 2002, 495.
22 For example see: C. Menkel-Meadow, *The sense and sensibilities of lawyers: lawyering in literature, narratives, film and television, and ethical choices regarding career and craft*, McGeorge Law Review, 31, 1999, 1.
23 See for example: N.A. Sprinthall, Counselling and role taking: promoting moral and ego development, in J. Rest and D. Narvaez (eds.), *Moral development in the professions: psychology and applied ethics*, Lawrence Erlbaum Associates, 1994, 85.
24 F. Bloch, *The andragogical basis of clinical legal education*, Vanderbilt Law Review, 35, 1982, 321.
25 F. Quigley, *Seizing the disorienting moment: adult learning and the teaching of social justice in law school clinics*, Clinical Law Review, 2, 1995, 37.
26 See: D. Nicolson and J. Webb, op cit., Chapter 2.
27 M.A. Noone and J. Dickson, *Teaching towards a new professionalism: challenging law students to become ethical lawyers*, Legal Ethics, 4, 2001, 127.
28 For pertinent and contrasting views see: R. Condlin, The moral failure of clinical legal education, in D. Luban (ed.), *The good lawyer: lawyer's roles and lawyer's ethics*, Rowman & Allanheld, 1983, 332; and N. Duncan, Responsibility and ethics in professional legal education, in R. Burridge, K. Hinett, A. Paliwala and T. Varnava (eds.), *Effective learning and teaching in law*, Kogan Page, 2002, 105.

29 For example see: M. Rees, *Clinical legal education: An analysis of the university of kent model'*. The Law Teacher 12, 1975, 125, 136.
30 Further discussed in: D. Nicolson, Learning in justice: ethical education in an extra-curricular law clinic, in Robertson et al (eds.), *The ethics project in legal education*, Routledge, 2010, 171.
31 H. Brayne, N. Duncan and R. Grimes (eds.), *Clinical legal education: active learning in your law school*, Blackstone Press Ltd, 1998, 47.
32 D.A. Kolb, *Experiential learning: experience as the source of learning and development*, Prentice Hall, 1984.
33 See: D. Nicolson, *Education, education, education: legal, moral and* clinical, The law teacher, 42 (2), 2008, 145; and D. Nicolson, *'Our roots began in (South) Africa': modelling law clinics to maximise social justice ends*, International Journal of Clinical Legal Education, 23, 2016, 87.

Part 2 – Teaching legal ethics under the civil law

José García-Añón

5.2.1 Introduction

In the film *Philadelphia* (1993), there is a discussion about justice in a case of discrimination. One of the actors (Andrew Beckett) explains why he loves the law and what makes a good lawyer (implying of course that he is!). He says: "It's that every now and again – not often, but occasionally – you get to be a part of justice being done. That really is quite a thrill when that happens." Behind this fragment is linked the idea of professionalism and the fight for access to justice. Lawyers are clearly the gatekeepers in this regard.

How can we transmit this idea to our students? I use this film as a part of the methodology to teach legal ethics precisely because it makes the connection between professional legal ethics and need for (and moral right to) access to justice.

In this contribution I intend to show that there are differences in approach between teaching and learning about ethics in the civil law system as compared with the common law yet there is much shared ground.

There are three kinds of issues relating to legal ethics, professionalism and learning: first, the place of legal ethics in the law curriculum; second, the content of that curriculum; and third teaching methods.

In the first part of this chapter, Nicolson talks of the 'what, how and why?' of ethics teaching. I would add a fourth question – who?

In my own country (Spain) and probably most other civil law countries, the 'who' is a crucial issue. Who has the power or control to decide when, what and how legal ethics is learned/taught? Often decisions about the form and content of the law curriculum lies in the hands of government and/or the legal profession.

I would also add further questions – where and when?

5.2.2 Where (and when) to teach legal ethics?

In Spain, as in other civil law jurisdictions, legal ethics is, and has been, almost non-existent in terms of the law curriculum.[1]

Legal education continues today anchored in the accumulation of knowledge and information that, whilst undoubtedly useful, is not enough especially if a graduate wishes to join the legal profession.

It is true that the Bologna Process has had an impact on methods and content.[2] The main objective was meant to ensure a more comparable, compatible and coherent system of higher education in Europe. It included several action lines and priorities to achieve its objective, including a focus on lifelong and student-centred learning, mobility of staff and students; effective quality assurance, comparable criteria and methodologies and cross-border recognition of qualifications. However, the need for ethics is noticeable by its absence.[3]

A number of reports indicate the importance of legal ethics in the education and training of lawyers in Europe.

The Council of Bar Associations and Law Societies of Europe's report on European Legal Education and Training states:

> It is of fundamental importance for lawyers to have full knowledge and understanding of professional and ethical rules, as expressed in national codes of conduct, as well as in the CCBE cross border code of conduct.[4]

In the LETR Report, *Setting Standards: The Future of Legal Services Education and Training Regulation in England and Wales,* the need for legal ethics to be included in the curriculum is singled out for its significance in the legal education context.[5]

One of the premises that has to be taken into account in this overall development is the competence approach of learning that is said to better reflect the connection between learning methods and assessment – providing more effective learning. That is, learning is better served when there is an alignment between learning outcomes, teaching activities and assessment.

> This 'whole-task' approach is reflected in the current competency movement. A competency is the ability to handle a complex professional task by integrating the relevant cognitive, psychomotor and affective skills. In educational practice we now see curricula being built around such competencies or outcomes.[6]

In 2014 a separate legal ethics and professionalism course was introduced at my university. Ethics was previously referred to in other modules for example the Legal Theory course (compulsory in the first-year law degree) and the Philosophy of Law course (compulsory in the fourth year in the law degree). The content of this new course is about the relationship between and the problems of and limits to law and morals.

5.2.3 Undergraduate degree(s) in law

There have been a number of reforms to the legal education curriculum in Spain with a reduction in the number of compulsory subjects but with the inclusion of additional material including legal ethics. But professional ethics or deontology has never been a separate course. Interestingly, the Degree in

Law Curricula of Spanish Universities recently adapted as part of the European Higher Education Area process in 2010 reveals that:

- Private law schools account for 37 percent of the institutions offering law degrees in Spain and half of them expressly include Legal Ethics as a compulsory or optional subject.
- By contrast only one public university does so. Where taught legal ethics is so found it is only in the relatively newly established universities (post 1993).[7]

So what is happening in the majority of universities – the ones that do not take on board ethics?

Ethics does appear in a minority of institutions either as part of new Fundamental Legal Skills course – this subject was introduced in the last reform of the Bologna Process – or as part of other modules.[8]

The remaining majority of institutions do not teach Legal Ethics and Professionalism at all (and neither do they appear to intend to).

I suggest that this is a lost opportunity. Why do we have to wait for the postgraduate stage to do so? Ethics, as Nicolson has already argued before in this section of the book, needs to be addressed at the earliest part of a student's studies and then (ideally both discretely and pervasively) throughout.

5.2.4 Master's degrees and becoming a qualified lawyer

Until November 2011, becoming a lawyer was a simple process. Spanish law students graduated from their five-year Spanish Law degree and automatically became eligible for admission to the local bar association, without any further requirements for training or examination. The system contrasted with many other European jurisdictions that require further vocational training and assessment and possibly a period of apprenticeship.

Partly due to the Bologna Process and in part with an eye to improving overall quality, since November 2011 new requirements have applied. These are in themselves problematic. The Spanish Law of Access to the Legal Profession (Ley 34/2006) sets out the content and regulations of a Master's degree focused on obtaining practical skills for the legal profession. Under the new regime, aspirant lawyers must obtain a master's degree and pass a state bar examination in order to qualify as a lawyer (*abogado*). Among the various legal competences required prior to admission is an understanding of ethics and professional responsibility including:

> To know and apply the professional ethics rights and duties in the relationship between lawyer with client, the other parties, the court or public authority and among lawyers.

To know and evaluate the different responsibilities related to the exercise of the professional activity, including the basic functioning of legal aid and the promotion of social responsibility of lawyers. (and)

To know how to identify conflicts of interest and know the techniques for their resolution, set the scope of the privilege and confidentiality, and preserve the independence of criteria.

(Article 10)

All master's programmes will have to address these issues. Anticipating this requirement, some universities have already introduced relevant courses. For example, at the University of Valencia there is a compulsory subject called *Professional Ethics and System of Liability for Lawyers*. In the Universitat Pompeu Fabra, a 3-credit course called "Professional Ethics and Regulatory Framework" is offered and at the University Carlos III de Madrid, there is a 9-credit module called: "Professional practice: organization, legal status and ethics".

5.2.5 Clinical legal education

On the University of Valencia's law degree, the content of Legal Ethics course is offered as part of the Legal Clinic for Social Justice option. The main reason for this introduction was that previously students finished their studies without having any contact with professional ethics, and yet their main role in the clinic required them to behave as lawyers. It therefore seemed necessary to expose students to the subject of professional responsibility. We were concerned not only that they understood what it means to be a lawyer but that the role of the lawyer, from the ethical point of view, transcends the relationship with the client and must include concern for the interests of wider society.

5.2.6 How can ethics be taught experientially?

At Valencia we seek to engage the students through learning with others (*peer learning*); case-based study (learning through *problems*); focusing on personal experience (*reflective and active learning*); and self-directed learning from information already received (*constructive learning*).

The problem-based learning method, combined with others, provides an effective interactive learning environment "based on constant feedback to the student."[9] Through a weekly reflective journal – a portfolio that must be uploaded in the virtual classroom – the student takes responsibility for the results of his or her learning through a clearly articulated and structured process of reflection on what has been learned, if the students have found it useful and in what way.[10]

Our face-to-face contact with the students usually begins with an activity in which we reflect on clinical models and teaching methodologies. A scene of a film is watched, *The Paper Chase* (1973), where a teacher in a very well-known American university announces to his students that he will not be teaching through traditional lectures but instead, will use the Socratic method.

Using a collaborative teaching method sometimes referred to as the 'jigsaw', the students are allocated to one of three groups that represent different methods of learning and must discuss a given scenario.[11] Each group is given one of three teaching methods to evaluate. These are:

- the deductive method, in which the students learn and study theory as provided by the professor (the lecture);
- the inductive method, which consists of an active class where the professor asks questions about the content of the course (the case method); or
- a situation where the students, with some tutor input, dissect and analyse issues arising in a given problem (problem-based learning).

The students inevitably conclude that each method has its place in the learning armoury but also the students vocalise their appreciation of the chance to apply theory to practice. The problem-based learning scenario is regularly identified as the 'best' teaching and learning strategy. We intend to build on the 'PBL' potential.

For it to work effectively, the PBL process needs to be structured. Ideas for doing this are set out elsewhere (and in Hedlund's contribution in this book).[12] The steps in the process fit closely with the classification of learning objectives in Bloom's Taxonomy:

Steps	*Bloom's Taxonomy*
1. Read carefully, clarifying whatever you do not understand.	1. Knowledge (recognizing)
2. Identify parties and interests.	2. Comprehension (understanding, summarizing, classifying . . .)
3. Set out chronology.	2. Comprehension
4. Brainstorm issues.	2. Comprehension
5. Organise issues.	4. Analysis (comparing, organizing)
6. Name the problem.	5. Evaluation (checking, judging, hypothesising . . .)
7. Define the learning outcomes/ research questions.	6. Creation (planning, designing, producing . . .)
8. Agree on a research plan.	3. Application (applying, implementing, carrying out . . .)
9. Carry out research.	3. Application
10. Share outcomes.	3. Application (applying, implementing, carrying out . . .) 4. Analysis (comparing, organizing . . .) 5. Evaluation (checking, judging, hypothesising . . .)
11. Conduct further research and produce final report.	6. Creation (planning, designing, producing . . .)

With this methodology, the student is introduced to experiential learning and through the subject matter of the given problems, to the world of professionalism and ethics.

5.2.7 Reflective learning and assessment

The discussion of using experiential methods to teach ethics would not be complete without mentioning assessment. At Valencia and elsewhere, increasing use is made of reflective portfolios. The clinic uses the following schema for assessment:

(1) informal (giving feedback during case supervision);
(2) weekly reflective journals posted on the Virtual Platform (reflective learning and self-assessment); and
(3) monthly rounds (peer and tutor assessment).

We use several different approaches in assessing: self-assessment, peer-assessment and team-assessment. When assessing formally (where marks or grades are given) we use rubrics as grading tools to ensure that standards of performance are based on concrete, objective and well-defined competences/learning outcomes.[13]

As law professors, we don't have strong evidence about the relationship between learning and assessment. In fact, in our years of experience teaching by following traditional methods and using exams as the primary performance-measuring device, the general conviction may be that we are not doing things in the wrong way, although other alternatives in teaching and assessing exist.

The use of a reflective journal as portfolio is the main tool we use as a part of on-going and frequent (if not precisely continuous) assessment. The portfolio is a weekly individual report to be uploaded in the Virtual Classroom platform. The content of this report is, first, a description of the activities that the student has done that week in this subject (in class and outside class). All of them are evidence of a student's learning that must be shown at the end of the term. Second, it must include the report done by the team on the PBL scenario they have been working on or the other activities carried out in the clinic (which ever may be relevant at the time). Third, a reflection and assessment of everything the student has learnt or thinks that he/she has to learn has to be set out. It must include the problems and difficulties found in this process.

Additionally, each month we hold a "round" in which students talk and discuss their cases together, and highlight the problems they encountered, including ethical issues. Rounds in law clinics are meetings in which all the students discuss their real work with their classmates and professors. Participants exchange information about what they have done, discuss issues they are working through and what next steps are to be taken.

5.2.8 Final remarks

Why has Legal Ethics have not been fully included in the law curriculum in many jurisdictions?

First, because the tradition of legal science and positivism that are part of civil law tradition and have influenced curricular content.[14] In the civil law system, and probably in other jurisdictions, the old way is often the accepted one. Change requires effort and resources and poses threats to those comfortable with tradition. This means that not only do subjects that do not form part of the standard curriculum get missed (such as legal ethics) but alternative and innovative teaching and learning methods fall by the wayside too.

Second, law as an academic discipline is seen by many as a body with a multitude of different and separate parts. This general framework does not lend itself readily to the inclusion of additional subjects, especially those such as legal ethics that might be seen as more pervasive than discrete and possibly multifaceted and interdisciplinary.

The third problem is that legal ethics inevitably involves teaching values or even dogma. The university frequently portrays itself (as an institution at least) as apolitical (particularly in the public sector) and untainted by the vested interests of others, including the practising professions. Access to justice, for example, is a political minefield for the unwary. That said, it will be clear from what I have written above that the work of the lawyer from the ethical point of view transcends the client relationship and must include concern for the interests of society. Legal education should integrate the teaching of doctrine, skills and values in order to produce responsible and effective lawyers: what makes an excellent lawyer is that "you get to be a part of justice being done".

Notes

1 See: C. García-Pascual, *El tiempo de la deontología, El buen jurista*, Deontología del Derecho, Valencia, Tirant lo Blanch, 2013, 13.

2 See: D. Blázquez-Martín, *La educación jurídica clínica en el contexto del proceso de Bolonia: su aplicabilidad en España, Opinión Jurídica*, Publicación de la Facultad de Derecho de la Universidad de Medellín, 5 (10), 2006, 161.

3 J. García Añón, A. Llabrés Fuster, J. Martín Pastor, G. Palao Moreno, C. Salcedo Beltrán and C. Alfonso Mellado, in J. García-Añón (ed.), *Los estudios de Derecho en Europa: Alemania, Francia, Italia, Reino Unido e Irlanda*, Valencia, Servei de Publicacions de la Universitat de València, 2008.

4 CCBE (Council of Bars and Law Societies of Europe), *CCBE Comments on European legal training*, Brussels, 2010.

5 J. Webb, J. Ching, P. Maharg and A. Sherr, *Setting standards: the future of legal services education and training regulation in England and Wales*, London, Legal Education and Training Review, 2013, 34.

6 C.P. Van der Vleuten and L.W. Schuwirth, *Assessing professional competence: from methods to programmes*, Medical Education, 39, 2005, 309.

7 Data from personal research and presented as *Legal ethics and professionalism in the Spanish legal education and training system*, International Legal Ethics Conference, London, July 2014.

8 In the first year of a law degree, students usually study a course in Legal Theory, including "Law as a system of norms" and "Problems of Justice" In the fifth year, "Philosophy of Law" is taught and looks at legal values, including human rights. See Royal Decree 1424/1990.

9 A. Font Ribas, *La incidencia del aprendizaje basado en problemas (ABP) en la integración laboral de los licenciados en Derecho*, Revista de Derecho Mercantil, 2013, 237.

10 Variously see: J. García-Añón, *Transformaciones en la docencia y el aprendizaje del Derecho: ¿La educación jurídica clínica como elemento transformador?*, Teoría y Derecho, Revista de Pensamiento Jurídico, 15, 2014, 12; J. García-Añón, *La integración de la educación jurídica clínica en el proceso formativo de los juristas*, REDU: Revista de Docencia Universitaria, número extraordinario 'Formación de los licenciados en Derecho', 12 (3), 2014, 153; García-Añón, *How do we assess in clinical legal education? A 'reflection' about reflective learning*, International Journal of Clinical Legal Education, 23 (1), 2016, 50; and, J. García-Añón, *Aprendizaje experiencial y reflexivo utilizando la metodología de aprendizaje basado en problemas en el primer curso del Grado en Derecho*, experiencias docentes en el grado de Derecho, Barcelona, Editorial Octaedro, 2016, 75.

11 This is the initial scenario: "In 2020, after 10 years of Bologna Plan, the Ministry of Education in Spain has realized that it does not work. Therefore, it has commissioned a group of academics to research the models of education that might be used at universities with a view to identifying the relative advantages and disadvantages and which model(s) might be adopted in the future."

12 See: A. Font-Ribas, *Líneas maestras en el aprendizaje por problemas*, Revista interuniversitaria de formación del profesorado, 49, 2004, 79; A. Font-Ribas, *Aprendizaje basado en problemas en la Facultad de Derecho de la Universidad de Barcelona*, en Buenas prácticas en docencia y política universitaria, Universidad de Castilla-La Mancha Servicio de Publicaciones, 2009, 113; and R. Grimes, *Clinical legal education and problem-based learning: an integrated approach to study fit for purpose?*, en Jose García Añón (ed.), *Transformaciones en la docencia y el aprendizaje del Derecho*, Actas del Quinto Congreso Nacional de Docencia en Ciencias Jurídicas, Valencia, 11–13 de septiembre de 2013, Unitat d'innovació educativa, Facultat de Dret, Universitat de València, 291.

13 García-Añón, *How do we assess in clinical legal education? A 'reflection' about reflective learning*, International Journal of Clinical Legal Education, 23 (1), 2016, 50.

14 C. García-Pascual, op cit.

Part 3 – Ethics, professionalism and the law

Laura Bugatti

5.3.1 The legal profession and legal education: the role of legal ethics

In most common law countries, ethics and professional responsibility can be found in the curriculum (even if much of it could be drastically improved – as Nicolson's part of this chapter clearly shows) but in countries of the civil law teaching legal ethics at university is patchy, inconsistent[1] and, where it does exist, is of relatively recent origin.[2] For both systems this represents particular challenges.[3]

Currently, in the majority of civil law jurisdictions law graduates discover the existence of legal ethics and professional practice rules in the lead up to sitting a bar examination – the passing of which is required in order to be admitted to the legal profession.[4] Even worse, they start to face moral dilemmas when they have just received their license to practice law. In fact, the ethics dimension to legal education struggles to be recognised not only at the academic level, but also in the so-called vocational training. Whilst it is true that whilst national bar associations may highlight the importance of legal ethics and the professional codes of conduct, nevertheless, in many, if not most, jurisdictions insufficient attention is paid to the actual study of the topic.

At most, a law graduate aiming at becoming a legal practitioner – starting his/her own traineeship under the supervision of a senior professional (*dominus*) – may absorb, by instruction and/or osmosis, the morality of the law firm in which he/she is working. However, the lack of what Nicolson refers to as 'sensitivity' to matters ethical leads to a stunted level of moral development at least in the context of the practice of law.

Nevertheless, more than ever, it is crucial that the professions emphasise their ethical priorities and achieve an authentic awareness of their identity and role within the society.[5] In fact, the intellectual professions in general and the legal profession in particular must now face a new working environment marked by increasing globalisation, competition, technological advances and deregulation. Furthermore, the economic perspective imposed by membership of the European Union – which in this context leads us to consider lawyers as commercial beings as well as professionals – is having a profound impact on national regulation and in particular, in the legal field.

During this period of change, professionals are now required to abandon aspects of their traditional attitudes (including resistance to change and remorse for perceived loss their previous *status* in terms of power, privilege and economic importance)[6] and get involved proactively to reinstate their own ethical values, enhancing the public and social relevance of the legal professional's role.

In such a setting, law schools cannot remain on the margins, as they are an essential building block in the growth of future professionals. In order to be able to play an active role in such an evolving situation, universities are now being asked to reconsider – where necessary – the goals and nature of 'academic' teaching.

It appears that the strict division between exclusively theoretical study and post-university, vocational, training is unsustainable.[7] The dialogue between law schools and professional organisations has to become more intense: by underlining each other's roles as well as shortcomings. The mission of law schools and post-university training organisations (bar associations, professional schools and in some instances universities) seems increasingly in conflict: they each provide skills for a defined market; and, students are expected to be able to master theoretical concepts of law whilst at the same time being able to meet standards of technical competency. An appropriate blend of legal knowledge, practical skills and ethical awareness provides the essential grounding required to achieve requisite quality and morality for a legal professional as well as to actually understand law in its operational context.

One must comprehend the cultural background of the civil law to appreciate why ethics is currently accorded such a low priority in law schools. As seen elsewhere in this book, notably in Genty and Amato's contributions, that context is clearly set out. Whilst the reasons for the omission of ethics from the law curriculum may be explained historically, this is no excuse for further inertia.

5.3.2 The role of the law schools in ethics education

If the new mission of law schools is, at least in part, to contribute to the creation of legal practitioners,[8] the academy cannot carry on deeming the teaching of legal ethics as someone else's responsibility.[9] Prospective legal professionals do not only require an adequate knowledge of legal rules and the ability to apply them correctly in specific cases but they must also, in order to be responsible and effective, be able to understand the context in which they operate. They need to manage interactions with other stakeholders (clients, colleagues, judges and the wider community) and behave appropriately, taking into account applicable codes of conduct, as well as the wider ethical values and ideals of the profession.[10] Further, through their behaviour, legal practitioners contribute to societal perceptions of the legal system as well as its actual operation – they help to shape the culture of the law including the need for improving access to justice and identifying issues requiring law reform. In other words, how people perceive law and the legal system is, in part, determined by how lawyers behave. As noted elsewhere:

> Lawyers who know how to think in legal terms, but have not learned how to behave, are a menace to society and a liability, not an asset to the administration of justice.[11]

Therefore, it is not enough to provide to the students what is strictly necessary to pass the exam to get into the legal profession and to obtain a professional licence: it is fundamental to teach them how to be legal professionals and, consequently, how to act as responsible and accountable practitioners.

Teaching legal ethics at the university stage is not just a new responsibility and a challenge. From a practical point of view, it is also an opportunity to build links with the practicing profession and introduce students at the earliest possible stage to a holistic education.

Law schools are important and privileged institutions, often funded by the state, and they are 'place where the learning can be guided, can be structured, can be taught rather than merely learned'.[12] An adequate training in ethics and professional responsibility – under the guidance of competent mentors – should allow students to develop awareness on their own morality; conversely, such a result, although desirable, is not always achievable during the traineeship, through the neutral observation of other's professional behaviour. In fact, due the lack of general tools for constructing and understanding the context, trainees' choices are often affected by the law firms' views.[13]

In addition, during their academic studies, students are particularly receptive and malleable, whereas in the course of their professional lives, the development of the ethical dimension may be distorted by 'professional observation of bad habits of legal thinking, legal application, or dubious ethics',[14] and also by personal and other interests – like having to charge clients fees and the need to make a profit. If ethical values have not been grasped and internalized, poor judgment may result.

The emergence and recent expansion of legal clinics in Europe makes even more urgent the task of taking legal ethics on board. For most students at university, this will be their first exposure the profession and to clients. In this context, knowledge of the law and trying to apply it is not enough. As students are required to perform as legal practitioners (albeit under professional supervision) they should be aware of the social role they are influencing and must, for their client's sake (as well as their own and the university's), know how to act accordingly, assuming responsibility for their actions and facing the consequences, albeit it in a supervised setting.

5.3.3 Legal ethics education: content and goals

Despite the growing interest expressed by some academics in teaching legal ethics, opinions may differ about what the content, the mode of delivery and the main objectives of such teaching should be.

Expressions such as 'legal ethics' and 'professional responsibility' are sometimes used interchangeably and refer, at least in part, to rules, expectations and sentiments found in the largely self-regulatory codes of conduct and to related disciplinary proceedings. They can, of course, encompass far wider issues, some pertinent to the practice of law and the concept of professionalism but others more fitting to an overtly educational context. Here moral considerations and dilemmas and 'philosophical ideas about justice, social and environmental responsibility, minimising harm and respecting others' can be studied in safety and in depth.[15]

The interface between what is required (according to a code of conduct) and what is 'right' or 'wrong' (as encountered in the moral maze) is not unproblematic – for example, under the Italian legal system (and similar situations arise in other civil [and common] law jurisdictions)[16] the Bar Association Code of Conduct prescribes expectations that should shape relationships with professional colleagues, clients, judges and third parties. However, as also underlined by the Italian High Court, these provisions:

> are merely clarifications of the general principles – mentioned in the law governing lawyers and in the Code of Conduct itself – of dignity, fairness, probity and professional decorum.[17]

Dignity, integrity and probity[18] are surely part of the ethical backdrop of all professionals - lawyers and otherwise. The same might be said for a doctor or teacher (and not only Italian, but European and globally as well);[19] they constitute some of the essential values that should inspire and guide professional conduct, as well as behaviour in private life. The importance of these principles in the work of a professional is demonstrated by the numerous disciplinary decisions which have identified infringements of such duties in a broad range of cases. Consider the following cases:

- after agreeing to lease his property to a colleague and handing him the keys, a lawyer then demanded that the tenant vacate the property unless he was willing to sign, within three days, a lease for a much higher rent than previously agreed. The lawyer was eventually sanctioned with two months' suspension;[20]
- the importance ascribed to the conduct of a lawyer who had issued bank cheques in absence of sufficient funds;[21]
- the lawyer who had carried out real-estate brokerage's activities and then has qualified them – in an invoice – as legal counsel' activities, in order to justify his conduct;[22]
- the use of inappropriate language by a law firm in defence of their client, or in criticism of a judgment under appeal;[23]
- a law firm offering unavailable or inappropriate services to attract clients;[24]
- and interestingly, given our competitive world, the lawyer who offered his professional services at very low predetermined costs, violating the

expectation of proportionality between the activity carried out and the compensation requested.[25]

None of the above were specifically outlawed by the relevant code of conduct. There are no doubt countless other situations where a lawyer has to take decisions the 'correctness' of which does not depend on slavish adherence to professional rules, but this implies something more. This uncertainty may be caused, for example, by a difficult interpretation of rules, vague wording of legal provisions, a lack of rules or guidance or by the nature of the dilemma itself. The satisfactory resolution of such issues (from the viewpoint of all affected) necessarily depends on the implementation of a set of ethical values and standards already internalized, as well as any individual moral stance adopted.

For this reason, the teaching of legal ethics cannot be considered as 'a knowledge attribute'[26] and 'just another substantive black letter domain':[27] Paying close attention to professional ethical rules is the basis of a lawyer's 'knowledge of how to be'.[28] In order to ensure that legal practitioners are able to maintain behaviour 'appropriate to the prestige of the legal profession which imposes individual conduct inspired by positive values and immune from any possible judgment of civil, ethical and moral reproach',[29] the goals of ethics teaching must be extended to include the 'mode of ethical decision-making employed'.[30] Students should be educated to be able to consciously deal with the ethical issues and moral dilemmas that they may encounter during their professional and private lives, so as to be ready to recognize – in each instance – what is right from what is not, and what should be done in consequence.[31]

Through the teaching of legal ethics students should be made aware of how to consciously deal with the four basic elements that characterise ethical decision-making process[32]: i) the ability to recognize the existence of ethical problems in complex and ambiguous situations and sense the consequent need to adopt a moral decision ('moral sensitivity'); ii) the ability to handle mature ethical reasoning suitable to a morally defensible decision ('moral reasoning')[33]; iii) the ability to have the moral decision prevail over other interests at stake, such as, for example, personal ones ('moral motivation'); iv) the ability to effectively implement in practice that moral decision ('effective implementation').[34] A means by which decisions can be made and can be justified is therefore essential. The more this process is understood and consolidated, the greater the opportunity is for a professional to adopt ethical behaviour 'automatically'.

5.3.4 From theory to practice

There are of course different ways of designing and delivering classes and programmes on ethics and professional responsibility. The models that are available generally belong to the common law tradition. I suggest, as others do in this volume (see in particular Grimes and Sibony) that in spite of the contrast in history and form of the two legal traditions, there are in fact few real obstacles that should stand in the way of taking and adapting (as Rocarro elsewhere in the book suggests) such models for civil law countries.

The emerging pressure on continental law schools to move towards a more skilled and values-based curriculum and the need to consider the employability of students (on this see Daniel's contribution) and the needs of the legal profession mean that we have a starting point for the re-thinking of legal education in general and the teaching of ethics in particular.[35] The choice of how to implement and structure such a re-think clearly depends on the desire to achieve defined objectives.[36]

The literature on legal ethics education, which often refers to already-tested experiences, suggests that the preferable approach to teaching and learning legal ethics is a 'pervasive approach'.[37] This has the undeniable advantage of helping students to self-develop throughout the entire curriculum, through a learning path that is guided, rational, structured and incremental. Furthermore, the pervasive approach clearly conveys the importance of legal ethics teaching, attributing it a central role in the future legal professional's education. Legal ethics – in addition to meriting the same consideration of the other law school courses – can be also addressed in other (if not all) substantive and procedural courses

> because it arises in all . . . areas. A faculty which declines, explicitly or implicitly, to address ethical issues encourages future practitioners to do the same. To confine professional responsibility discussions to a single required course marginalizes their importance and undermines their most important message: professional responsibility is a crucial constituent of all legal practice.[38]

Considering the ethical dimension can also enrich learning elsewhere in the curriculum, the educational goal needs no longer be limited to doctrine and rules but encompass considerations a wider and socially relevant framework – including lawyering skills and ethics.

Despite the undeniable merits of this approach, numerous obstacles hinder the full implementation of such a review. A reconsideration of teaching priorities is required, as is the wholehearted commitment of the academic community. There may also be a need for induction and training, especially if adjunct faculty are used. Material needs to be designed and programmes perhaps need to be accredited.[39] The overcoming of these barriers, although desirable, will require time, effort and the deployment of resources. I suggest those will be well spent if the end result is better-educated students.

On a pragmatic level and as a starter in order to encourage the introduction of the legal ethics teaching in the European civil law tradition, legal clinics are an extremely useful and cost-effective way of beginning.[40] The link between clinical and ethical teaching is evident: in legal clinics: 'the connection between what lawyers do, the law that governs how lawyers may do it, and the professional environments within which lawyers do what they do'[41] become clear.

With clinical experience, the students are compelled to behave as real lawyers (or if they don't, to have their shortcomings identified – education indeed!). It is highly likely, even in the typical low-value clinic case (in economic terms at least), that students will face ethical issues and dilemmas at every turn – for example, is there a conflict of interest, what is client confidentiality, is the client being fair/reasonable and do I (the student) empathise with the client (and does it matter)? Addressing the problems directly and personally experiencing the consequences of the choices made inevitably brings home the meaning of legal ethics in a way that being told in a lecture or watching a qualified professional under pressure in the office may never do.[42] To thoroughly understand and appreciate the conflicting obligations and responsibilities inherent in the actualization of rules, students must utilize them in practice. Put differently, one can only fully understand the rules in theory if one has experienced them in practice.[43] Creating a strong connection between clinical and ethical teaching can be the first and immediate step for the development of a civil law educational framework devoted to consider not only legal knowledge and professional skills but also the moral and ethical dimension.

5.3.5 Conclusion

The growing awareness in legal practice and legal education relating to the importance of the ethical dimension in the education of future legal professionals is a fundamental turning point. Nevertheless, law schools and law professors must now seriously assume a formative role in promoting their students' identities as legal professionals and to reflect upon which teaching methods and structures are suitable in order to combine 'conceptual knowledge, skill, and moral discernment . . . into the capacity for judgment guided by a sense of professional responsibility'.[44] In fact, I suggest, it is not enough to praise the importance of legal ethics: it is time to translate those thoughts into curricula priorities.

Notes

1 Among the criticisms leveled at the teaching of legal ethics in American universities, it is often stressed that "many law schools satisfy the ABA requirements with a single, doctrinal course focused solely on learning the Model Rules of Professional Conduct"; see N. Duncan and S.L. Kay, *Addressing lawyer competence, ethics, and professionalism*, in F.S. Bloch (eds.), *The global clinical movement: educating lawyers for social justice*, Oxford, Oxford University Press, 2011, 183; see, also, D.L. Rhode, *Teaching legal ethics*, Saint Louis University Law Journal, 51, 2007, 1043.

2 US, Australia and Canada require professional ethics in law degrees; see R. MacCrate, *Preparing lawyers to participate effectively in the legal profession*, Journal of Legal Education, 44, 1994, 89; G. Powles, *Taking the plunge: integrating legal ethics in Australia*, Law Teacher, 33, 1999, 315; Federation of Law Societies of Canada, *Task force on the Canadian common law degree* (FLSC, 2009), available at: http://flsc.ca/wp-content/uploads/2014/10/admission8.pdf, accessed 19 October 2016.

3 In England and Wales, The Lord Chancellor's Advisory Committee on Legal Education and Conduct (ACLEC) emphasised the importance of the ethical dimension (see ACLEC, *First report on legal education and training*, 1996 and ACLEC, *Continuing professional development for solicitors and barristers: a second report on legal education and training*, 1997). This was followed in 2001 by the Law Society of England and Wales' consultation on a new training framework (see Law Society, *Consultation: training framework review*, London, Law Society, 2001); See also, *Legal Education and Training Review (LETR), Setting standards: the future of legal services education and training in England and Wales June 2013* available at: www.letr.org.uk/wp-content/uploads/LETR-Report.pdf, accessed 19 October 2016.

4 I refer in this paper to the term 'legal professionals' instead of lawyers as in most civil law countries a 'lawyer' may become an advocate, a notary public, a judge, a prosecutor or an in-house lawyer in a commercial company.

5 See: J. Webb, *Ethics for lawyers or ethics for citizens? New directions for legal education*, Journal of Law and Society, 25, 1998, 134–135: 'In such an age of doubt and deregulation there is a certain inevitably in the growing calls for legal education to develop a more distinctively moral voice'.

6 See: L. Speranza, *I poteri delle professioni*, Catanzaro, Rubbettino editore, 1999; M.R. Carillo and A. Zazzaro, *Innovazione, ricerca della rendita e prestigio sociale: verso una teoria dinamica delle professioni*, 2002, Working Paper n. 4/2002, available at: www.depa.unina.it/depa/wpcarzaz.pdf, accessed 19 October 2016.

7 See B. Hepple, *The liberal law degree*, Cambridge Law Journal, 55, 1996, 474, especially 484. See also: N. Irti, *La formazione del giurista nell'università del "saper fare"*, Rivista giuridica degli studenti dell'Università di Macerata, 2010, 29.

8 In Italy, for example, the National Agency for the Universities and Research's evaluation (ANVUR) has started to evaluate the quality of the Academia taking into account also the so called "Third Mission" activities – direct interaction with the society.

9 See D.L. Rhode, *Legal education: rethinking the problem, reimagining the reforms*, Pepperdine Law Review, 40 (2), 2013, 451.

10 See G. Pascuzzi, *How to become lawyers and able to do so: teaching the ethics of the legal professions through narrative*, 2012, Research Paper n. 11, available at: http://eprints.biblio.unitn.it/4003/1/11._Pascuzzi.pdf, accessed 19 October 2016.

11 See W.E. Burger, *The role of the law school in teaching of legal ethics and professional responsibility*, Cleveland State Law Review, 29, 1980, 377, especially 390.

12 J.E. Moliterno, *Experience and legal ethics teaching*, Legal Education Review, 12, 2001, 3–9 – Faculty Publications. Paper 930, available at: http://scholarship.law.wm.edu/facpubs/930, accessed 19 October 2016.

13 See J.B. Brooks, *Legal ethics*, The Yale Law Journal, 19 (6), 1910, 441–444.

14 W.E. Burger, *The role of the law school in teaching of legal ethics and professional responsibility*, Cleveland State Law Review, 29, 1980, 377, at 390.

15 C. Parker and A. Evans, *Inside lawyers' ethics*, 1st ed., Cambridge, Cambridge University Press, 2007, 4. See also D. Nicolson and J. Webb, *Professional legal ethics: critical interrogations*, Oxford, Oxford University Press, 1999, 4.

16 See the Italian National Bar Association Code of Conduct, as amended in 2014 (Gazzetta Ufficiale, no. 241 of 16 October 2014).

17 This currently refers to Article 9 of the Code of Conduct for Lawyers, entitled "Duties of probity, dignity, decorum and independence" and to the closing rule in Article 3, paragraph 2 of the law governing lawyers no. 247/2012.

18 These could be extended to other values intrinsic to the figure of the legal professional, including: '(a) independence and freedom to ensure the defence of his client; (b) professional secrecy and confidentiality; (c) avoidance of conflicts of interest between different clients or between the client and the lawyer himself; (. . .) (e) loyalty to the client; (f) correctness in charging fees; (g) professional competence; (h) respecting one's

colleagues; (i) respecting the rule of law and contributing to the proper administration of justice; and (j) self-regulation of the legal profession' (see CCBE, *Charter of Core Principles of the European Legal Profession*).

19 The principles referred to are the same broad principles that the Council of the Bars and Law Societies of Europe (CCBE) decided should be shared by the various European legal systems, as demonstrated by the reference to "*Principle (d) – the dignity, integrity and probity*" found in the Charter of Core Principles of the European Legal Profession of 2006.

20 CNF, November 19, 2012, no. 156.

21 CNF, December 12, 2013, no. 208; CNF, March 15, 2013, no. 44.

22 CNF, May 3, 2016, no. 112.

23 CNF, September 2, 2013, no. 150; CNF, September 30, 2013, no. 163; CNF, March 20, 2014, no. 31.

24 CNF, June 6, 2013, no. 89; in general, CNF, May 7, 2013, no. 74.

25 CNF, March 15, 2013, no. 37.

26 J. Webb, *Ethics for lawyers or ethics for citizens? New directions for legal education*, Journal of Law and Society, 25, 1998, 134, especially 139.

27 Ibid., 46.

28 See C. Parker and A. Evans, op cit.

29 Among many references: CNF, February 21, 2014, no. 11; CNF, December 30, 2013, no. 220.

30 "*Teaching of integrity*" is constantly referred to as one of the highest goals of teaching legal ethics. See: J.V. Tunney, *Is the bar meeting its ethical responsibilities*?, San Diego Law Review, 12, 1975, 245, specially 247, teaching of virtue (see J.R. Elkins, *The pedagogy of ethics*, Journal of the Legal Profession, 10, 1985, 37, specially 37–38); teaching of values (D.C. Mulcahey, *A plea for moral education in law schools*, Journal of Law and Religion, 2 (1), 1984, 101, specially 102). See also the opinion of those who see '*developing moral character*' as the ultimate goal of teaching legal ethics; as main reference, see D. Nicolson, *Teaching legal ethics: what, how and why: Ensenar etica juridica: que, como y cuando. Revista De Educacion Y Derecho*, Education and Law Review, 1, 2009, 171.

31 See J. Webb, *Ethics for lawyers or ethics for citizens? New directions for legal education*, Journal of Law and Society, 25, 1998, 134, at 139.

32 See: J. Rest, *Moral development: advances in research and theory*, New York, Praeger, 1986; J.R. Rest, Research on moral judgment in college students, in A. Garrod (ed.), *Approaches to moral development*, New York, Teachers College Press, 1993, 201–211; J.R. Rest, Background: theory and research, in J.R. Rest and D.F. Narvaez (eds.), *Moral development in the professions: psychology and applied ethics*, Hillsdale, NJ, Lawrence Erlbaum, 1994.

33 See, especially, L.A. Kohlberg, *The psychology of moral development: the nature and the validity of moral stages* (vol. 2), San Francisco, Harper & Row, 1984; Id, A current statement on some theoretical issues, in S. Modgil and C. Modgil (eds.), *Lawrence Kohlberg: consensus and controversy*, Philadelphia, Palmer, 1986, 485–546. See, also, J. Rest, D.F. Narvaez, M.J. Bebeau and S.J. Thomas, *Postconventional moral thinking: a neo-Kohlbergian approach*, Mahwah, NJ, Erlbaum, 1999.

34 See: C.D. Cunningham, Learning professional responsibility, in R.V. Magee, M.A. Lynch, R. Boyle and A.S. Lopez (eds.), *Teaching the newly essential knowledge, skills, and values in a changing world, section E: intercultural effectiveness building on best practices: transforming legal education in a changing world*, Lexis Nexis, San Francisco, 2015, 289, available at: http://works.bepress.com/rhonda_magee/7/, accessed 19 October 2016, from which the phrasal expressions "*moral sensitivity*", "*moral reasoning*", "*moral motivation*" and "*effective implementation*" were derived.

35 With regards to the American experience, this objective is expressly considered in the *America Bar Association's Standards for the Approval of Law Schools 2016–2017*, Standard 301.

36 On the importance of defining the educational objectives in the project design of an educational training program, see G. Pascuzzi, *Avvocati formano avvocati: Guida all'insegnamento dei saperi forensi*, Bologna, Il Mulino, 2015, 69 ss.

37 The pervasive method involves the introduction of the teaching in ethics in all the various aspects of a legal curriculum. See in particular: D.L. Rhode, *Into the valley of ethics: professional responsibility and educational reform*, Law & Contemporary Problems, 58, 1995, 139; D.L. Rhode *Professional responsibility: ethics by the pervasive method*, 2nd edn, U.S., Aspen Publishers, 1998; D.L. Rhode, *Ethics by the pervasive method*, Journal of Legal Education, 42 (1), 1992, 31; and R.G. Pearce, *Legal ethics must be the heart of the law school curriculum symposium: recommitting to teaching legal ethics- shaping our teaching in a changing world*, Journal of the Legal Profession, 26, 2002, 159.

38 See: D.L. Rhode, 1995, op cit., 140.

39 Ibid., 141.

40 See C.M. Venter, *Encouraging personal responsibility: an alternative approach to teaching legal ethics*, Law and Contemporary Problems, 58 (3/4), 1995, 287–296; L. Wortham, *Teaching professional responsibility in legal clinics around the world*, KLINIKA, 1, 2000, 195.

41 See J.E. Moliterno, *On the future of integration between skills and ethics teaching: clinical legal education in the year 2010*, Journal of Legal Education, 46, 1996, 67, specially 68; with reference to the American experience.

42 The reference should be extended beyond the legal clinics, so as to involve all the types experiential learning, such as simulations and externships; see, in this sense, N. Duncan and S.L. Kay, Addressing lawyer competence, ethics, and professionalism, in F.S. Bloch (eds.), *The global clinical movement: educating lawyers for social justice*, Oxford, Oxford University Press, 2011, at 188 ss.; J.E. Moliterno, *On the future of integration between skills and ethics teaching: clinical legal education in the year 2010*, Journal of Legal Education, 46, 1996, 67.

43 N. Duncan and S.L. Kay, op cit., 187.

44 See W.M. Sullivan, A. Colby, J. Welch Wegner, L. Bond and L.S. Shulman, *Educating lawyers: preparation for the profession of law (Carnegie Report)*, Stanford, CA, Carnegie Foundation, 2007, 12.

Chapter 6

Regulation and jobs – universities, the legal profession and other employers

Part I – Of tribes and territories – an employer and regulator perspective on re-thinking legal education

Chris Maguire

6.1.1 Contested territories

The history of legal education and services is populated with initiatives, enhancements and reviews of all varieties, leading to iterative, evolutionary and structural changes. However, the last decade has seen an unprecedented level of scrutiny of the sector, across the world, resulting in significant pressure for radical change in the regulation, structure and delivery of legal services and education. What follows is jurisdiction specific (England and Wales) but may help explain the past and present and what awaits in the future.

I focus in particular on three key developments: the introduction of the Legal Services Act 2007 (and with it the Legal Services Board), the Legal Education and Training Review, 2013 (LETR), and the publication in September 2016 of the Legal Services Board's paper, *A vision for legislative reform of the regulatory framework for legal services in England and Wales* (Sept 2016). What these developments have brought or are likely to bring is a single regulator for legal services, the fragmentation of legal services, regulation primarily through the 'entity' of the business organisation, qualification by segment and most pertinently given the content and aims of this book, a major opportunity for a review of how we educate lawyers. Interestingly, given increased focus on regulation, law schools in the UK, unlike many of their civil law counterparts, are not so tightly controlled, especially in terms of how legal education can be delivered.

Legal education in England and Wales comprises contested territories, with porous borders. These territories are usually defined in oppositional terms: education/training, academic/professional, new/old universities, city/high street, knowledge/skills, Bar/Law Society.[1] Underpinning this are the debates that characterise knowledge dichotomously as either intellectual or practical, theoretical or applied, transferable or contextual, academic or vocational. The legal education 'tribes' analyse, review and agonise about the purpose(s) of legal education, its relationship to law and legal practice and their roles within it. To some this reflects a rich and healthy tension underlining the importance of law as a discipline with diverse and rich influences. To others it reveals a dystopia of conflicting and harmful self-interests of academics, practitioners and regulators that obstruct creative and meaningful solutions.[2]

6.1.2 Routes to qualification

Before turning to an analysis of the possible future(s) of legal education, for readers unfamiliar with it, it may be worth rehearsing in outline how it is structured and regulated in England and Wales.

Historically, qualification as a lawyer (a barrister or a solicitor) required a form of apprenticeship, where the student would 'devil' in a lawyer's office or chambers. More recently qualification depended on studying (cramming) for either the Bar or Law Society Finals, a range of unseen examinations dealing with legal knowledge and reasoning. Since the late 1980s and early 1990s, aspirant entrants to legal practice, through the Bar Council for barristers or Law Society for solicitors, required an honours degree in law or an honours degree in another discipline plus the Graduate Diploma in Law (GDL) (also known as the Common Professional Examination). The GDL is an intensive one-year full-time or two-year part-time programme that, covers the seven foundations of legal knowledge and an eighth legal subject; i.e. the subject matter that the professional bodies, in agreement with the law subject associations and learned societies, have determined must make up the core part of the academic stage of legal education (roughly 180 UK or 90 ECTS credits, or half of a law degree). Following the law degree or GDL students must obtain a place on the Legal Practice Course (LPC) for intending solicitors or Bar Professional Training Course (BPTC) for intending barristers. The BPTC and LPC comprise the vocational stage of training and offer a one-year equivalent programme in practical legal knowledge and skills. Finally, students compete to enter the professional stage of training in a law firm or set of chambers. For intending solicitors this is normally a two-year training contract,[3] in a law firm or in-house legal department, usually comprising four 'seats' of six months each, where the trainee works within different areas of practice offered by the firm directly or through placement externally. Intending barristers enter pupillage under the supervision of a pupil-master in a set of chambers or employed practice. Pupillage comprises two six-month periods. During the second-six the trainee is permitted to undertake work of their own under supervision, though the practicality of doing so depends on the area of practice. Following successful completion of the professional stage, the trainee becomes an independent practitioner, although solicitors cannot practice on their own for the first 3 years. In addition to the two routes outlined above, a student may qualify as a Chartered Legal Executive by completing three years in legal employment and passing the CILEX Professional Diploma in Law and Practice (at Level 3 of the Framework for Higher

Education Qualifications) and subsequently the Professional Higher Diploma in Law (set at level 6).

The players involved in these routes to practice include the law schools who offer qualifying law degrees (QLDs), the GDL, the LPC and the BPTC; the regulatory arms of the professional bodies; the Solicitors Regulation Authority for the Law Society and the Bar Standards Board for the Bar Council, and the Chartered Institute of Legal Executives. Since 2007 the professional bodies' regulatory arms (Approved Regulators) are overseen by the Legal Services Board.[4]

6.1.3 Drivers for change and the regulatory landscapes

Government rhetoric in relation to the provision of legal services echoes that in relation to higher education. Despite the lauded benefits emanating from both institutions – the significant contribution to GDP, international standing, underpinning democracy, maintaining and enhancing the social structure – the lexicon of marketisation, value for money and measurable practicality pervades. Law, at the sharp end of practice at least, is a business.

The drivers for change in legal services and practice are a constant: quality assurance and the need to reduce the costs of legal advice and the pursuit of litigation while ensuring access to justice. As with higher education, the government is seeking to reduce the financial burden on the state and shift more of it from the public to the private purse. This has resulted in a range of efficiency measures and initiatives, including the simplification and tightening of civil procedure rules (based on the Woolf reforms) introduced in 1999, the ever-present emphasis on alternative dispute resolution and the continuing and severe reductions in Legal Aid availability.[5] For the current government in the UK it appears that 'competition is god' and the key to reducing costs and enhancing access:

> The government's vision is for a strong, competitive legal services market in which innovative businesses can flourish to ensure good quality, affordable legal services are accessible to consumers, while ensuring consumers and the public interest are protected by effective regulation.[6]

In 2001 the Office for Fair Trading presented its report on competition in the professions, which identified unjustified restrictions in competition within the legal services market and recommended that they be removed. In July 2003 the government responded with its own report: *Competition and regulation in the legal services market: A report following the consultation "In the public interest?"* The report concluded that the (then) present framework was outdated, inflexible, over-complex and insufficiently accountable. This led to the establishment of an independent review led by Sir David Clementi, which reported in December 2004.[7] The report concluded that "existing regulatory arrangements were inconsistent, complex, lacking objectives and underpinning principles and had insufficient regard for the interests of consumers"[8] and recommended the establishment of the Legal Services Board with statutory objectives and regulatory powers to oversee the front-line regulators and to require the separation of their representational and regulatory arms; the establishment of the Office of Legal Complaints as a single independent body, and the establishment of alternative business structures to encourage innovation in the market.

In consequence, the Legal Services Act 2007 (the Act) was introduced, setting out the legislative framework for the regulation of legal services in England and Wales. Its objectives are:

- protecting and promoting the public interest;
- supporting the constitutional principle of the rule of law;
- improving access to justice;
- protecting and promoting the interests of consumers;
- promoting competition in the provision of services;
- encouraging an independent, strong, diverse and effective legal profession;
- increasing public understanding of the citizen's legal rights and duties; and
- promoting and maintaining adherence to the professional principles.

There were three primary mechanisms by which these objectives and Clementi's recommendations would be progressed. The first was to introduce a more effective and simplified regulatory framework. This was achieved through the separation of the representational from the regulatory arms of the Bar Council and Law Society and the formation of the Bar Standards Board and the Solicitors Regulation Authority respectively. This was never going to be entirely satisfactory and now has been overtaken by the proposal from the LSB that it and the approved regulators be replaced by a single regulator. The second measure was to establish an effective and independent complaints mechanism. This was particularly important to restore public confidence and trust given the issues surrounding the Law Society's complaints handling process. Third, competition, with all that term offers, would be through reforms, enabling Alternative Business Structures (ABSs) to compete in the legal services market. This, at the time, appeared the most radical proposal and the most effective in shaking up legal services.

Initially ABSs were regulated more closely than traditional providers of legal services, but in July 2016, the Conservative Government issued a consultation paper on proposals to 'level the playing field' by removing the additional regulatory burdens on ABSs to enable more to enter the market and for traditional firms to become ABSs. The proposed changes delegate more authority to the licensed regulators to set their own rules and use their discretion in vetting potential new entrants.

The government's justification for removing the additional checks on ABSs was that they had received no more complaints than the traditional sector. The risk was therefore equivalent, and consequently there was no justification for treating ABSs differently or causing the regulatory bodies additional and, it is implied, unnecessary work. The logic of this reasoning is supported in the principles of better regulation, adopted by the government and pursued by the LSB:

> The Government will regulate to achieve its policy objectives only:
>
> (i) having demonstrated that satisfactory outcomes cannot be achieved by alternative, self-regulatory, or non-regulatory approaches
> (ii) where analysis of the costs and benefits demonstrates that the regulatory approach is superior by a clear margin to alternative, self-regulatory or non-regulatory approaches
> (iii) where the regulation and the enforcement framework can be implemented in a fashion which is demonstrably proportionate; accountable; consistent; transparent and targeted.
>
> There will be a general presumption that regulation should not impose costs and obligations on business, social enterprises, individuals and community groups unless a robust and compelling case has been made.[9]

That reluctance to interfere in the markets and the Government's Better Regulation principles shaped, it is argued, the LSB's approach to addressing risk through the identification of key themes. The first of these is the collection and publication of performance information to identify risks to quality. This is followed by analysis of the data collected to identify the level of risk, and 'segmentation' of legal services to inform proportionate interventions that minimise adverse effects on innovation. In summary, regulatory activity should be evidence-based, tailored and proportionate and regulators will be judged on how lean, precise and effective their actions are.

The language used by the LSB and the requirement placed on the Approved Regulators to be aware of the challenges faced by their regulated communities reveals a switch from a primary focus on policing standards to one of enabling development, facilitating growth and supporting a diversity of approach. This is emphasised by the use of the term 'communities', which implies a mutual dependence and social obligation. This is the 'test' by which regulators will be judged. Roy and Handford argue that regulation should not be regulating inputs, e.g., lawyers' behaviour, but outputs, i.e., the satisfactory resolution of a legal problem. Rules of conduct and behaviour may, it is argued, actually obstruct a satisfactory outcome.[10] This approach supports a utilitarian philosophy where the means are justified by the ends. Roy and Handford note that the SRA has accepted the LSB's view that regulation should be outcome based and subsequently introduced a new Code of Conduct for Solicitors and a separate Code for Firms, which Rowlands, chair of the SRA, claimed would ensue that "Every solicitor will be absolutely clear about their personal obligations and responsibility to maintain the highest professional standards".[11] However, others disagreed:

> the new Code of Conduct is more like a set of teleological aspirations, written more in the style of civil code jurisdictions, and quite unfamiliar to the common law lawyer . . . this OFR is unworkable, unteachable and unfit for purpose.[12]

The regulatory impact of the LSA, as Duncan and Webb indicate, extends beyond legal services and the opening up of the market to new and more diverse entrants; it introduces a duty on the LSB and the Approved Regulators to ensure that their systems of legal education and training advance the regulatory objectives of the Act.[13]

One of the UK's senior judges, Lord Neuberger, has been forthright in his objection to the LETR report and its prioritising of two subsidiary objectives – the need to protect and promote the interests of consumers and to ensure an independent, strong, diverse and effective legal profession – over the two fundamental objectives: the need to protect and promote the public interest, and the need to support the constitutional principle of the rule of law, Neuberger considers the LETR team may have misdirected itself and its report may therefore be "unbalanced or worse".[14]

However, the same prioritising of the consumer was emphasised by the, then, Chair of the LSB, David Edmonds: "The basic purpose of the Act was to bring about a new system of regulation for legal services – a system of regulation by which the consumer – in all forms – was recognised as the essential beneficiary."[15] The LSB has recently stated that "having a large number of objectives can be problematic. They do not offer a clear focus, there is a risk of scope creep." Rather, "We think the overarching regulatory objective should be to safeguard the public interest by protecting consumers and ensuring legal services deliver outcomes in the interests of society as a whole." Addressing the issue raised by Neuberger this overarching objective now includes two elements, the first of which addresses the risk of harm to consumers while the second "would encompass outcomes such as the rule of law, access to justice and the effective and efficient administration of justice."[16] It is hard not to read that element 1 is primary and that element 2 an afterthought, and consequently that LETR had taken its direction accurately from the LSB and Approved Regulators. Deregulation and marketisation remain paramount.

The regulatory objectives, as they are currently framed, are translated into education and training through the following requirements:

(a) education and training requirements must focus on what an individual must know, understand and be able to do at the point of authorisation;
(b) providers of education and training have the flexibility to determine how to deliver training, education and experience that meets the outcomes required;

(c) standards are set which find the right balance between what is required at the point of authorisation and what can be fulfilled through ongoing competency requirements;
(d) regulators should strive to balance obligations for education and training between the individual and the entity, both at the point of entry and ongoing;
(e) regulators should not place inappropriate direct or indirect restrictions on the numbers entering the profession.[17]

The first three of these requirements represent the traditional areas of debate and contestation; the latter two, though familiar, are also prescient of where the debate over regulation is tending.

6.1.5 The issue of knowledge: quarts and pint pots

It is recognised that prior to LETR there had been no systematic, overarching review of legal education and training since Ormrod in 1971.[18] However, the professional bodies and providers themselves had undertaken numerous and repeated reviews of their areas and stages of legal education and training. The academic stage was under perpetual scrutiny with the content of the QLD a recurrent theme at sector conferences; however, the complexity of the issue meant that the *Joint statement on the academic stage of training* (the rules agreed by the professional bodies governing the QLD) were left largely untroubled. The vocational programmes, with their need to articulate between the academic stage and professional training, their expensive resource base and high fees and their position as a gateway to practice came under closer and more critical and political scrutiny, both internally and externally. In the early 1990s The Office of Fair Trading expressed concern about the monopoly of the Inns of Court School of Law over the (then) BVC and the restrictions on access that caused, leading to its validation in 1996. Access and costs had been raised by the Equal Opportunities Commission, and this was one of the spurs that led the Lord Chancellor's Advisory Committee on Legal Education and Conduct to review the vocational stage and investigate the potential for a form of common training.[19] The pressure then was, however, in the opposite direction with programmes becoming more specialised rather than generic, as evidenced by the emergence of the 'City LPC'. Within the Bar there were questions as to why the BVC should require both criminal and civil litigation when increasingly graduates would not utilise both. These pressures added to the impetus of internal annual and periodic review by the professional bodies themselves. The BVC, for instance, had a major review with input from the academic and practitioner community, as well as pedagogical and resource experts on an almost biennial basis. The standards and quality of all BVCs themselves have, been monitored annually, with individual annual visit reports on each provider and a summary annual overview report presented to the Bar Council's (now BSB's)

Education and Training Committee. The case was similar with regard to the SRA's oversight of the LPC, where as early as 2001 the Training Framework Review discussed the introduction of day one outcomes, alternative pathways to qualification and the possible abolition of the QLD and LPC as the gold standard.

However, it was not until 2011 that, following discussions after the implementation of the Legal Services Act that the Bar Standards Board, Solicitor's Regulation Authority and CILEX, prompted by the Legal Services Board, established and funded the Legal Education and Training Review (LETR).

LETR does provide a systematic literature review that catalogued the existing research material in the field. However, as Maharg notes, the material was highly variable, with significant gaps and 'disturbingly chaotic'.[20]

So what should be included in 'legal education'? The dragon represented by content of law degrees remains a key theme but the difficulty of slaying it only seems to have grown. Professional body groups met with academics with the sincere intention of reducing the core of what is taught in law schools, but usually ended trying to add to it. In recent commentary on the subject, Neuberger has argued for the inclusion of civil procedure and human rights in the QLD, Susskind for jurisprudence, others for company law, business awareness, advocacy against a lay client and soft skills. There is also the question of the development of cognitive and intellectual skills, the ability to think like a lawyer, to think on one's feet in action and to be a reflective practitioner throughout. Allied to this is the recognition that much of what is taught outside the principles of law is factual knowledge that has a limited shelf-life and consequently is only valuable to provide the material for contextual learning and application. In addition, and contrary to requirement (c) above, the profession in general wants more subject content delivered earlier in the process (i.e., before the trainee fumbles with their new security pass at the gates of the cathedrals of practice).

Twinning characterised this as the problem of Pericles and the Plumber. What was the purpose of legal education in relation to law and what type of lawyer was it seeking to educate or train? Was it to be a detached critic and censor of law in society or the educational support service "for a profession that is itself caught between noble ideals, lucrative service of powerful interests and unromantic cleaning up of society's messes"?[21] Is the lawyer (and how we train a lawyer) to be modelled on Pericles, full of noble intentions and emancipatory ideals; or the plumber, a technician in the functioning of legal practice?

Our plumbers are doubly unfortunate. Not only are they denied the richness of the liberal tradition in their own training, but their professional accreditation and licence to practice requires them to submit annually for reassessment of their skills and knowledge to protect the consumer from the risk of, for example, a gas explosion, or carbon dioxide poisoning. The costs of such reaccreditation are significant.

These dichotomous characterisations of lawyers are, of course, as Twining points out, too sharp, crude and over-simplistic.[22] They represent the poles of a continuum of a profession's members, or even a day or week in the range of experience in the professional lives of those members, and it is that continuum as a whole that legal education must seek to deliver.

The scrutiny of the effectiveness or otherwise of legal education in its contribution to professional formation led both the BSB and SRA to specify what it was that a new entrant was expected to be able to do on day one of practice. As mentioned above, the SRA had been working on 'day one competences' since the last century. Following the publication of the LETR report in 2013, and building on an earlier report in 2005, it again reviewed its expectations of the competences that newly qualified solicitors are expected to demonstrate and approved the publication of its *Statement of Solicitor Competence* on 11 March 2015.[23] In the foreword to a subsequent consultation paper, the chair of the SRA states that that the next stage of its work will be to review the process for qualification as a solicitor and to develop a mechanism for assessing the Competence Statement prior to qualification. The Bar both through the BSB and the Council of the Inns of Court has done the same.

The proposals that have since emanated from the SRA to hold a centrally set assessment for all aspiring lawyers, the Solicitors Qualifying Examination (SQE), have not been well received by legal education providers or large parts of the profession. It raises more questions than it answers and poses more problems than it solves, not least because, while nodding towards the strong legal education tradition that has previously supported the profession, the SQE may be attempted, like the old Law Society Finals, without the candidate having undertaken any formal course of study. In many ways this is a principled approach. In theory a candidate could take the exam drawing only on life experience, natural ability and application, thereby addressing the diversity issues and costs burden of legal education for which the profession is roundly criticised. However, the absence of process is seen by many commentators and respondents to the consultation paper as sidestepping the complexities and challenges of addressing the question of the what, when, where and how of the legal education process, including the contradictory behaviour of the profession itself.

Given their traditional focus on the academic rather than the practical, it is perhaps ironic, then, that the profession prefers to recruit from the elite 'Russell Group' of universities, rather than those modern universities that have actively tried to address the gaps in employability skills and practical legal knowledge identified by the profession. Or is it the case that in practice, while tut-tutting at gaps in instrumental and declarative knowledge and skills for their particular area, practitioners actually find that the liberal approach to legal education produces more independent and intellectually able and adaptable trainees? If so, the process of education is key and can give greater confidence to the meaningfulness of the naturally limited and snapshot assessment of complex learning outcomes.

The BSB and the Council of the Inns of Court (COIC) have been more circumspect in their deliberations than the SRA, and their 2015 consultation paper offers three broad approaches which both retain and liberalise the current structures, these comprise an 'evolutionary option' that seeks to increase flexibility in pupillage and reduce prescription in the BPTC; 'the managed pathway option' which in addition to the integrated LLB and BPTC, offers an integrated BPTC and pupillage and also a modular approach to qualification enabling candidates to commit to training 'one step at a time'; and finally 'the Bar Specialist option' that introduces an open entry qualifying examination on legal skills and knowledge. Successful candidates would then be admitted to a skills-based course which would prepare them for pupillage.

Of course, the devil is in the detail, but so is the drama. It is thought that option 3 is the preferred option of the Inns if not the BSB. It is a 'back to the future' option that reinstates a form of the old bar finals as an aptitude test for entry to a skills-based course (a shorter form of the current BVC) with the Inns as the exclusive provider, a return to the monopoly provision of the Inns of Court School of Law, raising issues of geographical accessibility that the validation of the then BVC sought to resolve and raising the prospect of a 'golden route' to practice which would, effectively, make any other route uncompetitive and unappealing. It firmly relocates the responsibility for the education and training of barristers to the Inns and reaffirms the Inns' position, through COIC, as much more than the landlords or livery companies of the Bar.

However, what remains true of both the SRA and the BSB/COIC's proposals is that both in different ways sidestep the challenges and opportunities that engaging with stakeholders about the principles of education and pedagogy for complex professional practice offers. This is where the future(s) of legal education and legal practice lies. The questions that we might ask in beginning such a debate should centre on not, to quote Susskind, where the puck is now but where it might be.[24]

In addressing these questions, we must be willing to consider that we might not have advanced in the service of our students or of the professions for two decades. Bell's work on Graduateness in Law[25] revealed that, unlike other subjects, law students had a slavish attitude to learning time-limited facts rather than principles or approaches. Whilst humanities students were painfully aware that their deep knowledge of Greek theatre, or the socio-economic effect of the Corn Laws, would be unlikely to aid them in the world of work, their ability to research an issue, analyse the literature, evaluate opposing views, synthesise an argument and propose a resolution would. Consequently, we need to be clear about what type of knowledge and skills we deliver when, where and how. Returning to the future, is there anything so wrong in the trivium and quadrivium of classical education: logic, rhetoric and ethics, disputing the broad principles of law as a foundation of cognitive and conceptual knowledge and skills followed by a narrowing of the syllabus to practice skills, procedural knowledge (of either civil or crime but not necessarily both) and optional areas of law depending on which area or segment of law the student wished to pursue? There is a rub, of course. The nature of law, legal practice and indeed the regulatory structures within which they operate are changing as fast as syllabuses can be updated. So, while we consider the nature of knowledge in modern (or indeed postmodern) society, we also need to consider the changing nature of legal practice and regulation.

With the de-regulation of strictures surrounding multi-disciplinary partnerships (MDPs) and alternative business structures, will the law firm or chambers survive? Or will lawyers become knowledge workers in larger, one-stop-shop, service entities, addressing client needs and problems holistically, e.g., from a financial, accountancy, management as well as legal perspective, and in a personal and private capacity as well as that of a business?

Wider questions arise about the future socio-cultural and economic position of the lawyer in society given the rise of MDPs and ABSs. The lawyer can no longer control the culture of the legal profession. But much like the academic profession, new managerialism in the form of executive business heads, non-law experts in IT, HR, communications and client management, separate the lawyer from the business and cultural context of legal practice, leaving them to deal with legal problems or elements of legal problems. The law firm in the future will be like the wristwatch is to the iPhone.

The technological analogy does not stop there because technology itself will facilitate new approaches to legal practice that will change the landscape of provision of legal services. While the city elite will look over their shoulders at the big four accountancy firms (the new dragons of coverage), they will be looking over their other shoulder at the hornets of sole practitioner firms or small MDPs and ASBs, at the ability of lawyers to operate independently through new technologies that will put them on an even footing with larger practices because of: access to cloud technology; e-discovery software; increasingly sophisticated and affordable mobile technology hardware; legal research through sophisticated and intuitive artificial intelligence robots, and outsourcing of routine, non-expert and commodifiable business to specialist companies utilising suitable but less qualified and cheaper staff in labour-efficient geographies. These will be lawyers able to effect a work/life balance, to work virtually anywhere in the world while living anywhere else in the world.

But technology will not only be a boon to practitioners but also to clients. While firms will be able to drive down costs through cheaper and more efficient ways of document analysis and management and legal research technologies, the client will have increasing access to these technologies themselves and given the LSA's objective of transparency, to the costs associated with these areas of case management. As an example, IBM has developed a robot, software platform called Watson that is already having a profound effect on areas such as medical diagnostics.[26] Watson has spawned Ross,[27] an equivalent application in law that has the ability to receive commands or search requests in vernacular language and to provide an answer that includes all relevant citations, recent changes, distinguishing factors and a recommendation with a measure of confidence. This is tailored wiki-law. Put in your search question and a sophisticated answer emerges. This has the potential to guide clients in the initial stages of their legal problem; to enable them to distinguish when they need legal advice and when a matter is more straightforward. Similarly, like NHS choices, one can see this becoming a tool available to the general public, funded by opportunity costs and adverts.

Legal education must surely grasp the changing working environment as firmly as it does basic principles of contract and tort.

6.1.6 Legal identities: educationalists, practitioners and regulators

Clementi's discomfort with the representative bodies regulating themselves was only partly addressed by their division into distinct arms, separated by Chinese walls. The LSB is now proposing that regulation should ensure accountability independent of the professions and government. Without such independence there is greater complexity in the relationships between the regulators and the regulated; greater potential for distraction; reduced credibility in the eyes of the public; less transparency; more opportunity for inertia and obstruction on the part of the professional bodies; greater confusion around which bodies are responsible for what; higher costs; greater uncertainty and disincentive for investment; and, perhaps, most tellingly, these disadvantages arise against a background where market changes are reducing the relevance of regulation in relation to representative bodies.[28]

The LSB proposes that an independent review should be established to determine which activities should be regulated and that the new regulator should be answerable to parliament to ensure its independence. It also proposes that risk should determine whether regulation occurs before, during and after the event, i.e., high-risk events such as the conduct of litigation and the performance of advocacy should be regulated in advance via entry standards; low risk regulation, such as consumer protection, may be served by after the 'event regulation' in the form of redress.

If the direction of travel sketched out above is to be believed, the culture and identity of legal practice will change, perhaps unrecognisably. The primacy of entity regulation will obscure the individual. The co-location of practitioners within such entities will erode the distinctions of practitioner culture and history, particularly as they will be regulated by either a single regulatory body or bodies which are wholly independent of practice itself and therefore of membership or representational bodies. The consequent demise of the Law Society and the Bar Council will further erode distinctions in identity and with it the architecture and protections around the current structures of education and training.

The segmentation of legal practice and its interface, if not integration, with other professional practice such as finance and accountancy, together with the previously high costs of qualification and the gaps in legal provision, will drive the demand for the ability of students to qualify in segments of legal practice, with the opportunity to build segment licensing into broader areas of qualification. Students will be familiar with this approach because it already applies in higher education through the modular approach to programme design, with individual modules, stages and exit awards being regarded as valuable in their own right, as well as the final qualification of the bachelor's or master's degrees.

Ironically, educationalists will then face the same problems as they do now in deciding the balance and chronology of development between underpinning, meta-cognitive knowledge and skills that form a base for future understanding and development, and the instrumental knowledge and skills that non-cognate, new-managerialist employers will require of their staff tomorrow.

The government's new 'trail-blazer' apprenticeships appear an apt solution to this disaggregated model of education (an issue addressed by Stephen Levett later in this chapter); offering an immersive, context orientation and a just-in-time rather than just-in-case, knowledge and skill specific approach to workforce development. Given the government's tax levy on business, it would appear that apprenticeships will be a zero-cost and attractive option and provide the adaptable, hybrid professionals of future legal/finance/business practice. With the financial drivers of practice acting as a catalyst for the outsourcing of routine, low-level legal work the advent of the apprenticeship may also provide a way to keep it in-house and utilise it both as a training benefit and a sustainable income stream. Perhaps some entities will take training back in-house entirely if it is the entity and not the individual which is regulated, for most areas of practice at least.

Which returns us to perhaps the fundamental issue in predicting these futures. With questions over the future conception of the identity of a legal practitioner, the nature of the business structures in which they will work, their status as autonomous individuals, the identity and nature of regulation, how it will be conducted and how this will affect the current approved regulators, and perhaps more importantly, the professional bodies from which they have emanated, questions arise also as to the future form and identity of the legal education provider. Will we be looking at a PWC University or even the University of the Big Four? Or will the provision of legal education to a segmented, disaggregated market cause the segmentation and disaggregation of legal education itself? Even if the regulatory objectives are retained that provide for legal education providers to have control over how to meet the specified outcomes of education, it is not now clear who will specify those outcomes, how they will be differentiated across segments and areas of practice and what critical mass will be determined as an entry threshold and for what. Will such courses and their providers continue to fall under the remit of the traditional higher education regulators, the Higher Education Funding Council and the Quality Assurance Agency for Higher Education, or whatever their new form under the Office for Students will be, or will this be of no consequence to training that is dictated by an entity's needs? These futures raise questions about the fundamental nature of legal practice and conceptions of what it is to be a lawyer – if that identity is to survive at all.

Notes

1 See: R. Burridge, K. Hinnett, A. Palliwalla and T. Varnova, *Effective learning & teaching in law*, London, UK, Stylus Publication, 2002, 5; and, more generally: W. Twining, *Law in context: enlarging a discipline*, Oxford, United Kingdom, Oxford University Press, 1997.
2 See in particular: A. Boon, J. Flood and J. Webb, *Postmodern professions? The fragmentation of legal education and the legal profession,* Journal of Law and Society, 32 (3), 2005, 473.
3 Recent changes to training regulations now mean that other forms of work-based experience may count towards the apprenticeship stage for aspirant solicitors.
4 The acronyms here need explanation. The QLD is a qualifying law degree – one that meets the standards (currently) set by the regulatory bodies for barristers and solicitors. Obtaining a QLD qualifies the graduate for taking the overtly vocational stage of their legal education – the Legal Practice Course (LPC) (for solicitors) and the Bar Professional Training Course (BPTC) (for barristers). A non-law graduate can take a conversion course – typically called the Graduate Diploma in Law (GDL) passing which then entitles them to sit for the LPC or BPTC.
5 These reforms and developments are jurisdictional-specific (England and Wales) although their effect may be felt internationally.
6 J. Ching, P. Maharg, A. Sherr and J. Webb, *The future of legal services education and training regulation in England and Wales*, Legal Education and Training Review, 2013, 155.
7 See: D. Clementi, *Report of the review of the regulatory framework for legal services in England and Wales*, Ministry of Justice, 2014.
8 D. Clementi, *Report on the review of the regulatory framework for legal services in England and Wales*, 2004, Chapter E, available at: www.webarchive.nationalarchives.gov.uk/+www.legal-services-review.org.uk/content/report, accessed 20 February 2016.
9 H.M. Government, *The Government's principles of regulation: better regulation framework manual*, 2015, available at: www.gov.uk/ . . . /publications/better-regulation-framework-manual, accessed 20 February 2016.
10 A. Roy and C. Handford, *Reserved and unreserved Lawyers' Activities Legal Services Board*, 2011, 5, available at: www.legalservicesboard.org.uk/news_publications, accessed 20 February 2016.
11 E. Rowlands, *Looking to the future – feasibility and public protection*, SRA June 2016, 51, available at: https://sra.org.uk/sra/policy/future/position, accessed 26 July 2016.
12 J. Ching, P. Maharg, A. Sherr and J. Webb, A*n overture for the well-tempered regulators: four variations on a LETR theme,* The Law Teacher, 49 (2), 2014, 157.
13 N. Duncan, J. Webb, *Editorial,* The Law Teacher, 45 (3), 273.
14 Lord Neuberger of Abbotsbury, *Lord Upjohn Lecture 2012: reforming legal education,* The Law Teacher, 47 (1), 2013, 4, 7.
15 D. Edmonds, *Training the lawyers of the future- a regulator's view,* The Law Teacher, 45 (1), 2011, 4.
16 Legal Services Board, *A vision for legislative reform of the regulatory framework for legal services in England and Wales*, 2016, 10–11, available at: www.legalservicesboard.org.uk/news_publications, accessed 14 September 2016.
17 Legal Services Board, *Quality in legal services*, LSB, 2012.
18 See: Committee on Legal Education, *Report of the Committee on legal education*, Cmnd 4595, 1971.
19 See: Lord Chancellor's Advisory Committee on Legal Education and Conduct, *First Report on Legal Education and Training*, 1996 (the ACLEC Report], London, Millbank House.
20 P. Maharg in J. Ching et al, 2014, op cit., 12, 146.

21 W. Twining, *Blackstone's tower: the English law school*, London, United Kingdom, Sweet & Maxwell. 1994, 2.
22 W. Twining, *Law in context*, 1997, Oxford, 83.
23 *Statement of Solicitor Competence*, June 2016, available at: www.sra.org.uk/solicitors/competence-statement.page, accessed 14 July 2016.
24 See: R. Susskind, *Provocations and perspectives, a working paper submitted to the UK CLE Research Consortium*, 2012, available at: www.letr.org.uk/wp-content/uploads/Susskind-LETR-final-Oct-2012, accessed 20 February 2016.
25 John Bell and Jennifer Johnstone, General Transferable Skills in the Law Curriculum: Report of a DfEE funded Discipline Network project, 1998.
26 Stephen Baker, *Final jeopardy: the story of Watson, the computer that will transform our world*, Mariner Books, 2012.
27 A. Arruda, *Artificial intelligence systems and the law*, Peer to Peer, ILTA Summer 2016, available at: file:///C:/Users/cmaguir/Documents/Alternative%20Provider%20Literature/ROSS%20Intelligence%20-%20Artificial%20Intelligence%20Systems%20and%20Law%20(1).pdf, accessed 12 January 2017
28 LSB, 2016, op cit.

Part 2 – Degree apprenticeships – a way forward?

Stephen Levett

There have been some significant recent policy developments in the UK recently which could provide opportunities for the wider application and development of experiential learning and clinical legal education and may suggest possible development routes for other jurisdictions. I wish to focus on one – the government's commitment to increasing the numbers of apprenticeships in England to 3 million by 2020.[1]

6.2.1 Apprenticeships in the modern context

Apprenticeships fell out of use and fashion in many sectors of the economy in the UK in the latter part of the 20th century. They were associated with manual labour in failing old-fashioned industries like steel and coal production, or in traditional blue collar trades like carpentry or building. As a result, for many of the aspirational lower and middle classes, the perception was that the best way to achieve social and economic progress was to go to university. This dream of higher education became a real possibility for increasing numbers of people as the number of institutions and student places expanded (particularly post-1992 when vocationally focused polytechnics were accorded university status). The proliferation of 'new' universities offering courses delivered in a wide variety of ways (including part-time study) made it easier than ever before for people to choose a course that matched their lifestyle and dreams.

And yet, far from quenching British industry's thirst for a supply of highly qualified graduates equipped with the skills, attributes and mind-sets that business said it was crying out for, there were continuous murmurings of discontent; universities were "too easy" to get into; there was "grade inflation" as the number of students getting first- and second-class degrees increased;[2] too many graduates had to be "retrained" as soon as they entered employment. Some employers complained that graduates' skills and knowledge were out of date even before they graduated, as university courses struggled to keep up with the dizzying pace of technological change.[3]

One engineering company based in the North East of England, for example, told me that whilst they were satisfied with the general quality of engineering graduates, they did not have the specific skills they needed to enable them to add value to the business from day one. In particular, they lacked computer-aided design skills and had to be trained to use the software which the company had adopted. This could take anything up to a year, so represented a considerable investment on the part of the company in the new recruit. There was a palpable sense of frustration on the part of this employer that universities did not seem able to respond to that company's specific needs.

There was then a sense of disconnect in some areas between what universities were teaching and what businesses felt they needed. Employers' organisations and industry representative bodies claimed that the employers they represented wanted much closer contact between business, industry and educational institutes, and that their members were willing and able to give time to develop that partnership.[4] Universities, by contrast, they said were remote, difficult to talk to and isolated in their 'ivory towers'. Simply finding the right person to speak to about a possible collaboration was seen as too much like hard work.

6.2.2 Apprenticeships and higher education

Meanwhile important changes to the way higher education was funded (especially in England) were (inadvertently?) preparing the way for a stronger alliance between business and education. From 1998, far more of the cost of obtaining a university education was being pushed onto students. (The argument was that because students benefitted from better pay over the course of their working life when compared to non-graduates, they should bear some of the cost too.)[5] In 1998 tuition fees for undergraduate programmes were introduced, with universities in England being able to charge up to £9,000 per year from 2012 for an undergraduate university programme. A Student Loan Company was set up to provide loans to students to cover the costs of tuition and maintenance, with the loans becoming repayable only when a graduate's annual earnings exceeded a specified amount. From 2016 maintenance grants for students from poorer backgrounds were also replaced by additional student loans.

The implication for students contemplating continuing onto higher education is that whilst they have more chance of attending university than ever before, the cost of doing so is soaring and in the case of English students, could be in the region of £50,000. Little wonder, then, that many students are looking for ways of securing the higher-level qualifications they need without being saddled with high levels of student debt. In some cases, this has resulted in UK students applying to study on English-speaking courses elsewhere in Europe, where fees and the cost of living may be far lower. In other instances, students are actively seeking courses and programmes that will enable them to combine work and study, such as part-time degrees or online programmes that at least do not incur the cost of studying away from home.

A third and relatively new option though, especially as far as the legal services sector is concerned, is to complete a degree apprenticeship. Degree apprenticeships are like any other kind of apprenticeship; the student is an employee of a business and works for that employer. At the same time, he or she engages in substantial on-the-job training (the ultimate hands-on learning experience) whilst also studying to complete the requirements of a university degree.

The model for the development of degree apprenticeships, which has been adopted by the government, involves businesses in the creation of "standards". These standards are designed by employers "to meet their needs, the needs of their sector(s) and the economy more widely".[6] Standards are meant to be short and easy-to-understand documents (typically no more than 2 pages). They focus on the key Knowledge, Skills and Behaviour (KSBs) required to undertake a specific occupation; they indicate how an apprentice will show mastery of an occupation; and they set out how an apprentice will meet any relevant or necessary professional registration requirements.

In practice, those standards which have been designed to date have been put together by "trailblazer" groups of employers, often alongside professional associations or representative bodies and, where the standards are at a sufficiently high level to incorporate a degree as part of the apprenticeship, with one or more higher education institutions. The early involvement of businesses and stakeholders from the relevant sector (in this case the legal one) is key to the government's approach to modern apprenticeships. Without that support an apprenticeship will not see the light of day.[7]

There are currently relatively few degree apprenticeships. At the time of writing, less than 20 degree-level apprenticeship standards had been approved as ready for delivery (a necessary precursor to an educational body being able to deliver a degree apprenticeship based on that standard). However, this is likely to change rapidly, as from April 2017 the government will be imposing a levy on all businesses with a wage bill in excess of £3 million pounds (approx. US$4 million) to create a fund to support the development and delivery of apprenticeships including degree apprenticeships.[8]

The introduction of the levy has not been without its critics. But in announcing this approach as its preferred method of funding apprenticeships, it has had the effect of generating greater awareness of, and interest in, developing apprenticeships in general and degree apprenticeships specifically. Put simply, businesses (including public sector institutions such as universities and hospital trusts) are going to have to pay this tax, so they might as well derive some benefit from it. Higher education providers have in the meantime seen that the levy offers a real business opportunity,[9] and this has resulted in a much more proactive approach to attracting businesses to work with them on the development of new higher-level qualifications. Interestingly, of the few degree apprenticeships which had been developed at the time of writing, 3 exist in the legal services sector, with others already developed in professional services sectors, such as banking and accountancy.[10] This suggests that these areas (perhaps because of their tradition of post-qualification training) are more receptive to this approach than others.

6.2.3 Apprenticeships and the law

In the legal sector, standards have been developed so far for apprenticeships which will lead to qualification as solicitor, legal executive, licensed conveyancer and paralegal; and these new routes into the profession have been broadly welcomed by the profession. For example, the Solicitors Regulation Authority has said that apprenticeships are likely to "drive up quality and improve access to the legal profession".[11] A number of high-profile law firms have also embraced the idea of legal apprenticeships, including, for example, Freshfield Bruckhaus Deringer, which in announcing its first paralegal apprenticeship, agreed that it saw apprenticeships as offering wider access to the law by offering "a flexible route for talented students to join the legal profession".[12]

The advantage for the student is two-fold. The first is that the student gets to study for a degree which has been designed in partnership with an employer. This should enable the student both to apply their theoretical learning to their workplace, and at the same time draw on their practical experience to enhance their understanding of that theory. Moreover, the fact that the student's learning is set in the context of a modern legal practice means that employers' concerns about the currency of the knowledge and skills being delivered by the educational institution are addressed. The second advantage is financial. Because the student on a degree apprenticeship has to be employed, he or she is "earning while learning" and the cost of the degree is met by the employer. As a result the student can qualify debt-free.

There is an additional benefit to some degree apprenticeships in that, because the standards are frequently developed in partnership with a professional association, students who complete a degree apprenticeship often come out dual-qualified with a degree and an accompanying industry-recognised accreditation.[13]

How then does the development of higher level apprenticeships in the legal sector link with experiential learning? Of course, an apprenticeship is, literally, a case of "learning on the job". However, there is considerable potential for an effective interface to be established with university clinical programmes.

The basic model of clinic sees students working together in groups on relatively straightforward legal problems that have been carefully selected for them to ensure they are able to derive the maximum educational benefit. Students are closely supervised and given the opportunity to develop their skills and knowledge in a safe environment which is permissive of mistakes and which sees error as a learning opportunity, to be analysed and corrected before the client is given any advice or information. Reflection and the gathering of evidence to support that reflection is frequently key to the student's development. Time scales are sometimes longer than those that would ordinarily apply in practice precisely to allow this reflective process to run its course. Close supervision by suitably qualified professionals ensures quality control for client and student alike.

Practice has very different priorities. As commercial entities, the pace of work in a legal service provider is necessarily much faster, enabling fee-earners to achieve challenging targets; there is (rightly so) an intolerance of error; team-working can sometimes be relegated in the drive to get things done. Reflection can be more of an aspiration than a day-to-day practice. As a result, the environment in which an aspiring solicitor studying tor a degree apprenticeship will be based will be very different from the environment at most universities for students studying on traditional law degrees.

Yet the level of investment that a legal service provider will be contributing in supporting a student through a degree apprenticeship will be substantial, and as a result, ensuring the best possible return on that investment will be a priority.

Clinical legal educators have the advantage of having delivered precisely the kind of hands-on legal education which degree apprenticeships will demand. Their experience of supervising inexperienced law students in a diverse range of legal settings and on a variety of types of case, means they are ideally placed to support law firms in developing their own approach to supporting students on degree apprenticeships.

This could, of course, involve university student law clinics working with law firms to provide law students with opportunities that a firm offering a degree apprenticeship is unable to offer. For example, for a number of years, one city law firm which was unable to offer its legal trainees opportunities to develop their advocacy skills, worked with a leading vocational course provider's student legal advice centre in London. Trainees were attached to the student law firm for a number of weeks in the course of which they were given the opportunity to represent clients in tribunal cases.[14] Such arrangements can be mutually beneficial – the law firm is able to give its trainees experience in a key skill, often on the kind of case that the firm would ordinarily tackle only as part of its commitment to pro bono; and the law clinic can derive an income to support its activities whilst at the same time delivering a high-quality service in a neglected area of legal practice.

6.2.4 Conclusion: apprenticeships and experiential learning

There is an opportunity here for clinical legal practitioners to support legal service providers as consultants, in helping them to develop their own understanding of how best to support student learning in the workplace. Clinical legal educators have a range of skills and approaches which can only be developed over time – the ability, for example, to stand back and allow students to work to find the answer (or not as the case may be) themselves without jumping in to provide an immediate response and solution for them. In a profession which prizes the ability to instantly assess a scenario, identify the problems and provide an immediate solution to a client anxious not to be kept waiting, such an approach to learning can be frustrating for an experienced practitioner. Similarly, it takes skill and patience to be able to identify good work in the midst of an unsatisfactory analysis, and to offer praise and encouragement. In an environment where success is judged by billable hours and reward is primarily financial, finding the time to develop a learner can be a distraction from the "main job".

Degree apprenticeships then are heading our way and, as legal educators in general and clinicians in particular, we should welcome them. By working closely with the legal sector, by engaging in a positive and supportive way with law firms and other legal service providers, and by sharing the wealth of our experience in developing the essential skills and attributes of a practicing lawyer, we can ensure that those students lucky enough to secure a degree apprenticeship experience a rich and deeply rewarding work-based learning experience.

Notes

1 See: www.gov.uk/government/uploads/system/uploads/attachment_data/file/482754/BIS-15–604-english-apprenticeships-our-2020-vision.pdf, accessed 26 October 2016.
2 See for example: A.D. Barrett, *Dumbing down of University grades revealed*, www.telegraph.co.uk/education/universityeducation/8235115/Dumbing-down-of-university-grades-revealed, accessed 21 October 2016.
3 The BCC workforce survey 2014 reported for example that 54 percent of employers thought graduates were "not ready for work". See: www.britishchambers.org.uk/assets/downloads/J4990%20-%20A4%20BCC%20WORKFORCE%20SURVEY%20INFOGRAPHIC%20final.pdf, accessed 21 October 2106.
4 See for example: *A model for school and business partnerships to promote young people's career prospects lessons from the school business partnerships project*, CBI, 8 March 2016.
5 For an early example of media discussion of this issue see The Telegraph, 19 November 2002 "All students should pay tuition fees", available at: www.telegraph.co.uk/news/uknews/3304776/All-students-should-pay-tuition-fees.html, accessed 25 October 2016.
6 See: *Apprenticeships guidance for trailblazers*, www.gov.uk/government/uploads/system/uploads/attachment_data/file/487350/BIS-15-632-apprenticeships-guidance-for-trailblazers-december-2015.pdf, accessed 25 October 2016.
7 Ibid., 19.
8 Department for Education, *Apprenticeship levy: how it will work*, www.gov.uk/government/publications/apprenticeship-levy-how-it-will-work/apprenticeship-levy-how-it-will-work, accessed 20 October, 2016.
9 See: A. Westwood, Why colleges and universities should be offering more and better apprenticeships, in T. Lanning (ed.), *Where next for apprenticeships?*, available at: www.cipd.co.uk/binaries/where-next-for-apprenticeships_2016.pdf, accessed 22 October 2016.
10 A full and updated list of apprenticeship standards can be found here, available at: Skills Funding Agency, *List of all the Apprenticeship Standards*, www.gov.uk/government/uploads/system/uploads/attachment_data/file/546991/Apps_standards_list_190816.pdf, accessed 23 October 2016.
11 SRA News release, 3 Sept 2015.
12 *Law Society Gazette*, 16 August 2016.
13 See for example the Chartered Manager Degree Apprenticeship the standard for which was developed with the active support of the Chartered Management Institute.
14 See Legal Week, 'Linklaters starts up litigation training deal', available at: www.legalweek.com/sites/legalweek/2003/11/06/linklaters-starts-up-litigation-training-deal/?slreturn=20170010112709, accessed 25 October 2016.

Chapter 7

Assessment in legal education

Qualification or quantification?

Jenny Gibbons

7.1 Introduction

There has been growing uniformity in both common law and civil law countries across Europe in the terminology used in higher education assessment as a result of the Bologna Process, and the development of the eight levels of the European Qualifications Framework.[1] This creates a useful comparative framework, whilst maintaining considerable academic freedom within universities on what content to assess and how. The majority of institutions choose, for a combination of legacy, administrative and convenience reasons, to teach legal topics in hermetically sealed modules using point-in-time assessments, such as exams. The final degree classification derives from credit-counting, whereby students receive a mark or grade for each module they undertake and university rules dictate the qualification award from this calculation. Experience within the UK indicates that, although there is scope within individual law schools for the creation of innovative assessment and for exceptional students to obtain consistently strong marks across numerous assessment points, the vast majority of students graduate with what is termed an Upper Second Class degree (a 2.1 – equating to an average of 60–69 percent in all of the modules undertaken).[2]

Why, though, does a university qualification involve so much quantification? Why is the focus of the assessment of legal knowledge on counting and measuring the product of the students' learning at a particular point in time? Can we re-imagine legal education assessment and evaluation to design high-quality assessment that has relevance to the students and is integrated into the process of their learning in a more sophisticated way? This chapter will explore how we might move away from the assessment of 'learning what', towards the assessment of 'learning how' and 'learning why'.[3] To do this, we need to make a mind-set shift from seeing assessment as a form of 'science' (where quantification may be appropriate) towards a model where legal education is a reflective and developmental practice aligned with the motivation of individual students, and with an emphasis on learning-oriented assessment (LOA), as advocated by Carless.[4]

The traditional approach to the assessment of legal knowledge in both civil and common law jurisdictions has been the 'closed book' exam, and this remains a popular format for assessment in both. Many educators (and many more students) argue strongly that it is not appropriate that assessment is defined solely by past practice, when the retention and recall of factual knowledge was of paramount importance. Instead we need to give consideration to what is needed now, and acknowledge that in a world where factual knowledge is readily accessible, particularly online, we have the opportunity to develop legal education assessment practice that is more fitting for the 21st-century lawyer and/or graduate citizen. As explored below, this involves a progression from the assessment of the recall of legal knowledge to assessment of the application of legal research to defined problems and issues. It is difficult to envisage for how long the 'closed book' exam can be maintained in the modern environment, so robust alternatives need to be explored by all of the stakeholders of legal education.

7.2 The purposes of legal education assessment

As Carless identifies, there are three main purposes for assessment in all disciplines. These are: (i) judging achievement; (ii) maintaining standards; and (iii) promoting learning.[5] All of these are important and have their place in legal education assessment design, but historically they have not been equally regarded or weighted. In the current climate, where increasing numbers of students study law at university level, where a lower percentage of law graduates enter the legal profession, where students are increasingly willing to travel abroad for their education and where the cost of funding education now rests primarily with the students themselves, it is worth giving greater consideration to the third of these factors as a way to enrich the learning experience of all.[6]

In the legal education world, it would appear that academic staff, most notably module leaders, have a tendency to overemphasise the first of the purposes of assessment identified by Carless. Unfortunately, the judgment of what achievement looks like is often evaluated using the module leader's own experience of studying and teaching law and as too strong a frame. For example, for substantive legal assessments, most module leaders create a 'model answer' which is given to the marking team, and against which the students' submissions are evaluated, marked and graded. Years of experience have led the module leader to categorise the canon of legal knowledge in their area and consciously or unconsciously, ranking it in a hierarchical way. For the students new to the discipline, it is only after they have undertaken an assessment that they will have an insight into the module leader's interpretation of the wealth of material to which they have had access during the teaching term. Where feedback is provided, students are often bewildered when they receive comments such as "You failed to mention [case X]" or "You should have given more emphasis to [authority Y]". The judgment of one person's achievement by another in a legal assessment is thus always subjective, regardless of whether it is packaged as an objective process and uses clear criteria. When re-thinking legal education assessment, it is worth giving increased attention to what 'achievement' looks like; how, and by whom, it should be judged and for what overall purpose.

Legal regulators are, quite rightly, most interested in the second of the three purposes identified by Carless. In most jurisdictions, the academic stage of legal education contributes to the qualification route into the legal profession, so the regulators have an interest in maintaining the standards of university-based legal education. However, where the regulators change their approach to qualification standards, this has a filter-down effect on assessment design in universities.[7] For some this equates to 'the tail wagging the dog', meaning that the dog needs to be of a robust and recognisable breed to prevent this from happening. Forward-thinking university law departments need to have a clear pedagogically model of legal education that prepares students for, amongst other things, the rigours of the standard setting designed by the regulators, without diluting the educational experience of the undergraduate programmes or deflecting from rigorous intellectual debate. The tension between law as a liberal socio-legal study subject and law as a vocational education pervades this discussion.

The third purpose for assessment identified by Carless, promoting learning, has often been overlooked within legal education, particularly given the traditional approaches to both teaching methods and assessment. Closed-book exams are more a test of recall than learning and in the current environment the proliferation of easy access revision guides for all law topics can lead students to achieving high grades in exams for papers based on momentary, superficial and transitory knowledge. There has also been an exponential rise in hard-to-detect 'cut and paste' content in coursework tasks, particularly for essays based on frequently assessed aspects of modules. For these and a myriad of other reasons, it is time to re-imagine assessment design in legal education to re-emphasis the role of learning. Before doing this, it is worth considering what the current practice of assessment design in legal education is and exploring the innovations that are already taking place.

7.3 The practice of legal education assessment

Not all law schools continue to use closed-book exams as the only, or main, method of assessment, and there is increasing credit given on university programmes to alternative formats, including essay-style coursework tasks, client letter drafting, presentations and portfolios. This is in part due to a greater engagement by legal educators with educational theory, including constructivist and social realist approaches to learning; and an increasing number of international networks and conferences where legal educators share ideas about pedagogic practice.[8] This discipline-specific conversation also feeds in to the wider debate about the purpose of assessment in higher education and the increased emphasis on embedding the assessment of skills into university programmes, in what is often termed the 'employability agenda'.[9]

For too long in legal education, the assessment of skills has tended to be interpreted narrowly as the need to practice legal skills with a view to employment in legal practice. In the UK this has meant 'learning what' in the academic stage, and 'learning how' during (typically) subsequent vocational training. I suggest that today this is not sufficient for the majority of students who will not (and often do not wish to) progress to the vocational stage, and who need the opportunity to be assessed on their ability to 'learn how' (and indeed 'learn why') at an earlier point. This is because they need to enter the workplace, in whatever role they choose, with a wider repertoire of knowledge, skills and values than just the ability to recall rules at a given moment.

7.4 Learning-oriented assessment in legal education

LOA is a useful concept to consider when designing assessment in legal education. As Carless explains, the first and most crucial strand of LOA is represented by the term 'assessment tasks as learning tasks'. He explains that for assessment to be meaningful, the tasks should promote the kind of learning dispositions required of graduates and should mirror real-world applications of the subject matter. In a legal context, this is most obviously a 'messy' legal problem that would be seen by a lawyer in practice, but could also include legal issues as seen by graduates in related fields, such as civil servants, business people and the general public. A curriculum based on problem-based learning (PBL), as is seen at York Law School and looked at in detail elsewhere in this book, is one (and I would add, powerful) way to design such 'assessment tasks as learning tasks'.[10] Using integrated curriculum design, it is possible to spread the assessment of substantive legal knowledge across a period of study, rather than allow students to rely on short-term bursts of sustained study for an end of module assignment that may not be studied, assessed or applied again whilst at the law school.

The second component of LOA is involving students actively in the evaluation and assessment process so that they develop a better understanding of learning goals and engage more directly with applicable criteria and standards. For Carless the emphasis here is mostly on peer feedback and peer assessment, but this component can also include a focus on reflective practice and self-evaluation in relation to the learning process and assessment activities.[11] Reflective practice is an important aspect of many experiential learning models, including those advocated by Kolb and Schön, but it can be problematic to assess as a stand-alone task, as will be explored further below.[12]

For assessment to promote learning, Carless maintains that the third component of LOA is that students need to receive appropriate feedback. In a recent, and timely, literature review on assessment feedback in higher education, Evans identifies and discusses dominant themes and discourses in the research literature and explores the notion of the feedback 'gap'.[13] She makes a distinction between different conceptions of feedback, and the links between these and the epistemological perspective of the marker. For some, and I would include here many legal academics in universities, feedback is seen as an end product, as a consequence of performance. This plays out in many universities where the task of producing feedback on summative assessments (if any feedback is given at all) is often delegated to junior staff and/or includes the production of standardised comments. These, and the model answers they are based upon, are reproduced for a similar task at a similar time of the academic term, year after year after year. This type of end-product feedback is often too general, too late and insufficiently related to the relevant marking criteria.

Evans, like Carless, advocates for the conceptualization of feedback as part of an ongoing process to support learning both in the immediate context of higher education and in future learning gains into employment beyond the university. This conception of feedback is captured in the increasingly ubiquitous terms 'feed-forward' and 'feed-up', respectively.

Many universities now actively promote this feed-forward approach. For many academic staff the idea that feedback should be individualised, forward facing and involve an ongoing dialogue with students is seen as an additional and problematic responsibility. For example, the need to individualise feedback can dramatically increase workloads, especially during busy marking periods, and can, in practice, lead to the types of unhelpful feedback comments referred to above. Despite these practical considerations, an active engagement with feedback not only helps to promote learning but can also help students to understand what counts as achievement, and in what way this is being judged. Strong feedback models can also be used during the teaching term, particularly for group activities and tasks. Carless emphasises that peers can and should be usefully deployed as givers of feedback, and that they are often an under-used resource in assessment design.

7.5 The future of legal education assessment

The combination of a changing higher education environment and a more activist and theoretically informed group of legal educators can help to generate an innovative approach to assessment design, including engagement with LOA. The suggestions below are by no means a definitive list but set out some examples to consider, and the rationale for their consideration.

There has been a technological revolution in legal practice as much as elsewhere, meaning that practising lawyers perhaps do not need to know law in the same way as they did. They do, of course, need to know where to find it, and what to do with it. Technology can certainly help in that process. In this environment, as set out above, appropriate assessments could be more based on 'messy' problems using simulated clients, which all students need to approach as an exercise in legal research, rather than an initial test of legal knowledge. This approach would do away with some of the arbitrary distinctions between the sub-categories of law (obligations, public, contract, land etc.), and the imbalance associated by the equivalent weighting within curricula of contested and uncontested legal concepts (for example equitable versus contractual doctrines). It would also put less emphasis on the role of the module leader, and their reliance on their own education and teaching experience. That is not to say that there is not a role for the 'expert' in legal education, just that they should be the curators of knowledge, rather than the traditional view of the 'fount of all knowledge'.

Where legal essay coursework tasks are pre-set, it is worth giving some thought to the purpose of this activity, and its alignment with students' motivation.[14] There is without doubt value in many aspects of the preparation for such tasks, for example, the process of constructing a legal argument, attributing relative weight to source material, evaluating and analysing the credibility and persuasiveness of the arguments of others and writing with a clear and coherent style. What is more problematic is the idea that there is a 'correct' model answer, or indeed that the question that has been set by another person is a question that student needs or wants to answer. To link with the second component of LOA, why not let students have greater choice in the selection of essay-type tasks? This would allow students to explore their own motivation and interpretation of the world and conduct realistic legal research using a range of resources beyond those prescribed by a module leader. If the result is appropriately referenced and coherently argued, there is no reason to penalise students whose interpretation of the world does not conform to the established view. Achievement in this task would need to be judged using criteria other than the expectations of content anticipated by the academic staff. Peer feedback could be a useful tool to develop in this context. This may be a shocking suggestion for civil lawyers given the historical view of law as science, but even in continental Europe there is surely room within the codes, as under the common law, for interpretation, analysis and reasoned conclusion.

Importantly, there is space for the inclusion of skills-based assessments in LOA, particularly where students feel that the development of the skill is relevant to their own plans for the future, in legal practice or otherwise. The assessment of legal and transferable skills in legal education can take many forms, and its nature lends itself to innovation as there is less focus on the 'right' answer and more on developing the skill in question. Consider this list and then think of the most suitable assessment format: advocacy, interviewing, legal drafting and letter writing, time management or negotiation. Would any of these be best assessed by a closed-book exam? There can also be tasks that develop other more generic skills, such as public speaking, project management and group work, and even what are rather unsatisfactorily referred to as 'soft' skills, such as empathy. An interesting point is whether the assessment of these types of tasks is based on the competence of the performance of the student as evaluated by an external observer; or is an assessment of the reflection by the student of their own performance. Should a student be given credit for recognising what was wrong with a particular performance and how he or she might improve in future? The LOA approach would advocate the later, despite the problematic nature of assessing and marking reflective work.[15]

Examples of innovative assessment practice which successfully use a LOA model can be found in both live-client and simulated-client work undertaken in law school clinics in both common law and civil law countries. Law school clinics have been early adopters of experiential approaches to legal education, and clinical legal education practitioners have explored a variety of ways to capture the process of learning that takes place in the clinical environment. Popular approaches include reflective learning portfolios and research diaries.[16] More recently law schools, including York Law School, have introduced a group oral examination (*viva voce*) in an attempt to facilitate and capture the reflective element of experiential learning.[17]

No matter what approaches to assessment are taken, current UK university requirements stipulate that each student must receive an individualised grade, which in most cases is calculated on the basis of the cumulative marks given by module leaders based on their subjective judgment of the student's achievement. This tends to lead to a pseudo-scientific approach to assessment in legal education, and an emphasis on quantification. In the future greater consideration needs to be given to the students' motivation, the process (rather than the product) of learning and reflective, experiential learning. It is hoped that this will go some way to putting a greater emphasis on quality in the assessment of legal qualifications.

Notes

1 See further: http://ec.europa.eu/education/policy/higher-education/bologna-process_en, accessed 21 October 2016.

2 The highest classification is called a first-class degree. More information is available from the Quality Assurance Agency for Higher Education about the UK classification system: available at: www.qaa.ac.uk/en, accessed 21 October 2016.

3 For recent overviews of assessment practice in higher education, see S. Brown, *Learning, teaching and assessment in higher education [electronic resource]: global perspectives*, London, New York, Macmillan Education, 2015; V. Bamber, *Enhancing learning, teaching, assessment and curriculum in higher education [electronic resource]: theory, cases, practices*, Maidenhead, Society for Research into Higher Education & Open University Press, 2009; and D. Boud and N. Falchikov, *Rethinking assessment in higher education: learning for the longer term*, London, Routledge, 2007.

4 D. Carless, *How assessment supports learning [electronic resource]: learning-oriented assessment in action*, Hong Kong, Hong Kong University Press; London, Eurospan distributor, 2006.

5 Ibid., 8.

6 For more on the changing environment of legal education, see M. Thornton, *Privatising the public university: the case of law*, London, Routledge, 2012.

7 This is currently happening in the UK where the Solicitors Regulation Authority is proposing changes to the routes to qualification. See further: www.sra.org.uk/t4t/, accessed 21 October 2016.

8 Resources on approaches to learning include J.B. Biggs, *Teaching for quality learning at university: what the student does* Maidenhead, England, New York, McGraw-Hill/Society for Research into Higher Education & Open University Press, 2007 and P.L. Berger, *The social construction of reality: a treatise in the sociology of knowledge*, Penguin, 1984. More on social realist approaches can be found M.F.D. Young, *Bringing knowledge back in: from social constructivism to social realism in the sociology of education*, London, Routledge, 2008; and J.M. Case, *Researching student learning in higher education: a social realist approach*, Abingdon, Routledge, 2014.

9 For more on employability, see: www.heacademy.ac.uk/workstreams-research/themes/employability, accessed 21 October 2016. See also G.W. Hinchliffe and A. Jolly, *Graduate identity and employability*, British Educational Research Journal, 37, 2011, 563.

10 For more on PBL, see M. Savin-Baden, *Facilitating problem-based learning: illuminating perspectives*, Society for Research into Higher Education & Open University Press, 2003. For more on the PBL model at York Law School, see R. Grimes, *Delivering legal education through an integrated problem-based learning model – the nuts and bolts,* 21 IJCLE, 2014, 228.

11 See further, A. Campbell and L. Norton, *Learning, teaching and assessing in higher education: developing reflective practice*, Learning Matters, 2007 and J.A. Moon, *A handbook of reflective and experiential learning: theory and practice*, London, RoutledgeFalmer, 2004.

12 See further, D.A. Kolb, *Experiential learning: experience as the source of learning and development*, Prentice-Hall, 1984, and D.A. Schön, *The reflective practitioner: how professionals think in action*, Ashgate, 1991.

13 *C. Evans, Making sense of assessment feedback in higher education*, Review of Educational Research, 83, 2013, 70.

14 For more on the impact of student motivation on their learning, see M. Baeten, F. Dochy and K. Struyven, *The effects of different learning environments on students' motivation for learning and their achievement*, British Journal of Educational Psychology, 83, 2013, 484 and C. Koh, *Motivation, leadership and curriculum design: engaging the Net Generation and 21st century learners,* Springer, 2015.

15 See further: J. Gibbons, *Oh the irony! A reflective report on the assessment of reflective reports on an LLB programme,* The Law Teacher, 49, 2015, 176.

16 For more on experiential and simulated approaches in legal education, see P. Maharg, *Transforming legal education: learning and teaching the law in the early twenty-first century*, Ashgate, 2007; and C. Strevens, R. Grimes and E. Phillips (eds.), *Legal education: simulation in theory and practice*, Ashgate, 2014. On the analysis of reflective journals, see J. Rué, A. Font and G. Cebrián, *Towards high-quality reflective learning amongst law undergraduate students: analysing students' reflective journals during a problem-based learning course,* Quality in Higher Education, 19, 2013, 191.

17 See further: R. Grimes and J. Gibbons, *Assessing experiential learning – us, them and the others,* International Journal of Clinical Legal Education, 23, 2016, 111.

Part C

Countries and cases

Examples of re-thinking

Introduction

The final section of the book is a collection of case studies that sets out ideas and models for re-imagining (or actually realising) a new and improved legal education approach and structure.

The contributions are many and varied in terms of both identified challenges and concrete examples of what could or, in fact, does work.

The recent emergence and rapid growth of legal clinics in Spain (and indeed the rest of continental Europe) is picked up in Chapter 8 by Jose García-Añón, Pilar Fernandez and Ruth Mestre. Developments in this part ofWestern Europe have been both impressive in nature and extent but, as importantly, indicate what is needed for longer-term sustainability.

In Chapter 9 the situation in 3 jurisdictions of Central and Eastern Europe is examined by, respectively, Michal Urban (Czech Republic), Luba Krasnitskaya (Belarus) and Katarzyna Kowalska (Poland), all of whom comment on the influence of the former Soviet Union and membership of the European Union and how this is being reflected in developments in law schools of the region. Whilst the description of situations on the ground is necessarily brief, the material is rich in both analysis and ideas.

Chapter 10 crosses the North Atlantic, where Sue Prince looks at legal education in Canada, a country influenced by both the civil and common law traditions and by its former and current influences – the UK and the USA – with some interesting results in terms of actual and proposed reforms to legal education.

Moving down the continent in Chapter 11, Juan Beca gives a fascinating insight into legal education in Chile. The turbulent and often-violent history of that country, especially during periods of dictatorship have, perhaps surprisingly, produced innovative legal education models – ones that have survived and even thrived despite other pressures. Clinics for example can be dated back to a period in the mid twentieth century – long before such developments in much of the rest of the world.

Chapter 12 travels to sub-Saharan Africa. In charting recent changes to Nigerian legal education, Ernest Ojukwu looks at how the entire curriculum for the vocational stage of legal education in that country has been reviewed and changed with much beneficial effect. A key component of the new programme is simulated and live-client experiential learning.

Such is the gap between rich and poor in many parts of the world that law school–based clinics are an important and indeed vital service for those with unmet legal need. Shuvro Prosun Sarker looks at the situation in India in Chapter 13 and calls loudly and clearly for legal education reform despite some recent developments aimed at achieving that. Once again competing interests appear to get in the way of constructive change. His conclusions centre on the need for greater discourse between the regulators and law schools in order to meet the needs of law students and the wider society.

Chapter 14 goes to Australia, where there has been a long-standing and well-developed clinical presence but also notable challenges in terms of teaching and learning the law. Jeff Giddings recounts the problems facing legal education in his country and makes credible and important recommendations for improvement – building on many of the excellent experiential programmes already in existence in that country. His analysis of the present and immediate future for legal educators will ring true with many.

The final chapter is devoted to concrete examples of how to teach experientially. First, David McQuoid-Mason provides a valuable and clear example of experiential learning through a rendition of how mock trials can be organised and run. Although much of his work has been based in South Africa, David also has extensive experience of legal education and access to justice reforms elsewhere, and this part-chapter concludes with a mock trial that can be (and has been) used across the civil and common law. The second part takes us back to the innovative law school mentioned in Chapter 4. Here, Katarzyna Gromek-Broc, an experienced academic educated in the civil law tradition but now working at the University of York, UK, significantly, in the civil and common law context, takes the subject of European Law and demonstrates how this subject, can be taught experientially. Through an actual example of learning and teaching concepts and doctrine, the author shows how and why such an approach to study could be suitable in law schools found in either system – very much returning to the arguments set out at the beginning of this volume (particularly in Part A, Chapter 3).

The book then concludes with brief final words.

Chapter 8

The birth, growth and reproduction of clinical legal education in Spain

Pilar Fernández-Artiach, José García-Añón and Ruth M. Mestre i Mestre

8.1 Clinical legal education as a transformative tool

As a starting point, in our view, clinical legal education (CLE) is more than a teaching methodology. It is also a place, physical and psychological, for active learning, in which the opportunity for law students to learn from experience is designed, presented and analysed, in a real or realistic context. Students are expected to take responsibility for the outcomes of their learning through a process of reflection.

CLE is also an important tool for the transformation of legal education, from three perspectives. First, it calls for innovative teaching methods; second, it can serve the university's mission in working within and for society, beyond simply their role in teaching and research; and third, it can promote access to justice and human rights.

Considering the first aspect, CLE challenges tradition through the integration of theory and practice, by combining a formal education with the introduction to a professional environment in which knowledge, skills and ethics can be studied holistically. This can be done with exercises that simulate real life and/or with real clients with unmet legal needs.

Legal clinics are also the place where students can learn about the local community and its legal needs, about how the law and lawyers can (or should?) tackle these needs and how can they research, manipulate and articulate the legal content in addressing those needs.

CLE is a tool to show students that the law can be used in many ways and they (under supervision and in the context of clients' wishes) have to decide what needs to be done. Students soon come to realise the extent of protection the legal system might present to its citizens and that this depends, to a large extent, on the use lawyers make of the relevant rules and procedures.

8.2 Legal education in Spanish public universities

Although our analysis refers to public universities in Spain, we think it can be applicable in other contexts. B. De Sousa Santos has identified a triple crisis facing the universities: hegemonic, legitimatic and institutional.[1] That universities are no longer the only higher education educators is the result of a contradiction between what had been considered for centuries the role of universities in the civil law world and the new order in which there are many private education providers and where a free market predominates. While universities are still responsible for the production of critical thinking and technical knowledge, their traditional role was (and some might say still is) in educating an elite. The university's role has been undermined, leading to a crisis in legitimacy because society has, until relatively recently, prized (if not fully appreciated) the university's role. The reality is, in legal education and elsewhere, that instead of high-quality, discerning provision the academy has seen rampant discrimination (especially against women and minority groups), overbooked classrooms and low expectations and realisations of student performance. The university therefore can be said to lack legitimacy.

The institutional crisis refers to the fact that the autonomy of universities is now subject to growing requirements of competency, effectiveness and productivity, and market criteria like employability. Although it is true that law schools need to "produce" good technicians, this is problematic because "giving legal education a mere technical aspect responds to an authoritative design in which law faculties become professional schools without providing the element of critique to positive law."[2] As Santos points out, universities diverge from other centres of education because they are meant to be critical in their approach and not professional or technical as such.[3] In Spain, and elsewhere we suspect, public universities face this crisis, and we suggest that law clinics provide an intelligent way of addressing the problem – and perhaps even a way out.

More profoundly, if, as a public institution, the university is to engage with the development of democracy under the rule of law, to combat discrimination and defend pluralism in our ever-complex and diverse world, law schools surely have an important role to play. When it comes to law, and its procedures and processes, the legal clinic is a vehicle through which conflicts, expectations and needs can be highlighted. CLE is one of the ways in which public law schools can deliver knowledge to society and help produce valid responses and strategies for the better protection of the country's citizens. For us, this constitutes a solid framework to re-thinking of the kind of education that is needed for our future lawyers.

Of course, as seen at various points in this volume, many academics appear trapped, by chance or design (or inertia) in the old ways of the university and the production of 'valid' knowledge: the law is a particular animal of this species – produced by recognised and accepted authority, be it legislation or adjudication, with no other legal reality to check or discuss about-no valid knowledge beyond doctrine. The rhetoric continues: how can lay people understand high theory? How can they pretend to know what is best for them or what legal strategy is correct? But if our objective were to create non-critical technicians who know the norms but ignore *the rest,* what role is there for the law teacher?

Because that is not our objective, we had better re-think what and how we teach law and clinical legal education is one methodology that can help us.

Here are some initial guiding thoughts:

- We are preparing lawyers that will, in a very short period of time, be responsible for administering the law. We are not preparing possible jurists for some task in the distant future in some possible world but actual legal operators in a particular legal culture and context.[4] Today that particular legal context is a dynamic, complex one which faces challenges and changes with previous practices, technologies and markets – from basic human rights through to high commerce and finance.
- As Ferrajoli points out, the jurist needs to be critical of law because the knowledge of 'valid' law can no longer can be separated from the knowledge of law as fact, both in its source and application.[5] So, the jurists we need are critical ones who can uphold and protect the concepts and institutions enshrined by the law in its widest sense. Nothing less will do.
- It is not new to say that law is the product of the activity of legal practitioners, be they in the law office, in parliament or in the courts, so it is important to determine the learning process of these people who will be deciding what the law actually is and how it should be applied. It is not new either to say that the law is the exclusive preserve of what legal operators do. Arnaud considers that, when educating lawyers, we should take into account not just the law, in the positivist tradition, but all the phenomena associated with it, including legal and related skills, ethics and professional values and how to use the law in argument. In doing so there is more chance that the student will be able to connect law and the study of law to the rest of human concerns.[6]
- Llewellyn once said that "technique without ideals might be a menace, but ideals without technique are a mess; and to turn ideals into effective vision, in matters of law, calls for passing those ideals through a hard-headed screen of effective legal technique".[7] We doubt that a lecture or series of lectures can do that. We need to re-think how we deliver and not just what we deliver on.
- In the same way, in the legal realist challenge to the case method and formalism tradition, Jerome Frank once said that it was important to understand the "atmosphere of a case" or "cases as living processes" *vs.* the case method because "the practice of law and the deciding of cases constitute not sciences but arts – the art of the lawyer and the art of the judge. Only a slight part of any art can be learned from books. Whether it be painting or writing or practicing law, the best kind of education in an art is usually through apprentice-training under the supervision of men some of whom have themselves become skilled in the actual practice of the art."[8] Some lawyers of the civil tradition might disagree, but we are interested in his emphasis on the importance of lawyering tasks as a part of how students

should learn law and how the law school would resemble a sort of sublimated law office even if in Spain we are not wedded to the concept of judicial precedent.
- Moreover, the development of the CLE movement from the 1960s onward focuses on the connection between learning and the provision of a service to society. This activity can hardly be achieved without a connection with reality, and with the needs borne out of the difficulties of accessing justice. For this reason, CLE aims to relate the teaching of knowledge, skills and values to the social justice issues that law students experience through dealing with the disadvantaged and marginalized and "to make students socially aware of the problems faced by poor people in society and how these can be addressed."[9]

So, in re-thinking legal education in Spain, several activists, ourselves included, looked to a methodology that would link theory to practice, that was based on real or realistic scenarios, that would focus attention on not just what the law is but what it could be and needs to be, and that required the active engagement of all – professors and students.

If methods shape substance, then selecting a methodology is a crucial decision and nowhere more so than in legal education. We chose clinic.

8.3 The evolution of clinical legal education in Spain

In recent years, the number of Spanish universities offering clinical legal education has increased, developed and consolidated incrementally. In parallel, legal professionals have begun to engage in *pro bono* activities, often in collaboration with legal clinics.[10] In what follows, we point out some of the characteristics of the recent movement of clinical legal education in Spain, together with the challenges ahead, in relation to its growth and sustainability in a university context.

The first wave of clinics in Spain came in the years 2003 to 2006. This was part of a response to the Bologna Process and an opportunity for a change in the curriculum with the creation of the European Higher Education Area. However, this discussion reinforces previous discussions on the failure of the university educational model that were taking place as well. At this point, the undoubted influence and relationship of Latin American clinics in the foundation and support of Spanish clinics should be noted.[11] Two different sets of clinics developed during this early stage of CLE in Spain: those in relatively new universities founded in the nineties (for example Rovira i Virgili University [2003] in Tarragona, or the Carlos III University [2005] in Madrid), and those established in the older established institutions (such as the University of Barcelona [2005] and the University of Valencia [2006]).

Later, from 2012, other universities joined the CLE movement coinciding with an increasing concern amongst professionals for developing pro bono activities and after changes brought about by the Bologna process, noted elsewhere in this book, to law degree curricula in 2010. In some cases, these probono activities are linked to new or existing clinics. Such is the case of the clinics at the University Pablo de Olavide in Sevilla, the University of Alcalá, the University of Balearic Islands, the International University of La Rioja, the Legal Clinic of Icade Pontifical University of Comillas; Legal Clinic of Villanueva University Center, Legal Clinic of IE University, the University of Valladolid and the European University of Madrid. The development of clinics is also not restricted to public universities with clinics now operating in 20 universities across the country.

The second phase of clinical development was due to a number of circumstances, including improving national networks and the exchanging of experiences. The structuring and consolidation of the clinical movement through national and international meetings on legal clinics was also a key factor. Clinicians have been very active in conferences about innovative methods of legal education. Furthermore, several clinical meetings organized between 2007 and 2014 planted the seeds for an extended development of clinics, for example: the International Clinical Legal Education Seminar, organized at the Faculty of Legal Sciences of the University Rovira i Virgili in Tarragona (2007); the Workshop "Experiences of legal clinic in the Spanish Universities" at the Faculty of Law of the University of Valencia (2010); the Third Meeting of Legal Clinics of Spanish Universities held in 2013 under the Fifth National Congress on Legal Education in Valencia,[12] and the Fourth Meeting organized by the Carlos III University and the Bar Association of Madrid (2014). As in other countries and contexts, one of the priorities was to create a community of support, this is a network of legal clinics to promote visibility and foster recognition by public institutions. This community of clinicians has focused on the establishing good practices; the training of trainers, the development of research strategies and the development, where possible, of joint projects amongst clinics. An informal Legal Clinics Network of Spanish Universities has also been set up.[13]

Clinical development in Spain has also benefited from participation in regional and international networks. A milestone was achieved with the holding in 2011 of the sixth World Conference of the Global Alliance for Justice Education and the ninth Conference of the International Journal of Clinical Legal Education (IJCLE) at the University of Valencia. This combined meeting gave a definitive boost to the clinical movement in Spain. Although clinical legal education has spread throughout the world, with different models and procedures, a recent European clinical perspective has been developed that has facilitated the cohesion and relationship amongst clinics. With the support of the NGO PILNET and the European Pro Bono Forum (which held a meeting in Madrid in 2012) focus was rightly placed on the European dimension.

This was followed by the establishment of a pan-European group ENCLE (the European Network of Clinical Legal Education).[14]

The translation into Spanish of the book edited by Frank S. Bloch, *The Global Clinical Movement. Educating Lawyers for Social Justice,* was another milestone because it showed a collection of experiences in other parts of the world and provided important training material.

Finally, the implementation in 2010–2011 of new degree in law curricula, as a consequence of the Bologna Process called for the development of active methodologies for which the evolving clinical movement had concrete ideas.

All of these developments and activities have promoted and supported the Spanish CLE movement. However, many challenges remain, including: improving the exchange of information and dissemination of ideas, improving sustainability – for example, securing adequate resources, integrating legal clinics into the curriculum or setting standards and best practices, providing training for new clinicians and developing research on clinical methodologies and related activities.

To illustrate what Spanish clinics can do and how they operate, let us look briefly at the University of Valencia.

8.4 The legal clinic for social justice at the University of Valencia

From a practical perspective, each Spanish clinic has its own structure and methodology; some of them are multidisciplinary clinics, others specialize in a certain topic; some are live-clinics, others are not. Our aim here is not to discuss the types and virtues of each clinic but to focus on the work done at the Legal Clinic for Social Justice of the University of Valencia, as a mere example of how clinical legal education can be put into place and developed in Spain.[15]

The *Legal Clinic for Social Justice* is a university project which started in 2006. As a learning project, it has been included in the *Campus d'Excellencia Internacional* "VLC/CAMPUS" programme, supported by the Ministry of Education, Culture and Sport (www.vlc-campus.com). The clinic belongs to the networks mentioned above. Around 50 students take part each year with 3 pro bono lawyers and 30 professors supervising in 9 different areas of law, all with a social justice focus.

We have been using a variety of active methodologies, from moot courts, mock trials and other simulations to live-client work, including individual advice and representation and public legal education classes (*Street Law*). All of this work is underpinned by the need for thorough research, high-quality communication and structured reflection.

It is our view that the quality of learning is improved when consideration of legal doctrine, lawyering and other skills and ethical considerations are studied together and when structures to ensure adequate supervision and personal/group evaluation are in place as procedural requirements of the programme. In our experience, learning is better-served when there is an alignment between learning outcomes, teaching activities and assessment. Learning outcomes specify what the student is expected to learn (as a minimum) on completion of the course and must be capable of attainment and measurement. As Biggs in his theory of constructive alignment states:

> When there is alignment between what we want, how we teach and how we assess, teaching is likely to be much more effective than when it is not (aligned). . . . Traditional transmission theories of teaching ignore alignment.[16]

It is not only important to decide what the objectives and learning outcomes of a course and its design are, taking into account study levels/areas of knowledge in the process of learning, but also their relationship with the methods of teaching used and their evaluation. For this reason, in CLE the link between assessment and learning is made very clear to both professors and students. As a principle, assessment is part of learning, and reflective learning is a part of assessment. From a civil law perspective, there may be challenges in that the state or institution may require certain modes of assessment at particular points (normally the end of the period of study in question), but we very much agree with Gibbons in her chapter in this book that where possible, assessment should be for learning. Where rules exist that prevent this being readily adopted, informal assessment (that perhaps does not count towards marks or grades) may be possible – formative assessment in its truest sense.

Miller's *Pyramid of Assessment* provides a framework for assessing clinical competence in legal education and can assist clinical teachers in matching learning outcomes with expectations of what the learner should be able to do at any stage. From the point of view of the professor, it implies multiplicity of assessments or and reflections on learning. Various sources of information or evidence of learning are necessary to evaluate complex outcomes and competencies.[17]

Our assessment regime is based on several different and complementary methods: close supervision (giving regular feedback to individuals, groups and the whole clinic cohort), weekly reflective journals using e-portfolios (where students post their reflections online for tutor input) and monthly rounds (where clinic students discuss issues arising on their and other cases).

The use of a reflective journal as portfolio is the main tool we use as a part of the on-going assessment process. The *portfolio* is a weekly individual report uploaded to the *Virtual Classroom* platform. The content of this report is, first, a description of the activities that the student has done that week in the clinic. Second, it must include a report by the team on a given scenario or on particular activities carried out in the clinic, and third, it should contain the student's own reflections on what he or she has learnt and what still needs to be done in that respect. It must include the problems and difficulties encountered in the clinic.

Additionally, each month we hold a "round" in which students talk and discuss their cases together, and discuss the issues and problems they have encountered, including, importantly, professional practice and ethical considerations.

For us, the use of general assessment rubrics is an effective tool for both students and professors. Students don't usually know what their performance levels are or how assessments are carried out. The students tend to be focused on what has to be written in a final exam. With the rubrics and samples provided, they should know what is expected of them in the activities that require different levels of performance and probably things that cannot be easily "measured" in an exam. Rubrics include grading criteria that indicate what a student must demonstrate to achieve a higher grade. These statements help to differentiate the levels of performance of a student. By making these criteria clear to students, it is hoped that students will aim for the highest levels of performance.

In the case of professors, we use rubrics for two reasons. First, to mitigate against unacceptable degrees of subjectivity in the assessment and as a tool that justifies and gives reasons for a mark, grade or comment. Second, it also makes transparent the assessment process and should be an indicator and reassurance of fair treatment amongst students.

Within the Valencia clinical programme, we work primarily on prison cases, public interest issues, migration matters and international human rights, helping individual clients and supporting NGOs who are active in the field. Our students learn through clinics as a part of a compulsory module on the law degree but also as part of the criminology course and the joint degree in law and business. We also have clinic students from the master's programme in human rights, democracy and international justice. We have volunteers too. This makes the clinic a very special place since students from different backgrounds, interests and levels share cases and it is literally (as noted above) a place for discussion and joint learning. Students who have already graduated are able to participate in the clinical programme as volunteers.

From its origin, the clinic project has required students to consider most if not all parts of the curriculum. Such is the variety of work that they encounter.

The clinic is open every working day from October to May. Students work in pairs or in teams, depending on the case, under the supervision of a tutor. Cases arrive by different means: the clinic has signed agreements with a number of NGOs for the general provision of legal advice and/or working on specific cases for their individual members. The clinic also gives advice to Valencia University students providing there is no conflict of interest with the university.

Cases are selected according to a series of criteria, such as the means of the client, the urgency of the case, whether or not we have capacity (students and supervisor), whether social justice issues are at stake or if there is something we can use educationally: a new methodology to work with the students, a new problem to discuss or an ethical issue to think together. If a case is accepted, it is assigned to a group of students under a tutor's supervision with a deadline for any action that is required.

There is a set of regulations, which lay down how the clinic must operate, including a protocol for students and templates for different parts of the process (research, reports, letters, etc.). We have a sophisticated record and archive system to enable us to act as a proper law office and meet professional standards.

8.5 Conclusion: challenges in sustainability

When we started the Legal Clinic Project at the University of Valencia some 10 years ago, as noted above, three things were clear: first, it was for us a new methodology for teaching and learning law; second, the clinic's work could be understood as part of a public university's social function; and third, we intended to improve access to justice. If we are being frank, we initially had little idea of how the clinic was going to operate and develop because most of us had not been practitioners. Our challenges were significant. We still face many, and as a conclusion, we would like to reflect on the idea of sustainability of clinics. What do we mean by 'sustain'?

If sustainability means 'to support, hold, bear up from below, bear the weight of, as a structure', it is clear that in these 10 years, five professors and one administrator have been sustaining the clinic, doing pro-bono work and inviting pro-bono lawyers to get involved in the process. Our success in showing our academic colleagues the power of clinics has perhaps been less impressive precisely because sustaining also means to undergo, experience or even suffer loss. In the main our academic careers have suffered and our research and publication rates have gone down, affecting institutional recognition and possibly promotion.

At one time we did consider closing the clinic, taking into consideration the effect it had on our academic position and the volume of work involved – but the community in the locality has sustained us: NGOs working with us, our grateful clients, former and current students and the wider, caring and sharing national and international clinic community.

CLE is a great way to learn and teach law that reaches aspects, issues and concerns other methodologies don't. However, when you lack recognition and support, you need to develop strategies to keep going (sustain) and in order not to give way. We have developed strategies to cope, such as making sure the clinic fitted in with institutional language, building strong alliances with academics and practising lawyers, having an advisory board, producing an annual report and feeding into local, national and international discussions. The result is a sustainable clinic albeit hard work but one that all who participate in (and some or watch from a distance) greatly appreciate.

Notes

1 B.S. Santos, *La universidad del Siglo XXI: Para una reforma democrática y emancipadora de la Universidad*, México, UNAM, Centro de Investigaciones Interdisciplinarias en Ciencias y Humanidades, Coordinación de Humanidades, 2005; and B.S. Santos, De la idea de

la Universidad a la Universidad de las ideas, in Santos, *De la mano de Alicia: lo social y lo político en la postmodernidad*, Siglo del hombre editores, Uniandes, 1998, 225–281.
2 M. Barberis, *Filosofia del Diritto*, Bologna, Il Mulino, 2000.
3 B.S. Santos, 2005, op cit., 62.
4 L. Gianformaggio, *Filosofia e critica del diritto*, Torino, G.Giappichelli editore, 1995.
5 L. Ferrajoli, *Derechos y garantías, la ley del más débil*, Madrid, Trotta, 1999.
6 See: A.J. Arnaud, *Los juristas frente a la sociedad (1975–1993)*, Doxa 15–16, 1995.
7 Quoted by Cooper, 2001. The quote is from a 1944 report that Lewellyn wrote for the AALS, published in 1945 in Comission on curriculum, Assn. Am. L. Sch., *The place of skills in legal education*, Columbian Law Review, 45, 1945, 345.
8 J. Frank, *Why not a clinical lawyer-school?*, University of Pennsylvania Law Review, 81, 1933, 907.
9 D. McQuoid-Mason and R. Palmer, *African Law clinicians' manual*, Open Society Foundations/University of Kwazulu-Natal/Institute for Professional Legal Training, 2013, 81.
10 D. Blázquez Martín and J. García Añón, Las Clínicas jurídicas españolas en el Movimiento Clínico Global, en F.S. Bloch (ed.), *Elmovimiento globalde clínicas jurídicas: Formando Juristasenla Justiciasocial*, TirantloBlanch, Valencia, 2013, 11–22.
11 See for example: F. González Morales, B. Londoño, M. Böhmer, J.M. Otero, C. Courtis, G. Gonzáles, J.C: Marín and G. Rodríguez, *Clínicas de Interés Público y Enseñanza del Derecho: Argentina, Chile, Colombia, México y Perú*, Cuadernos de análisis jurídico, Centro de Derechos Humanos, Universidad Diego Portales, 2003, 15.
12 See: www.uv.es/innodret, accessed 21 October 2016.
13 See: http://clinicas-juridicas.blogspot.com, accessed 21 October 2016.
14 See: www.encle.org, accessed 21 October 2016.
15 For a discussion of this important point see: J. García-Añón, *Laintegracióndelaeducaciónjurídicaclínicaenelproceso formativo de los juristas*, REDU: Revista de Docencia Universitaria, númeroextraordinario 'Formación de los licenciados en Derecho', 12 (3), 2014, 153.
16 J. Biggs, *Aligning teaching and assessing to course objectives: teaching and learning in higher education: new trends and innovations*, University of Aveiro, Aveiro, April 2003.
17 Discussed in more detail in: J. García-Añón, *How do we assess in clinical legal education? A 'reflection' about reflective learning*, International Journal of Clinical Legal Education, 23 (1), 2016, 50.

Chapter 9

Re-thinking legal education in Central and Eastern Europe

Michal Urban, Liubou Krasnitskaya and Katarzyna J. Kowalska

Despite all the rhetoric about the necessity and willingness to change the way we educate our future lawyers, the truth is that in number of places, reality changes slowly. Educational systems tend to be a window to our past rather than to our future. The curriculum in education – in its organization and content – tends to be entrenched. Change, after all, is challenging. It is true, in our region especially, that major reforms have been carried out in the past two and a half decades, but they have not proved to be radical enough. But after all, this is how progress is often made – in an evolutionary, rather than revolutionary, way.

Bearing this in mind, we would like to describe aspects of the Central and Eastern European legal education systems, highlighting similarities and making comparisons across the civil and common law worlds. We base our contribution on many years of practical experience with legal education in Belarus, the Czech Republic and Poland, but believe that the conclusions drawn in the chapter are, to a substantial extent, applicable in other countries of the region and possibly beyond.

When considering Central and Eastern legal (and other) education, we have identified the following aspects that stand out as issues and challenges in re-thinking how we educate our lawyers. Some of them may also be true elsewhere.

9.1 Resourcing

Funding education is like investing in the future economy of the country. Unfortunately, most, if not all, countries of Central and Eastern Europe are not in the top ten of places that invest significantly in education today to achieve long-term results in the future. The majority of countries that spend the most on education have the most-educated populations. As in previous years, the best-educated countries tend to spend the most on tertiary education as a percentage of gross domestic product (GDP). For example, the Belarusian government spends about 5 percent of the GDP on education at all levels. Tertiary education is even less supported by the state, receiving only 12 percent of all spending on education. By comparison, the Organization for Economic Cooperation and Development (OECD)'s Education at a Glance 2015 report estimates that public expenditure devoted to the tertiary education amounts to 26 percent of the education budget on average across OECD countries.

Education has never received substantial funding in the Czech Republic either. It is true for all the levels of education, including law. According to the Education at Glance OECD report, the Czech Republic spent just over 10 percent of its public spending on education, whereas the OECD average accounts for 13 percent. In terms of GDP, Czech Republic is investing just over 4 percent of its GDP in education, which is also well below the OECD average.[1] Each faculty of a university receives money not only for staff, but also for every student enrolled into the faculty. The Ministry of Education, Youth and Sports, however, does not distribute the money evenly. It has worked out coefficients which are supposed to reflect financial requirements of particular study disciplines. Whereas faculties preparing future doctors or dentists receive up to 3.5 more for one student than a law school, many other disciplines, such as natural sciences, mathematics and physics, enjoy coefficients between 2 and 3. Even human science disciplines such as translation and media studies are better funded per student than law schools.[2]

At the same time, the ministry in the Czech Republic has steadily increased the number of financed students in order to increase the total number of university graduates. Law schools have reacted economically and started to accept more students, resulting in more than 700 students enrolled, for example, in one year at the Faculty of Law of Charles University.[3] Limited funding and large number of students understandably do not easily lend themselves to interactive methods of teaching. Lectures for the whole study year and seminars for up to 40 students are still more or less the norm, at least for compulsory subjects.

Insufficient funding is reflected in relatively low salaries for academics, especially at the early stages of their career,[4] and this has also impacted on career choices. Since law schools are located in the larger Czech cities, where good lawyers have many other career opportunities, law teachers stay at law schools because they enjoy teaching and writing, because they perceive their role at a law school as a form of public service or because they do not want to or do not trust themselves to do well in competition in the legal market. In practice, relatively low salaries lead most law teachers to have at least part-time jobs outside of law schools – be it at another law school or university, in the public sector, with the judiciary or having their own legal practice.[5] In all cases it limits the amount of time and energy law teachers are able and willing to put into teaching and writing for their home law school. It does, on the other hand, enrich them with experience from outside of the law school, but the extent to which it limits their ability to concentrate on their academic duties is, we suggest, unhealthy for future development of law schools. Restricting opportunities to devote their time to other activities, as is the practice at some foreign institutions, however, would not work in Czech law schools, unless it was accompanied by a significant salary increase or system of accessible grant opportunities.

In Poland, the problem is similar. Data from 2006–2009, presented in the report conducted by Ernst & Young and Instytut Badań nad Gospodarką Rynkową, indicates that there were 102,000 university teachers of whom 98,000 were full-time.[6] This report states that "the essential barrier to the proper development of academic staff is a pay system based on low basic pay, the level of which, in the case of young academics, does not guarantee an acceptable standard of living".[7]

It has to be stressed that:

> The main source of financing of higher education in Poland is the public purse. Financing higher education from the state budget is done by determining the total amount of authorized expenditure, and this is then distributed among schools according to the Adopted Principles described in laws and regulations.[8]

Since 2008 there has been a significant increase in budgetary expenditure on science.[9] Last year the Minister of Science and Higher Education proposed a new strategy of changes based on three pillars: "Constitution for science, which will bring systemic changes in higher education, Innovations for the economy, which combine research and commercialization partnerships with business . . . (and a) . . . programme of corporate social responsibility of science".[10]

We wait to see what impact this has in real resourcing terms.

9.2 Access to legal education

Although Belarus is a country at the centre of Europe, pan-jurisdictional influence and innovation in education is rarely discussed, at least at the levels of power and influence. However, it would be incorrect to claim that the state doesn't guarantee accessible education. Quite the contrary, according to international data, Belarus is a country with a high percentage of people with a university degree[11] – more than in Italy, Hungary, Austria and the Czech Republic. Currently there are 54 higher education institutions in Belarus, and 9 of them are private, with almost all private institutions focusing, at least in part, on legal education. Similar to the situation elsewhere in Europe, legal studies are highly popular, with over a third of all university students studying economics, management or law.[12]

Strange as it may sound, there is no private law school in the Czech Republic.[13] Czech lawyers receive legal education[14] at one of four public universities, which are all free for the students. There have been serious attempts to introduce university fees, but they have never succeeded.[15] The debate over university fees remains controversial. Some believe it would spark student motivation to study and increase levels of expectation, leading to a better quality of legal education. Some, however, fear that it would sooner or later lead to social exclusion of certain students and turn education into goods sold on the open market – going to those with the money.

In Poland, in the academic year 2008/2009, there were 456 higher education institutions, of which 131 were public and 325 private.[16] Full-time study is free at public universities. In addition, students can choose part-time and evening classes, but both of these carry a fee. Social science, economy and law are extremely popular as subjects of study.[17]

9.3 The size of law school classes

As law is one of the most popular studies at higher education institutions, numbers of enrolled students tend to be high. As suggested above, this mitigates against innovative teaching methods. Lecturers are typically given to the groups of 50, and often considerably more, students, depending on the year of study. Many classes greatly exceed this number. Even 'small' group sessions (for example seminars) typically have upwards of 30 students. Undoubtedly the size of a group affects the nature of the learning and opportunities for innovation.

Czech law schools have for cultural and financial reasons large intakes and class sizes, certainly in comparison with their British or American counterparts. To teach cohorts of up to 800,[18] traditional teaching methods – lectures and large group seminars – are used.[19] These conditions understandably do not foster alternative teaching methods. Of course, as we know from the work of innovators such as Michael Sandel at Harvard Law School, even large audiences may – at least to a certain degree – be educated interactively. It is, however, a far more demanding task, requiring expertise, resources and good training in pedagogy.

9.4 Theoretical knowledge at a price

Although the long-term plan of the Prague law school talks about the unity of "knowledge, skills and values" that needs to be developed through an effective combination of teaching methods and it is still legal knowledge that stands at the core of what Czech law schools really demand their students to learn.[20] Alternative teaching methods are allowed and sometimes feature in optional and voluntary activities, such as moot courts, role-play and externships, but the majority of the compulsory subjects, which form up to 80 percent of what law students need to pass in order to graduate, end with exams focused mainly on knowledge. Students are sometimes still required to learn key paragraphs of the law by heart and be able to quote them at an oral exam. For some exams, they are provided with the relevant regulations but in most situations the text of the law remains firmly in the hands of the teacher or examiner.[21]

Alternative assessment methods (including portfolios, writing essays, analysing cases, presentations, or awarding credit for good work at seminars) are being used, and in this area over the last decade there has been significant progress.

But the mainstream diet of lectures and exams for compulsory subjects changes very slowly, being deeply connected with the education and pedagogical views of the teachers. Even the deans have limited powers in this area; they may open discussions and provide domestic and foreign examples of best practices, but their true ability to push through changes against the will of the teachers is constrained, unless they want to run the risk of being dictatorial and paternalistic.[22] Paradoxically, the emphasis on knowledge of concrete provisions survived even the so-called "legislative cyclone", which was a governmental reaction to the slow implementation of EU legislation in the lead up to and on becoming an EU member. The Czech parliament has passed a large number of statutes since 2000 – in some years, more than twice as many laws were created than on an annual basis before 2000.[23] This surely makes it even more important to concentrate on legal values and principles rather than particular pieces of legal knowledge, which may change before the graduate leaves the law school or not too much later. This is well illustrated by the adoption of new criminal and civil codes, which both came into existence around 2010.[24] In an ever-complex world, it is simply unrealistic to know all of the law. A lawyer, of course, must know the basics and be able to recognise issues, research them and come to credible and sustainable conclusions.

By way of partial contrast in Poland there has been progress in terms of the development of the curriculum. The implementation of the National Qualifications Framework re-focused attention from education based on topics to education based on "learning outcomes". These set out, across the education sector, including in law, what a student is expected to achieve on graduation. The move to an outcomes-focused model using language and structures found elsewhere across the EU allows for developments that are not limited simply by history and tradition.[25] This is a positive building block for future development.

9.5 Academics are not necessarily good teachers

Although doctoral studies may serve to prepare someone to gain employment in a university, they rarely involve a study (or practice) of teaching methodologies. In the curriculum for doctoral studies for lawyers in Belarus, there is a course titled "Pedagogy and psychology in higher education" which looks at the general theoretical knowledge around pedagogy, but this course does not provide doctoral students with teaching skills or any real understanding of student-centred learning. Consequently, we have qualified academics with little or no teaching skill.

To become a law teacher in the Czech Republic, a candidate needs to fulfil required criteria, which include a completed master's in law programme, usually an agreed topic for a PhD and evidence of publication activity. Pedagogic experience is welcomed, though mostly not insisted upon or tested. The ability to teach is therefore low on the priority list. It is assumed that a candidate is able to teach based on his or her other attributes and qualifications.

Since most of the Czech law teachers start their careers close to completing their PhD studies (or even before that), it would not be fair to expect them to be teaching stars at the time of their selection, especially when they have received little or no prior pedagogic guidance. Because many such students are required to teach during their studies, they are offered basic pedagogic training at some law schools, although even these courses have been introduced only recently.[26] Thanks to EU or other grants, some new teachers do take up such courses on a voluntary basis, which gives the opportunity for the keen, but even this financial support fails to motivate most, thus having limited impact on the general level of teaching standards at law schools.[27]

In Poland teaching quality is supposedly monitored through periodic evaluation. The legal bases, the Act of Law on Higher Education, as well as the statutes and rules of individual universities, lay down the relevant rules. Ability to teach is tested e.g. by the following questions (taken from an evaluation forms): "Does the teacher use measures to facilitate the understanding of program content?" or "Was the content of the course communicated clearly and accessibly?"

Evaluation is conducted by the entity indicated in the statutes of the university, at least once every four years or at the request of the head of the organizational unit in which the academic teacher is employed. Evaluation criteria exist, and the process may include the use of experts from outside of the university and the assessment feedback from students at the end of each cycle of classes. Despite the apparent check on teaching quality, there is at best considerable inconsistency in the evaluation process and at worst a failure to take the purpose seriously. There is also little by way of a strategy to support the development of teaching best practice.

9.6 The communist legacy

The countries we are discussing here share many things in common, including periods when they were either part of the Soviet Union or members of the Soviet Bloc. Belarus, for example, inherited a heavily management-oriented approach to education from Soviet days. According to the Code on Education in Belarus, governance in higher education is the responsibility of various people, from the President to national and local public authorities; for example, the Council of Ministers defines the general rules of the annual centralised enrolment test, the President, by decree, formulates the criteria of acceptance for higher education institutions. The coordination and control of the system of education is delegated to the Ministry of Education. However, some actions of the Belarusian public authorities do not fit comfortably with international standards and expectations. In 1973 Belarus ratified the International Covenant on Economic, Social and Cultural Rights which defines the human right to education (art.13). Guidance on the article states that the enjoyment of academic freedom requires the autonomy of institutions of higher education. Autonomy is that degree of self-governance necessary for effective decision-making by higher education institutions in relation to their academic work, standards, management and related activities.[28] Belarus is regularly criticised by international experts on education for a lack of autonomy in higher education institutions. It was one of the reasons the application of Belarus to join the Bologna Process in 2011 was rejected.

For example, the Ministry of Education designs and approves the standards for quality education and model curricula and programmes. A model curriculum on, for example, jurisprudence defines the duration of period of study, its content and the academic schedule and serves as the template for all types of higher education institutions regardless of its form of ownership, status and affiliation. These models are detailed documents which are comprised of a list of mandatory subjects, stating the number of study hours, how many field placement law students must complete along with learning outcomes and required forms of assessment.

Such regulations apply, as a rule, for 5 years. After that they are revised if required. Higher education institutions annually compose their own programmes of legal subjects based on the templates approved by the Ministry of Education. Universities have some discretion in relation to one-third of the entire programme (i.e., they can modify only optional subjects but must follow the Ministry template for the majority of the course content). Universities also have some discretion over the content of postgraduate studies.

A model and inflexible curriculum does little to motivate either students or teachers. Typically the same lectures are presented every year unless legal provisions have been changed. Such standardisation impacts on students' creativity and initiative to learn the material beyond the framework. What is more surprising is that to prepare law students for examinations, there is a list of questions set and approved by the members of the faculty. In the exam, the law students are assessed by being asked to answer 2 to 3 questions from the list. If a teacher asks a question which is not included in the list, the students often face difficulty in answering because students memorise the answers to the exam questions. Their knowledge is therefore very limited and decontextualised.

It is interesting to compare a Belarusian policy with the Standards and Guidelines for Quality Assurance in the European Higher Education Area (EHEA)[29] and 2015–2016 Standards and Rules of Procedure for Approval of Law Schools[30] in the USA. Standard 1.2 of EHEA provides that institutions should have processes for the approval of their programmes which should be designed so that they meet the objectives set for them, including the intended learning outcomes. There is no mandatory instruction, however, on what and how law shall be taught.

The American Standards prescribe in general terms what an accredited programme of legal education shall consist of, but they do not define, in whole or part, the actual content of the programme, nor recommend particular assessment methods. What they do state is that to be accredited as a law school in the USA, an institution must provide students with a chance to encounter work-based learning either through placement (externships), pro bono opportunities or legal clinics. Of course, in the USA, a law graduate must pass the applicable bar exam for the state he or she intends to practice in. These are not set or administered by the law school.

The content of a set of new legal study programmes needs to be agreed in the Czech Republic by the Accreditation Commission, an independent organ established by the Higher Education Act of 1998. The standards set out minimum requirements for study programmes, but within these boundaries, law schools are free to design their content and form of law programmes. This, for example, has allowed Olomouc Law School to get accredited with a more skills- and values- based curriculum.

In the field of higher education in Poland, after 1989, changes were based on provisions of the Law on Higher Education Act 2005 (Dz. U. of 2005 No. 164, item. 1365). These apply to both public and private law schools. In addition, there are rules laid down in the National Qualifications Framework for Higher Education – including, importantly, the need for learning outcomes for all programmes and modules. Whilst law schools do have some discretion on form and content of their programmes the core is determined centrally.

The heavy prescription of legal education in terms of form and content, typically found in civil law countries, including in Central and Eastern Europe, mitigate against creativity and possibly open-mindedness to new ideas, particularly in higher education. It is always easy to blame the past for everything. It is worth remembering that many older academics, practitioners and members of the judiciary are the product of Soviet times. That said, more than 25 years now separate us from the Communist era. Membership of the EU has opened up particular opportunities in educational terms and nowhere more so than in law schools. The admittedly slow, but we suggest steady, introduction of alternative teaching methods and changes to law school curricula is starting to make its presence felt.

9.7 The need for work-based experience

Many students seek work-based experience out of choice or necessity. There have, however, been moves across the continent to encourage or even require the acquisition of practical experience.

One of the common requirements in law schools in Belarus is now a mandatory field placement during the law degree. The model curriculum for jurisprudence and commercial and international law includes 3 field placements starting in the second year of legal studies. The first and second placements last a month and are to be completed by the end of the second and third academic year accordingly. During this time students observe professionals at work, gain practical skills and undertake simple tasks under the supervision of a qualified lawyer. The placements may be in law firms, industry, prosecutors' offices, with Bar Associations or with government bodies and the courts. Few law schools in Belarus, however, count time spent in a law clinic as a field placement. In most law schools, clinics are voluntary, extra-curricular, activity. Within the last and fifth year of studies, law students work on their final thesis and participate in a 2-month field placement. Those students who have started paid employment during their studies usually organise their placement in their workplace.

Czech law schools are also becoming far more practical. Unlike 10 or even 15 years ago, when there were very few externships offered to students, currently placements are the norm rather than the exception. Czech law schools, however, differ in their approach to such a practical dimension of study. Some see it as a compulsory element every student should go through but leave it up to students to find the placements (for example Brno Law School), whilst others offer a variety of externships at various public and private law institutions, but leave the decision to take part at a placement with the student (for example Prague Law School). There are also differences in the amount of supervision students receive whilst on placement from faculty members, ranging from almost none to regular contact and feedback. Supervision from the faculty generally increases the quality of the externship and learning outcomes of students, but may, of course, become very time-consuming.

In addition to the above, in Belarus every intending lawyer, in whatever capacity, needs to serve a post-graduation apprenticeship (internship). The periods stipulated depend on the career destination but varies from 3 to 12 months. This mandatory work-based experience stems from Soviet times when all graduates started their careers where the state commission dictated – in accordance with perceived need at the time. With limitations on internship opportunities and reluctance on the part of aspirant lawyers to work anywhere other than the main urban centres, increasing numbers of Belarus graduates are now looking for work opportunities abroad.

In the Czech Republic, there is also the need to complete a substantial period of work-based, post-graduation, pre-qualification experience. During three years of professional training after the graduation, aspirant lawyers have to deal with significant level of uncertainty of future employment prospects, since they are not guaranteed a job even after graduating and passing the bar exam. Wages are also relatively low even if work is found.[31] That was one of the reasons why the current Minister of Justice received strong criticism after introducing a proposal to expand the training period of future attorneys-in-law from three to five years. Even though this proposal was not passed, there still remains at least three years between the graduation and the time a judge, state prosecutor or an attorney-in-law is fully qualified to perform his or her job.

The situation in Poland is somewhat different. The National School of Judiciary and Public Prosecution, which is located in Krakow, is the base for the training of judges and prosecutors. The course, interestingly (as compared with the mode of delivery of undergraduate law classes), is an example of the extensive use of simulated cases, mock trials and other interactive study methods. Due to recent legislative changes (Dz. U. 2016, poz. 150) judicial and prosecutors trainings now lasts 36 months.[32]

Those intending to practice, for example, as an attorney or legal counsel must take a training course which is organised and run by the regional bar association and includes an internship. Before entering training, the candidate has to pass a state bar exam. Recruitment for this programme takes place once a year and is highly competitive.

From the experience in all three discussed countries, we can see that on the one hand, work-based experience is increasingly seen as a necessity at both the academic stage and in post-graduate vocational training. Placements and internships familiarise students with the realities of the law and the work of judges, prosecutors, public defenders and private practitioners. The internships aim at developing or even polishing the practical skills of lawyers and deepening understanding and ability to apply the law in practice.

9.8 The EU/European influence on legal education

In 2003, Russia signed the Bologna Declaration (1999), and Ukraine signed it in 2005. Until May 2015 Belarus remained the only country in the Eastern Europe which didn't participate in the Bologna Process.[33] Committing itself to Bologna is clearly an important development and will bring benefit to whoever it may concern – the government, the educational system or the individual students and citizens of Belarus.

The harmonisation of legal studies requires measures which can attract foreign students, create possibilities for international academic exchanges and promote higher education on the international stage. As suggested above, especially given the lack of autonomy in universities in Belarus, its law schools are not ready to compete on equal terms with law schools in Poland, the Czech Republic or indeed, other European countries.

The percentage of foreign citizens studying in Belarus is currently just 4 percent regardless of the specialisation.[34] All of them study in the Russian or Belarusian language and have an annual preparatory language course prior to the first academic year. There is no law school in Belarus where legal subjects are taught in English. International simulations like moot court or mock trial are not popular due to a lack of fluency on the part of staff and students in foreign languages. Case studies based on Belarusian legislation are rare and role-play and other simulations only very occasional events in law schools. Faculty staff often considers such as extra-curricular activity and as a burden, and many are not eager to exceed their workload beyond the normal day. Lectures and presentations by invited professors from non-Russian-speaking countries are also unusual events.

This situation affects both the image of the country in the international context and the competence of law students to work in the international environment or in a multilingual group. Frequently innovation and new ideas are only developed through collaboration and networking. Although law students are interested in participation in the international exchanges and competitions, conditions are imposed by the government and related institutions. According to the database, from 2010 to 2015 there were 670 scholarships within Erasmus Mundus for Belarusians: 224 undergraduate students, 173 master's students, 127 PhD students, 54 researchers and 92 faculty staff.[35] These numbers are a drop in the ocean in comparison with the total number of students and teachers in Belarus.[36] How many of them study law it is not known. There is clearly much catching up to do, and re-thinking legal education in Belarus is going to take time.

By contrast the Czech Republic and Poland have engaged much more fully with European initiatives, a fact reflected in recent changes to the law curriculum.

9.9 Legal writing and scholarship

The skill of legal writing is an essential characteristic of a successful lawyer. Lawyers must, in order to do their job properly, have to know how to write accurately and effectively to meet the demands of the particular situation – be it a client letter, a court document or a commercial agreement.

Given the importance of this task, do law students learn to draft legal documents, and if so, how and when? Of course they may develop these skills during their studies and later during their working lives. It may come as no surprise for the reader to learn that too little attention is paid to the skills of legal writing in the law schools of Central and Eastern Europe. These skills are typically not part of the compulsory curriculum and are mostly practised, where they do exist, in optional courses.

The situation is further complicated by the fact that in Czech law schools, assessment has traditionally been done by oral examination. The lawyer – it is still believed – should especially be able to speak well, structure their speeches, formulate their thoughts and present their arguments coherently in spoken form. Although many exams are now preceded by written tests or case analyses, more than one half of all exams in the Czech Republic are by oral examination. Written parts either simply test basic knowledge or require the explanation of the content of a basic legal document. Students are generally not taught to write essays (i.e., argumentative and persuasive texts which test their legal thinking and their ability to formulate concise arguments in words). They are, however, expected to finish their degree programme with a thesis, for which they receive only partial preparation during seminars towards the end of their studies. Although the number of written assignments has increased over the years, it is still not the norm that every student has to annually undertake, say, an essay, for which they receive detailed feedback. Students may choose elective courses, which may be concerned with the substance of or otherwise require legal drafting skills, but the capacity of these courses is not sufficient to provide such instruction for every law school student.

Like at Czech law schools, Belarusian students are mostly assessed orally. Students have to present a structured and logical justification on given topics. Unfortunately, analytic and argumentation skills are less evident than memory recall, because the list of examination questions is always available to students before exams, and they prepare a script based on that. Nevertheless, each student must submit an annual thesis. Students are free to select the topic and subject. An individual supervisor is assigned to each student, and he or she assesses the paper at the end of the year. The final thesis is often the cumulative result of the annual papers together with an analysis of relevant judicial decisions and recommendations on how the law might be improved.

In Poland things are similar. Exams are generally both written and oral. A master's dissertation is written and has to be "defended" orally. Entrance exams for training to become an attorney, judge or prosecutor are in writing.

9.10 Legal clinics as a part of curriculum

The final section of this chapter looks at one particular form of interactive learning – the law clinic. If we, and as many in this book have also asserted, believe that any consideration of improving legal education lies in experiential learning then it is clear from the wealth of published work and the international prevalence of legal clinics, that this form of learning by doing has much to commend it. The law clinic is a powerful example of experiential learning and one that addresses many of the issues discussed above.

Although the value and significance of clinical legal education in the education of lawyers is commonly acknowledged on the international stage, legal clinics in Belarus still operate as extra-curricular activity. The reasons for this are many and varied – limited resources, prescriptive curricula, cultural inertia, lack of motivation and discomfort with innovation.

Legal clinics are, however, slowly finding their way into Czech law schools and have been prevalent in Poland for many years. In the Czech Republic, no law school has yet embraced clinics to such an extent that they are compulsory for every student, but they are forming an important addition to the learning diet. They take the form of simulations, externships, legal literacy projects (*Street Law*) as well as live-client advice. Where part of the curriculum, they are accredited and taught by the staff of the law schools. In the last 10 years, there has been a steady rise in the number of clinics in the Czech Republic, and now it is the exception rather than the rule not to have a clinic. Although there are sceptics, the enthusiasm that clinics engender amongst participating staff and students is clear indeed.

The situation in Poland is very different. Clinics have been part of the fabric now for many years, dating back to the fall of the Communist regime and the injection of financial and human resource-backing from the USA and other sympathetic countries. There is now a formal clinic network - the Polish Legal Clinics Foundation - which not only promotes and supports clinics but sets standards and provides limited grant funding. There are at least 25 clinics supported by this network.[37] Depending on the decision made by individual law schools, law clinics are optional or mandatory. Either way they carry academic credit.

9.11 Conclusions

Each country discussed here has chosen its own way of educating future lawyers. There are nevertheless common features that they share. To re-think legal education in Central and Eastern Europe, it is important to place more emphasis on legal skills and values and less on legal knowledge, reduce size of law school classes and of state control and, overall, increase funding. The quality and quantity of training for law teachers needs to be improved, and emphasis should be placed on alternative teaching methods, including legal clinics. Luckily, there are many pieces of good practice to find inspiration in. Many are even described in this book.

Notes

1 The World Bank, *Government expenditure on education, total (% of GDP)*, 2016, available at: http://data.worldbank.org/indicator/SE.XPD.TOTL.GD.ZS?view=map, accessed 23 October 2016.
2 Ministry of Education, Youth and Sports, *The table of with coefficients*, available at: www.msmt.cz/file/25115/download/, accessed 23 October 2016.
3 Faculty of Law, Charles University, *Annual Report 2010*, available at: www.prf.cuni.cz/dokumenty-download/1404044556/, accessed 23 October 2016. Since then, the amount of accepted students at Prague Law School started to drop slightly, reaching the level of cca 550 in 2016.
4 The differences in salaries in the private and public sector are smaller at the beginning of a teaching career but tend to rather quickly increase in senior positions reaching a point that is comparable with a partner of a private law firm. See T. Richter, *He who pays the piper: the conflicts involved in combining careers in legal academia and legal practice*, Právník, 2013, 127.
5 In 2012, there were about 24 percent of Czech law school teachers who were members of the Czech Bar Association. See T. Richter, *He who pays the piper: the conflicts involved in combining careers in legal academia and legal practice*, Právník, 2013, 128.
6 Ernst and Young/Instytut Badań nad Gospodarką Rynkową, *Diagnoza stanu szkolnictwa wyższego w Polsce (Diagnosis of the condition of higher eduaction in Poland)*, 2009, 4, available at: www.nauka.gov.pl/g2/oryginal/2013_05/fa5b19e372e1bed45db817b8380c8468.pdf, accessed 23 October 2016.
7 Ernst and Young/Instytut Badań nad Gospodarką Rynkową, *Diagnoza stanu szkolnictwa wyższego w Polsce (Diagnosis of the condition of higher eduaction in Poland)*, 2009, 7, available at: www.nauka.gov.pl/g2/oryginal/2013_05/fa5b19e372e1bed45db817b8380c8468.pdf, accessed 23 October 2016.
8 Ernst and Young/Instytut Badań nad Gospodarką Rynkową, *Strategia rozwoju szkolnictwa wyższego w Polsce do 2020 roku – drugi wariant (Strategy for the development of higher education in Poland by 2020 – the second variant)*, 2010, 23, available at: www.nauka.gov.pl/g2/oryginal/2013_05/59579f9e6efaec82014d6d5be081ca23.pdf, accessed 23 October 2016.
9 The National Research Programme Assumptions Science and Technology and Innovation Policy (Annex to resolution No. 164/2011 of the Council of Ministers dated

16 August 2011, 4, available at: www.ncbr.gov.pl/gfx/ncbir/pl/defaultopisy/23/1/1/ krajowy_program_badan.pdf, accessed 23 October 2016.

10 Ministry of Science and Higher Education, Republic of Poland, *Nowa strategia dla nauki i szkolnictwa wyższego*, 2016, available at: www.nauka.gov.pl/aktualnosci-ministerstwo/ nowa-strategia-dla-nauki-i-szkolnictwa-wyzszego.html, accessed 23 October 2016.

11 The Organization for Economic Cooperation and Development calculates annually the proportion of people between the ages of 25 to 64 with a university degree (i.e., tertiary education) in the EU and a few Non-EU nations. While in the developed countries, the average percentage of adults with tertiary education experience is about 33 percent, Belarusian graduates form 25 percent of population at the age of 20–64 according to the National Statistics data from 2014. See more OECD, *Education in a glance 2014*, Table A1.4a, available at: https://data.oecd.org/, accessed 7 February 2016.

12 National Statistical Committee of the Republic of Belarus, *Annual statistics data on education in Belarus*, Minsk, 2015, 143.

13 It is hard to tell exactly why. The formal reason is that no applicant has ever received accreditation by the Accreditation Commission. A private law school would need to gather a large group of legal experts willing to teach at the law school and provide the evidence of "*appropriate staff, financial, material, technical and information support*" for the study programme (Section 79 subsection 1c of the Act No. 11/1998, the Higher Education Act.) Unofficial reasons include a presumption that a population of 10 million in the Czech Republic does not need another law school, since the needs of legal market are satisfied with the existing four public law schools, and that there are not enough experts to guarantee high-quality legal education at another law school. The last and one of the best-prepared attempts to accredit a private law school in the Czech Republic took place in 2012. The application was declined with the explanation that the applicant had insufficient scientific activity in the legal area, there were too few professors working in the institution and other members of the new law school had their working and scientific activities primarily at other institutions, which cast, according to the Accreditation Commission, doubt on their willingness to transfer their activities to the new institution. See Accreditation Commission, Minutes no 1–12 from the session of the Accreditation Commission. Available at: www.akreditacnikomise.cz//attachments/ article/339/zapis_ak_01_2012.pdf, accessed 23 October 2016. It appears rational for the future accreditation of a 5-year master law degree to first have a bachelor law degree and possibly a following master's degree, which would demonstrate financial, scientific and pedagogic abilities of the institution, as well as the amount of research produced by the institution. Consequently, there are only private bachelor degrees, which are, however, not regarded as full legal education by the Czech Bar Association or the Ministry of Justice since they do not allow its holders to proceed their career in judiciary or as an attorney-in-law. According to respondents of one study, more than 80 percent of all master's degree law school graduates continue in the traditional legal professions in the judiciary, the state prosecutor's office, as notaries, in academia or as advocates. In this chapter, we therefore write about these master's programmes, unless stated otherwise. See Faculty of Law, Masaryk University, *Research Report. Knowledge and skills of law school graduates in the Czech Republic*, Brno, 2015.

14 Several public as well as private universities offer bachelor law degrees. The same applies to branches of Slovak private universities located in the Czech Republic, although their main focus should be on Slovak, not Czech law.

15 The last serious attempt took place in 2010 and provoked large student protests.

16 Ernst and Young/Instytut Badań nad Gospodarką Rynkową, *Diagnoza stanu szkolnictwa wyższego w Polsce (Diagnosis of the condition of higher eduaction in Poland)*, 2009, 27, available at: www.nauka.gov.pl/g2/oryginal/2013_05/fa5b19e372e1bed45db817b8380c8468. pdf, accessed 23 October 2016.

17 Ernst and Young/Instytut Badań nad Gospodarką Rynkową, *Diagnoza stanu szkolnictwa wyższego w Polsce (Diagnosis of the condition of higher eduaction in Poland)*, 2009, 78, available at: www.nauka.gov.pl/g2/oryginal/2013_05/fa5b19e372e1bed45db817b8380c8468.pdf, accessed 23 October 2016.
18 Some school years cohorts were as large as that in between 2003–2010 at Prague law school.
19 Apart from two largest law schools in Prague and Brno, there are also two smaller law schools in Olomouc and Pilsen, which accept no more than 300 students every year. Our focus will be primarily on the two large law schools, which produce about two-thirds of all law graduates in the Czech Republic.
20 Prague Law School, *Long-term plan of the Prague Law School for the period 2011–2015*, available at: www.prf.cuni.cz/dokumenty-download/1404044562, accessed 23 October 2016.
21 A survey among law school graduates confirmed that relatively recent law school graduates (42 percent finished their studies before 2008) believe law schools are able to teach them to orient themselves in law but they (the students) are unnecessarily forced to know the wording of selected legal acts. They lack soft (and other more overtly lawyering skills) skills, such as public presentation, negotiation, legal writing, ability to analyse and teamwork. See Faculty of Law, Masaryk University, *Research report: knowledge and skills of law school graduates in the Czech Republic*, Brno, 2015, 14, 33–34.
22 The most progressive in this regard is the Olomouc law school. It benefits from its relatively small size (cca 250 law students in one year).
23 It includes law published in the Collection of Laws and international treaties published in the Collection of International Treaties.
24 Act No. 40/2009 Coll, Criminal code, effective since 1 January 2010, and new Civil Code (Act No. 89/2012 Coll.) entered into force on 1 January 2014.
25 E. Chmielecka, Z. Marciniak and A. Kraśniewski, *National qualifications framework for Polish higher education system*, Warsaw, 2010, 1 in: *Program autonomy of higher schools: Qualifications framework for higher education*, Ministry of Science and Higher Education.
26 At the Prague law school, they receive a course (*circa* 12 hours) in pedagogy and didactic of law teachings and presentation skills. In Brno, they are offered similar provisions. Olomouc law school introduced didactic courses for PhD students in 2016.
27 At the Prague law school, these activities are initiated and coordinated by the Interdisciplinary Centre for the Development of Lawyering Skills.
28 UN Committee on Economic, Social and Cultural Rights, *General comment 13: the right to education (Art. 13 of the Covenant)*, 8 December 1999, E/C.12/1999/10.
29 The standards were adopted by the ministers responsible for higher education in May 2015, Brussels, Belgium.
30 Programme of legal education – Chapter 3, [w:] ABA Standards and Rules of Procedure for Approval of Law Schools, ABA Book Publishing, 2015, 15–26.
31 An average wage in the Czech Republic in autumn 2015 was around 27,000 CZK and university graduates were earning on average 36,000 CZK. Trainee lawyers were receiving around 20,000 CZK, with the exception of trainee lawyers in large law firms, which pushed the average to 27,000 CZK for all trainee lawyers. See Právní prostor, *Survey Wages of Trainee Lawyers Fundamentally Differ*, available at: www.pravniprostor.cz/clanky/ostatni-pravo/mzdy-advokatnich-koncipientu-se-zasadne-lisi, accessed 23 October 2016 and *Ministry of Labour and Social Affairs*, available at: www.mpsv.cz/ISPVcharavypis.php, accessed 23 October 2016.
32 *National School of Judiciary and Public Prosecution*, available at: www.kssip.gov.pl/angielski, accessed 23 October 2016.
33 The first application of Belarus to join the Bologna process in 2011 was rejected. The main reason was a lack of respect of the principles and values of the Bologna Process,

such as academic freedom, institutional autonomy and student participation in the governance of universities. Other social and political facts in the country, such as harsh dispersion of the peace demonstration after the President's election, the growing sanction, and the EU ambassadors leaving Belarus in protest, didn't help support Belarus's application to join the 47-nation club.

34 National Statistical Committee of the Republic of Belarus, *Annual statistics data on education in Belarus,* Minsk, 2015, 160.

35 *Belarusian higher education institutions will participate in 4 new projects within the programme Erasmus+*, BELTA – Belarusian Telegraph Agency, News on Society, 5 October 2015. Available at: www.belta.by/society/view/belorusskie-vuzy-budut-uchastvovat-v-4-novyh-proektah-po-rezultatam-konkursa-programmy-erasmus-165266–2015/, accessed 6 March 2016.

36 National Statistical Committee of the Republic of Belarus, *Annual statistics data on education in Belarus,* Minsk, 2015, 137. The total number of students of the I and II level of education is over 370,000, excluding PhD students and faculty staff.

37 Fundacja Uniwersyteckich Poradni Prawnych, available at: www.fupp.org.pl, accessed 23 October 2016.

Chapter 10

The same but different

What can we learn from Canadian attitudes to legal education?

Sue Prince

10.1 Introduction

The impact of a worldwide recession, legal aid cuts, globalisation, technology and financial efficiencies have led to a fundamental transformation in the way the legal profession provides legal services. Commentators such as Richard Susskind predict that these differences will only increase as we move into a future where the only certainty is on-going adjustment and change.[1] In addition, higher education bodies have had to come to terms with marketisation and the high cost of providing education within a more aggressive and competitive worldwide arena. Such changes have caused the regulators to reflect upon the best way of providing legal education in such a challenging environment to best suit clients, lawyers and the growing numbers of students all too eager to embark on legal studies.[2] One big issue is access. These more recent consultations are a pragmatic response to the changing situation and the 2013 Legal Education Training Review (LETR) was an earlier joint response to this ambiguous future.[3]

In Canada, the Canadian Bar Association (CBA) has recently looked across the Atlantic at the developments in the UK and seen changes in business structures introduced through the Legal Services Act 2007 and are keen to consider the application of these to their own practices. In *The Legal Futures Initiative*,[4] (2014) the CBA considers how legal services in a future Canada will be delivered. In Canada, several new law schools have recently opened, and a pioneering post-law degree programme has been validated which, since September 2013, delivers a Legal Practice Program (LPP), combining vocational teaching with practice, in a bid to reduce the pressure on apprenticeships in large law firms.

Canada offers a useful comparator for English legal education. It is predominantly a common law system and being a member of the Commonwealth, much of the way in which the law is established is based upon the 'English' model. Yet there are strong influences from the USA, with which Canada does most of its business, and much of legal education looks south of the Canadian border. There are, of course, strong French connections too in parts the East of the country. Like their American counterparts, legal education is currently provided as a postgraduate programme. The difference then is that traditionally aspirant lawyers in Canada undertake an apprenticeship (articles) within the province in which they have studied. The cost to the students is high, and the cost to the profession of supplying articling and training is also expensive to undertake. Canada is therefore creating its own vision of what a future legal system will look like and how legal education should respond.

Canada is historically a pioneering state with all the legacy that that brings, and there is much to be learnt from their recent reflections and developments here. Can a country that grew from the English legal model (but has civil law ties) offer any suggestions for a future direction for legal education in the rest of the common and civil law worlds?

10.2 The background

The impact of global as well as local economic changes, austerity and recession has transformed the Canadian commercial legal market and the profession. Top Canadian firm Heenan Blaikie, which was founded in the 1970s, collapsed sensationally in 2014, and its demise was taken as a key indication of the significance of a shifting legal marketplace as well demonstrating the tough environment in which law firms now operate.[5] Troubling times have opened the door over the last few years for international US and UK enterprises to merge with, or take over, prominent Canadian firms.[6] Changes at the top of the profession are coupled, at the other extreme, with difficulties for self-represented litigants and a lack of legal aid impacting more generally on the public – reducing access to justice.[7] The indications are that legal service provision in Canada is going to be radically different in the future, with certain consequences for legal education.

Canadian legal education traditionally tends to follow the Langdellian case-method. As seen above, law is studied at postgraduate level using an English 'liberal law' approach.[8] Case-method teaching places emphasis upon the students' analysis of judicial reasoning through Socratic questioning rather than the development of a wider range of graduate skills and attributes. Yet, Canadian law schools are increasingly looking critically at their educational provision to see whether it is suitable training for the 21st-century lawyer.[9] This is in part due also to the decline in law student numbers and the corresponding lack of lawyer employment, which the New York Times has described as a 'crisis in legal education'.[10]

There are 23 law schools across Canada which offer what is described as a 'professional degree': equivalent to a combination of the qualifying law degree (QLD) and the Legal Practice Course (LPC) in England and Wales. This is a low number of providers given the high numbers of students wishing to study law. Law programmes are offered in either common law, which is the system in place in all of the Canadian provinces other than Quebec. The Barreau du

Quebec regulates the practice of law in that province which mainly operates under a civil law system for private law; criminal law matters and public law and constitutional issues fall under the common law of the federal state.[11] Quebec is therefore distinctive in having a mixed jurisdiction. There are only six law schools that offer civil law programmes, and the law schools in Quebec teach both the civil and common law processes, a 'transystemic' method,[12] so that students who have studied in the province have an advantage when it comes to employment in Québécois law firms. Canada therefore does not operate a uniform system.

Across Canada, the 14 provinces and territories each regulate their own law firms and sole practitioners. The Federation of the Law Societies of Canada (the Federation) has imposed standards for the learning of law through a 'National Requirement' statement and all approved programmes are reviewed annually to ensure that the standard is met.[13] The power to award the law degree is therefore held by the institution and the province, but the regulation of the professional-facing bar programme and, therefore, to become a Canadian lawyer, is governed by the Federation. In essence, a Canadian law degree is a three-year postgraduate taught programme with a greater emphasis on producing 'practice-ready' lawyers: heavily built around analytical legal content, but with additional elements involving legal skills and professional responsibility. It therefore differs from most English law degrees in that it pursues a strong emphasis on the practice and ethics of law through the learning and application of cases as well as limited skills development.[14] As a postgraduate programme, most students are looking to a specific vocation rather than a programme that is akin to a general academic or liberal law degree.[15] In many other parts of the common law world, the division between the so-called 'academic' stage of undergraduate study and a practice-focused graduate vocational course still persists.

In the past Canadian law schools offered a LLB degree, but since the early 2000s most now offer a JD, which is the common designation used in the USA. This title indicates the graduate nature of the programme and signifies that in some respects the degree programme mirrors US education provision rather than any other common law system.[16] Similarly, Canadian law schools require students to pass the LSAT (Law Schools Admission Test) prior to entry. This exam tests ability to analyse, think critically and reason. It has a reputation for being difficult and establishes a high bar for legal study in Canada and reinforces a positive reputation for law schools.

The Canadian degree is measured through competencies rather than through the teaching of specific core modules as in most common and civil law jurisdictions. Such is the tie now between the two neighbours that when changes are made to legal education in the US these tend to be incorporated by Canadian law schools. An example of this is the growth in the integration of pro bono or experiential modules.[17] It is common for Canadian law students to look to the US bar as a pathway to qualification.[18] For this reason, although Canadian law has its origins and traditions in the common law system of England and Wales, geographical attachment to the US means that Canada's legal education provision is admired as well as dominated by the US perspective.

Once a student has graduated with a JD, the most usual and traditional way of becoming a lawyer in Canada is to pursue an articling position: a 10-month supervised professional placement with a law firm. Articling is the means of fulfilling the practical and experiential learning of hands-on legal skills which equip the burgeoning law student to become a lawyer. Each Canadian province has different rules on qualification as a lawyer, but generally, following articling, a student would take provincial bar exams which confirm the eligibility to practice in a particular province.

10.3 Impact of changes in legal services on the delivery of the Canadian law degree

In *Tomorrow's Lawyers* Richard Susskind argues that the domain of the law is globally in a state of flux because of market-driven, regulatory and technological challenges to the traditional understanding of the role of the lawyer.[19] The global impact on the market has significantly affected the delivery of legal services, especially through the growth of multi-jurisdictional practices so that increasingly, there are more large law firms that cross national boundaries. Multi-jurisdictional practices take time zones in their stride and offer international clients a service to match their own desire to tackle legal issues across borders easily and effectively. In England and Wales, the Legal Services Act 2007 came into effect in 2011. Changes in regulatory structures introduced in the act allow for the emergence of new types of law firms and a more innovative approach to delivery. The Act introduces 'alternative business structures', which allow for non-legal ownership of law firms. Such an initiative has been watched with particular interest elsewhere in the world, and although such liberalising processes are not currently in place in Canada, the changes introduced in the UK have been commented upon positively as a means of opening up the market to further investment and innovation.[20] The market itself has been significantly impacted by the growth of technology, which has been a disruptive if significant instrument of innovation. In the US, for example, Legal Zoom offers an online resource for small businesses and consumers who want to access a range of different legal services. This arrangement challenges the traditional view of a law firm even without statutory change. In Canada, the trends driving change are stated similarly: globalization, technology, client expectations and decline in access to legal services.[21] One major change, for example, is that the commoditisation of law will lead to a much more systemic approach to the delivery of legal services and less one-to-one bespoke provision.[22] It is not just commercial legal practice that is impacted by such changes as there is also a marked shift in focus in court procedure globally towards a more proportionate, problem-solving justice system.

In Canada there is a specific emphasis in civil justice on alternative, out-of-court processes, such as arbitration and mediation, partly because mediation is mandatory in Ontario, and these practices have an impact on the type of skills required by lawyers. Thus, there is less emphasis on adversarialism and more on problem resolution and informal dispute resolution through negotiation.[23] Julie Macfarlane states that the lack of trials is emblematic of the new world of legal practice so that courtroom skills for lawyers give way to new specialisations.[24] The impact is huge because the legal world has been hit by so much change that it encompasses 'the structural, economic and procedural character of legal practice'.[25]

When so much change has happened and is still envisaged, there are clear implications for legal education, which needs to prepare students for the future vision of what working in law will look like. The Canadian Bar Association sees an urgent need to identify the new opportunities and roles for those who have undertaken legal education and aims to move the debate towards a discussion as to how collaboration between the profession and universities can help to develop proper and suitable provision for legal education of the future.[26] This might include, for example, new routes to admission to law school other than through the LSAT to encourage diversity and a wider and different experience. It is likely to bring to an end articling as the final step on the route to qualification.

The Canadian Bar Association is the body that represents lawyers across Canada: the equivalent of the English Law Society or Bar Council. It has an on-going initiative currently considering how the sorts of changes discussed above are going to impact on the delivery of legal education in the future.[27] It has been influenced by other developments in the profession more regionally. For example, the Law Society of Upper Canada has recently recommended the introduction of 'alternative business structures' along the lines of those already available in the UK and Australia.[28] Their report highlights the changing nature of legal practice and trends in consumers' approach to legal services, for example the growing use of technology as a gateway.[29] The aim is to create an agreed vision for the future development of law in Canada, with legal education forming a strategic element of this. Even before the potential introduction of alternative business structures, there have been significant changes to the profession through the increase in the use of paralegals; the growth in online legal services, and the reduction in opportunities for articling clerks. These are just small indications that in a few years' time there will be more than one pathway to becoming a lawyer. It has led Canadian authorities to reflect upon whether the idea of law as a postgraduate degree is still appropriate and whether law skills should be more pervasive and multidisciplinary. For example, combining legal study with business skills might expand the reach of the profession and enable more flexibility for law students in choosing a future career.

Another response to a changing world is the need for greater emphasis on continuing professional development. In this sense the Canadian model is echoing the recommendations of LETR made to legal regulators in England and Wales.[30] In instructing the lawyers of the future, educators will need to design programmes that can respond to modern challenges. This includes the need to produce lawyers who are more adaptable to change and more able to tackle creative problem-solving and negotiate/mediate empathetically rather than focus mainly on rhetoric and legal argument. Therefore, educators need to take a more innovative approach to designing programmes of study and modules and to also be horizon-scanning so they are cognisant of the tasks that will need to be undertaken by lawyers of the future such as "legal risk management, legal process analysis and legal risk engineering".[31]

10.4 The impact of *pro bono* on Canadian legal education

The seminal North American report of the Carnegie Foundation on Legal Education published in 2007 calls for reform in the shape of a more practical curriculum and emphasises the need for the teaching of 'civic professionalism'.[32] This term is used to describe the integration of practice, policy and theory to create a more comprehensive approach to educating lawyers. Such an approach necessarily calls upon the use of practicums and *pro bono* opportunities as a cornerstone of learning law in action. The report's authors criticised the huge focus of most North American law schools on case method and analysis, which is usually prioritised over practical problem-solving, ethics and professional responsibilities. Not only is a more practical approach useful in a system where there is no additional vocational level of study, it can also be more rewarding for those students who are paying to study for a vocational programme. Since 2015, the Canadian Federation of Law Societies National Requirement has become more outcome-based and embraces a more experiential approach to legal education.[33] This approach is very different from the one taken when clinical education was first introduced in the early 1970s. It was initially opposed by the legal profession for, amongst other things, fear of putting the reputation of qualified lawyers at risk.[34]

The move away from a heavily doctrinally based curriculum and towards one that integrates a more reflective and practical approach has been readily embraced by the foremost law schools in Canada, as a means of focusing students on the need for awareness of ethical issues, and professional responsibility. Although it originally started out as extra-curricular in nature, Osgoode Hall Law School, which has a tradition of clinical practice, was the first to introduce the requirement for all students to engage at some level with *pro bono* or public interest activity in order to pass the degree. This means that there is now a mandatory experiential element injected into the JD programme.[35] The types of clinical programme on offer are innovative and emphasise both academic knowledge in an applied setting alongside the practice of skills, competencies around problem-solving and the development of a set of values centred on professional responsibility and ethics.[36] Law clinics and experiential learning can straightforwardly address these requirements but can be expensive to provide. *Pro Bono Students Canada* is an umbrella organisation that provides *pro bono* opportunities for all law students in Canada and enables law schools to meet some of their regulatory requirements.[37] Innovation in assessment is also encouraged and students are evaluated through non-exams methods and can also gain marks for taking part in simulation competitions, for example, in negotiation and mooting.[38]

10.5 From articles to the LPP

Taking all of the above into account, Canadian legal education can be said to be in flux. There are good experiences offered at law schools in Canada, but these are limited and many students are keen to study law but cannot get a place on a Canadian university programme. Increasingly, large numbers of law students are choosing to study law outside of Canada, in Australia and the UK, and then return to home to practice.[39] Within Canada there has been a small growth in the number of universities offering innovative professional law programmes over the last few years – Lakehead University, Thompson Rivers University, Trinity Western University and the Université de Montréal in Quebec. Lakehead University in Ontario is an example of one of these universities offering a new and more integrated programme, designed to respond to changes in the legal profession, and the consequent different requirements for a provider of legal education.[40] At Lakehead there is a skills-oriented pathway approach so that as students go through the degree they build on skills developed in each year of study. The course integrates a practical legal practice element into the JD programme and as the university is situated in rural Northern Ontario it aims to build on a lawyer shortage in the area by developing student placements that supplement the region's unmet legal need.[41] Lakehead may not seem particularly novel from other perspectives, but in the Canadian context, it represents a highly innovative approach and a clear move towards a different style of legal education than found in the more traditional case-method processes employed by most Canadian law schools. Others are considering how their curricular might be shaped and perhaps altered by such developments.[42] The Canadian Bar Association affirms that a more mixed economy of practice and academic learning is preferable for students who need to manage change and cope in different environments, using a variety of skills, and that this will be more efficacious than the traditional route of articling with a law firm.[43]

In 2014 the Law Society of Upper Canada introduced the Legal Practice Program (LPP) as an alternative to the articling route. This is a controversial development because, as stated above, the traditional route to qualification is through a period of articling and employment at a law firm. However, articling positions are becoming harder to source, and for a student, who may have to pay huge fees to attend law school, the lack of articling positions can be a real obstacle. The Law Society of Upper Canada Task Force that investigated the articling crisis found that 15 percent of students had trouble finding articling positions.[44] As a result, there has been a concomitant decline in the number of students wishing to study law.[45] In order to provide an alternative pathway to legal qualification the province of Ontario created the LPP, offered by Ryerson University in Toronto and the University of Ottawa.[46] These programmes seek to solve the difficulty of the rapidly rising numbers of law students who cannot find articling. The LPP is a taught, competency-based, course lasting for 4 months, which is then matched with a 4-month experiential work placement. Paid and unpaid work placements can be offered in a wide range of services, and the intention includes using these placements to provide aspiring lawyers for organizations such as NGOs that are looking to expand access to justice, as well as the serving the interests of the more usual commercially oriented law firms. The programme is controversial as many qualified lawyers believe that it mainly exists to serve those aspiring lawyers who are not good enough to obtain articles in the conventional manner.[47] In its report recommending the LPP alternative pathway, the Task Force opened a door towards abolishing articling completely as a route into the profession.[48] However, more recently the Law Society of Upper Canada's Professional Development and Competency Committee has recommended ending the LPP and returning to the traditional articling system.[49] It suggests that the LPP creates a second-class form of training and that the programme itself is too costly to the profession. The committee's criticism leaves the future of the practical element of training exposed as articling opportunities remain limited, and the present system is unsustainable. There is clearly more work to be done by legal educators to devise a suitable programme that can meet the needs of law firms without carrying the stigma of an inferior form of training.

10.6 Conclusion

Canadian law historically takes its lead from its common law, English, inheritance. However, it is and has for many years been heavily influenced by its geographical attachment to the US. This chapter has outlined the indicators that show that Canadian legal education is in a period of rapid change. Yet, it is not just to the US that Canada is looking, for as this book demonstrates, the wider world is also considering how to make legal education fit for current and future purpose. Both the Canadian Bar and university law schools have acknowledged that change must take place. Multi-disciplinary approaches, technological developments, clinics and other forms of active and experiential learning will likely inform the future of legal learning in Canada. The more traditional law schools can no longer afford to rely on the tried and trusted case-law method supported by some extra-curricular pro bono work. An examination of the developments and conversations around Canadian legal education demonstrate to the rest of us that any innovation in legal provision must be matched by contemporaneous innovation in legal education and work on the attitudes of a more traditional profession as to the efficacy of such skills to reflect changes in educational approaches. It is clear that any complacency about the current changing situation is simply not an option.

Notes

1 R. Susskind, *The end of lawyers?*, London, Butterworths, Oxford University Press, 1998.
2 Solicitors Regulation Authority, *A new route to qualification: the solicitors qualifying examination*, SRA, 2016 and Bar Standards Board, *Future bar training – consultation on future training for the bar: future routes to authorisation*, BSB, 2016.
3 Legal Education Training Review (LETR), *Setting standards: the future of legal services education and training regulation in England and Wales*, IPS, BSB and SRA, 2013.
4 Canadian Bar Association, *The legal futures initiative: trends and issues*, 2013 and Canadian Bar Association, *Futures: transforming the delivery of legal services in Canada*, 2014.
5 *Death of a law firm: behind the collapse of Heenan Blaikie*, The Globe and Mail, 7th February 2014.
6 For example, one of the top five law firms in Canada, Gowlings recently merged with Wragge, Lawrence, Graham in the UK to create a huge international law firm. See further, *Gowling WLG announce international board as merger goes live*, The Lawyer, 22nd February 2016.
7 See further The Canadian National Self-Represented Litigants Project (NSRLP), available at: https://representingyourselfcanada.com, accessed 21 October 2016.
8 LETR, op cit.
9 A. Woolley, *Legal education reform and the good lawyer*, Alberta Law Review, 51, 2014, 801.
10 *Too many law students, too few legal jobs*, The New York Times, 25th August 2015.
11 F.P. Walton, *The legal system of Quebec*, Columbia Law Review, 13, 1913, 213.
12 A. De Mestral, *Bisystemic law teaching: the McGill programme and the concept of law in the EU*, Common Market Law Review, 40, 2003, 799, 800.
13 Federation of Law Societies of Canada, *National requirement*, November 2015.
14 In the UK over 60 percent of students do not go on to get a job in the legal profession after graduating from a law degree (Source: HESA data, 2013–14).
15 B. Hepple, *The renewal of the liberal law degree*, Cambridge Law Journal, 55, 470, 471.
16 S. Yandle, *An old model adapted for a new era: preparing law school graduates for the global legal profession*, CELJ, 3, 2014, 65.
17 For example, Osgoode Hall Law School introduced an experiential education requirement in 2012.
18 H.W. Arthurs, *Poor Canadian legal education: so near to Wall St so far from God*, Osgoode Hall Law Journal, 38, 2000, 381.
19 R. Susskind, *Tomorrow's lawyers*, Oxford: Oxford University Press, 2013, 3.
20 Canadian Bar Association Legal Futures Initiative, *Futures: transforming the delivery of legal services in Canada*, Canadian Bar Association, 2014, 41. See further the discussion below.
21 Ibid., 4.1.
22 R. Susskind, *Key trends in the legal marketplace*, Canadian Bar Association Legal Futures Initiative, September 2012.
23 For example, mediation is compulsory in several cities in Ontario, Canada. See further, S. Prince, *Mandatory mediation: the Ontario experience*, Civil Justice Quarterly, 26, 2007, 79.
24 J. Macfarlane, *The new lawyer: how settlement is transforming the practice of law*, UBC Press, 2008.
25 Ibid., 4.
26 Canadian Bar Association, 2014, op cit., 7.0.
27 Canadian Bar Association, 2013, op cit.

28 *Alternative business structures and the legal profession in Ontario*, Law Society of Upper Canada, 2014.
29 Ibid., 17.
30 LETR, op cit.
31 R. Susskind, 2012, op cit, 27.
32 W.M. Sullivan, A. Colby, J. Welch Wegner, L. Bond, L.S. Shulman, *Educating lawyers: preparation for the practice of law*, The Carnegie Foundation for the Advancement of Teaching, Wiley, 2007, 4.
33 Federation of Law Societies of Canada, *National requirement*, November 2015.
34 J. Giddings, R. Burridge, Sam Gavigan and C.F. Klein, The first wave of modern clinical legal education: the United States, Britain, Canada and Australia, in F.S. Bloch (ed.), *The global clinical movement: educating lawyers for social justice*, Oxford: Oxford University Press, 2011, 10.
35 *Shaking up the academy*, The National Magazine, 11th March 2016.
36 Federation of Law Societies of Canada, 2015, op cit.
37 Website of Pro Bono Students Canada, available at: www.probonostudents.ca, accessed 24 October 2016.
38 See, for example, Osgood Hall Law School, York University, *Student Handbook*, Summer 2016, available at: www.osgoode.yorku.ca/wp-content/uploads/2014/03/Student-Handbook-2016–2017.pdf, accessed 26 October 2016.
39 *Want to be a lawyer? Go down under*, Maclean's, 24th February 2009.
40 Bora Laskin Faculty of Law, available at: www.lakeheadu.ca/academics/departments/law, accessed 20 October 2016.
41 Lee Stueser, *The future for Canadian law schools*, Manitoba Law Journal, 37, 2014, 155.
42 See, for example: *The future of law school*, Conference held at the University of Alberta in September 2013 to mark the first century of the Law School.
43 Canadian Bar Association, 2014, op cit., 7.8.
44 *Pathways to the profession: a roadmap for the reform of lawyer licensing in Ontario*, Law Society of Upper Canada Articling Task Force Final Report, 25th October 2012, 18.
45 *Shortage of articling positions for students up for debate in law society elections*, The Globe and Mail, 21st April 2015.
46 Law Society of Upper Canada, 2012, op cit.
47 *Critics fear Ontario's articling plan will create two-tier system for students*, The Globe and Mail, 23rd November 2012.
48 Law Society of Upper Canada, 2012, op cit., 70.
49 Law Society of Upper Canada, Professional Development and Competency Committee, Report to Convocation, September 2016.

Chapter 11

The civil law tradition . . . but with clinics – a case study from Chile

Juan P. Beca

11.1 Introduction

Let me begin with a personal experience, to which many lawyers in my country, and many Latin American countries, may relate. My first job was at the Ministry of Public Works in their legal department. I was asked to look at a contract and see if it was legally 'correct'. I studied, learned and passed with merit a course in administrative law, and I had contractual theory and doctrine under my belt. I knew what the civil code and administrative regulations said about contracts. Was I well-equipped? Certainly not. This was the first time in my life I had ever seen a real contract – and the contract was a multimillion-dollar one, regarding the construction of a highway!

I managed, of course, but only after calling in help and losing much sleep! Now I teach law, and I do not want (or consider it necessary) for this to happen to my students. What use are they to their clients (which in my case was the country of Chile itself) if they have no experience grounded in reality?

11.2 Tradition and politics in law teaching

The way we teach law, and maybe this is true in other professions too, is heavily influenced by tradition. We are aware of the civil law and common law differences, but what I am talking about is more profound. It has to do, at least in part, with political, ideological and historic elements, and also with the way we perceive and understand law itself. As Jerome Bruner reminds us, pedagogy is never innocent.[1]

In most Latin American countries, this tradition has two primary characteristics. First, the conception of the legal system, which is considered complete in itself, with all the characteristics axiomatic systems possess, being coherent, complete and independent.[2] Therefore, the legal system is seen, and consequently taught, as something already established that can be learned as an object of study, not as something that evolves over time and is responsive to demands and pressures. In my view, and I am not alone in thinking so, law is effectively created by legislators but also by intellectuals, professors, legal professionals and students.[3] Of course under the civil law, we do not entrust judges with the same law creative capacity but the reality is they too, through their pronouncements and interventions, affect how law is perceived and therefore acted upon.

The second involves the role of the elite. In the 19th century, there was a small ruling class that knew how the system works, while the public at large was ignorant about it. Relevant to the issue we are discussing, they had to remain ignorant, so the elite could retain its privileges. Legal professionals had a key role in preserving this hierarchy.[4]

Considering the above, it is not difficult to understand why the law was considered as to be beyond question and consequently taught and learnt as a fixed set of rules that one simply needed to digest and accept. There is a strong tradition too that states that the law curriculum must have an encyclopaedic approach, meaning that it should be extensive – very extensive indeed – and that it should cover all areas of domestic (and even international) law. This phenomenon can be observed not only in Latin America, but also widely across other civil law (and also most probably common law) countries.[5]

Professors were those who knew and students were those who did not – in other words, they were as ignorant as the general public but of course could transcend this position by becoming lawyers. They could be initiated and become part of the exclusive group who knew the legal system and could then use it for specific purposes. Nevertheless, it should be stated that actually using the system was something not addressed at universities. Knowledge was understood as something to be transmitted, not created in any sense, to a passive student body. The knowledge to be transmitted was theoretical, not experiential. It was the law!

Experience – experiential learning – was, if encountered at all, provided outside of the lecture room. It was the responsibility of practicing lawyers, not lecturers or law schools themselves, to introduce this dimension. In many cases these practicing lawyers were at the same time lecturers, but they did not give away their experience, or let students 'put their hands' on the law, in their capacity as university professors. They did so as members of the practicing lawyers' community.

The profession owned practical knowledge. Therefore, experiential learning occurred in a professional setting, at lawyers' offices. So the elite – the professional community – retained power and could share it with whom they wanted. In some sense it was not only a social and economic elite, since knowledge was shared based on meritocracy.[6] It was possible for somebody coming from outside the elite to go through the university, graduate in law, get some experiential learning in a lawyer's office and became part of the privileged group who knew the system – the 'legal elite'. Power is a different issue; it was not (and still is not) necessarily shared so easily.

Changing the way law is taught is strongly intertwined with social and political factors.[7] Given this, we must consider that there is a very important ideological component of the picture we are portraying. Latin American countries became independent in the early 19th century and were built, at least from the official point of view,[8] on the foundation of law.[9]

In the civil law tradition, codes and regulations – written legislation – is the main source of law, so who gets to write the law is a major political issue. The group who drafts the law has political, social and economic power, not necessarily those who adjudicate on its application. So we must consider that being part of the 'legal elite' does not mean to be part of the elite in a sociological or political sense. Power, not only political power, was on the side of the group who created the law.

Political power, at this time, was in the hands of a relatively small group of very rich men – the citizens. Even though a formally democratic system was eventually established, citizenry was reduced.[10] Since voters were only wealthy men, women and other social groups were not considered citizens and therefore excluded from any kind of political power. The general public was expected to obey the law, not create it.

In this setting, knowing the law, sometimes by heart, was relevant. We can then understand, historically at least, why sometimes, even today, especially during examinations, students are asked to recite the law, without questioning it or even interpreting, let alone applying, it to a practical case.

Creativity was not, and unfortunately sometimes still it is not, a competency or ability expected to be developed by law students. This approach clearly places obstacles in the way of experiential learning. Students were expected to learn a given system, not necessarily understand it or know how the system worked.

Judicial decisions, in the civil law tradition, are well known to be less significant than legislation. "Precedent has lesser value in the civil law than in the common law because a judge's decision is not intended to provide definitive interpretation of the law."[11] Law was (and often still is) understood as what has been written by the legislator and not dependant or even, in principle, affected by what judges do with those rules. A sort of cult for the legislator was created.[12] Therefore, in a traditional setting, judicial decisions were barely considered during law studies.

Since the study of law was therefore approached, and in some cases is still approached, as something unrelated to practice,[13] there was a little or no opportunity for experiential learning. Judges are indeed those who give life to law, applying it to practical cases. Legal life was, however, absent from legal studies. Experiential learning requires interacting with real (or realistic) cases and with people and their problems, in other words, with a living legal system – even if that were simulated for the purposes of teaching. Interaction was neither encouraged nor seemingly possible in the traditional setting we are presenting, so experiential learning was not possible either.

There was (and at times still is) strong resistance to any innovation in pedagogy. It was not only a matter of teaching and learning methodologies; ideological issues, political power and even the established order itself were at stake in the way law was taught. Therefore, along with resistance, there was also strong suspicion on any attempts to change the customary law-teaching system.

11.3 The 1960s and legal clinics

In the 1960s a wave of change shook the world, and of course universities, as part of the real world, were profoundly affected by it, even the ultra-traditional law schools. Radical ideas abounded, liberal thoughts were promulgated, protests were commonplace, human rights were high on some agenda and communication techniques were improving. The world was a smaller place in consequence. In this time of social change, some (mainly the new and young) professors introduced a number of interesting innovations in the way law was taught, including, besides the traditional lectures, small group discussions about, for example, law reform and the relevance of judicial decisions. Here students would be actively encouraged to express their views and to voice their own opinions – even produce articles and commentaries.[14]

Legal clinics were introduced in Chile in this context.[15] Besides being a vehicle for students' experiential learning, they were a way to connect the university with the community, getting both students and professors out of the so-called ivory tower. Students went into the *poblaciones* (poor neighbourhoods) offering legal assistance and poor people went to the clinics (usually located outside university campuses) seeking help with their legal problems, especially the need of an attorney to appear in court for them. Clinics in Chile are therefore not a recent creation – as in many other civil law countries – but a direct product of the 1960s.

A very important goal of the clinics, not always present in other countries,[16] was to provide legal service to the poor. Initially, this was the case due to a political commitment by universities in order to give to the wider community some of the benefits that other people and institutions had enjoyed for decades-sharing them with traditionally excluded groups. In those days, poverty was the only relevant fact to be considered when defining the exclusion. Ethnic and sexual minorities, women, children, people with disabilities and other disadvantaged people, although having their particular problems, were not seen at all as specific groups to target. Poverty was such an urgent concern that other problems were set aside.

The 1973 *coup d'état*, led by General Pinochet and the armed forces, that overthrew President Allende, had a tremendous impact on Chilean life. There was a profound change not only in the political system but also in the social and economic structures. We have already stated that law teaching is intertwined with political issues, so is not surprising that the effect of the *coup d'état* was felt in every walk of life, including law schools. Reform was brought to an end violently and abruptly; and as regards the teaching of law, the traditional order was re-established.[17] Seminars, discussions and workshops were banned. Questioning the newly established political regime, with all the legal changes implied, was extremely dangerous.

But interestingly legal clinics survived, albeit some not necessarily in the comfort of the law school, but they generally did not suffer the same fate as other innovative initiatives. This may be puzzling, but it has an explanation. The need to offer legal assistance to the poor was also important for the dictatorial government, and clinics were a way to deal with this problem. Wilson importantly recognises the quality and value of Chilean clinical programmes and their pedagogic sophistication.[18]

Legal assistance for the poor was traditionally a responsibility of the Bar Association, known as College of Advocates. Professional associations, and among them the College of Advocates had, in the past, important political influence. They were responsible for the ethical behaviour of their members, and membership was required to practice any profession. Some of them, like the College of Advocates itself and the College of Medical Doctors, had been very critical of the previous regime and were seen by Pinochet and his government as an important ally. But at the same time, associations, or any group with political influence, were potentially dangerous. So these associations were not banned, but membership was no longer a requirement to practice, as is still the case in Chile today. Therefore, professional associations were profoundly weakened.

The College of Advocates suffered and became unable to deliver legal aid to the poor. A public office (Judicial Assistance Corporation [JAC]) was created to intervene and still exists, working with a small number of attorneys and a large cohort of *egresados,* meaning students who have finished law school but are not yet licensed lawyers. To be fully qualified, an exam has to be passed and a period of apprenticeship with the JAC completed.

This situation allowed law schools to shelve innovation and focus on theoretical aspects, leaving to the Judicial Assistance Corporation the role that private lawyers' offices had in the past performed. Therefore, once again experiential learning was not considered in the law curriculum. The work of the *egresados* is designed and used to provide legal aid, and not for them to learn. Learning occurs, basically among peers,[19] but is not assessed or monitored by the institution. Experiential learning may occur in this context but is not structured or overt.

This historical digression brings us to the present day. Of course there has been the overthrow of the dictatorship and the introduction of a modern democracy. However, the law school continues largely as of old. Some clinics remained at law schools, surviving the banning of innovative reforms, justifying their role as a means of giving legal aid to the poor, rather than being a deep experiential learning opportunity for students. This might have been a positive collateral effect, but clinical work was not conceived or designed in this sense.

The clinical experience in this setting does not have a metacognitive effect, through which students really learn from what they do, reflecting on the outcomes of their actions and becoming aware of their learning. Going through a clinic, which in most cases is now mandatory in Chile, can be a demanding experience in which a student may see dozens of similar cases, providing legal assistance to many desperate people, but with no time to discuss the cases with professors and classmates, or reflect on her/his learnings.

11.4 A new wave of change

At the end of the 20th and the beginning of the current century, a new wave of changes arrived in Chilean law schools. This may not have been as dramatic as those in the 1960s and 1970s, but I believe is much more structural and profound. The dictatorship came to an end and democracy was re-established. During the last years of the dictatorship, regulations were liberalized and numerous universities were created, many of them establishing law schools, since it was a cheap programme to offer and was very popular amongst prospective students. In 1980 there were only 5 law schools in Chile, and in 2016 there were 49, some offering law programs in more than one location. In the 25 years from 1983, the number of students in higher education quadrupled.[20] Democracy opened the door to dialogue and the possibility to challenge the way things were done. The new universities paved the way to innovative ways of teaching law.[21]

Traditionally, law professors were lawyers with a very active private practice who also taught. These professors still teach some courses, but the main responsibility in teaching, research and administration has been taken by a professional group of academics, meaning people whose main (and sometimes only) job is with the university.[22] Law teaching has been professionalised. This group is formed by young professors who are being hired, both at traditional and new universities, most of them with post-graduate studies and degrees from foreign universities. Socially it is a diverse group and very different from the traditional elite.[23]

Besides studies and training in law itself, is also necessary to undertake a course on teaching methodologies. Wilson observed, a decade ago, a "nearly total ignorance, if not active resistance by the legal academy in the United States, in Chile, and elsewhere to the careful study of teaching and learning theory and methods, and to the incorporation of these methods in their pedagogy."[24]

Universities have been investing in training their professors, and not only in law schools,[25] in teaching methodologies. We can observe nowadays a powerful combination of people working full time at the university, with a solid knowledge of legal issues and awareness of the need to use a pedagogy that is student centred and supports both learning and teaching. It needs not only structure and form but also clear outcomes.

The elements mentioned above have produced a new movement for rethinking legal education, reflecting on the 1960s experiences but going beyond it.[26] More recent reforms have focused on market needs, and not on public function as prior reforms had. Lawyers were expected to play a key role in state institutions. Most of the representatives and senators were indeed lawyers and prior to the 1973 *coup d'état* (from 1851 to 1973), 19 out of 24 presidents were lawyers as well, but this is not true anymore. After the return of democracy, in 1990, only 2 out of 6 of our presidents have been lawyers. The latter has had an impact on legal education; since society expects a different role for the profession, the new movement needed to respond to that social demand, so curriculum and methodology were assessed according to market needs.[27]

It might be seen as contradictory that a professionalised academic body, which does not practice law actively, is more aware of the practical component of teaching, and is more inclined to experiential learning. These professors know how students learn, and their goal is precisely students' learning. Students learn from what they actually do and not just (if at all) from what is done by their professors. Academics are better prepared than practicing lawyers to design programmes and delivery methods that foster the best that experiential learning can offer.[28]

11.5 Opportunities and challenges at the present time

Without being in any way complacent, after centuries of challenge and many more recent difficulties, we now have fertile ground on which to plant and nurture more effective legal education and harvest the rewards in society as a whole. We can start from a democratic foundation. We can turn to other disciplines and learn that students are not a *tabula rasa*. They have indeed some knowledge, which is a sort of scaffold to build understanding upon.[29] With guidance and support, students begin to reflect increasingly the depth of their understanding in consequence, with help from both their professors and peers. In this sense, knowledge is more democratically distributed, not emanating just from the professors' side; students have something to say about their education and learning process, and what they say[30] is that they learn more when they practice than when they just listen or watch.

The student body is very heterogeneous, due to the widespread increase in university enrolment. Many form the first generation in their families to have access to the university. A not-insignificant number of these students have difficulties with their reading abilities, so they rely on oral and visual ways of learning to make the most of their experiences.[31] "It is not by chance that Kolb's learning cycle begins with the concrete experience."[32] Experiential learning is precisely the way they can get these experiences and learn, helping them to overcome difficulties they are not responsible for. For the bulk of these students who are not from the elite, they need to learn as much as possible in a university setting, since they don't have the chance outside.[33]

Knowledge is not considered, under this paradigm, as something to be transmitted; it is rather considered something that each student must build by her/himself, albeit with the support and encouragement from their peers and academic members of the staff. We are persuaded that the best way to build knowledge is by doing, and doing is done precisely through experiential learning.

Experiential learning, in legal studies, is much more than a clinical experience. It has to do with experiencing and juggling with the law. In the old set-up this was not possible, since law was considered as something to be learned and not something to be used. But as this has changed and, in principle, depending on learning outcomes and resources, students can engage in active and experiential learning from Year 1. It is not necessary to wait until the final stages of the law degree to do this – which is where legal clinics are usually located in the curriculum.

Students should be challenged to use the law, build norms and find out which norms have been built by others, especially in judicial decisions, in order to solve problems and in that way, learn the law. And this is not, or should not be, done only in clinics. Students, to learn law, are not expected just to know regulations. They should indeed know them but also learn how to use them, bringing law into life. The careful use of simulation can be a very effective (in terms of resource input and learning outcomes) way of introducing experiential learning.

This approach, however, presupposes that the traditional law studies' content has to be covered by students. If we want students to work with the law, then we should be sure that they know it. Using Twining's metaphor, we do need both Pericles and the plumber;[34] but do students need to know all of the law? I suggest not – basic principles and essential doctrine – yes, of course. The finer detail – probably not. Surely we are educating students to think and act like lawyers, not become an encyclopaedia of law. Even the most experienced lawyers need to research that detail, as our students should. Sacrificing some substantive law in favour of skills and values might just be a price worth paying.

In order to be plumbers, students must learn the 'nut and bolts; taps and washers' of the legal system. In other words, they need to know how things really work, what to do to solve problems. But they are going to be professionals, not technicians, meaning they must be able to find solutions to new problems and not just repeat solutions that others have arrived at. The traditional approach reduced lawyers' role to being experts on regulations, not able to face new situations.[35] What is needed is a balance between conceptual teaching (legal theory and legal dogma) and the development of skills and values for the legal profession.[36]

How do we teach students to use already given solutions to simple problems and at the same time prepare them to find solutions to new and complex problems? How do we teach students to be creative and to question the *status quo* when there is a need to do so? I strongly believe that the only way is through experiential learning, letting them solve problems and not just learn regulations and theories, throughout the whole legal curriculum and not only in isolated courses or experiences, as even clinics can be in some cases. Clinical legal education is indeed a form of experiential learning[37] but is not the only one.

Experiential learning needs, obviously, experience. Students need to experience for themselves what they are learning, which can be done in different contexts, either real or simulated. A real context, such as a clinic, is better but is often allocated at the end of the curriculum, so initial experiences are also needed.

There is a difference between live-client clinics and other forms of experiential learning. Many real client clinics focus so much on service delivery (understandably) that they may ignore the learning, and the clinic can become little more than a placement. In the converse, simulation (e.g., role-play) can carry more learning value, but none of them, pure simulation or pure service delivery, are enough. Effective Clinical Legal Education does both – service delivery and learning.

Experiential learning also helps to create professional identity. To generate passion for the discipline that is being studied, the apprentice must be able to connect contents with real, live experiences.[38] Through experiential learning students can get a sense of what it is to be a lawyer, which is important for any student, but especially for those with no family background in the legal profession, or indeed in any profession at all. Very helpful in this sense has been a course on lawyering, allocated in the first semester of the curriculum, in which students can experience different ways of practicing law (through mock trials, simulations of interviews with clients, writing simple contracts, etc.)[39]

Competency-based curricula which currently seem popular with some academics and many university administrations,[40] may provide a great opportunity to introduce experiential learning. Competencies are understood as being able to do something in a given context, using acquired knowledge and other resources, as well as knowing how to activate this when required. They can seldom be achieved only by studying theory. In order to do things, students must have a strong theoretical background but this must be coupled with experience of and an ability to effectively apply that knowledge or skill. Therefore, the goal is to have better prepared lawyers, and not just people that can use a given 'recipe' on a given set of ingredients.[41] Students, going through a number of experiential learning activities, not only clinics, can be prepared to for the professional world as well as showing their mettle in exams.

Law schools have to be responsible enough to send fully prepared legal professional to the labour market and not people who are willing to learn but not to work and solve problems. Students should never be in my position and encounter a contract for the first time in the law office.

Assessment too is critical to competency-based learning. Evaluation should be consistent with and linked to the expected outcomes.[42] Both students and professors need to know what is expected of them and when set outcomes have been achieved (or if they have not, why not). Assessing competencies needs the student to demonstrate that he or she can perform relevant activities in which competency can be observed; and there is no better, or even other, way than an experiential approach.

Notes

1 R. Coloma, *El ocaso del profesor Binss: Un ensayo acerca de la enseñanza del Derecho en Chile*, Ius et Praxis, 11 (1), 2005, 162.

2 E. Bulygin, *Teoría y Práctica de la Legislación*, Análisis Lógico y Derecho, Madrid, Centro de Estudios Constitucionales, 1992.

3 B. Bravo, *Estudios de Derecho y Cultura de Abogados en Chile 1758–1998: Tras la Huella Ius Commune: La Codificación y la Decodificación en el Nuevo Mundo*, Estudios Histórico Jurídicos, 1998, 20.

4 I. De la Maza, *Los Abogados en Chile: Desde el Estado al Mercado*, Santiago, Centro de Investigaciones Jurídicas, 2002.
5 E. Solari, *El Currículo Chileno de Estudios Jurídicos*, Revista de Derecho de la Universidad Católica de Valparaíso, XXXIX (2), 2012, 703–734.
6 Admission to most universities was, and it is still, based on the results of a national test. Nevertheless, the result in the test is highly influenced by family income. (F. Meneses and J. Toro, *Predicción de Notas en Derecho de la Universidad de Chile: ¿Sirve el Ranking?*, Isses, 10, 2012, 43–58).
7 R. Wilson, *Three law school clinics in Chile, 1970–2000: innovation, resistance and conformity in the global south*, Clinical Law Review, 2002, 8.
8 S. Villalobos, *Portales: Una falsificación histórica*, Santiago, Editorial Universitaria, 1989.
9 F. Campos, *Historia Constitucional de Chile*, Santiago, Editorial Jurídica de Chile, 1983.
10 S. Grez, *La Ausencia de un Poder Constituyente Democrático en la Historia de Chile*, Tiempo Histórico, 1 (1), 2010, 15–35.
11 R. Wilson, *Three law school clinics in Chile, 1970–2000: innovation, resistance and conformity in the global south*, Clinical Law Review, 8, 2002, 521.
12 B. Bravo, *Estudios de Derecho y Cultura de Abogados en Chile 1758–1998: Tras la Huella Ius Commune: La Codificación y la Decodificación en el Nuevo Mundo*, Estudios Histórico Jurídicos, 1998, 20.
13 The traditional approach has been ingeniously described by Professor Coloma, using the figure of Harry Potter's Professor Binns. Among other features, it considers the encyclopaedic approach, an exaggerated emphasis on memorisation, the abuse of lectures and the conception of the lawyer as a mere applicator of rules. (R. Coloma, *El ocaso del profesor Binss: Un ensayo acerca de la enseñanza del Derecho en Chile*, Ius et Praxis, 11 (1), 2005).
14 R. Coloma, *El ocaso del profesor Binss: Un ensayo acerca de la enseñanza del Derecho en Chile*, Ius et Praxis, 11 (1), 2005.
15 As early as 1922, in Universidad de Chile's Law School, students took a course called Forensic Practice and offered their services through a legal aid office. R. Wilson, *Three law school clinics in Chile, 1970–2000: innovation, resistance and conformity in the global south*, Clinical Law Review, 2002, 8. The programme disappeared, but it can be considered the first seed of a native clinical program.
16 See: R. Wilson, *Three law school clinics in Chile, 1970–2000: innovation, resistance and conformity in the global south*, Clinical Law Review, 2002, 8; and more generally: S. Sarker. *Clinical legal education in Asia*, New York, Palgrave Macmillan, 2015.
17 De la Maza says that, along with the *coup d'état*, the weak organization of the universities and the lack of an academic community should be taken into account. (I. De la Maza, *Los Abogados en Chile: Desde el Estado al Mercado*, Santiago, Centro de Investigaciones Jurídicas, 2002).
18 R. Wilson, *Three law school clinics in Chile, 1970–2000: innovation, resistance and conformity in the global south*, Clinical Law Review, 8, 2002.
19 K. Miller et al, *Response switching and self-efficacy in peer instruction classroom*, Physical Review Special Topics – Physics Education Research, 11 (1), 2015, 1–8.
20 F. Meneses and J. Toro, *Predicción de Notas en Derecho de la Universidad de Chile: ¿Sirve el Ranking?*, Isses, 10, 2012, 46.
21 It must be stated, nevertheless, that many of the new law schools were created only as a way to make money, and just repeated what was being done in older universities, hiring their professors and using their curricula.
22 F. Muñoz, *¿Hacia la academización de las Facultades de Derecho en Chile? Un análisis teórico y comparado del conflicto de las profesiones*, Revista de Derecho, XXVIII (1), 2014, 9–25.
23 But it must be said, with the risk of becoming a new intellectual elite.
24 R. Wilson, *Three law school clinics in Chile, 1970–2000: innovation, resistance and conformity in the global south*, Clinical Law Review, 8, 2002, 573.

25 Law professors are usually more reluctant to take part in these programs than colleagues from other schools and departments.
26 R. Coloma, *El ocaso del profesor Binss: Un ensayo acerca de la enseñanza del Derecho en Chile*, Ius et Praxis, 11 (1), 2005, 169.
27 I. De la Maza, *Los Abogados en Chile: Desde el Estado al Mercado*, Santiago, Centro de Investigaciones Jurídicas, 2002.
28 F. Muñoz, *¿Hacia la academización de las Facultades de Derecho en Chile? Un análisis teórico y comparado del conflicto de las profesiones*, Revista de Derecho, XXVIII (1), 2014, 23.
29 L. Shepard, *Linking formative assessment to scaffolding*, Educational Leadership, 63 (3), 2005, 66–70.
30 Sometimes they don't say it clearly, but this is what research shows. (A. Valle et al, *Las Estrategias de Aprendizaje: Revisión Teórica y Conceptual*, Revista Latinoamericana de Psicología, 31 (3), 1999, 425–461.
31 R. Coloma and C. Agüero, *La Liebre y la Tortuga: ¿Cómo Trabajar con Estudiantes que Poseen Distintos Niveles de Dominio de Competencias Básicas al Iniciar sus Estudios de Derecho?*, Nuevos Desafíos de la Enseñanza del Derecho en Chile, Santiago, Libromar, 2013.
32 J. Beca, *Teaching legal ethics to law students: why, what, how and who might teach?*, Asian Journal of Legal Education, 3 (1), 2016, 92.
33 R. Coloma, *El ocaso del profesor Binss: Un ensayo acerca de la enseñanza del Derecho en Chile*, Ius et Praxis, 11 (1), 2005, 149.
34 W. Twining, Pericles and the plumber, in *Law in context: enlarging a discipline*, Oxford, Oxford University Press, 2012, 63–88.
35 B. Bravo, *Estudios de Derecho y Cultura de Abogados en Chile 1758–1998: Tras la Huella Ius Commune: La Codificación y la Decodificación en el Nuevo Mundo*, Estudios Histórico Jurídicos, 20, 1998, 100.
36 E. Solari, *El Currículo Chileno de Estudios Jurídicos*, Revista de Derecho de la Universidad Católica de Valparaíso, XXXIX (2), 2012, 722.
37 R. Wilson, *Three law school clinics in Chile, 1970–2000: innovation, resistance and conformity in the global south*, Clinical Law Review, 8, 2002, 569.
38 R. Coloma, *El ocaso del profesor Binss: Un ensayo acerca de la enseñanza del Derecho en Chile*, Ius et Praxis, 11 (1), 2005, 164.
39 The course was introduced in 2004 at Universidad Católica de Temuco, modeled on a similar course at New York University. Some other law schools in Chile have introduced this course in their curriculum in the last few years.
40 M. Zabalza, *La Universidad de las Competencias*, Revista de Docencia Universitaria, 10 (2), 2012, 11–14.
41 C. Jamin, *Le Cuisin Du Droit. L'école de Droit de Science Po: Une expérience françai*s, Paris, Lextenso Éditions, 2012.
42 R. Coloma and C. Agüero, 'La Liebre y la Tortuga: ¿Cómo Trabajar con Estudiantes que Poseen Distintos Niveles de Dominio de Competencias Básicas al Iniciar sus Estudios de Derecho?', in Libromar (ed.), *Nuevos Desafíos de la Enseñanza del Derecho en Chile*, Santiago, 2013.

Chapter 12

Making a real change

Legal education in Nigeria – partly re-imagined?

Ernest Ojukwu

12.1 Introduction

Legal education began in Nigeria in 1961 when the first law faculty at the University of Nigeria[1] was established. Following the enactment of the Legal Education Act in 1962,[2] the Nigerian Law School was established.[3]

Before 1962, the legal profession in Nigeria was made up of lawyers who were either called to the English Bar or enrolled as solicitors in England[4] and under the 1896 Supreme Court Ordinance laypeople (with some court-clerkship experience) were permitted by the Chief Justice to practice as lawyers on a renewable 6-monthly basis.[5]

Due to its former colonial connections, Nigeria's legal education and the legal profession is generally modelled after that of the English system.

12.2 Legal education before 1990

Before 1990 in Nigeria, legal education was divided into two parts. The first – the Academic Part – was a 3- to 4-year study at university for a bachelor of laws degree. The second part – the professional/vocational stage – was one-year training course at the Nigerian Law School preparing students for call to the Nigerian Bar.[6]

The academic programme

At the undergraduate stage, each university had autonomy in terms of duration, content and teaching methodology. In reality, however, universities had similar programmes.

The academic programme content was a set of substantive law modules, some compulsory (the core subjects) and others optional. The first year generally focused on non-law courses presented in combined large classes of law and non-law students. Most of the teaching of these non-law courses was seen as foundation subjects that all students should undertake, but the actual teaching was done without any serious attempt at achieving any educational goal. Core law courses like contract, torts, constitutional law, equity and trusts, land/property law and criminal law were taught during the remaining part of the academic programme.

Teaching was mainly teacher-centred, using lectures and note dictation. There was limited tutorial and seminar contact. There were few in-course assignments and exercises, and these were largely unassessed and without feedback being given to the learner. Assessment was by one-off, summative examinations at the end of a year. Classes were large – typically over one hundred students and sometimes many more.

The law faculties did not set goals or outcomes for legal education. There were no clearly stated objectives and the overall aim seemed to be to provide students with a mass of definitions, principles and case law with no thought given to its relevance beyond covering the syllabus.

The professional/vocational programme

The one-year vocational training at the Nigerian Law School focused on some adjectival law, such as civil and criminal procedure. The teaching methodology was also almost exclusively based on dictating notes to the students in a lecture format. Again, there was much rote learning, and assessments were by summative examination at the end of the course.

12.3 Legal education from 1990

After 1990 it is still divided into two stages but now runs as follows.

The academic programme

From 1990 the National Universities Commission in Nigeria prescribed a uniform minimum standard for all undergraduate law degree programmes at the country's universities.

These prescriptive standards introduced many more compulsory and optional non-law courses and encouraged a more multi-disciplinary approach to study. The standards also increased the number of mandatory law (core) courses.

In terms of the content of the core and overall teaching methodology, however, nothing has really changed.

The uniform minimum standards were later reviewed and called Benchmarks and Minimum Academic Standards. All university faculties, including law, were required to develop curricula based on subject benchmark statements and minimum academic standards. Regrettably, the law faculties have continued to use the content-driven benchmark statements and minimum academic standards as if they constitute curricula with little thought given to either the interrelationship of subjects or the mode of delivery of the curriculum. The law faculties have also generally not set goals or outcomes – what they expect students to be able to do on completion of certain modules or the entire programme.[7]

I wish to critique these seemingly positive developments from two perspectives – curricula and pedagogy.[8]

At this level of education, best practice suggests that curricula should be regularly reviewed and at least every 2 to 5 years. What has happened with the law faculties in Nigeria is the introduction of additional subjects to the minimum standard imposed by the National Universities Commission. Minimal effort has been put into designing and reviewing the curriculum as a coherent whole. This failure has resulted in an uneven product that is neither consistent nor logical. It has also seen the introduction of more and more law (a greater number of core and optional subjects) without adequate rationale or thought being given to what is trying to be achieved.

As stated earlier, the introduction of a uniform minimum academic standard did not alter the teaching methodology followed by the law faculties pre-1990. The lecture and note-dictating format largely continued as the teaching methodology. Lecturing can only be an effective way of teaching if it is used together with other active teaching strategies.[9] The lecturing format, as the principal methodology for teaching, does not lend itself to giving any, let alone adequate, feedback to the learner. It is teacher-centred, does not actively engage students and in consequence, does not effectively develop knowledge. The lecturing method cannot be used to develop skills, competencies and values in the learner.

This has led to widespread criticism including: "public and private employers of university graduates, as well as the government itself, consider the quality of university graduates to be inadequate."[10] Of about thirty public university law faculties in Nigeria, only one (University of Lagos) achieved full accreditation consistently from 1990 to 2014.[11] The National Universities Commission has three categories of accreditation – full, interim and failed. Most of the law programmes continued and continue to receive interim accreditation, and some that received full accreditation have this downgraded at some point to interim accreditation. Those that failed accreditation were barred from admitting new students until they remedied their status.

The professional/vocational programme

The organisation of the one-year professional/vocational programme at the Nigerian Law School remained the same from its inception until much later. In 2008 a major review took place, and nothing short of revolutionary reforms resulted. Apart from evidence of general complaints about the quality of lawyers and legal training in the country,[12] the impetus for the Nigerian Law School's desire for reform can be seen in the Request for IDF Financing Basic Information document that states:

> The Nigeria National Economic Empowerment and Development Strategy 2004 (NEEDS) recognizes that its success rests on three pillars, one of which is improving the Nigerian legal environment. It draws a clear

> link between a stable, predictable and good quality legal framework, strong judicial system and economic growth. NEEDS also emphasizes upon improving access to justice and legal aid. A qualitative improvement in legal training better equips the lawyers to meet the society's challenges and respond to its concerns.
>
> The Nigeria Country Partnership Strategy 2005–09 (CPS) builds on the NEEDS Report and recognizes the inadequate legal and regulatory framework as one of the major impediments to Nigeria realizing its full growth potential. The CPS emphasizes the need to improve the quality of the Nigerian legal system to improve the business environment and encourage investment flows into the country. Improving the quality of legal services available within Nigeria forms an integral part of this effort.
>
> The Nigeria competitiveness and Growth Report 2006 (i.e. Country Economic Memorandum) . . . highlights the delay and cost of enforcing contracts in Nigeria. It suggests the need to reform the law and court systems, expand the use of alternative dispute resolution system, and more importantly, to build capacity of legal professionals.
>
> The Insolvency and Creditor Rights ROSC Report . . . also recognises the propensity of some lawyers to raise frivolous arguments and unnecessarily delay cases. While this secures temporary relief for their clients, the overall impact on society is very negative. Improving the training that lawyers undergo will make them understand the costs this imposes on society and strengthens the ethics of the legal professionals.[13]

It was possible to make changes at this time because there was new leadership at the Nigerian Law School with the desire to reform and the will to translate that desire into reality.

The features and characteristics of the introduced reforms and curriculum for the professional/vocational programmes have been summarised as follows:[14]

1. There is a guiding vision and a mission statement.
2. There are set and clear objectives for the curriculum and for each module.
3. It is outcomes-based.
4. It is learner-centred, providing case studies and interactive activities (though still heavily content-driven).
5. It addresses learning in an integrative way that focuses on knowledge, skills and values.
6. There are clear rules and measures for formative and summative assessments even though the programme is still heavily reliant on end-of-programme examinations.
7. It provides opportunities for experiential learning and the development of clinical legal education.
8. There is potential for an evaluation mechanism and quality standardization and assurance.

9 There is a relatively small and focused curriculum – 5 subjects: criminal litigation, civil litigation, property law practice, corporate law practice, and law in practice.
10 The curriculum provides for 40 weeks of activity – a mix of theory and practice, including: one week of induction (use of library and other issues), one week of moot and mock trial before the lessons, 12 weeks of externship (placement in courts and law firms), 3 weeks of externship portfolio assessment, one week of post-lesson moot and mock trials and one week of final examination.
11 An externship programme that is assessed on a pass/fail basis and a failure grade deprives the student a bar certificate.

This development, in terms of both form and content (pedagogy and curriculum), has been described as follows:

> What (has been) designed and implemented at the NLS accords with many of the principles of best educational practice for a law school in terms of curriculum design, teaching methodologies and assessment regimes. It should produce students who are equipped with the knowledge, skills and values to become competent and ethically aware practitioners. The programme does however need to be monitored to ensure that what is being implemented meets local and national needs and continues to develop in a robust way.[15]

A major aspect of these reforms is the integrated externship programme. The main features[16] of the Externship Programme are as follows:

1 There are clear goals for the programme – developing the extern's lawyering skills; helping the extern' to understand various aspects of the legal system and legal profession; inculcating in the extern', the sense of professional responsibility and values; developing the extern's ability to reflect on and learn from their experiences.
2 The rules of engagement affecting the law school, students, assessors, supervisors and mentors are very clear. Both students and field supervisors have detailed handbooks to guide them through the programme.
3 For the first time in the history of the school, each student now has a mentor to support them and give feedback. The mentor is usually a full-time teacher or an adjunct.
4 Students must keep a log of activities as part of their portfolios for the externship.
5 The programme encourages reflective learning, particularly on ethical dilemmas and law office management.
6 Students' portfolios are assessed by teachers and legal practitioners at the end of the placement period and there is a pass or fail mark. If a student fails, he or she cannot progress to enrolment at the Bar.

7 Students' portfolios include: a log book of daily activities, reflective essays (themes usually provided by the school), a law firm or court survey to be completed by externs, samples/evidence of work performed by the extern during the placement and a confidential law firm/court field supervisor's evaluation of the extern's performance. The aim of the surveys is to assist the Nigerian Law School to assess law firms and courts for the purposes of the externship programme. Law firms that receive negative reports may be delisted, and students would not be sent there for externship programmes while feedback will be sent to heads of the courts concerned. This will serve as a form of court and law firm monitoring. Students would also learn from discussing and reflecting on the results of the survey.
8 The Externship programme is designed to provide a clear opportunity for formative assessment and growth of the professional learner.
9 There are clear rules for the accreditation of law firms (though yet to be implemented).
10 A code of conduct for students, mentors, assessors and field supervisors has been provided under the programme.

Since 2013 the new curriculum at the Nigerian Law School has been reviewed though the only change has been altering the title of one of the modules from law in practice to skills and professional ethics.

In spite of the successes of the new curriculum, it is "still heavily . . . contents-driven" with "dominant summative assessment".[17] The future of professional/vocational legal training in Nigeria at this level will be best served if the curriculum moves from "a dominant contents-driven curriculum to a more qualitative outcome-based one" focusing more client values, "ethics, trial advocacy skills, communication skills, justice education and knowledge and skills for delivering services in a global context".[18]

12.4 The future of the academic programme of legal education in Nigeria

I have written of legal education in Nigeria before in these words:

> Traditional legal education in Nigeria separates legal education between a liberal art bachelor of laws programme at the law faculties and the bar programme at the Nigerian Law School. I describe this process of compartmentalisation as the "oil and water approach" to learning. It may be too late (or too early) to suggest an abolition of one part but the best practice requires that law should be taught at any and all levels of education both as a liberal art and as a vocation during which learning should be interdisciplinary integrative of knowledge, skills, competencies and values.[19]

Late in 2015, the National Universities Commission in Nigeria released a draft 'Benchmark Minimum Academic Standards for Undergraduate Programmes in

Nigerian Universities'.[20] This document, when approved, is to drive the development of new curricula and teaching methodologies for all disciplines of tertiary institutions in Nigeria, including undergraduate law programmes.

The document's philosophy and rationale is captured in the document itself as follows:

> After more than a decade of using the Minimum Academic Standard (MAS) documents as a major instrument of quality assurance, the Commission in 2001 initiated a process to revise the documents. The curriculum review was necessitated by the fact that the frontiers of knowledge in all academic disciplines had been advancing with new information generated as a result of research. The impact of Information and Communication Technologies on teaching and learning and the dynamics of the skills set required to face the challenge of competition engendered by globalization were also compelling reasons for the curriculum review.
>
> Other compelling reasons included the need to update the standard and relevance of university education in the country as well as to integrate entrepreneurial studies and peace and conflict studies as essential new platforms that will guarantee all graduates from Nigerian universities the knowledge and appropriate skills, competencies and dispositions that will make them globally competitive and capable of contributing meaningfully to Nigeria's socio-economic development. Recognising that the content-based MAS documents were rather prescriptive, a decision was taken to develop outcome-based benchmark statements for all the programmes in line with contemporary global best practice. To actualize this, the Commission organized a stakeholders' workshop to benchmark each programme in all the disciplines taught in Nigerian universities. Following comments and feedback from critical stakeholders in the universities indicating that the Benchmark-style Statements were too sketchy to meaningfully guide the development of curricula and were also inadequate for the purpose of accreditation, the Commission put in place the mechanism for the merger of the Benchmark-style Statements and the revised Minimum Academic Standards into new documents referred to as the Benchmark Minimum Academic Standards (BMAS).
>
> The resultant documents, an amalgam of the outcome-based Benchmark statements and the content-based MAS clearly enunciates the learning outcomes and competencies expected of graduates of each academic programme without being overly prescriptive while at the same time providing the requisite flexibility and innovativeness consistent with institutional autonomy.

This proposed minimum standard sets out the philosophy and fundamental principles of the bachelor of laws programme. The philosophy states that:

> the main focus of the Law programme is to create an environment that encourages intellectual rigour, analytical and critical engagement as well

> as profound ethical standards. The programme will produce law graduates who can compete actively in legal, social, economic and political developments on a global scale.

The document also sets out general learning outcomes for the bachelor of laws degree programme in these broad categories:

a Analytical skills

> Graduates of law are expected to develop high cognitive abilities and skills. With the growing complexities in society, law graduates are expected to identify related socio-economic challenges and demonstrate ability/competence in proffering practical relevant solutions.

b Research skills

> Graduates of the programme are also expected to exhibit commendable research skills, with significant ability to find, consult and analyse legal texts and other materials.

c Advocacy skills

> As 'ministers in the temple of justice', graduates of law are expected to demonstrate commitment to societal harmony and the administration of justice at all levels utilising their analytical and advocacy skills.

d Application

> Graduates of law are expected to have the ability to apply their knowledge and skills in solving academic and practical social problems.

12.5 Conclusion

The proposed change in the benchmarks and minimum standards for undergraduate law programmes is an impetus for reform and transformation of legal education in Nigeria. The minimum standards are not the reform in itself. Legal educators and the legal profession must seize the opportunity to design programmes that will bring about the reform and the much-needed transformation to established best practices.

Meaningful legal education must 'focus' on 'forming legal professionals who are both competent and responsible to clients and the public',[21] creating opportunities for developing in our law graduates deep knowledge in an interdisciplinary manner, skills, attitudes and values.[22]

The final words here are this:

> The bigger picture transformation of legal education in Nigeria must focus on reformation of legal education at the bachelor of laws degree level where the trainee spends 5 years of a 6 years legal training preparing

for the profession. The Law Student from the first year should be trained holistically using an integrated liberal art and vocational approach. This is whether or not the trainee intends to join the profession or not. Medical schools or engineering schools do not separate their students during training between those who intend to finally become medical practitioners or not and between those who plan to be practicing engineers or not. Learning must be student-centred, interactive, and active with heavy doses of experiential learning- to prepare for the profession.

More than 50 years after independence, it is time for us to set goals for our legal education. Law Faculties must set goals for their legal education. Law Faculties must design curricula that are complete with objectives, outcomes, and assessment and evaluation mechanism. Law teachers must be trained in teaching skills and curriculum development to begin to approach legal education from a facilitator's learner-centred perspective rather than from the "sage on stage" attitude.[23]

Notes

1 See: www.law.unn.ng, accessed 13 April 2016. In 1962 Obafemi Awolowo University Ife and University of Lagos established Law Faculties. See: www.unilag.edu.ng, accessed 13 April 2016 and www.oauife.edu.ng, accessed 13 April 2016.

2 Legal Education Act, 1962.

3 J.K. Jegede, A historical perspective of the Nigerian Law School, in Tahir Mamman and others (eds.), *Nigerian Law School – four decades of Service to the legal profession*, Nigeria, Council of Legal Education, 2003, 5.

4 E. Ojukwu, *Trends in legal education: a comparative analysis of Nigeria, USA, UK and South Africa,* in Tahir Mamman et al, op cit., 133.

5 J.K. Jegede, op cit., 6.

6 J. Olakunle Orojo, *Forty years of service to the nation*, in Tahir Mamman et al, op cit., 24.

7 See R. Stuckey and others, *Best practices for legal education*: a *vision and a road map*, New York, Clinical Legal Education Association, 2007, 8.

8 W. Saint and T.A.H.E. Strassner, *Higher education in Nigeria: a status report*, available at: wenr.wes.org/2004/09/wenr-septemberoctober-2004-higher-education-in-nigeria-a-status-report/, accessed 15 June 2016.

9 See George Mason University, *Teaching strategies*, available at: www.gmu.edu/resources/facstaff/part-time/strategy.html, accessed 23 October 2016.

10 Ibid.

11 See: http://nuc.edu.ng/accreditation-results/, accessed 15 June 2014. The University of Lagos Law Programme was given interim accreditation in 2014.

12 See 2007 Report of Council of Legal Education Legal Education Review Committee.

13 See E. Ojukwu, *Legal education in Nigeria: a chronicle of reforms and transformation under Tahir Mamman*, Abuja, Council of Legal Education, 2013, 311–312.

14 Ibid., 312–313.

15 R. Grimes, in Ernest Ojukwu, 2013, op cit., 313.

16 See: E. Ojukwu (ed.), *Externship handbook for supervisors*, Abuja, Council of Legal Education, 2014.

17 See: E. Ojukwu, 2013, op cit., 515.

18 Ibid.

19 See: E. Ojukwu, 2013, op cit., 519–520.
20 See: http://nuc.edu.ng/, accessed 25 October 2015.
21 W.M. Sullivan and others, *Educating lawyers: preparation for the profession of law*, The Carnegie Foundation for the Advancement of Teaching, 2007, 14.
22 Ibid., 22.
23 See: E. Ojukwu, 2013, op cit., 519–520.

Chapter 13

A reform agenda for Indian legal education

Shuvro Prosun Sarker

13.1 Introduction

Legal education in India has been described as a 'sea of institutionalized mediocrity with a few islands of excellence'.[1] There are often calls for reform of legal education – for a system which is of excellent quality, is responsive to modern needs but is also sensitive to the large underprivileged sections of Indian society. Engagement with social needs and their challenges, problems and movements makes legal education relevant and contextual. For this to happen, a liberal, holistic, approach to curriculum planning and development of experiential and clinical teaching is necessary.

However, institutional mechanisms for, and vested interest in, legal education itself form a veritable battlefield. Such a suggestion of conflict is, I suggest, an appropriate description of the contemporary reform initiatives of Indian legal education – a process which is as poorly coordinated as it is lacking in vision. In this chapter, the present status of legal education in India will be analysed with particular reference to intellectual wars between various commissions, council, committees and expert bodies, and finally an agenda for meaningful reform is proposed.

13.2 The mechanics of legal education in India

There are three bodies that, to differing extents, control and affect legal education in India.

Bar Council of India

The Bar Council of India and the State Bar Councils came into existence after the passing of the Advocates Act, 1961. This legislation was enacted to amend and consolidate the law relating to legal practitioners. The Act created an all India Bar with only one class of legal practitioners, namely advocates, who are sub-classified as senior advocates and other advocates. The principal responsibility of the State Bar Councils is to ensure that ethics and etiquette is maintained within the profession. By contrast, one of the main functions of the Bar Council of India is to lay down standards of legal education and accredit law schools. Further, the Bar Council of India has the power to frame rules to secure its objectives, including dictating the legal education curriculum including, but not limited to, the subjects to be taught, the mode of assessment and the qualification to be conferred on successful students.

University Grants Commission

The University Grants Commission (UGC) is a statutory organization, established under the University Grants Commission Act 1956,[2] for the coordination, determination and maintenance of standards of university education. The Act provides that the UGC shall, in consultation with universities, take such steps as it may think fit for the promotion and coordination of higher education and for the maintenance of standards in teaching, examination and research. For the purpose of performing its functions, the UGC may make grants to universities and other educational institutions for maintenance and development. It can also advise the central government, state governments and institutions of higher learning on the measures necessary for the promotion of university education and make rules and regulations consistent with the Act.[3] Non-university institutions can enjoy the academic status and privileges of a university without having to be a multi-faculty educational provider and are able to strengthen their activity areas of their own choosing.

Further, professional councils are responsible for recognition of institutions serving that calling and provide grants to undergraduate programs. Such bodies include the Bar Council of India. Thus, the University Grants Commission recognises the Bar Council of India as partly responsible for legal education.

Committee of Judges

The Committee of Judges, currently consisting of Justices A. M. Ahmedi, M. Jagannadha Rao and B.N. Kirpal, periodically suggests appropriate steps to be taken to improve the quality of lawyers, including the need for practical experience before joining the Bar. The Bar Council of India has been called upon by the committee to take appropriate steps to enhance the prestige of legal profession by ensuring a higher quality of legal education.

13.3 Introduction of an integrated course in law

Against this backdrop, and during his tenure in early 1980s as the secretary of the Bar Council of India, Prof. N.R. Madhava Menon took the duties and powers of the Bar Council and the judges' proposals and framed an educational curriculum for the law students over an extended period (from the then 3-year course to a 5-year course) that was a rigorous programme, equivalent to that found in medicine or engineering and drawing on best practice from elsewhere in the world. This curriculum required students to study law subjects alongside the humanities and social science subjects for the first two years and then engage in experiential learning through a structured clinical legal education component. However, Prof. Menon's proposal met with opposition.[4]

Instead, the idea of an independent law school was born where the best students from all over the country would come to study alongside the best faculty and where new, innovative, methods of teaching would be devised to improve legal education provision.[5]

The need for an independent law school was, in part, a response to the need for a new curriculum, but also it involved something more fundamental – the concept that professionalism and ethics and legal doctrine and lawyering skills needed to be taught together and at a point in a student's education well before joining the Bar. With the profession's support and the backing of the judiciary, the National Law School of India University (NLSIU) was set up in Bangalore in 1987. This was an attempt to implement the radical proposals that had failed to be adopted on a national level. A key component was the integration of experiential learning. Legal clinics were seen as essential in giving students the opportunity, under requisite supervision, of putting theory into practice. At the same time, social justice could be served through the provision of free help to the indigent.[6] This new law school was the only one in India that would be managed by the people from the Bar and the bench – by legal professionals.

The National Law School initiative has led directly to the setting up of similar institutions across India – now totalling over 20 – and all using the extended, integrated, 5-year study programme.[7] Despite these positive changes, the situation elsewhere in India is very different. Though there was a reform movement within legal education in India, there still remained (and remains) many institutions which fall below acceptable standards.[8] The Bar Council of India has failed to stem the abrupt growth of law schools in India, which often provide part-time programmes using inexperienced and even unqualified staff.[9] Teachers here tended to be advocates who, after a tiring day in practice, resort to the classroom to pass on their knowledge and earn extra income.

13.4 The 184th report of the Law Commission of India

In 2002, amongst rising concern about the general standard of legal education provision, the Law Commission, under the chairmanship of Justice M. Jagannadha Rao, decided to review the situation. The powers and duties of both the Bar Council of India and the University Grants Commission were both highlighted, as were the failings in current legal education provision.[10] The link, if not causal, between the two was obvious – why were the regulators not taking firmer and more effective action to remedy the situation?

The Law Commission consulted widely, including with law teachers, and went on to recommend amendments to the Advocates Act 1961, and the University Grants Commission Act 1956, with the objective of laying down clear standards, for the quality of teaching, the content of the curriculum, assessment regimes and admission requirements.[11]

Finally the commission recommended that:

> the Bar Council of India must consult a body which effectively represents all universities and that such a body should be constituted by the University Grants Commission.[12]

and that there was an urgent need for greater co-ordination between the Bar Council and the UGC and between them and law teachers.

13.5 More recent developments

During the period 2006–2009, the National Knowledge Commission (NKC) also reviewed Indian legal education provision and suggested that legal education must aim at preparing legal professionals not only as advocates practising in courts, but also as academics, legislators, judges, policy makers, public officials, civil society activists, as well as legal counsel in the private sector. All should maintain the highest standards of professional ethics and a spirit of public service. Legal education should prepare professionals equipped to meet the new challenges and dimensions of law and legal practice in modern times. The NKC recommended setting up a new regulatory mechanism under the Independent Regulatory Authority for Higher Education (IRAHE), which would be vested with powers to deal with all aspects of legal education, and the decisions of the IRAHE would bind the institutions teaching law and state governments.[13]

The NKC recommended that autonomy may be granted to universities, the National Law Schools (NLSUs) and other providers to decide the core and optional courses to be offered. Curriculum development should reflect issues of social justice.

Rules of Legal Education 2008

In part as a reaction to the preceding reports and criticisms, the Bar Council of India produced the Rules of Legal Education 2008, in an attempt to address apparent shortcomings.[14] The most important aspect of these rules has been to prohibit a student simultaneously registering for a law degree programme whilst being enrolled on any other course of study run by the same or any other institution.[15] The rules also stipulate the minimum marks needed in qualifying examinations for admission to the Bar.[16] The rules specify the need for full-time study under a semesterised system.[17] In addition, a student is not be allowed to take an end-of-semester examination if he or she does not have 70 percent attendance.[18]

The rules also provide for mandatory accreditation by the Bar Council of India for any institution offering courses on law.[19] A Directorate of Legal Education has now been established providing continuing education and training courses and conducting research on legal education issues.[20] The Legal Education Committee of the Bar Council of India is now the dispute resolution body for all disputes relating to legal education.[21] The course content of the two law degree courses (i.e., the 5-year integrated course and the 3-year programme) has also been revised.[22] Moot courts and internships are also now mandatory.

Committee on Legal Education

These developments have also been the subject of recent litigation.

In *Bar Council of India v. Bonnie FOI Law College & Ors* [SLP 22337 of 2008],[23] the Supreme Court has addressed the issues of the inspection, recognition and accreditation of legal education providers. The court noted, with concern, the diminishing standards of professional legal education and identified the importance of overall quality and standards of infrastructure. The order of the Supreme Court reads:

> This petition filed by the Bar Council of India raises very serious questions regarding affiliation and recognition of law colleges by the Bar Council of India. . . . The entire future of the legal profession depends on the ultimate product of these . . . providers). . . . Looking to the gravity and seriousness of the matter, we request the learned Solicitor General and President of the Bar Association and Chairman, Bar Council of India to look into the matter seriously and submit a report to this court as expeditiously as possible. They would be at liberty to associate experts or any other person which they deem it appropriate.[24]

In response, the Bar Council has established a Legal Education Committee with the remit of keeping the state of legal education in India under on-going review.

Curriculum Development Committee (CDC) report 2010[25]

The next development in this plethora of reports and recommendations is the Bar Council's proposals for the improvement and standardisation of legal education provision.[26] This report, significantly, recognises the success that the National Law Schools (NLS) movement has had in linking the theory of law with its practice and the use of innovative and contemporary teaching and learning methods.[27]

Such is the success of the NLS that legislation has been drafted to sustain and support the development.

The preamble to the National Law Schools Bill 2010, sets out the aims of these educational institutions as:

> [providing] ... legal education through setting up of world class law schools with the co-operation of States, in every State where no such law schools exist, to provide for justice-oriented legal education essential to the realization of values enshrined in the Constitution of India, prepare professionals equipped to meet the new challenges and dimensions of internationalization; and to seek path breaking legal research to create new legal knowledge and ideas to help meet the emerging challenges in a manner responsive to the needs of the country and the ideals and goals of the Constitution.[28]

The Bill proposes National Law Schools to be set up in every state, and where no such national law school exists, this will be done by the central government,[29] and sets out the powers[30] and functions[31] of the National Law Schools – which closely resemble those of the existing National Law Schools. One of the important functions in the Bill requires National Law Schools to coordinate with the Centre for Advanced Legal Studies and Research (proposed in the National Knowledge Commission Report) on matters of legal research. Funding for the new schools is to come from a mix of national government and the state government coffers,[32] although the possibility of public-private partnership (and presumably shared cost) is acknowledged.[33]

However impressive the NLS movement has been, much-needed curriculum development can only take place if there are infrastructural changes and all legal education providers are closely regulated. Amongst all of the reviews and reports cited above, it is only the National Knowledge Commission Report and the 3-member Committee on Legal Education that have highlighted the need for the such strategic development if there is to be an effective overhaul of legal education in India. The tension between the perceived and actual roles of the University Grants Commission and the Bar Council of India is palpable and unhelpful in this regard.

13.6 Let noble thoughts come from everywhere[34]

What the reports mentioned above all have in common is that they attempt to reform legal education either without thought to institutional capacity and/or with no consideration of delivery as opposed to content. If we are to make progress first, it is necessary to understand and root out the basic problems relating to curriculum design and associated administration and pedagogy.

Reforming the curriculum

It is inappropriate to continue to have a 3-year and 5-year LLB programme coexisting with one focused on the integration of knowledge, skills and values whilst the other is, at least on the face of it, doctrine-driven. If there is to be effective quality assurance, there needs to be commonality in what is delivered. Given the vested interests at stake, perhaps the only solution is to end both of these programmes and replace them with a degree that runs for sufficient time to allow for a holistic approach to study. The USA and Australia may have the answer through a graduate-only programme, such as the Juris Doctor (JD). Typically this is a 3- to 4-year offering.[35] Students would enter this programme with life skills and an enhanced education background. The slightly shorter study period (4 rather than 5 years) would take into account these attributes whilst allowing more time (than on the 3-year programme) for the inclusion of a strong clinical component.

There must be emphasis on clinical legal education. If 6 subjects were studied in each semester over an 8-semester course, there would be space (taking into account the likely core and optional subjects) for at least 6 overtly clinical courses. In other words, every law school could operate a set of clinics on different themes which might include human rights litigation, legal literacy, women's empowerment, law reform, criminal litigation, disability law, public policy, consumer rights, refugee law and alternative dispute resolution. In addition, whilst not having the same social justice/unmet need focus, other subjects of a more commercial nature, such as intellectual property and corporate law, could also feature, being studied in experiential fashion.

Thought might also be given to requiring an externship component prior to sitting the Bar exam. Lessons may be learnt from the Nigerian experience (see Ojukwu's contribution to this book) where students undertake placement with law firms and the courts as an integral part of their studies. This could be an assessed component and one which, if the student fails, prevents them from qualifying. Law schools might create a database of lawyers accredited to take externs with clear guidance given on the operation of the system. It would also need to be monitored to ensure compliance and consistency. Of course, this could be done as a formal apprenticeship following the lines of work-based learning used in some parts of the civil and common law worlds, but the link between the practice experience and the law school is an important connection that should ensure a realistic opportunity for analysis and reflection.

Reforming administration and accreditation

It is clear that Indian legal education is suffering from multiple controlling authorities. On one side there is the University Grants Commission and on the other the Bar Council of India. It is time for a reorganisation. The Bar Council of India understandably, given its brief, should control entry to the profession, but their wider remit of accrediting law schools is unnecessary unless there is evidence of actual quality control – as is the case, for example, with the ABA in the United States. Legal education is both an academic subject for study and a professional, practice-oriented one too. Given historical failings, it is now time to establish a new professional body (may be an All India Council of Legal Education) to look after matters like accreditation of law schools, setting standards for education and research, prescribing syllabi, developing pedagogy and training teachers. Membership should reflect all interests, the Bar, the judiciary, the academy and the wider public.

The process of accreditation of law schools in India, if properly done, would, given the variance in quality of provision, undoubtedly see the demise of some current providers. In India there are more than 1,000 law schools, and many, possibly most, do not meet the standards as required by the Rules of Legal Education 2008. Most of these providers suffer from poor infrastructure, part-time teachers, limited library and IT facilities and no funding for development. It is true that India, as a large country with a large population, needs lawyers to cater for the whole population; however, at the same time, India does not need poorly educated and ill-equipped lawyers who are unable to discharge their duties properly. With fewer but better-quality law schools, funding could be more effectively targeted.

13.7 Conclusion

The present status of legal education in India is unsatisfactory. There are the national law schools and some wealthy private institutions that have good reputations, excellent facilities and high-quality faculty. These are in the minority, and the private law schools tend to be the preserve of a privileged elite who pay dearly for the experience. There exist, however, a large number of law schools with temporary campuses, little or no library provision, inexperienced faculty and poor reputations. This latter category of law schools represents around 90 percent of provision. This must change, and only the systematic reform of governing structures will achieve that. Once this is in place, we, in India, can look forward to a socially relevant curriculum delivered in a way that provides students with the maximum opportunity to learn – and not just legal rules but the skills a lawyers requires (whether he is she is a practitioner or in some other career), an appreciation of the importance of sound ethical values and a keen sense of professional responsibility.

Notes

1 N.R. Madhava Menon, *To go from mediocrity to excellence*, The Hindu, 18th July 2010.
2 University Grants Commission Act, 1956.
3 Section 12, University Grants Commission Act, 1956.
4 J.K. Krishnan, *Professor Kingsfield goes to Delhi: American Academics, the Ford Foundation, and the development of legal education in India*, American Journal of Legal History, 46, 2004, 478, 480.
5 Ibid., 480–484.
6 N.R. Madhava Menon, *Why yet another law school?*, National Law School of India Review, 1, 1988, 1–4; See: G.M. Gopal, *Prof. N.R. Madhav Menon's reflection on legal and judicial education*, Universal Law Publishing Company, 2009, 217.
7 There have been many institutions in different states that have been modelled on the National Law Schools. For instance if we take the state of West Bengal, the National University of Juridical Sciences (NUJS) experience has led to the setting up of many

institutes that offer a 5-year law course, and the course curriculum has also been designed in the manner which NUJS or other National Law Schools follow.

8 Law Commission of India, *184th Report on The Legal Education & Professional Training and Proposals for Amendments to the Advocates Act 1961 and the University Grants Commission Act 1956*, 2002.

Law Commission of India, 184th Report states that (Para 10.7):

> *We cannot, however, rest content with a few star colleges. We must be concerned with all the rest of the hundreds of law colleges located in cities and district headquarters all over the country. It is these students who come to the bar in great numbers at the grass root level. . . . A few bright star colleges with limited number of student intake in an All India selection is not the end and may not result in an over all change in the level of legal education.*

9 A.K. Avasthi, *Legal education – role of Bar Council of India, judicial intervention/suggestion*, Indian Bar Review, 29, 2002, 27.

10 Ibid., reference may be made to the Forwarding Letter of the Law Commission Chairman to the Minister of Law, government of India.

11 Ibid para 2.3.

12 Ibid, para 2.22.

13 National Knowledge Commission, *Report to the Nation*, 2006–2009.

14 Rules of Legal Education 2008, rule 4.

15 Ibid r 6.

16 Ibid r 7.

17 Ibid r 10.

18 Ibid r 12.

19 Ibid r 14.

20 Ibid r 34.

21 Ibid r 43.

22 Ibid Schedule II.

23 Report of the 3- Member Committee on the Reform of Legal Education, 2010.

24 Ibid i.

25 Bar Council of India, *Curriculum Development Committee Report*, 2010.

26 The steps include (a) overhauling the Education Rules by introduction of New Education Rules from the academic session of 2009 to strengthen the standard of legal education after reviewing the standard of professional legal education in various countries; (b) proposing to establish the Accreditation Committee for national and state level accreditation of the Law Schools; (c) proposing to establish the Directorate of Education at the BCI under the leadership of a senior Professor of Law as Director of the Directorate for conducting Faculty Improvement Program for academics and continuing legal education program for the legal professionals; (d) constituting a Curriculum Development Committee (CDC) to design a standard curriculum of various courses to be run by the Law Schools across the nation; and (e) planning to conduct an All India Examination for enrolment of Indian Students studying and obtaining degree from a foreign recognized University.

27 Curriculum Development Committee Report Bar Council of India, 11.

28 The National Law Schools Bill 2010.

29 Ibid Section 4.

30 Ibid Section 5.

31 Ibid Section 6.

32 Ibid Section 23.

33 Ibid Section 25.

34 Rig Veda, Verse 1.1.

35 This is now a popular discussion among the visionaries of Indian legal education reform.

Chapter 14

Beyond the boom

Prospects for Australian legal education

Jeff Giddings

14.1 Introduction

'Boom and Bust' is the natural state of Australia's arid interior, with occasional heavy rains punctuating the prevailing dry heat. Australia's fauna and flora have evolved to make the most of this unpredictable environment. Early European settlers benefited from rainfall beyond the average and suffered when the cycle turned and droughts returned. This chapter considers the prospects for Australian legal education following what can be described as the boom for Australian law schools since changes to higher education regulation in the late-1980s. In 1989, there were 12 law schools in Australia. By 2016, there were 39 law schools operating across 45 campuses – a pattern of development that can be found elsewhere in common and civil law worlds.

This law school expansion coincided with a prolonged economic boom through the second half of the 1990s and the 2000s, driven in large part by Australia's resources sector and growth in trade with China. The resources boom is now over, leaving a range of structural changes to be made in difficult circumstances. Likewise, Australian legal education grew and changed during the boom and now faces the challenge of adjustment in a crowded and increasingly globalised market. All this growth diverted the attention of legal educators from the challenges raised by such developments and the best ways forward from here are not particularly clear or palatable. This chapter seeks to explain the context for the changes made to Australian legal education over the past quarter century. It then considers the changes now needed to enable legal education to satisfy various interested parties. In particular, I argue for a comprehensive and integrated approach to the use of experiential learning methods and for a more cooperative approach to developing a coherent legal education framework. Legal education is in demand, but is it fit for purpose?

The argument is that the various groups interested in legal education, including the academy, practising profession, regulators and judiciary, need to work at developing content, pedagogy and resourcing. It will take time, effort and a collaborative mind-set to develop the necessary working partnership. In 1990, Weisbrot described the relationship between Australian legal academics and practitioners as uneasy and 'the most significant division within the profession'.[1] Clinical legal education has a distinctive contribution to make in bringing together the various interested parties. The capacity of clinics to combine client service, community engagement and skills development is yet to be embraced fully by the academy. Some academics dismiss learning by doing as being an educational fad or only about practice when the reality of Australian clinical legal education has been very different with its lasting focus on effective pedagogy, holistic and contexualised study and social justice.

I will now consider the need for a more coherent framework to underpin and integrate the various stages of Australian legal education and then address the implications of the dramatic recent changes in the legal education landscape – in terms of law schools and law students. Finally I look at the changes needed to enhance legal education and the relationships that underpin a model legal profession.

14.2 Square pegs in round holes: seeking a more coherent legal education framework

There have long been concerns about the lack of coherence in the legal education framework and the lack of integration between the academic phase usually undertaken as part of a university law degree and vocational phase(s), be it a training course, a bar exam and/or an apprenticeship. Australia is no different. The focus of regulation in this country has been on content coverage rather than on how students learn and how future professionals can best be prepared for the work they will encounter. The Australian Government Productivity Commission's 2014 *Access to Justice Arrangements Inquiry Report* recommended that the Australian government conduct a review of the current status of the three stages of legal education in consultation with the state and territory governments, jurisdictional legal authorities, universities and the profession.[2] The Productivity Commission also emphasised the importance of law students learning more about Alternative Dispute Resolution.

In Australia law graduates must complete a practical legal training (PLT) program or a workplace traineeship in order to be eligible for admission to the legal profession. While a small group of programs (most notably the Professional Program at the University of Newcastle) have been designed to jointly satisfy both the undergraduate law degree (LLB) and PLT requirements, today almost all graduates complete a separate PLT program and many complete most of their PLT study online. Depending on the provider, PLT programs involve a supervised workplace experience of between 2 and 18 weeks, but these programs tend not to integrate the work placement with the rest of their simulation-based program which would enable students to make use of their placement to better understand the dynamics of the practice of law.[3]

Supervised legal practice is a statutory requirement in all Australian states and territories. Legislation requires that newly admitted lawyers engage in supervised legal practice for two years (for those who have completed a PLT program) or 18 months (for those who completed a traineeship).[4] Unfortunately, this requirement is not well understood. The term 'supervised legal practice' is not given any useful definition, nor has it been the subject of any judicial consideration. While supervised legal practice guidelines have been published by some law societies and regulators, they provide virtually no practical guidance in relation to: the meaning of supervision; appropriate supervision practices; or the training and developmental aspects of supervision.[5] The contribution of supervised legal practice as the third stage of legal education needs to be more clearly comprehended.

There have also been serious concerns raised by law schools regarding the poor fit with broader regulatory requirements for the higher education sector. The Australian Qualifications Framework (AQF) is the national policy that sets the specifications for regulated qualifications in Australia. University of New South Wales's law dean, Professor David Dixon, described the AQF as providing 'a series of round holes into which our square pegs don't fit'.[6] The AQF specifications for honours and master's degrees were identified as likely to damage law programs without benefit, especially in relation to providing significant disincentives for international students to study law in Australia.[7] A key reason for the law school interest in attracting international students is the inadequacy of federal government funding of law schools.

One of the key reference points for the operation of the AQF in terms of law studies is the Threshold Learning Outcomes (TLOs) for law published in 2010 as part of the Learning and Teaching Academic Standards component of the AQF. TLOs have been developed for a range of disciplines and are defined in terms of minimum discipline knowledge, discipline-specific skills and professional capabilities including attitudes and professional values that are expected of a graduate from a specified level of program in a specified discipline area. The law TLOs are:

- understanding a coherent body of knowledge;
- developing understandings and abilities related to ethics and professional responsibility;
- developing relevant thinking skills;
- developing research-related skills;
- being able to communicate and collaborate; and
- being able to self-manage.[8]

The Law Admissions Consultative Committee (LACC) is the key entity responsible for facilitating development of the requirements for admission to the legal profession in Australia's states and territories. It is responsible to the Australian and New Zealand Council of Chief Justices, which appoints the Chairman of the Committee, and consists of representatives of each admitting authority, the Council of Australian Law Deans and the Australasian Professional

Legal Education Council. In late-2014, LACC released a discussion paper proposing a limited review of academic requirements for admission to the legal profession.[9] The discussion paper raised the possibility of removing requirements for law degrees to include prescribed coverage of four substantive areas – civil procedure; company law, evidence and ethics and professional responsibility. The possibility of removal of these areas of required coverage received almost no support from the various individuals and entities that responded to the invitation to make written submissions.[10] The proposal relating to ethics and professional responsibility attracted very strong opposition.

The discussion paper also raised the possibility of strengthening the requirements for law degrees to address statutory interpretation following serious concerns from senior judges regarding the poor standard of drafting by practitioners.Various responses to the LACC Discussion Paper contended that statutory interpretation is better taught through integration with existing substantive courses rather than on a stand-alone basis. Others queried why statutory interpretation should be taught differently to other important skills, such as client interviewing, negotiation and advocacy. Learning activities related to statutory interpretation are perhaps best used as a vehicle for active student engagement and the understanding and application of laws. The LACC's review discussion paper and consultation process are indicative of missed opportunities for serious engagement around how interested parties can work towards a more effectively integrated legal education framework. There is a need to consider issues beyond the substantive legal content that must be addressed in a law degree program.

It appears that LACC may be moving towards taking a more systematic approach to addressing the assurance of competence of practising lawyers in a way that should address the various stages of legal education including the need for continuing professional development. As mentioned elsewhere in this book the influence of the Legal Education and Training Review in England is being felt further afield. In Australia the LACC is also now proposing a review of requirements for practice, including the threshold level of competence needed of entry-level lawyers. The review now proposed by LACC would involve 'substantial consultation with a wide range of key groups'.[11] Advocates for a change of approach to legal education will need to take this opportunity to engage closely with this review process.

14.3 Significant change in Australian legal education

Let us now move on to consider ways in which Australian legal education changed through the 'boom times'. As mentioned earlier, the 'boom' saw the number of law schools more than treble from 12 in 1989 to 39 in 2016. Barker refers to this as an 'avalanche of law schools'.[12] There was a dramatic increase in student numbers, from 11,254 studying law in 1984 to 36,331 studying law or legal studies in 2000.[13] Between 2001 and 2012, law student numbers increased by 31 percent, with some 36,000 graduates in 2012.[14]

Changes in law schools

In 2001–2002, Johnstone and Vignaendra completed a detailed 'stocktake' of curricula and teaching and learning in Australian law schools. Their report noted significant change during the late-1980s and 1990s, most notably in a strengthening focus on ethics, legal theory and generic and legal skills teaching as well as a more informed and 'student-focused' approach to pedagogy, along with greater rigour in subject design. They also noted a lack of systematic co-ordination, in part due to resource constraints and the competing views of stakeholders as to what legal education should address.[15]

Since this appraisal, the key areas of development in law teaching have been the sector-wide move to greater engagement with digital technology (especially in the PLT field, most notably at the Australian National University) and changes generated by globalisation. Law students are now much more likely to engage in 'study abroad' and LLB/JD curricula are now much more likely to address global legal issues and content in both core and elective courses. This appears to have been driven more by growing interest in other legal cultures than developing student understanding of, say, inquisitorial legal processes. Some Australian law schools have relinquished their stand-alone faculty status and become part of a larger group or division within their university, often with partners from Business, Commerce and Justice Studies. Such changes have seen law schools lose some autonomy within their institution, and this has resulted in some being 'square pegs' in university efforts to comply with the 'round holes' prescribed by the AQF referred to earlier. There have also been significant impacts on law teaching generated by the intensifying university focus on research and publication outputs. While research imperatives have fostered greater scholarship of learning and teaching, they have created particular challenges for legal academics with heavy teaching loads.

The *Juris Doctor* qualification was just emerging as Johnstone and Vignaendra completed their review in 2002. The JD is now much more prominent but has not yet developed the strong focus on learning by doing in preparation for legal practice that characterises the JD in many US law schools. Growing interest in experiential models of legal education is yet to be matched by deep engagement and understanding of the strengths, limitations and resourcing needs of such models. Research conducted in 2010–2012 for the *Australian Clinical Legal Education Best Practices Guide* revealed considerable variation among clinical programs in terms of the responsibility given to students, supervisory processes and the classroom component accompanying the clinic experience.[16] In an effort to reduce costs, some Australian law schools have relied on unpaid, untrained and unsupported external supervisors. To work well, external placements require careful structuring in terms of the supervision arrangements and the academic component linked to the placement. Without close attention to effective pedagogy, Australian law schools may end up in a 'race to the bottom' for student placement opportunities that emphasise practice-oriented experiences without revealing the ethical and justice-oriented insights generated by those experiences.

Changes in law students

The 21st century has also heralded significant change for Australian law students, particularly in terms of less certainty about their professional pathways. While some in the practising legal profession lament the rapid growth in the number of law graduates, law schools take a very different view. However, it appears undeniable that students see themselves as facing greater challenges in securing the types of professional opportunities they are seeking. The requirements for contemporary professional work are probably more demanding now than in the past and are constantly changing, indicating that the possession of specific doctrinal knowledge is insufficient on its own as preparation for practice. Without knowing where these individuals will find employment on graduation it is difficult to make them 'job ready'. Most law graduates now complete a predominantly online PLT program, a form of preparation for supervised legal practice that was not available 15 years ago. Yet, dramatic changes to law firm structures now seriously limit the opportunities for law graduates to engage in a closely supervised, personal transition to professional practice.

Students are also incurring greater debt in the course of their studies, and all indications are that course fees will rise rather than fall in the future. The student fee focus in higher education has clearly contributed to students seeing themselves as consumers, with increased expectations as to the levels of service, flexibility and accessibility they can expect from their law school. Students are also responding to changes in law firm hiring practices by seeking employment in firms long before graduation as this is seen as the most promising route to subsequent entry to the profession through continuing employment with the firm in question.

Australian law students are also less likely to attend classes than previously. The move to digital delivery has contributed to this shift and students increasingly expect to be able to 'control how they engage with their studies, particularly in relation to attendance' and also expect there to be some 'value in prioritising these activities over their other interests'. Research by Corbin, Burns and Chrzanowski highlighted that the real issue with attendance is student engagement, noting that 'a critical element of engagement is attendance'.[17] They found that students choose not to attend lectures and tutorials if they consider such attendance will interfere with assessment-related work or if they do not see a benefit in such attendance. Other significant contributors to non-attendance were family and work obligations as well as illness.

Recognition in Australia of issues related to the mental health and wellbeing of law students has grown dramatically in the past decade. The 2009 Courting the Blues project reported that 35 percent of Australian law students recorded elevated levels of psychological distress as compared to 13 percent of the general population. Almost 40 percent of those students with high or very high levels of psychological distress reported distress severe enough to warrant medical or clinical intervention. Studies of law students at the Australian National University (ANU) and Melbourne University found that students entered law school with rates of wellbeing no lower than those among the general population but that levels of psychological distress rose significantly in their first year of law.[18] The Tristan Jepson Memorial Foundation[19] and the Wellness for Law Forum[20] have both been important in publicising the mental health challenges faced by law students and lawyers.[21] There is a clear need to move beyond the consideration of wellbeing as a subject for scholarship to harness the insights to inform our approaches to legal education and improve teaching and support practices.

It is clear that a wide range of factors are impacting significantly on law teaching in Australia. Digitisation and globalisation have dramatically changed the work of law schools, law students and law firms. Sector-wide regulatory change related to the AQF has also affected law schools along with the expectations of both universities and students that a law degree will prepare graduates for work in a range of professional contexts. It is also useful to identify what has not changed significantly during the 21st century. Most notable in this regard is the continuing reliance on lectures and large group classes, even when student attendance has markedly declined.

14.4 How experiential methods can enliven legal education

We can now turn to delivery of the curriculum and in particular the contribution clinics and other forms of experiential learning can make to legal education. Learning by doing and reflecting can complement conventional classroom-based coverage of many basic subject matters, thereby addressing limitations of the standard law curriculum. Clinical methods are well suited to providing a counterpoint to approaches that currently dominate law teaching, including the case-dialogue method popular in the US[22] and the large class lecture relied on across much of the globe. Clinical methodologies can be a 'breath of fresh air' for students who tire of passive approaches to learning.[23]

Legal professional skills development

An array of authors has articulated the value that clinics can bring to student skill development. A wide range of practice skills arise with clinic-based experiences, including trial advocacy, interviewing, problem-solving, client counselling, negotiating, mediating, lobbying, drafting, fact management, legal research, time management, teamwork and strategic planning. Such teaching should 'provide models for the exercise of these skills, rather than simply focussing on how-to-do-it'.[24] Skills development 'takes on an entirely different dimension' when it involves working with real clients in a clinic, filling 'the gap that so many lawyers feel between what they were taught in law school and what they do in practice'.[25] Close supervision of students is significant to providing the scaffolding learners need in order to further develop their professional skills.[26] Frameworks that use simulations to prepare students for real-client work, with complexity increasing over time as students develop their skills and understandings, are important here.

Dealing with unstructured situations

Various authors emphasise the use of clinics to enable students to develop the analytical frameworks they will need to effectively structure their work on behalf of clients. Modes of planning and analysis for dealing with unstructured situations are described by Amsterdam as 'conceptual foundations for practical skills'. Two such skills ideally suited to development in the clinic are: the structuring and application of doctrine to situations involving unclear or developing facts; and problem-solving through 'a thorough canvass of one's goals and an equally thorough study of the ways in which those goals might be accomplished'.[27] Students need to develop their understanding of the demands, constraints and methods for analysis of situations where the issues have not been pre-identified.[28]

Self-awareness and the capacity to learn from reflection

Almost all law students and novice practitioners benefit from guidance around how to learn from experience. The close supervision enabled by the typically low student-teacher ratios used in clinics can foster such student reflection. The flexibility of clinical methods also enables students to engage in wide and deep experiences, providing greater opportunities to acquire wisdom. Reflective learning and self-awareness are also important in fostering resilience, a quality increasingly recognised as significant in the work of professionals in a range of disciplines.[29] Even in larger group sessions, the clinic's reflective practice can be used by prompting students to share their experiences and discuss what happened and why and what they might do differently next time.

Exploring and critiquing 'lawyering' and legal systems

The nature of the clients represented by clinics (often the poor and disenfranchised) highlights to students 'the way in which status often disadvantages their client, sometimes as a result of legal doctrine or other times because of the prejudices of judges or other actors in the legal system'.[30] Such exploration and critique can extend to the various roles that can be played by lawyers – from 'collaborative' work to 'facilitative' roles to 'integrative' work and 'activist' approaches.[31]

Awareness of clients and contexts

Clinic-based experiences enable the impact of the law and legal processes to be very clearly demonstrated to students, many of whom will initially have little idea how the law affects people in practice.[32] 'Practical courses in lawyering and work in legal clinics are thus the logical complement to the forced decontextualisation that students experience in the standard first-year curriculum.'[33] Constructivist learning theory emphasises that learning is a matter of constructing interpretations of experiences and developing personal understandings that stay with the learner. Students will learn better 'when their opportunities to construct understandings are authentic, such as when their learning is anchored in a realistic context'.[34]

This extends further to illustrating to students the merit of adopting holistic and inter-disciplinary approaches to addressing legal issues, in both practical and theoretical contexts. Placing the client, rather than the law, at the centre also involves recognition of the limits of the law and the importance of other disciplines. Clinical legal education allows students to consider the relevance, viability and applicability of legal rules and principles in other professional contexts and provides opportunities for cross-disciplinary collaboration.

Collaboration

Clinics provide multiple opportunities to foster greater collaboration and the use of integrative frameworks, among students as well as between students and supervisors. 'The more one values and practices collaboration, the better one will collaborate. The better one collaborates, the more one will value and practice collaboration.'[35] Working together, students and supervisors can identify a range of options, and in that process, they learn another important lesson: that professional work involves exercising practical judgments under conditions of uncertainty. Collaborative learning also allows students to develop new ideas through dialogue with others.

Promoting ethical understanding and actions

The literature on clinical legal education emphasises the suitability of practice contexts for fostering ethics-related learning. Experiential education is a 'powerful tool for forming professional habits and understandings',[36] allowing students 'to critically analyse the law of lawyering including the various codes of practice and their rationales within a framework of access to justice issues, a client centred approach and a recognition of the public role of a legal practitioner'.[37] The legal practice context of the clinic gives rise to spontaneous and various ethical questions,[38] allowing students 'to judge their ethical standards not just by their ideals, but by their actual deeds'.[39] Students can also learn through observing the actions of their supervisor and other professionals involved in the clinic.[40]

Fostering student commitment to social justice

Clinics can also develop student sensitivity to social justice concerns generated by the law and legal processes. This is linked to promoting the engagement of students in *pro bono* activities, a contribution that I explore further below. A social justice-oriented clinical experience can create circumstances in which students will encounter 'disorienting moments' where their clinic experience cannot be explained by their previous understandings of how the world works. This relates particularly to students understanding the impact of laws on marginalised people. Quigley emphasises that a complete clinical education experience should include lessons about social justice.[41]

Clinics often pursue social justice objectives by working well beyond the traditional service delivery model of advice and representation for individual clients, for example by delivering public legal education classes. Some new approaches have been focused on enriching student learning, while others have been designed principally to enhance the community benefits of the work of clinic teachers and their students.

Clinic and 'capstones'

Clinics also have the potential to provide a valuable capstone experience for law students, 'integrating a body of relatively fragmented knowledge in a unified whole'. The focus on reflective practice can enable students to 'both look back over their undergraduate curriculum in an effort to make sense of that experience, and look forward to a life of building on that experience'.[42] A project on capstone experiences in legal education identified the following curriculum design principles:

- supporting transition by promoting self-management, developing professional identity and supporting career planning and development;
- providing integration and closure;
- responding to diversity by enhancing students' capacity to engage with diversity in professional contexts;
- promoting professional engagement;
- recognising the experience's culminating nature by requiring students to make appropriate use of feedback and to reflect on their own capabilities; and
- being regularly evaluated.[43]

Clinical courses in a student's final year have often fulfilled many of these capstone features. Making such courses accessible to all students who want to complete them raises significant resourcing issues that will require support from a range of interested parties.

14.5 Improving Australian legal education

This subtitle suggests changes that should be made to enhance Australian legal education. I call for the development of a more integrated legal education framework that articulates and harnesses the links between the understandings, skills and judgement that students need to develop as part of their LLB/JD studies, then through their PLT and supervised legal practice with a view to becoming effective and reflective in the workplace – whether that be in law or elsewhere.

The need for balance

The regulators of Australian legal education have been preoccupied with ensuring the coverage of substantive content in key areas and have paid insufficient attention to how students are taught and what those students learn. The focus on 'what the law is' needs to be balanced with understandings of how the law works and how it might be changed to work better. The focus on 'black letter law' has been underpinned by convenient but flawed assumptions about the effectiveness of traditional teaching processes. Law schools and the legal profession admitting authorities need to move away from substantive silos to address the law in terms of its impact on people. Legal education should not be confined to preparation for practice in a narrow, technical and doctrinal sense. This alternative view of the future of Australian legal education emphasises the importance of responsibility, integrity and creativity on the part of students and practitioners. It addresses the importance of students developing their ability to make wise judgements when acting on behalf of others.

Funding that supports experiential legal education

Funding issues are central to the future of Australian legal education. Since 1991, the federal government has used a Relative Funding Model to allocate operating grants to universities. This model disadvantages law, placing it in the lowest of five discipline funding clusters (along with economics, accounting and various humanities disciplines) with a weighting of 1. By contrast, the top cluster (comprising medicine, dentistry and veterinary science) has a weighting of 2.7. This has entrenched less expensive ways of teaching as the standard approach in Australian law schools.[44] At the same time, law students contribute to the Higher Education Contribution Scheme (HECS) at the highest of three differential rates.[45] The 2008 Report of the Bradley Review of Australian

Higher Education referred to law students are amongst the groups that make the largest contribution to the cost of their education through HECS payments. Law student HECS payments cover 84 percent of the amount a university receives from the federal government for each law student. This compares to 27 percent for nursing student HECS payments. The absence of a strong tradition of clinic-based experiential learning in law and the funding of law at a minimal level make it less likely that law schools will prioritise relatively expensive forms of legal education such as clinical programs. For experiential learning to become a major part of legal education, this funding framework needs to change.

Greater understandings of dispute resolution

Kathy Douglas draws on a range of sources to persuasively argue that alternative dispute resolution needs to be a key feature of the law curriculum in order to prepare graduates for contemporary legal practice.[46] This is important to overcoming the 'adversarial mindset' identified by the Australian Law Reform Commission in its 1997 Discussion Paper on Legal Education.[47] Skills and understanding of negotiation and mediation also build the capacity of law students to address conflict in their personal and professional lives. A range of teaching methods can usefully be integrated, including coverage in substantive areas such as civil procedure complemented by stand-alone elective courses on mediation and negotiation. Clinical experiences also have a valuable contribution to make in deepening student understanding of ADR, the dynamics of conflict and the importance of negotiation.[48]

A broader view of the globalised legal world

I have already made reference to the growing globalisation of legal education with Australian law students more likely to take up opportunities to study abroad as part of their degree. It will be valuable for Australian law schools to consider and build partnerships with institutions and organisations in 'developing' countries rather than relying on traditional destinations in the United Kingdom and North America. In making such arrangements, partnerships can usefully be nurtured with organisations such as the Global Alliance for Justice Education.[49]

Integrating effective clinical teaching practices

Legal education frameworks that effectively integrate clinical teaching methods have an important contribution to make in enhancing legal education. Clinical methodologies can make a more substantial contribution as part of an integrated and effectively sequenced program than on a stand-alone basis. Experiential learning frameworks also rely on effective supervision practices given that much of the potential of such learning can be lost if the student is not supported and guided to understand what they have encountered.

14.6 Conclusion – fostering constructive change in legal education

If we are serious about change, what steps can be taken to foster constructive engagement among the key participants in Australian legal education? What processes can be used to ensure that innovation is driven by design rather than convenience? The groups involved in legal education appear to have been more concerned with their 'ownership' of the issues and processes involved rather than with their shared 'custodianship' of legal education. These interested parties need to view legal education as a shared endeavour rather than each different stakeholder assuming that theirs is the most valuable and valid perspective. There also needs to be less preoccupation with the money side of legal education and a greater emphasis placed on the preparation of future professionals.

LACC and the admitting authorities that accredit law degrees should engage with the broad dimensions of legal education and support law school initiatives that foster higher levels of quality in legal education. Rather than simply setting requirements, the authorities could positively endorse those law schools that demonstrate extensive integration of clinical methods and insights. They should acknowledge the additional educational value of structured supervision arrangements that are focussed on preparing LLB/JD students and PLT students for the challenges of professional practice or other employment destinations. The full benefits of learning through doing will not be realised without a supervisor who supports the student to understand and reflect on their experiences.

The judiciary also has a key role to play in supporting legal education initiatives that foster the ongoing ethical development of law students and practising lawyers. *Pro bono* initiatives and clinical teaching methods both have important contributions to make in fostering ethical development. Clinical experiences are well recognised as providing students with opportunities to deepen their understanding of the dilemmas faced by lawyers in balancing the interests of clients with their over-riding duties to the administration of justice and issues of self-interest. Beyond their understandable concern with improving statutory interpretation, judges can contribute to legal education by sharing their distinctive experience with fact-finding, interpretation and decision-making more generally.

Legal professional organisations can be influential in building traditions of involvement in the education of tomorrow's lawyers. The long-term vitality of the profession will be enhanced if lawyers take the time to provide students with opportunities to develop their skills, knowledge and professional identity. Law schools clearly have an important role to play in explaining their work and engaging with the profession around their respective roles in preparing future lawyers and contributing to the development of legal knowledge. As I argued earlier, legal education must not be confined to preparation for practice in a narrow technical and doctrinal sense nor should it be focused on overtly 'legal' careers.

I have also argued there is a need for a more coherent framework to foster effective legal education with clear linking of the different phases – the LLB/JD, PLT and supervised legal practice. The lack of a coherent framework leaves too much opportunity for those responsible to play 'pass the parcel'. This highlights the importance of greater cooperation between the different stakeholders. Huxham and Vangen have described various bases for 'collaborative advantage', where it is in the interests of organisations to work together.[50] They refer to the importance of developing trust, communicating effectively and understanding that collaboration is a time-consuming process that requires compromise.[51] Australian legal education will be improved if that 'collaborative advantage' can be gained and 'collaborative inertia' avoided.

Notes

1 D. Weisbrot, *Australian lawyers*, Longman Cheshire, 1990, 146.
2 Australian Government Productivity Commission, *Access to justice arrangements inquiry report*, 2014, Chapter 7, 254. See Recommendation 7.1.
3 J. Giddings and M. McNamara, *Preparing generations of future lawyers for legal practice: what's supervision got to do with it?*, UNSWLJ, 37 (3), 2014, 1226, 1233–1236.
4 Ibid., 1236–1237.
5 Ibid., 1247–1255.
6 D. Dixon, *TEQSA, the AQF and the regulatory threat to Australian legal education*, available at: www.industry.gov.au/highereducation/Policy/HEAssuringQuality/Documents/Submissions/David%20Dixon.pdf, accessed 21 October 2016.
7 Ibid.
8 A. Huggins, *Incremental and inevitable: contextualising the threshold learning outcomes for law*, UNSWLJ, 38 (1), 2015, 264.
9 See: Law Admissions Consultative Committee, *Review of Academic Requirements for admission to the legal profession*, www.lawcouncil.asn.au/LACC/index.php/review-of-academic-requirements, accessed 23 October 2016.
10 I contributed to 2 submissions, those by Griffith Law School and Legal Ethics Academic Lawyers
11 Law Admissions Consultative Committee, *Assuring professional competence*, copy on file with the author.
12 D. Barker, *An avalanche of law schools, 1989–2013*, Journal of the Australasian Law Teachers Association, 6, 2013, 153. See also Margaret Thornton and Lucinda Shannon, *Selling the dream: law school branding and the illusion of choice*, Legal Education Review, 23 (2), 2013, 249.
13 G. Lansdell, *Have we 'pushed the boat out too far' in providing online practical legal training? A guide to best practices for future programs*, Legal Education Review, 19, 2009, 149, 151, fn 11.
14 P. Collins, *Australian legal education at a crossroads*, Australian Universities Review, 58 (1), 2016, 30, 32.
15 R. Johnstone and S. Vignaendra, *Learning outcomes and curriculum development in law*, A report commissioned by the Australian Universities Teaching Committee, 2003.
16 A. Evans, A. Cody, A. Copeland, J. Giddings, M.A. Noone and S. Rice, *Best practices: Australian clinical legal education*, 2013, 28–47.
17 L. Corbin, K. Burns and A. Chrzanowski, *If you teach it, will they come? Law students, class attendance and student engagement*, Legal Education Review, 20, 2010, 13, 20.

18 M. Townes O'Brien, S. Tang and K. Hall, *Changing our thinking: empirical research on law student wellbeing, thinking styles and the law curriculum*, Legal Education Review, 21, 2011, 149.
19 See: www.tjmf.org.au, accessed 24 October 2016.
20 See: www.wellnessforlaw.com/, accessed 24 October 2016.
21 See also the work of R. Field, *National Teaching Fellow*, available at: www.olt.gov.au/altc-teaching-fellow-rachael-field, accessed 20 October 2016.
22 W. Sullivan, A. Colby, J. Welch Wegner, L. Bond and L. Shulman, *Educating lawyers*, Jossey Bass, 2007, Chapter 1.
23 R. Wilson, *Training for justice: the global reach of clinical legal education*, Penn State International Law Review, 22 (3), 2004, 421, 429.
24 Association of American Law Schools (AALS), *Report of the Committee on the future of the in-house clinic*, Journal of Legal Education, 42, 1992, 508, 512.
25 F. Bloch and N.R. Madhava Menon, The global clinical movement, in F. Bloch (ed.), *The global clinical movement: educating lawyers for social justice*, Oxford, Oxford University Press, 2010, Chapter 18, 271.
26 Sullivan et al, op cit., 27. 'By making explicit important features of good performance through various conceptual models and representations, teachers can guide the learner in mastering complex knowledge by small steps. These devices of representation serve as scaffolds (in the language of learning theorists) to support efforts at improved performance.'
27 A. Amsterdam, *Clinical legal education—a 21st century perspective*, Journal of Legal Education, 34, 1984, 612.
28 R. Stuckey and Others, *Best practices in legal education: a vision and a road map*, Clinical Legal Education Association, 2007, 169.
29 Ibid., 29–36. See also D. Maranville, M. Lynch, S. Kay, P. Goldfarb and R. Engler, *Re-vision quest: a law school guide to designing experiential courses involving real lawyering*, New York Law School Law Review, 56, 2011, 517, 533. They refer to 'Promoting lifelong learning' as a potential goal for clinical experiences.
30 E. Milstein, *Clinical legal education in the United States: in-house clinics, externships and simulations*, Journal of Legal Education, 51, 2001, 375, 379–380. See also Rose Voyvodic, *'Considerable promise and troublesome aspects': theory and methodology of clinical legal education*, Windsor Yearbook of Access to Justice, 20, 2001, 111, 119, where she refers to the 'culture shock' students face when they enter a clinical program with 'no prior life experience of poverty or its racialized or gendered aspects'. See also Maranville et al, op cit., 533. They include 'Understanding unequal social structures and advancing social objectives' and 'Providing culturally competent client representation' as potential goals for clinical programs.
31 A. Cody and B. Schatz, Community law clinics: teaching students, working with disadvantaged communities, in F. Bloch (ed.), *The global clinical movement: educating lawyers for social justice*, op cit., Chapter 11, 181.
32 F. Bloch and M.A. Noone, Legal aid origins of clinical legal education, in F. Bloch (ed.), *The global clinical movement: educating lawyers for social justice*, op cit., Chapter 10, 164. They state: 'Providing legal services to the poor can have a transformative effect on students when they see firsthand the operation of the legal system and its imperfections and negative impact on certain sections of the population'.
33 Sullivan et al, op cit., 59. Maranville et al, op cit., also refers to the contribution of clinics through providing context. She refers to these five aspects of context: information about the people who find themselves involved in legal disputes; the institutions and practices giving rise to legal disputes; the processes in which legal doctrines are applied; familiarity with the legal tasks lawyers perform; and the firms, organisations and work settings in which lawyers perform their tasks. Maranville, op cit., 128–129.

34 M. Schwartz, S. Sparrow and G. Hess, *Teaching law by design*, Carolina Academic Press, 2009, 7.
35 D. Chavkin, *Spinning straw into gold: exploring the legacy of bellow and moulton*, Clinical Law Review, 10, 2003, 245, 254–255. See also D. Chavkin, *Matchmaker, matchmaker: student collaboration in clinical programs*, Clinical Law Review, (1), 1994, 199, for a valuable analysis of both the importance and challenges of fostering student collaboration.
36 Stuckey and others, op cit., 167.
37 L. Curran, J. Dickson and M.A. Noone, *Pushing the boundaries or preserving the status quo? Designing clinical programs to teach law students a deep understanding of ethical practice*, International Journal of Clinical Legal Education, 8, 2005, 104, 121.
38 S. Rice and G. Coss, *A guide to implementing clinical teaching method in the law school curriculum*, Centre for Legal Education, 1996, 21.
39 AALS, op cit., 514.
40 The AALS Committee on the Future of the In-House Clinic stated that 'students are able to observe the faculty member modelling how she would address the professional responsibility issue in question, and to learn that competent professionals take ethical responsibilities seriously'. AALS op cit., 514.
41 Ibid., 38. Ross also lists a series of articles on the explicit social justice agenda of US law school clinics. M. Ross, *A 'systems' approach to clinical legal education*, Clinical Law Review, 13, 2007, 780–781.
42 R. Durel, *The capstone course: a rite of passage*, Teaching Sociology, 21 (3), 1993, 223.
43 S. Kift, M. Sanson, J. Cowley and P. Watson (eds.), *Excellence and innovation in legal education*, Lexis Nexis Australia, 2011, Chapter 5.
44 J. Giddings, *Promoting justice through clinical legal education*, Justice Press, 2013, 121.
45 This means that while HECS payments by law students are at the highest level, government funding is at the lowest level. See D. Bradley et al, *Review of Australian higher education: final report*, 2008, 161. See also: A. Goldsmith, *Why should law matter? Towards a clinical model of legal education*, UNSWLJ, 25 (3), 2002, 722. Goldsmith noted that in 1998, the Federal Government paid universities less than $7,000 per law student while the figure paid for each dentistry and medicine student exceeded $18,000.
46 K. Douglas, *The role of adr in developing lawyers' practice: lessons from Australian legal education*, International Journal of the Legal Profession, 22 (1), 2015, 71.
47 ALRC, *Review of the adversarial system of litigation: rethinking legal education and training: issues paper*, 21, 1997, 52.
48 J. Giddings, *Using clinical methods to teach alternative dispute resolution: developments at Griffith University*, Australasian Dispute Resolution Journal, 9 (3), 1999, 206.
49 www.gaje.org, accessed 24 October 2016.
50 C. Huxham and S. Vangen, *Managing to collaborate: the theory and practice of collaborative advantage*, Routledge, 2005, 7.
51 Ibid., Chapter 3.

Chapter 15

Re-thinking at the sharp end – examples of experiential teaching and learning practice

Part 1 – Mock-trials in an accusatorial and inquisitorial context

David McQuoid-Mason

15.1.1 Introduction

This chapter is based on the writer's experiences when teaching about the criminal justice system in South Africa. The concept of mock trials is, it is suggested, however of equal relevance in the civil law world. The materials described here have been tried both at home and extensively in Central and Eastern Europe.

Born out of an African context, I offer the mock trial as a valuable form of experiential learning rich in potential and applicable regardless (providing there is a relevant form of judicial hearing) of the nature of the legal system.

Mock trials may be based on real cases or use hypothetical situations.[1] The format chosen depends largely upon the learning outcomes set for the exercise. The word 'trial' can be broadly interpreted to include preliminary matters such as plea or bail as well as formal hearings into alleged guilt. They can centre on either criminal or civil liability although the former may be easier to stage and is used here as the example.

Mock trials allow students to experience courtroom procedures and understand how the courts deal with and resolve disputes. Mock trials enable students to see how lawsuits are handled by lawyers and judges and how the procedures impact on lay witnesses, the accused and experts. They also help students to develop critical thinking skills, analyse problems, think strategically, formulate questions (through preparation and active listening), develop oral presentation skills, hone research capacity and importantly, think on their feet. This form of interaction also promotes co-operative learning and may prepare students for possible future involvement as parties and witnesses in trials. Mock trials help to lessen fear of the courts and provide students with the knowledge and skills needed to perform their roles in the simulated court effectively.[2]

Law school mock trials are often about individual performance, and many take the form of competitions. The model I am describing here is aimed more at a larger student cohort and as part of a specific learning and teaching vehicle. Sometimes termed '*Street Law*' (a form of public legal education often delivered by law students to community groups), mock trials are a means of educating students (and where applicable, others) in the workings of the judicial system. They are based on the sequence of events that have occurred or might occur in real courts.

As well as showcasing the mock trial as a powerful form of experiential learning, I also wish to show that it can be successfully used in both common and civil law countries – under both adversarial and inquisitorial systems. I will demonstrate how relatively large groups can be involved. This is done by constituting teams of prosecutors and defence lawyers to prepare, as appropriate to the jurisdiction, opening statements, questions for examination-in-chief, cross-examination, re-examination and closing addresses; and teams of judges to control the proceedings and prepare questions and judgments after they have heard the evidence. In addition, other participants play the roles of the defendant, witnesses and court officials. In inquisitorial jurisdictions, the judges play a much more active role in questioning the defendant and witnesses than traditionally in the case system, and the team of judges in the civil law trial can be expanded to reflect this.

Street Law mock trials can be used to teach law students, school children and lay people about the court system. I set out below the specifics of how to run mock trials in both common and civil law countries. Although much of the material here is available in printed and electronic form elsewhere, I reproduce it below to give a concrete example and template for readers and their students to use.

The *Street Law* mock trial requires around four hours: approximately three hours to train the participants in court procedure, evidence, an understanding of the relevant facts, the law applicable and trial advocacy; and one hour to present the trial. This can be done in one day with a morning training session and an afternoon trial, or as a series of six classroom lessons of 45 minutes each.[3] Criminal cases are ideal because the pre-trial procedures can be dealt with beforehand and policy questions concerning crime and society lend themselves to lively discussion. Also most people, particularly the young, can relate to the criminal context and even find it interesting and fun!

15.1.2 Learning outcomes for a *Street Law*-type mock trial[4]

As seen elsewhere in this book, clear learning outcomes are essential if the programme is to have requisite focus and is open to constructive assessment and evaluation. The learning outcomes for a mock trial will depend on the educator's objectives but might typically cover the following.

At the end of a mock trial students will be able to:

1 Explain the steps taken in an investigation which takes place before a trial is conducted.
2 Identify the participants in the trial – who does what and why and in what order?

3 Describe who must prove what in a trial.
4 (Depending on the roles allocated) prepare suitable questions, arguments and submission for the trial.
5 Explain how judges reach their judgments in a trial.
6 Respond appropriately to judges during the trial.
7 Explain to clients, witnesses or other parties what will happen, what did happen and what might now happen in and as a result of the trial.

15.1.3 Preparing for a *Street Law*-type mock trial

The following is a guide to setting up and running the mock trial.[5] (The terminology may need adapting to fit with particular jurisdictions.)

Step 1: Distribute the mock trial materials to the class

Read through the charge, indictment or summons, the facts of the case and the witnesses' statements with all the participants. The law teacher should:

(a) Make sure that the students understand the facts of the case, the nature of the offence and the applicable law.
(b) Get the students to read through each of the statements and to highlight those parts of the statements that favour the prosecution and those that favour the defence.

Step 2: Assign or select students for the various roles in the mock trial

Depending on the type of trial, students should be selected to play the roles, as appropriate, of lawyers, witnesses, experts, judges, registrars, clerks, court orderlies, time keepers, the press, welfare officers and court observers. For the role of judge, it is often helpful to invite a resource person, such as a lawyer or real judge. If this is not possible, law teachers, law students or other participants can act as judges.

Step 3: Prepare participants for the trial

The *Street Law* mock trial is designed to involve as many students as possible in preparation and presentation. This is done by ensuring that all the participants understand the facts and the law that must be established by the prosecution and/or defence. Thereafter each team of prosecutors, defence lawyers and judges must be given the necessary background to enable them to prepare their questions, arguments or judgments. The best way of doing this is to require individual participants to read out the statements of each witness, and then invite all the participants to identify those aspects of each statement that can be used by the prosecution and defence respectively when preparing their questions, arguments or judgments.

In order to achieve this, the law teacher should divide the class into training groups. Students should be divided into:

- Teams of lawyers, witnesses, experts and accused persons for the prosecution and defence. Each team has the responsibility for preparing its side of the case and needs to prepare opening statements, questions for their witnesses and those of the other side, and closing statements.
- Teams of judges (if more than one judge will be used), who need to know how to run the trial and must prepare questions for the witnesses and a preliminary judgment that will be subject to change after hearing the case.
- Teams of registrars, clerks, court ushers/orderlies and time keepers who need to be prepared for the various tasks in a trial (e.g., arrange time charts, call witnesses and generally keep order in the court).

15.1.4 Adversarial mock trials

I include here detailed instructions for running the trial. Much of what I say applies to both common and civil law jurisdictions, although the preliminary investigation and role of the judge at trial is significantly different in civil law countries. Where this is the case, it is noted in the shorter section that follows dealing with inquisitorial cases.

Steps in an adversarial mock trial

A number of events occur during an adversarial trial, and most trials must happen in a particular order.[6] Subject to domestic procedural rules, the following steps normally occur in an adversarial criminal mock trial:[7]

1. The court is called to order by the court usher/orderly.
2. The judge or judges enter and sit down.
3. The court clerk or registrar calls out the name of the case.
4. The clerk or judge puts the charge to the accused and asks him or her to plead.
5. The accused pleads guilty or not guilty.
6. The prosecution and defence teams introduce themselves.
7. If the plea is not guilty the prosecutor makes an opening statement.
8. The prosecutor presents the prosecution evidence case: The prosecutor calls the first witness and conducts the direct examination of the witness. The defence lawyer can then cross-examine the witness. Afterwards the prosecutor re-examines the witness if necessary. The judge may ask questions to clarify issues.
9. The steps in 8 above are completed for each of the prosecution witnesses.
10. The prosecutor closes the case.
11. The defence lawyer may make an opening statement.
12. The defence lawyer then presents the case in same manner as the prosecutor in 8 above: The defence lawyer normally calls the accused first (if he

or she is going to give evidence) and conducts the examination-in-chief (also known as direct examination). The prosecutor can cross-examine the accused. The defence lawyer re-examines the accused if necessary. The judge may ask questions to clarify certain issues. The same procedure is followed in respect of each of the witnesses for the defence.

13 In 12 above the accused must be called before the other defence witnesses if he or she is going to give evidence – to make sure that the accused does not change his or her story to make it fit with that of the other witnesses.
14 The defence lawyer closes the defence case.
15 The prosecutor makes closing submissions summarizing the evidence and relevant law.
16 The defence lawyer makes closing submissions.
17 The prosecutor may reply to the defence's argument but only on matters of law raised by the defence – not the facts.
18 The judge or judges adjourn the case to consider their verdict.
19 The judge or judges give their verdict and reasons.

In a *criminal case* the following steps occur if an accused is convicted (or pleads guilty):

20 The prosecution gives an outline of the facts (on a guilty plea) and then the defence offers a plea in mitigation (attempting to affect the nature or limit the severity of sentence).
21 The prosecution may be allowed to respond depending on the jurisdiction and to say why the sentence should not be reduced or why it should be increased or what the sentence should otherwise be.
22 The judge or judges consider the submissions and then sentence the accused.

Simplified rules of evidence

It is important for mock trial participants to understand that most legal systems have developed rules to govern the types of evidence that may be used in a trial, as well as the manner in which evidence may be presented.[8] These "rules of evidence" have been designed to ensure that accused persons have a fair trial. The judges are responsible for making sure these rules are obeyed.

Lawyers can attempt to make sure that the rules of evidence are followed by raising "objections" to evidence or procedures wrongly used by the opposing side. When an objection is raised, the lawyer stands up and says, "I object" and gives the reasons for the objection. The lawyer against whom the objection is raised will usually be asked by the judge to respond. The rules of evidence used in real trials can be very complicated. A few of the most important rules of evidence have been adapted for mock trial purposes. I suggest that if the aim of the mock trial is to introduce students to the realities of the criminal justice system, then a slavish adherence to the rules of evidence, whilst realistic, may be unhelpful and unnecessary – unless of course one of the learning outcomes is a specific grasp of the relevant rules of evidence. If the purpose is more general – to see how the justice system operates – then some flexibility can be introduced. That said, some rules are still required to make the trial work. These include the following.

Rule 1: Leading questions[9]

Leading questions may not be asked when direct evidence is being obtained by the prosecutor or defence lawyers from their own witnesses or the accused or experts. When questioning their own witnesses or other parties called by them prosecutors and defence lawyers should use "open-ended" questions beginning with "Who", "Where", "What", "Why", "When" or "How". The same applies to questions during re-examination. The question should not suggest the answer.

Rule 2: Witness goes beyond the question[10]

Witnesses' answers must be in response to the questions. Answers that go beyond the questions may be objectionable. This occurs when the witness provides much more information than the question calls for. It should be added, however, that there is considerable variance in practice here, with some judges more keen than others to allow a witness to expand on his or her evidence.

Rule 3: Relevance[11]

Questions or answers that are irrelevant and add nothing to the understanding of the issue in dispute are objectionable. Questions and answers must be related to the subject matter of the case. This is called "relevance". Questions and answers that do not relate to the case are "irrelevant".

Rule 4: Hearsay[12]

Usually statements made by people who are not going to be called as witnesses in court cannot be used as evidence in the court case, or if it is permitted, then it is subject to subsequent analysis as to relevance, reliability and weight. Only statements made by people who are going to be called as witnesses can be used. This is because if people are not called to give evidence as witnesses, the truth of their evidence cannot be tested by cross-examination in court. There are many exceptions to the hearsay rule, but for simplicity I suggest that only two apply in mock trials. These are:

1 A witness may repeat a statement made by the accused provided that the witness actually heard the statement.
2 Statements made by the accused which go against his or her interest may be used as evidence.

This is because in both instances the accused will have a chance in court to dispute the truth of the statements.

Rule 5: Opinion evidence[13]

Unless a witness is qualified as an expert in the area under question, the witness may not give an opinion about matters relating to that area of expertise. However, if the evidence is about something that ordinary people know about, an ordinary witness may give an opinion (e.g., whether it was a hot or cold day).

Rule 6: Beyond the scope of cross-examination[14]

In cases where the lawyer has reserved time to re-examine a witness after cross-examination, the lawyer on re-examination may only ask questions related to topics that the opposing lawyer raised during cross-examination.

Rule 7: Beyond the scope of the problem in the mock trial[15]

This only applies to mock trials. Questions that go beyond the facts contained in the mock trial problem are objectionable. However, minor details regarding a character's role may be asked and added.

This objection only applies to mock trials and not real trials.

Conducting a mock trial

The following steps should be taken before, and when, conducting a mock trial:[16]

Step 1: Lay out the courtroom

It is important for students to be familiar with the physical setting of the courtroom. The following diagram depicts the layout of a typical courtroom – but this may vary depending on the jurisdiction:

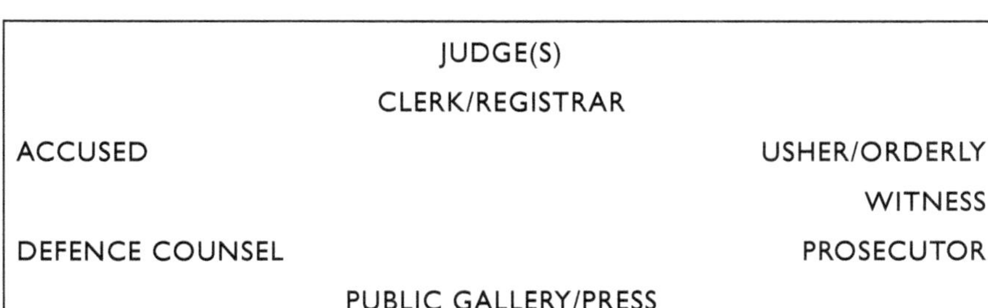

Witnesses, other than the accused, normally remain outside the courtroom until they are called to give their evidence (so they do not hear the prior evidence in case they are affected by it).

Lawyers conduct the trial while standing on their feet at the table for counsel. One lawyer remains seated while the other lawyer conducts his or her case.[17]

Step 2: Participants take their places

The lawyers, the accused (or parties in a civil case), witnesses, experts, registrar, court orderly, time keeper and courtroom observers (spectators) take their places. The witnesses may or may not be allowed in court before they have given their evidence.

Step 3: Orderly calls the court to order

As the judge or magistrate is about to enter the courtroom, the court orderly stands and says in a loud voice, "Silence in court! All rise". Everyone in court should stand and sit when the judge does. The judge and lawyers normally bow to each other as a sign of respect.

Step 4: The registrar or clerk informs the judge or magistrate about the case

"Your Lordship/Your Honour (judge) or Worship (magistrate), I am calling case (give name and number) for hearing."

Step 5: The charge is put to the accused

The judge or magistrate asks the accused to stand: "Will the accused please stand?". The judge or magistrate says to the accused: "Are you (name of the accused)? You are charged with the crime of (mentions the crime and puts the charge to the accused). How do you plead, guilty or not guilty?" The accused replies "guilty" or "not guilty". A trial only takes place, of course, if there is a not guilty (or no) plea. If there is a guilty plea, the procedure moves on to sentencing.

Step 6: Introduction of counsel

The judge or magistrate asks the counsel to introduce themselves (e.g., "Who appears?"). The prosecutor replies: "I am X and I appear for the State, My Lord/Your Honour (or Your Worship)". The defence lawyer replies: "I am Y and I appear for the defence, My Lord/Your Honour (or Your Worship)".

Step 7: Opening statements

The opening statement is the introduction to the case. Usually it is only done by the prosecutor who says what the charges are and what evidence will be brought before the court. In mock trials the defence lawyer usually opens by saying says what the accused person's defence is. The prosecutor always begins.

Step 8: Prosecution case[18]

The process of examining the witnesses begins. First the prosecution team presents its witnesses and evidence, then the defence team presents its witnesses and evidence.

Each time a witness is called to the witness stand, the court orderly asks the witness whether he or she has any objection to taking the oath to tell the truth. If the witness does not, the orderly administers the oath, by raising the right hand, and asking the witness to raise his or her right hand and asking: "Do you swear that the evidence that you are about to give is the truth, the whole truth and nothing but the truth? If so, raise your right hand and say, 'So help me God'." The witness should respond "So help me God". The wording and format of the oath may vary from country to country.

If witnesses do not wish to take the oath they may make an affirmation in which case they are asked: "Do you affirm that the evidence that you are about to give is the truth, the whole truth and nothing but the truth?" – without any raising of the hand.

The lawyer who calls the witness asks a series of questions called "direct examination" (or "examination-in-chief"). These questions are designed to get the witnesses to tell their stories, saying what they saw, heard, experienced or knew about the case. The questions must ask only for facts, not for opinions – unless the witness has been declared an "expert" in the area under question or is giving an opinion about things in common experience. During direct examination, the lawyer may only ask questions and may not make any statements about the facts, even if the witness says something wrong. Here the lawyer must use open-ended questions (e.g., What? Where? When? Why? Who? How?).

When the direct examination is completed, the lawyer for the other side then asks questions to show weaknesses in the witnesses' evidence through a process called "cross-examination". The purpose of the cross-examination is to show the judge that witnesses who give unfavourable evidence should not be believed because they: (a) cannot remember facts; (b) did not give all the facts during direct examination; (c) told a different story at some other time; (d) have a special relationship with one of the parties (maybe a relative or a close friend); or (e) bear a grudge against one of the parties. The cross-examination questions are designed to bring out one or more of these factors. Usually the questions are framed as statements with which the witness or the accused is asked to agree or disagree. Here leading questions are permitted.

Sometimes witnesses called by one side give evidence that helps the other side. The lawyer for the side getting the unexpected help should remember to use the evidence in the closing argument. After cross-examination, the prosecutor (or plaintiff's counsel) may "re-examine" the witness about matters that were raised in the cross-examination. During re-examination open-ended questions must be used. No further cross-examination is usually permitted after the re-examination.

When the prosecutor has closed the prosecution case, the defence opens its case.

Step 9: Defence case

The defence case is conducted in the same way as the prosecutor's case except that the defence calls witnesses for direct examination and the prosecutor cross-examines. If the accused is going to give evidence, he or she must be called as the first witness. Immediately after the accused and each defence witness has given evidence, he or she may be cross-examined by the prosecutor. The defence may re-examine the accused and each defence witness after the prosecutor has cross-examined them, but the prosecutor may not usually cross-examine them again.

Step 10: Closing arguments[19]

The purpose of the closing argument is to convince the judge that the evidence presented entitles the side that presented it to win the case. The closing argument should include:

(a) A summary of the charges against the accused and what the law requires to be proved;
(b) A summary of the evidence presented that is favourable to the presenting lawyer's case; and
(c) A summary of how the law, when applied to the evidence and facts in the case, should enable the judge to rule in favour of the presenting lawyer's case.

New information may not be introduced in the closing argument. In a *criminal case* the prosecutor closes first, then the defence, and then the prosecutor may reply to any points of law (not fact) raised by the defence but only with the consent of the judge.

Step 11: Deliberation and verdict

In making a decision, the judge considers the evidence presented and in order to determine the facts decides which witnesses were most credible or believable. Once having established the facts, the judge applies the law to the facts and comes up with a verdict – in a criminal trial guilt or innocence.

Step 12: Debriefing the mock trial

The instructor should begin debriefing by asking the participants whether or not they agreed with the verdict. What was the strongest argument for the prosecution? What was the strongest argument for the defence? What was the role of the prosecutors, defence lawyers and judges? Did the participants enjoy the role they played? Why or why not? Was it easy to be a judge in this case? Etc.

Time frame[20]

To ensure that the mock trials are completed within a reasonable time (in this instance one hour), the following time limits are suggested (and enforced by a time-keeper):

- Opening statement: 3 minutes each for the prosecution and defence.
- Direct examination: 7 minutes for each witness (or 5 minutes, with 2 minutes reserved for re-examination).
- Cross-examination: 4 minutes for each witness.
- Closing argument: 3 minutes each for the prosecution and defence.
- Reply: 1 minute by the prosecution.

If, during direct examination or cross-examination, a lawyer objects to a question of counsel or an answer of the witness, this time should not be counted as part of the allocated time. This means that when counsel argue about an objection and the judge rules on the objection, "the clock stops" and the time taken is not counted towards the 7 minutes of the direct examination or the 4 minutes of cross-examination.

If time limits are used, the time keeper should have time cards that read "3 min", "2 min", "1 min", "0". For each part of the trial that is timed, the time keeper should hold up the appropriate card to the judge and to the lawyer who is asking questions to let them know how much time is left.

Conclusion

Adversarial *Street Law*-type criminal mock trials enable substantial numbers of participants to experience the roles of prosecutors, defence lawyers, witnesses and judges play in the criminal justice system. All participants are involved in the discussions of the applicable law, the steps to be followed in a trial and the preparations for a criminal trial. This author has found that evaluations conducted after the mock trials indicate that participants regard mock trials as an invaluable learning experience. Where a class or workshop has more participants than roles, roles can be shared or additional trials run at a later stage to accommodate those who did not play a part first time round. Extra members can also help with preparation even if they don't get a speaking role.

15.1.5 Inquisitorial mock trial[21]

The concept of an inquisitorial or accusatorial mock trial as a mechanism for understanding how legal disputes are resolved in a courtroom needs to be explained to students. In inquisitorial jurisdictions proceedings can be very different from the mock trial process set out above. In a criminal case in a civil law country the roles of the police, the investigating officer, the public prosecutor and the investigating judge need to be explained. In addition the roles of the court officials, lawyers, judge, witnesses and parties in a trial should also be clarified, as well as who has to prove what and the extent of proof required.[22] The steps in the mock trial must also be made clear.

Pre-trial investigations

In criminal cases in inquisitorial trials the pre-trial procedure can be divided into four phases: (a) the role of the police; (b) the role of the investigator; (c) the role of the prosecutor; and (d) the role of the judge.[23] Each of these will be briefly discussed.

Role of the police

1 The police ask preliminary questions at the scene of the crime.
2 The police can require the suspect to go to the police station. (They may not if they think that there is insufficient evidence that an offence has been committed.)
3 The suspect and witnesses are asked to make statements at the police station.
4 The police send the file, with statements by the suspect and the witnesses to the investigator.
5 In serious cases (e.g., murder) the police may request the investigator to go directly to the scene of the crime.

Role of investigator

1 The investigator studies the police file and if satisfied that there is sufficient evidence will call in the suspect and explain the nature of the charge(s).
2 The investigator explains the accused's right to:

   (a) Have an attorney present.
   (b) Make a statement.
   (c) Remain silent.
   (d) Reject the statements made.
   (e) Raise any defence he or she wishes to make.

3 In serious offences (e.g., murder) the prosecutor could intervene directly in stage 2 above.
4 The investigator examines the accused and the witnesses: In some jurisdictions, a lawyer may be present for the examination of the accused.
5 The investigator prepares a file for the prosecutor by taking statements from the accused and witnesses.

6 The investigator also collects any evidence by visiting the place of the crime; he or she also gathers evidence (e.g., photographs, documents), holds identity parades, requests search warrants to search homes, etc.
7 If the investigator is of the opinion that the accused is guilty, he or she will:

(a) Write out a draft charge.
(b) Write a letter to the prosecutor recommending that the accused be charged.

Role of prosecutor

1 The prosecutor reads through the file and considers the investigator's recommendations.
2 If the prosecutor agrees with the investigator's recommendations, he or she will draft a formal indictment for the court, stating:

(a) What happened.
(b) Where it happened.
(c) When it happened.
(d) What crime has been committed.

3 If the prosecutor is of the opinion that there is insufficient evidence, he or she may ask the investigator to find further evidence or may refuse to prosecute.
4 If the prosecutor drafts an indictment, he or she also makes recommendations to the judge concerning:

(a) Which witnesses should be examined.
(b) Which evidence should be used.
(c) What other evidence the court needs.

5 The prosecutor sends the file with the indictment, the accused and witnesses' statements, and the recommendations in 4 above to the judge.

Role of the judge

1 The judge may send the file back to the prosecutor if the statements are inconsistent or require further elaboration.
2 If the judge is satisfied with the contents of the file, he or she may set a trial date.
3 The judge will request the accused, witnesses, the defence lawyer and experts to attend the court on the day of the trial to give evidence.
4 The prosecutor and defence lawyer can suggest that further witnesses be called, but the judge need not follow their suggestions if the witnesses were not examined during the investigation.
5 If the prosecutor of defence lawyer requests witnesses to be called who were examined during the investigation, the judge must call them even if

he or she only wanted their written statements read into the record and thought it unnecessary to examine them in person.

Steps in an inquisitorial mock trial[24]

In inquisitorial criminal mock trials the following steps are usually followed (although there may be jurisdictional variations):

(a) The accused is seated next to the defence lawyer on the left of the judge.
(b) The prosecutor is seated to the right of the judge.
(c) The court orderly calls for silence and tells everyone to stand.
(d) The judge enters.
(e) The judge checks the attendance of all interested parties (accused, witnesses, prosecutor and defence lawyer) by asking for proof of identity.
(f) The judge sends the witnesses out of the court.
(g) The judge opens the case.
(h) The judge asks the prosecutor to read the charge to the accused.
(i) The judge explains the accused's rights and asks how he or she pleads.
(j) The accused pleads guilty or not guilty.
(k) The judge asks the accused whether he or she wishes to say anything.
(l) The accused says anything he or she wishes to say.
(m) The judge questions the accused.
(n) The prosecutor questions the accused.
(o) The defence lawyer questions the accused.
(p) The judge requests the court orderly to call the first witness:

    (i) Before questioning the judge explains that the witness has a duty to tell the truth.
    (ii) The judge questions the witness.
    (iii) The prosecutor questions the witness.
    (iv) The defence lawyer questions the witness.
    (v) The accused questions the witness (optional).

(q) Steps (p) (i) to (v) are repeated in respect of each witness.
(r) Closing argument by the prosecutor on the merits of the case and sentence.
(s) Closing argument by the defence lawyer on the merits of the case and sentence.
(t) Closing statement by the accused on the merits of the case and sentence.
(u) The judge deliberates on the verdict and any necessary sentence.
(v) The judge delivers the verdict and sentence of the court – everyone stands.
(w) The judge advises the parties on the appeal procedures and deadlines.

In many civil law jurisdictions, assessors or lay judges are used in criminal trials, and in some cases victims may also be entitled to question witnesses and address the court.

In inquisitorial mock trials, the rules of evidence are less rigid than under the adversarial system because the judge has the statements of all the relevant witnesses beforehand. The judge knows what the witnesses should say and can prepare questions in advance. Many of the questions by the judge, prosecutor and defence are likely to focus on clearing up ambiguities and contradictions in order to establish the reliability of the witnesses. Much of this would already have been done by the investigator, the prosecutor and the judge during the pre-trial phase.[25]

Establishing the facts

In order to ensure that students understand all the facts of the case, they should be given a mock trial package which includes the indictment, a summary of the facts, a summary of the law, a list of witnesses and the witnesses' statements. Individual students should be required to read out the indictment, the summary of substantial facts and the individual witness' statements on each side. The instructor should then discuss each in turn to make sure that the students have a full understanding of the facts before proceeding to explain the relevant law.

Establishing the law[26]

Under the inquisitorial system, the criminal law is usually codified and the definitions of the different crimes, and the sentences apportioned to them are to be found in the criminal code. There is not the same emphasis on proving clearly articulated elements of the crime as occurs in adversarial systems. The focus is on whether or not the provisions of the code have been breached. The wording of the relevant articles of the criminal code needs to be explained to the students. The evidence necessary to be adduced by the prosecution to prove its case should be discussed with the students. Attention must also be drawn to the evidence that can be used by the defence.

As has been mentioned, in inquisitorial systems there is a conflation of the judgment on the merits of the case and the sentencing process. Indeed, many codes define the crime and at the same time specify the range of the sentence that must be imposed by the court. Thus students should prepare for both when presenting arguments at the beginning and end of the trial.

Under the inquisitorial system, the judge plays an active role. He or she takes the lead in asking questions and also controls the process. Therefore, to design a successful inquisitorial mock trial, scope should be found to involve as many students as possible in the roles of judges.

Time frame

It is important to control the timings to make the trial feasible. The following works well in practice:

(i) Judge checking attendance and identities, sending out the witnesses, and opening the case – 2 minutes.

(ii) Judge asking the prosecutor to read charge, and explaining accused's rights -2 minutes.
(iii) Accused's opening statement – 2 minutes.
(iv) Questions of each witness by judges – 18 minutes (3 minutes x six witnesses).
(v) Questions by each witness by prosecutors – 12 minutes (2 minutes x six witnesses).
(vi) Questions by each witness by defence lawyers – 12 minutes (2 minutes x six witnesses).
(vii) Closing arguments – 3 minutes.
(viii) Judgement – 2 minutes.

Conducting the mock trial

The steps in a mock trial should be explained and handed out to the participants before conducting the mock trial.

The room should be laid out as a courtroom in the following form: The judge's bench in the centre close to the front wall; the court orderly and judge's secretary (who can act as time-keeper) seated at a table immediately in front of the judge; the witness box to the judge's right; the accused seated with the defence team at a table in front of the judge on the judge's left; the prosecution team seated at a table in front and to the right of the judge; and the spectators seated behind the defence and prosecution teams.

The judge's secretary (time-keeper) should assist the judge, prosecutor and lawyers by indicating the number of minutes remaining during each phase of the trial, e.g., for the judge who checks the attendance of all the parties and opens the case; the judge who asks the prosecutor to read the charge and explains the accused's rights; the accused who makes an opening statement; the judges who question the accused and witnesses; the prosecutors who question the accused and witnesses; the defence lawyers who question the accused and witnesses; the closing arguments by the prosecution, defence and accused; and the judgment.

Debriefing the mock trial

At the end of mock trial, there should be time for debriefing – preferably immediately after the judgment, or at least at a subsequent lesson. Participants should be encouraged to give their views on the judgment of the court, the manner in which the prosecution and lawyers conducted the case, the demeanour of the witnesses, and their experiences in the different roles.

As has been mentioned the objective of the mock trial experience is to give participants and observers a better understanding of how the judicial process works.

Conclusion

Once again participants experience playing the roles of teams of prosecutors, defence lawyers, witnesses and judges in the criminal justice system. As in adversarial mock trials, all the participants are involved in the discussions of the applicable law, the steps to be followed in a criminal trial and the preparations for it. Likewise, I have found that evaluations conducted after the inquisitorial mock trials indicate that participants had very similar reaction as those involved in adversarial mock trials. In both instances, there is an appreciation of the value of learning through active involvement and a sense of enjoyment at acting out a realistic court case (albeit one that may be hypothetical and artificially time-constrained). As for the accusatorial mock trials, participants not allocated roles in the actual trial may still take part in one of the team activities and can always assume an active role in subsequent trials.

15.1.6 And finally . . .

Space in this publication does not allow for the inclusion of a fully worked example of a mock trial role-play. However, set out below is a scenario that has been successfully used in both civil and common law countries.

The 'instant' pub murder mock trial

This example is based on a short role-play in which a person is fatally stabbed. Following the incident, either the police arrive and arrest the suspect who is then questioned, charged and referred to the courts (common law) or the following arrest and questioning the investigator refers the matter to the prosecutor and then to court (civil law). Either way students can act out the preliminary matters and then follow the mock trial procedure set out above for either an accusatorial or inquisitorial system.

The scenario for the role-play is as follows:

> A bartender, a stranger, a local man and various bystanders are in a bar. The local makes comments to the bartender about not wanting strangers in his bar. The stranger objects, and an argument ensues. After a scuffle the stranger falls to the ground fatally wounded. The local, who has a knife on him, says the stabbing was accidental and he was only trying to fend the stranger off. The facts will emerge as the role play is acted out and the witnesses can give statements based on what they saw and heard.

Notes

1 See generally David McQuoid-Mason (ed.), with Lindi Coetzee, Lloyd Lotz, Malebakeng Forere and Rowena Bernard, *Street law: practical law for South Africans* (3rd edn), Juta & Co, 2015, 19–27 and David McQuoid-Mason, *Street law mock trial manual for Eastern and Central Europe, Russia and Former Soviet European and Central Asian Republics*, Street Law Inc, 2000, 7–16, available at: http://oalaw.tsingua.edu.cn/lilvoei/237822104823994.doc, accessed 6 April 2016; on which this chapter is based. Also see: Thomas A. Mauet, Warren D. Wolfson and Steve Easton, *Materials in trial advocacy: problems & cases* (7th edn), Aspen Coursebooks, 2011. For other examples of mock trials see: McQuoid-Mason et al, *Street*

law: practical law, op cit., 145–152 and McQuoid-Mason, *Street law mock trial manual*, op cit., 25–96. See also the following mock trial packages D.J. McQuoid-Mason *S v Switchitov*, a euthanasia case (unpublished 1997); D.J. McQuoid-Mason *S v Didna Doit* a medical negligence case (unpublished 1998); and *S v Bulala*, a death in police custody case in D.J. McQuoid-Mason and M.A. Dada, *The guide to forensic medicine and medical law*, Independent Medico-Legal Unit, 2004, 145–168.

2 McQuoid-Mason et al, *Street law: practical law*, op cit., 19.
3 Ibid., 145–146.
4 McQuoid-Mason, *Street law mock trial manual*, op cit., 7–8.
5 McQuoid-Mason et al, *Street law: practical law*, op cit., 19–20.
6 This section is based on McQuoid-Mason et al, *Street law: practical law*, op cit., 19–27 and 145–146.
7 Ibid., 20.
8 Ibid., 21–23.
9 Ibid., 21.
10 Ibid.
11 Ibid., 22.
12 Ibid.
13 Ibid., 22–23.
14 Ibid., 23.
15 Ibid.
16 Ibid., 25–27.
17 Ibid., 25.
18 Ibid., 26.
19 Ibid., 27.
20 Ibid.
21 This section is based extensively based on McQuoid-Mason, *Street law mock trial manual*, op cit., 7–16, which is available on open access at: http://oalaw.tsingua.edu.cn/lilvoei/237822104823994.doc, accessed 6 April 2016, which the copyright holders *Street Law* Inc, have given the present writer permission to reproduce.
22 Ibid., 7.
23 Ibid., 10.
24 The procedures to be followed in an inquisitorial mock trial were devised by the present writer with the assistance of ex-Judge Jan Hrubala, Partners for Democratic Change, Banska Bystrica, Slovakia in April 1998.
25 McQuoid-Mason, op cit., 10–11.
26 Ibid., 11–12.

Part 2 – Teaching EU law in an experiential way

Katarzyna Gromek-Broc

15.2.1 Introduction

As seen elsewhere in this book, the York Law School at The University of York teaches all of its core, and most of its optional, subjects through experiential methods, primarily problem-based learning (PBL). I will not repeat what is said there or elsewhere in this book and in publications referred to further analyse the PBL process as such, but I will look at how one important component of the curriculum – the law of the European Union – has been delivered there using PBL and go on to consider if this approach to study could be successfully adapted in countries of the civil law.

Before I look at the detail of teaching EU law through PBL methods, it is important to note that there is a global concern about whether legal education is meeting the needs of all concerned and how legal pedagogy can be improved in consequence. Duch observes that 'our role as educators is to prepare students to be comfortable in the new working environment'.[1] Our students must have a solid grasp of theory and doctrine but must also be equipped with a skill set and an appreciation of wider ethical concerns so they are more than mere technicians. Thus, legal education in any jurisdiction owes it to its students to consider both the form and content of the curriculum, what is taught and learnt and how that is best achieved.[2] For those who grapple with these issues, there is perhaps an additional responsibility as members of the wider academic community – to share effective practice with a view to stimulating debate and improving provision and subsequent quality.

There are barriers, of course, to following such a course of action. Regulation of what is taught and how it is delivered may exist. Where there is room for manoeuvre, it may be difficult to change attitudes and culture.

The traditional method of university teaching in both common and civil law countries is based on content-driven lectures. Assessment is predominantly through examinations, with emphasis placed on recollecting core cases or texts rather than evaluation and critical reflection. This 'spoon-feeding' of knowledge, relies on the teacher to supply the diet to hungry but passive students.[3] The method of teaching that worked decades ago 'will no longer suffice, for the simple reason that past approaches fail to develop the full battery of skills and abilities desired in a contemporary [world]'.[4]

As a related aside, and interesting in a teaching and learning sense, students could be exposed to both the common and civil law in a comparative way. Smits observes, using an example from Maastricht Law School[5] (where PBL is entrenched across the university) that "students addressing a specific problem by moving back and forth from one jurisdiction to another are much more conducive to the 'dialogue with otherness' than the sequential model."[6] Husa argues against 'mind fixing' – legal education based only on one legal system: 'The problem with the traditional law-teaching approach is that it constructs a primary epistemic foundation for legal understanding, which is based on one mother-system. This creates an implicit mono-epistemology, which makes lawyers regard their own system as "normal"' (and other systems as the exception).[7] If we are genuinely interested in opening students' minds, there is much to be said for studying, at least at the overt academic stage, both the civil and common law traditions.

But let us now turn specifically to PBL and EU Law.

15.2.2 PBL and the EU

Whether a subject can and should be taught comparatively is an interesting and important question. Whatever the answer, it does not preclude the use of experiential learning methods. I suggest that the relevance of such an approach would benefit from comparison and may, strategically at least, make the innovation more acceptable in the civil law world.

At York the overall educational aim is to marry substance with skills, to combine the theory with practice and to make the learning experience an interactive and student-focused one – bringing knowledge, skills and values together. As will be seen from the worked example set out below, the problems designed at York tend to extend to more than one legal topic and subject area. In this way we believe that the student sees law in its operational context rather than treating law as separate and unrelated compartments. This technique also means that the student can be asked on more than one occasion to consider principles and issues – avoiding the consequence that once studied, the matter in hand is over and done with and giving them the chance to revisit important concepts, thus testing and developing the depth of their understanding.

My choice of subject for analysis, EU law, is, of course, a commonly studied subject both in the UK and on the continent.[8] In my discussion, I will be using a concrete example: a joint EU/Public Law problem that appears at the start of the final year of a 3-year undergraduate law degree programme.

The York model can be described as an 'integrated approach' which, for the purposes of teaching EU law and PBL design, meant finding the most appropriate fit with another legal subject or subjects. The obvious candidate was seen to be Public Law, which is a second- and third-year subject (in civil law countries probably referred to as Constitutional Law).

The syllabus of the course addresses general principles of constitutional law and in particular the way in which the EU impacts on that so far as the UK and other current member states are concerned. Similarly, we look at 'sovereignty' on both an EU and a national level.

As subjects, at York, EU and Pubic Law are delivered predominantly through PBL, with weekly plenary sessions devoted to each subject designed to get the students to think through issues that have arisen in their linked PBL sessions. The programme is divided into 4 'blocks' with associated themes, and there is a block guide to give students suggested reading and guidance on the subject area. The example I set out below is taken from Block 2 and relates to the concept of citizenship and associated difficulties after the Lisbon Treaty was adopted. The problem is multifaceted and intellectually challenging as well as requiring detailed research. However, I believe it is appropriate for students in their final year of study. It was also the first time this particular problem had been used, so as well as sharing it here as an example of teaching through PBL that has direct relevance to the civil law, I wanted to evaluate its effectiveness.

Each PBL group (of which there are 12 with a membership of 10–12 each) received the following scenario at the start of the relevant PBL session:

> *PBL Year 3, Block 2, Problem 2*
>
> "You are studying in a university as a doctoral student. You have just received this memo from your supervisor:
>
>> Hi
>>
>> Thank you for all your recent help with my research. I would like you to help me again.
>>
>> I am presenting a paper at a conference next month which should fit with the general theme of the conference "The future of European Integration after the crisis and the role of individual". One of my ideas is that to move forward with the integration process we need a strong sense of belonging to Europe, a 'European Identity' which arises from national identities but then it takes its own shape inherent to the EU. My paper is in the form of a response to a recent paper written by Massimo La Lorre that I have found challenging, available here: La Torre, Massimo. 'A Weberian Moment for Europe? Constitutionalism and the Crisis of European Integration.' European Public Law 20, no. 3 (2014): 421–434.
>>
>> I would like you to help with my response to the following extract, which is taken from p423:
>>
>>> *""[. . .] national identity feeds a sense of belonging that is sometimes intractable through constitutional provisions, in so far as membership is not considered in terms of a self-defining citizenship, but rather as given through prepolitical commitments. Democracy could thus be rendered a fight for groups whose characters could be neither reshaped nor accommodated through constitutional rules. The commonality of the political space*

> *would either be equivalent to nationality or it would become just a prudential calculus of cost and benefits in a contingent and fully unstable arena of trade-off and compromise. The European Union has faced and keeps facing a rather similar problem.*
>
> *The principle of respect of national identity has been concretized in the Treaty of Lisbon (Article 4.2) as a safeguard of national constitutional identities. That article is dense in normative content. Among the many norms that could be said to be comprised in it, perhaps two are the most fundamental: the principle of equality of Member States; the mandate to the European Union, and all its institutions, to regard the constitutional and political structure of the Member States as part of the wider unity that is the European Union. The latter mandate reflects the implicit premise that the European Union is legally and politically built on the basis of the collective of national constitutions and political systems. Nationality is here a supportive principle of constitutionalism and democracy in Weberian terms."*

Please come and see me at the same time next week and make a presentation addressing the issues I have identified.

Notes to PBL tutor: Please divide your SLF into two and ask each group to prepare a presentation based on the extracts. This should enable them to identify and meet the LOs learning outcomes (LOs) for this problem."

The reference above to 'SLF' is to 'student law firm'. All PBL groups at York are called SLFs, and students stay with the same firm for all of their work for the entire academic year. They are allocated to different firms in subsequent years. The reference to 'LOs' is to 'learning outcomes'. Students are expected to identify what they need to find out as part of the PBL process. The LOs are therefore normally drafted as research questions.

A couple of other points by way of explanation are needed here:

A) The choice of the problem scenario.

The choice of scenario, the issues covered and the level of difficulty is the module team's decision. Every subject is taught collaboratively at York with typically 2–3 academic and adjunct staff (PBL tutors) in each team. In this particular case, the scenario must thematically cover relevant issues of EU and Public Law syllabi. This PBL problem sits well with the debate on the future of European integration and requires the students to analyse the relevant academic sources and treaty article. The context – a doctoral student helping a supervisor – is readily understood by the students, who may themselves aspire to further study. It adds necessary realism to the problem, making engagement easier.

B) Tutor guidance

It is vital for consistency and quality that all PBL groups have the same task and produce similar results in terms of module design outcomes. Hence

> the teaching team develops tutor notes, giving guidance on what the problem is about, what the students should consider and what the end result should be. The PBL process itself is, of course, left to the students, with tutor input, as and when necessary, to keep them on track. The tutors' notes need to be specific and detailed, including what learning outcomes the students are expected to identify and research.[9]

In this problem, the following LOs might be appropriate:

1. To identify the key theoretical underpinnings of the EU
2. To engage with the debate about the future of European integration
3. To reflect on how the economic climate and constitutional concepts impact individuals
4. To consider what is needed to develop a deeper sense of 'EU identity'.
5. To read and evaluate relevant academic articles in advance of end-of-course assessments.

Following the structure used at York for all PBL sessions, the students must first read the problem out loud and then identify any unclear terms. They must list all prospective interested parties and specify the relevant issues at stake for each. They then set out the chronology of events if relevant (it is not here), followed by a mind-mapping exercise in which they try to identify relevant legal issues. They then organise these into themes from which they draft their research questions (learning outcomes). They then agree a research plan, carry out the necessary research individually and report back on their findings and in this case, make the presentations. Presentations are not always included in PBL sessions but the report back always is, as this is the chance to see whether each student has addressed each learning outcome. The process is described in detail elsewhere.[10]

The students might be expected to come up with the following questions or outcomes – that is what they need to know to 'answer' the question. Of course, there may be no answers as such in the sense of right, wrong or complete:

1. What are constitutive elements of European Integration? How could/should they be modified to overcome current economic and constitutional crisis? What is needed to make EU integration progress again? How it could be achieved?
2. How can we achieve two goals: preserving national identity and moving towards a European identity a sense to belonging to Europe? Why it has been difficult to develop this? Why does it matter for the future integration?
3. What does Article 4.2 of the TEU say? Does it safeguard national constitutional identity?
4. What is the principle of equality of Member States? What is the evidence that this is upheld?

5 Is the European Union legally and politically built on the basis of the collective of national constitutions and political systems?
6 How do the constitutions and political systems of the UK and Germany compare?
7 What is meant by 'Weberian terms'?

The tutor notes might read as follows:

'At the end of the session students should be able to provide relevant answers to the questions raised by la Torre in the passage cited above.[11]

In brief, La Torre's position is:

- In the current political climate, European integration can no longer be assumed. (The students' suggestion could be that a new model of integration is needed.)
- When Max Weber was writing (1890–1920) it was in the context of fundamental theoretical and historical dilemmas. We can evaluate his writing, which addresses identity and religion ("roots" and "values") and learn from it.
- Weber also evaluated the role of the State and national identity. This issue is more controversial in the EU context due to the migratory movements across borders. How can we adopt his ideas to the current European structure and constitutional and economic crisis?
- National identity is a concept enshrined in Article 4.2 of the TEU. In this context, it is a supportive principle of constitutionalism and democracy in Weberian terms.
- The above idea implies an assumption that there is European Constitutional Law.
- National constitutional identity offers a shield to protect national constitutions against self-generated integrative pressure
- The principle of equality implies that European integration should be so structured as to avoid the will of one or a few member states being translated into the general will of the community
- European constitutionalism is now challenged by value pluralism and the tension between European integration, national constitutions and migration.
- This reminds us of Weber, who, when discussing the prospect of a republican constitution for Germany, was committed to a strong executive and a more homogeneous federal structure. . . .'

The list could go on.

The points raised above are just indicative. Students should be encouraged to develop their own ideas so long as they are backed by reference to relevant sources.

These tutors' notes would, in reality, also cover detailed information regarding the content of the Los, but I do not have the space here to go into this further.[12]

15.2.3 An evaluation – work in progress

The above scenario is, I suggest, a perfect illustration how theoretical issues, history, politics and constitutional dilemmas could be addressed in one PBL session. Admittedly it is a complex problem and may take the students a while to come to terms with. This particular example may well appeal to many colleagues on the continent given that it requires serious theoretical understanding and may convince them that PBL as a method is *not* simply based on practical issues. In other words the practical setting is just a vehicle for learning and teaching.

Given that this was a very challenging problem we, as the teaching team, sought feedback from each other and from the students – a very York thing to do!

The problem triggered some interesting discussion, and the response to it was quite uneven. Some groups did very well, but in some others attendance was weak, preparation was more superficial and pressing issues was insufficiently examined. Some PBL tutors had some specific interests in legal theory and were able to engage students in an interesting debate. For others this was more demanding. Overall the tutors liked the idea of requiring the students to read a complex article and to discuss basic and more sophisticated principles of EU law. They thought that the task encouraged the students to engage with academic commentary and would also be a great help preparing them for the Public Law examination.

Tutors also liked the idea that the students should be asked to prepare a presentation for the feedback session as this would also help to develop skills as well as having to justify their arguments.

Here is some of the tutor feedback:

1 Ideally a PBL session requires a problem for the students to unpick and for them to formulate learning outcomes based on their analysis. An article could do this if it was short enough to read and digest in 10–15 minutes max and it raised some legal research questions which are not blindingly obvious. Simply having the task of reading an article and explaining what it means is not PBL.
2 A good problem usually raises both substantive issues of law and normative considerations. Solely focusing on normative issues is however hard in a PBL context.
3 The Massimo La Torre's article is too long and too complex to read and unpick in 45 minutes. I found it difficult to understand in places and the language is challenging – I looked six words up in the first page! Many of the foreign students struggle with English language so they would be at an extreme disadvantage. It might be better to run this over 2 PBL sessions.
4 The article seems to touch on a large number of themes and problems without actually drawing any clear conclusions or offering any

> solutions. As such it is difficult to respond to but an excellent challenge for the students and the group discussion in the plenary session helped focus their minds.

According to the tutors, it is just not enough to say that we want to use the La Torra article and we want students to respond to it. We need to identify which principles we want the students to focus on and also how these principles play out in practice.

On reflection (another York trait!), an improvement might be to use specific CJEU cases where relevant principles have been identified and/or had an impact on the outcome, and then create a factual problem scenario based on these cases. The students could then start with a more practical setting which, with substantive research, would lead them to appreciate some of the bigger normative issues. Looking at the themes in the article, cases where national rights have prevailed or cases where equality of all Members States has been recognised or cases where the national constitutional rights/interests have not been allowed to override EU law would perhaps provide for a better study context.

15.2.4 Conclusion

In this contribution my aim was to provide some insight into design, process and evaluation of PBL in the context of EU Law and to show how it might be usefully adapted to a civil law context.

An important conclusion can be drawn from this example. Students at York are well-used to working with PBL. By their final year of study, they will have taken part in many such sessions – perhaps 50 or more. It is therefore possible for them to address complex and challenging issues in the PBL format. If this methodology is to be used elsewhere, for example in civil law jurisdictions, thought will have to be given to the induction of students into this method. PBL does not have to be fully integrated into the curriculum as it is at York and can be effectively used in isolated modules or as one-off encounters. What matters is that using PBL the students are placed at the centre of the learning process and are compelled by the regime to take responsibility for their and their peers' learning. That degree of engagement will inevitably have knock-on and positive effects on learning.

As suggested above, although York Law School is fully committed to PBL, the individual matchings of subject and theme and the extent to which the PBL regime is followed across each year of study (for example do Year 3 students need the same structure for learning as the First years?) is still a work in progress. I consider it a healthy and encouraging sign that it is. To be mindful of the need to critically evaluate our programmes in all respects keeps us on the proverbial ball and leaves us open to change and improvement.

If we are to improve legal education for the betterment of students and ultimately wider society, then we must be prepared to re-think what we do and how.

I maintain, as do others in this volume, that there is nothing intrinsic in the civil law system that renders it inappropriate for experiential learning to take place. Whether this is in the form of PBL or other interactive methodologies is a matter for the law school and possibly, other the regulators. Teaching EU law provides a good example of the suitability of PBL to both common and civil law countries.

Brexit or no Brexit, the discussions will continue, as will York's focus on learning experientially.

Notes

1 B. Duch, S.E. Groh and D.E. Allen, Why problem-based learning? A case study of institutional change in undergraduate education, in Stylus (ed.), *The power of problem-based learning*, 2001, 4.
2 R. Stuckey et al, *Best practices for legal education a vision and a road map*, 2007, available at: www.cleaweb.org/Resources/Documents/best_practices-full.pdf, accessed 17 September 2016.
3 L.H. Distlehorst and R.S. Robbs, *A comparison of a problem-based learning and standard curriculum students: three years of retrospective data*, Teaching and Learning in Medicine, 10 (3), 1998, 131.
4 B. Duch, S.E. Groh and D.E. Allen, op cit, 131–137.
5 K. Gromek Broc and R. Hedlund in Mutaz M. Qafisheh and Stephen A. Rosenbaum (eds.), *Experimental legal education in a globalized world: the Middle East & beyond*, Cambridge, UK, 2016.
6 J. Smits, *European legal education, or how to prepare students for global citizenship?*, 2015, available at: http://preview.ialsnet.org/wp-content/uploads/2015/08/Smits.pdf, accessed 15 September 2016.
7 J. Husa, *Turning the curriculum upside down: comparative law as an educational tool for constructing the pluralistic legal mind*, German Law Journal, 10, 2009, 913.
8 L. Khadar, *University law clinics and the growing demand for EU Law*, 30 October 2014, available at: www.opensocietyfoundations.org/voices/university-law-clinics-and-growing-demand-eu-law, accessed 13 September 2016.
9 S. Adam, *Learning outcomes current developments in Europe: update on the issues and applications of learning outcomes associated with the Bologna Process*, 2008, available at: www.ulb.ac.be/unica/docs/ECVET_Edinburgh_Feb08_Adams.pdf, accessed 20 September 2016.
10 R. Grimes, *Delivering legal education through an integrated problem-based learning model – the nuts and bolts*, International Journal of Clinical Legal Education, 21 (2), 2014, 1.
11 M. La Torre, *A Weberian moment for Europe? Constitutionalism and the crisis of European Integration*, European Public Law, 20 (3), 2014, 421.
12 R. Johnstone and S. Vignaendra, *Learning outcomes and curriculum development in law*, Department of Education, Science and Training, Australia, 2003.

Final words

There is much that could be said by way of a conclusion to this book, but as so many people have contributed so much already, I will be brief.

If we are genuinely interested in and are committed to make legal education fit for purpose in the 21st century we need to act and act now. As educators, students, the legal profession, employers, government and the general public who may, at some point, need a lawyer's help, we all have a responsibility to make legal education relevant and accessible. Gone are the days when we can complacently rely on lecture notes. Let us move to intellectually robust but, nevertheless, engaging forms of learning where students can usefully apply theory to practice and enhance their knowledge, skills and values in consequence, whatever their career destination may be.

The themes raised and followed in this volume ring with a certain resonance, especially given recent and on-going critiques and reviews of legal education worldwide. As mentioned in the Introduction, the contributors range from the experienced 'old guard' to the recent graduate, yet despite (or perhaps because of) this variance in experience and background, the messages are consistent – the need for greater student interaction in their learning and vehicles for study delivery that enable a teacher and learner to engage in a reflective dialogue, where prior experience can be deconstructed, revisited and re-evaluated in an on-going educational process.

Whilst there are common denominators running throughout this book – centred on the nature and value of experiential learning – it may come as a surprise, even disappointment, to some that little is said of the use of digital technology and e-learning. This is no oversight by the editor or other contributors. Computer and web-based facilities are clearly here to stay and should, where appropriate, be used to their maximum benefit. I maintain that however valuable such technology may be, unless the learning interface is an interactive one then there is little educational re-thinking going on. Let me give an example. There is, in higher education at least, great use made of the computer and the Internet for providing educational resources. A lecture may be recorded and placed online so it is accessible 24/7 and anywhere that has connectivity. This may be helpful or not depending on form and content, but it is unlikely to require the student's direct engagement beyond watching and listening. There are many examples of the use of e-technology in the study of law, ranging from blogs and chat rooms to highly sophisticated simulations that respond to student input in developing case or other scenario progression. Some may be in real time (for example an online seminar), and others may be asynchronous – with students exchanging views and arguments with their peers and teaching staff as time and opportunity permit. Providing these require students to take an active role in their learning then our view is that they have their rightful place on the learning menu. Space does not permit further discussion of this important issue, but for those interested, there are many examples of how technology can be effectively used in legal education and in an experiential way, to enhance engagement and learning.[1]

The other acknowledged omission in this volume is a discussion of research needs. I anticipate that reviews of this book will latch on to the authors' shared commitment, if largely unproven, to the worth of learning through experience in general and the value of clinical legal education in particular. We collectively plead guilty. We are hands-on learning enthusiasts, and we rely extensively on anecdotal evidence of the importance of learning by doing and reflecting on the doing. We also bed this belief in established education theory. Our plea in mitigation also rests on the similarly unproven significance of more traditional forms of legal education, in particular the use of the lecture and seminar. I think we have clearly shown in this work that using interactive teaching and learning methods promotes engagement and if a student is both interested and engaged in his or her studies, the extent of educational progress is likely to be commensurate with this. That said, there is a need for more research on the educational value of experiential (and other forms of) learning. The worldwide development, as evidenced by recent publications and the explosion of clinical provision in law schools, towards more interactive forms of learning is now a recognisable movement and one that is more rather than less likely to continue.

So what will legal education look like in a future, perhaps ideal, world? We are not naïve. Of course the popularity of law as a subject of study, the resulting sizes of law school classes, the resource implications of experiential learning methods and the prevalence and onward march of e-technology will all affect what legal education looks like in years to come. But this is also certain – if the relevant stakeholders want a sharper focus on legal knowledge, lawyering skills and ethical values, then the means through which to contextualise study and give the student the chance to experience the law in its reality must be developed. The experiential learning repertoire offers much in this setting.

And the civil common law divide? Despite the often frank and clear views expressed in this volume and elsewhere on the significant differences between the civil and common law traditions I remain convinced that there is nothing intrinsic in either system that renders an experiential learning component in legal education inappropriate. It may be different and challenging to teach and learn in this way, but there is a clear movement in that direction in the global north and south and across the civil and common law worlds. There are, of course, some important jurisdictions not covered in the text – notably Russia and China, but also in countries of the Middle East and across Southeast Asia (the book did not have enough space to accommodate all I wanted) – yet in these places too there is a discernible shift to experiential learning, at least in law, with legal clinics becoming all the more evident.

I very much hope that this book contributes to the development of more effective teaching and learning in law and stimulates much-needed debate amongst all those with a vested interest in high-quality and socially relevant legal education.

Richard Grimes
Goulzen d'en Haut
Montoulieu
Ariege
France

Postscript

Since the various chapters of book were written one of the contributors, Tanya Walker, has sadly passed away. She was just 42 year's old. Tanya was the epitome of a dedicated (if late-coming) student, a committed and active comrade and an inspiration to us all. She would, in her authentic, if blunt, Yorkshire style have probably said of this book's publication: "It's not bad lad now, let's get on with the real work". She would have been right of course. She is greatly missed.

Note

1. See for example: P. Maharg, *Transforming legal education*, Ashgate Publications, 2007, in particular Chapter 6; and more recently, R. Grimes, E. Phillips and C. Strevens (eds.), Ashgate Publications, 2014, especially Chapters 1, 2 and 7.

Index

For Product Safety Concerns and Information please contact our EU
representative GPSR@taylorandfrancis.com
Taylor & Francis Verlag GmbH, Kaufingerstraße 24, 80331 München, Germany

www.ingramcontent.com/pod-product-compliance
Ingram Content Group UK Ltd.
Pitfield, Milton Keynes, MK11 3LW, UK
UKHW020014200926
475702UK00014B/1876
9780367181932